The world has recently witnessed remarkable changes in Soviet domestic and foreign policy. Eastern Europe has sprung free of the country that held it in its grip for over forty years. The Soviet leadership has accepted the reunification of Germany and supported the US-sponsored resolution in the UN permitting the use of force in the Gulf against one of its former allies. Moreover, the leadership's quest for stability during a time of rapid technological, economic and political change has seriously weakened the position of the Soviet Union on the international scene.

This timely volume assesses these dramatic changes. It chronicles the debate within the Soviet Union over the success and validity of perestroika and the "new thinking" on foreign affairs, the policy alternatives supported by various groups within the elite and their likely impact on future policies. The authors, who comprise a broad range of leading analysts from Europe, North America, Africa and Asia also provide specific regional and country case studies. They examine changes in the Soviet–East European relationship, Soviet policy towards Northern Europe and the impact that shifts in Soviet policy are likely to have on a variety of developing countries.

Soviet Foreign Policy in Transitions

Selected papers from the Fourth World Congress for Soviet and East European Studies, Harrogate, July 1990

Edited for the
INTERNATIONAL COMMITTEE FOR SOVIET AND EAST EUROPEAN STUDIES

General Editor
Stephen White
University of Glasgow

Soviet Foreign Policy in Transition

edited by

Roger E. Kanet
University of Illinois at Urbana-Champaign

Deborah Nutter Miner
Simmons College

Tamara J. Resler
University of Illinois at Urbana-Champaign

Cambridge University Press
Cambridge New York Port Chester
Victoria Sydney

CAMBRIDGE UNIVERSITY PRESS
Cambridge, New York, Melbourne, Madrid, Cape Town, Singapore, São Paulo

Cambridge University Press
The Edinburgh Building, Cambridge CB2 8RU, UK

Published in the United States of America by Cambridge University Press, New York

www.cambridge.org
Information on this title: www.cambridge.org/9780521413657

First published 1992
This digitally printed version 2008

A catalogue record for this publication is available from the British Library

Library of Congress Cataloguing in Publication data

Soviet foreign policy in transition / edited by
Roger E. Kanet, Deborah Nutter Miner, Tamara J. Resler.
p. cm.
"Selected papers from the Fourth World Congress for Soviet and East European Studies, Harrogate, July 1990." – p.
Includes index.
ISBN 0 521 41365 6
1. Soviet Union – Foreign relations – 1985 – Congresses. 2. Europe, Eastern – Foreign relations – Soviet Union – Congresses. 3. Soviet Union – Foreign relations – Europe, Eastern – Congresses. 4. Soviet Union – Foreign relations – Developing countries – Congresses. 5. Developing countries – Foreign relations – Soviet Union – Congresses. I. Kanet, Roger E., 1936– .
II. Miner, Deborah Nutter. III. Resler, Tamara J. IV. World Congress for Soviet and East European Studies (4th: 1990: Harrogate, England)
DK289.S685 1992
327.47 – dc20 91-22135 CIP

ISBN 978-0-521-41365-7 hardback
ISBN 978-0-521-06341-8 paperback

Contents

Tables

Contributors

JAN S. ADAMS is a faculty associate of the Mershon Center, the Ohio State University, and Director Emeritus of International Studies at Ohio State University. She is the author of *Citizen Inspectors in the Soviet Union: The People's Control Committee* (1977), and more recently "Institutional change and Soviet national security policy," in *Soviet National Security Policy under Perestroika*, edited by George E. Hudson (1990).

PIERRE DU TOIT BOTHA is a researcher in political science and international relations at the Africa Institute of South Africa. He has published extensively in the Institute's journals on Marxism–Leninism in the Third World in general and Africa in particular, as well as in other South African journals on Soviet foreign policy toward the Third World.

ANURADHA MITRA CHENOY is associate professor at the Centre for Soviet and East European Studies of the School of International Studies at Jawaharlal Nehru University. Dr. Chenoy was a Fulbright Scholar at Columbia University and has published on various aspects of Soviet domestic and foreign policy, including most recently "New Soviet stances on conflict resolution," in *Independent Namibia, Problems and Prospects*, edited by Vijay Gupta (1990) and "Resurgence of ethno-nationalism in the USSR," in *Perestroika and the Nationality Question in the USSR*, edited by Shams-ud-Din (1990).

ZAFAR IMAM is professor of Soviet studies and chairman of the Centre for Soviet and East European Studies of the School of International Studies at Jawaharlal Nehru University and editor of the journal *Contemporary Affairs: A Quarterly Journal on Contemporary Issues in India and the Third World in a Global Context.* His publications also include *Restructuring Soviet Society* (1987) and *The USSR. Sixty Years: Economic and Political Development* (1982).

LENA JONSON is a research fellow at the Swedish Institute of International Affairs, Stockholm, where she specializes in Soviet affairs. Earlier she held a post as lecturer and research fellow in the Department of Political Science at the University of Gothenburg. Her recent publications include "What's in store for Northern Europe in the Gorbachev era?" in *Gorbachev and Europe*, edited by Vilho Harle and Jyrki Ivonen (1990) and "Russia and Europe: the emergence of a new Russian foreign policy," in *Peace and Security: Towards a New European Security Order*, edited by G. Herolf and B. Huldt (1991).

HO-WON JEONG is a research associate at Mershon Center and a Ph.D. candidate in Political Science at the Ohio State University. His primary research interests include Soviet policy in East Asia and Soviet relations with newly industrialized countries.

ROGER E. KANET is professor of political science and Director of International Programs and Studies at the University of Illinois at Urbana-Champaign. His recent publications include volumes coedited with Edward A. Kolodziej on *The Cold War as Cooperation: Superpower Cooperation in Regional Conflict Management* (1991) and *The Limits of Soviet Power in the Developing World: Thermidor in the Revolutionary Struggle* (1989).

GARTH T. KATNER is a Ph.D. candidate in the Department of Political Science at the University of Illinois at Urbana-Champaign. He is currently conducting doctoral dissertation research on the topic of international terrorism. He has contributed to a number of review essays that have appeared in *Osteuropa*.

STEPHAN KUX is a research associate at the University of Zurich. He has served as a Ford Foundation post-doctoral fellow at Columbia University and a resident fellow at the Institute for East–West Security Studies in New York. He is the author of *Language and Strategy: A Synoptical Analysis of Key Terms in the Strategic Doctrines of the Nuclear Powers* (1990) and *Soviet Federalism: A Comparative Perspective* (1990).

DEBORAH NUTTER MINER is professor of political science and Director of the Program in International Relations at Simmons College, Boston. She is also a research adjunct of the Center for Science and International Affairs of Harvard University and past president of the Northeast International Studies Association and past board member of the International Studies Association. Her recent publications include "The Soviet Union confronts an interdependent world," *Choix*, Québec (1990), and "What role for limited BMD?" in *Survival* (1987).

OLE NØRGAARD is associate professor at the Institute of Political Science of the University of Aarhus, Denmark. His current research focuses on the political transition in the Baltic republics; he is the author of numerous books and articles on Soviet and East European affairs, including *Politics and Reforms in the Soviet Union: From Khrushchev to Gorbachev* (1986) and *Gorbachev and Western Europe* (1989).

TAMARA J. RESLER is a Ph.D. candidate in the Department of Political Science at the University of Illinois at Urbana-Champaign. Her current research focuses on center–periphery relations and the nationality question in Soviet politics. She has contributed to several review essays published in *Osteuropa* and is the author of a forthcoming article on the impact of republic-level autonomy on Soviet foreign policy.

CAROL R. SAIVETZ is visiting associate professor of political science at Tufts University and a fellow at Harvard University's Russian Research Center. She has written extensively on Soviet policy in the Third World, with special focus on the Middle East. Among her publications are *Soviet–Third World Relations* (1985); *The Soviet Union and the Gulf in the 1980s* (1989); and *The Soviet Union in the Third World* (1989).

BILVEER SINGH is Director of the Institute of International Affairs at the National University of Singapore. His primary research interests include Soviet policy in the Asia-Pacific region. His major publications include *Soviet–ASEAN Relations, 1967–1988* (1989), *The Soviet Union in the Asia–Pacific Region* (1989), and *The Soviet Union in Singapore's Foreign Policy: An Analysis* (1990).

METTE SKAK is assistant professor in peace and conflict research at the Institute of Political Science, University of Aarhus, Denmark. Her research focuses on Soviet foreign policy and Soviet–East European relations. Her recent publications include *Kolos pa lerfødder. En undersøgelse af COMECON-landenes u-landspolitik* [Colossus on clay feet: an investigation into the LDC policy of the CMEA countries, 1989] and *Sovjetunionen og Østeuropa. Fra sovjetisering til europaeisering* [The Soviet Union and Eastern Europe: from Sovietization to Europeanization, 1990].

CARLYLE A. THAYER is associate professor in the Department of Politics, University College, Australian Defence Force Academy. He previously taught at the Faculty of Military Studies at The Royal

Military College, Duntroon. His recent publications include *War by Other Means: National Liberation and Revolution in Vietnam* (1989) and *The Soviet Union as an Asian-Pacific Power: Implications of Gorbachev's 1986 Vladivostok Initiative* (1987).

Preface

Initial drafts of the articles selected for publication in this volume were chosen from among those presented at the Fourth World Congress of the International Council for Soviet and East European Studies, held in Harrogate, England, July 1990. The articles focus on aspects of Soviet policy toward Northern and East-Central Europe, as well as Soviet policy toward the developing countries. As much as the editors would have wished to have provided more comprehensive global coverage of Soviet foreign policy – for example, including Western Europe and North America – contributions of publishable quality in these areas simply were not made available to them.

The chapters that follow are divided into four parts. The first section examines major trends in the current policy of the USSR. The four chapters that comprise part two assess changes in the Soviet–East European relationship, as well as Soviet policy toward Northern Europe and on the general issue of foreign policy neutrality. The third and fourth parts of the book deal with Soviet policy toward the developing countries and present both general overviews of shifts in Soviet policy, as well as more specific regional and country case studies.

The editors wish to express their appreciation to all who have facilitated the preparation of this volume. These include, first of all, the authors of individual chapters and those whose comments at the Harrogate Congress resulted in improvements in the original manuscripts prepared for presentation at the Congress. Sincere thanks go, as well, to Stephen White, general editor of all the volumes resulting from the Harrogate Congress, to Michael Holdsworth and his staff at Cambridge University Press, and to the anonymous readers for the Press who made suggestions for improving the volume. Finally, we are especially indebted to Brian V. Souders, who assisted in editing the original papers and to Fern Kurland of the staff of the Program in International Relations of Simmons College and to members of the secretarial staff of International Programs and Studies at the University of Illinois – especially Betty A. Bruns, Sheila A. Roberts and Karen R. Tempel – for typing and retyping the manuscripts and managing the flow of letters and manuscripts associated with the completion of this project.

ROGER E. KANET
Champaign, Illinois
DEBORAH NUTTER MINER
Boston, Massachusetts
TAMARA J. RESLER
Champaign, Illinois

Introduction

Deborah Nutter Miner

The chapters in this book were written over the period of an extraordinary twelve months from March of 1990 to March of 1991, a year which saw the last events of Gorbachev's reforms – the creation of the post of President of the USSR (eventually to be elected by popular vote) and of Presidential and Federation Councils, the end of the Communist Party's legal monopoly of power; and, in foreign policy the acceptance of the reunification of Germany, and the decision by the leadership to support the US-sponsored resolution in the United Nations permitting the use of force in the Persian Gulf by a US-led coalition against a former Soviet ally. The year also witnessed the beginning of what can only be called reaction caused by the unexpected consequences of Gorbachev's ambitious changes. This reaction took the form of an embargo against Lithuania, a long wait for resolution of the debate over economic reform, capped by the defeat in September 1990 of Shatalin's 500-day plan, Gorbachev's assumption of emergency powers in September, outbursts in the Supreme Soviet by conservative officers, the resignation speech by Foreign Minister Shevardnadze warning of impending dictatorship and his actual resignation, the appointment of conservatives to the posts of Minister of the Interior and Vice-President coupled with the abandonment of Gorbachev by important reformers, the placing of units of the armed forces to patrol the streets in the cities, and the death of fifteen people in Vilnius at the hands of the Soviet army in the course of storming the TV tower. And finally, these last months have witnessed the meteoric rise of Boris Yeltsin as the leader of the opposition to Gorbachev, as the leader of whatever might remain of reform in the Soviet Union. This was the period in which the long-prophesied occurred, although in a somewhat unexpected form: Gorbachev was not pushed out by the right; he chose to move to the right himself.

This dramatic, Janus-like year followed a truly remarkable year of foreign policy reform during which Eastern Europe sprung free of the Soviet Union, of the country that had held it in its grip for over forty years, a country that now stood still and watched, perhaps even lent support, as communist government after communist government fell in what is now called East-Central Europe.

Both the reform and the reaction, of course, are the result of the leadership's decision to deal head-on with the inheritance of the so-called era of stagnation under Brezhnev and actually to begin to dismantle the Stalinist system that had continued in place, albeit without the terror of Stalin, under both Khrushchev and Brezhnev. During these years, Stalin's hard-won battle to industrialize and become a global power, even a superpower, had been slowly reversed by a collective decision not to challenge the comfortable positions of either the party as a whole, the nomenklatura or the important institutional groups into which they had formed. In short, the choice by the leadership of stability for themselves as a group and, hence, policy stagnation during a period of rapid technological, economic, and political change in the rest of the world, seriously weakened the position of the Soviet Union in the international pecking order.

As the Soviet Union has struggled to deal with its decline or crisis of superpowerhood, as it has also been called, Gorbachev and others in the Soviet elite have set out to fashion and implement a foreign policy suitable, not for a superpower in decline, but perhaps for an injured superpower in the process of retraining for future competitions, still with its eye on the gold. It would appear that, although there has been an official, albeit flexible, policy, there have been alternative views within the Soviet elite both of the nature of the Soviet problem and of its solution.

It is not difficult to imagine the confusion and angst generated among the elite by the realization during the last years of the Brezhnev era and the first years under Gorbachev that the Soviet Union had not kept pace with, and had actually fallen far behind, the other industrialized states. The level of surprise, anger, and despair must have fallen along a broad spectrum. The energetic and optimistic Gorbachev of the early years, with his enthusiasm for a reformed socialism and his now discredited belief, expressed in perestroika, that most people in most countries would opt for socialism if given the choice, must have provided the discouraged Soviet elite with a vision and a plan under which they could go forward with some degree of unity and confidence. Now, of course, the internal parts of this plan lie in shambles; and the question is whether the external portion of Gorbachev's reforms will survive and in what form.

New thinking is a carefully thought out construction that integrates domestic and foreign policy and carefully links policy in all regions of the globe. In this sense it shares similarities with old thinking; but the changes in foreign policy growing out of the new thinking have been diverse and dramatic. Each region of the globe has been affected. The chapters in this volume analyze the new thinking, and assess its impact, as well as its likely longevity. They focus on the Nordic countries, Eastern Europe, the European neutrals, Central America, Africa, the Middle East, Southeast Asia, and South Korea. In short, they deal mainly with what might be called the regions rather than with the "great powers" – the United States, Japan, Germany, and China. The relationships among the great powers in the emerging multi-polar world, or what Joseph Nye has called the polycentric world, constitute the framework within which these states and regions will have to maneuver.

The authors of the following chapters answer a group of questions different from those generally asked from 1985 to 1989, which encompass the first two periods of perestroika and new thinking delineated by Roger Kanet and Garth Katner of the University of Illinois in chapter 6. The questions have gone from "Is Gorbachev sincere?" and "How long will he last?" to include "How far to the right will he go?" and "How much of new thinking will survive the conservative reaction?" The authors here have the advantage in their analysis of having been able to view more than five years of new thinking, as well as the advantage of the existence of a fairly open debate within the Soviet Union over its success and validity. These authors chronicle in sufficient detail and with insight these debates among the Soviet political and academic elite. These debates provide the clearest indication of the policy alternatives supported by various groups within the elite and hence the changes that we might see in Soviet foreign policy. Chapter 1 by Deborah Miner of Simmons College outlines the international imperatives for reform that will most likely continue to circumscribe the choices available to the Soviet leadership.

The contributors to this volume provide varying perspectives on Soviet foreign policy, in part because they are a truly international group, with different concerns and insights. Most are from the areas about which they write. Only four substantive contributions were written by Americans – those by Deborah Miner, Roger Kanet and Garth Katner, Jan Adams, and Carol Saivetz. Mette Skak and Ole Nørgaard are from the Danish University of Aarhus. Skak writes about the issues of cohesion and viability in the Soviet empire in Eastern Europe and looks at future Soviet relations with East-Central Europe, and Nørgaard focuses on changes in Soviet–Nordic relations. Lena Jonson from the Swedish Institute of International Affairs analyzes the role of signaling in Soviet–Nordic relations during the Lithuania crisis of 1990; and Stephen Kux, from the University of Zurich in Switzerland, looks at the

Soviet approach to neutrality and the role it could play in Soviet thinking about Europe and the Republics. Anuradha Chenoy of Jawaharlal Nehru University in India focuses on national liberation movements and the dramatic changes in the Soviet interpretation of these movements; and Pierre du Toit Botha of the Africa Institute of South Africa traces the Soviet reassessment of socialist orientation in Africa. Zafar Imam, also of Jawaharlal Nehru University, makes a striking case for the negative impact of new thinking on the position of the Third World; Carlyle Thayer of Australia's Defense Force Academy offers insight into the changing Soviet relationship with Indochina; Bilveer Singh of the Singapore Institute of International Affairs chronicles the evolving ASEAN policy of the current Soviet leadership; and Ho-Won Jeong, a South Korean Ph.D. candidate at the Ohio State University, analyzes the economic, political, and military dimensions of the emerging relationship between South Korea and the Soviet Union. Jan Adams of the Ohio State University examines the shifts in Soviet policy in Central America, and Carol Saivetz of Harvard University's Russian Research Center analyzes recent developments in Soviet policy in the Middle East. Finally, Tamara Resler of the University of Illinois pulls together the major strands of argumentation presented in the individual chapters.

In short, these are refreshing perspectives, approaches and insights that attest to the benefits of the growing global interdependence in social science research. Our epistemology holds that objectivity is our primary goal, but clearly the richness of varying experience and training continue to impress upon us the truth that our field encompasses the subjective as well as the objective, and that it is not sufficient to study our field from a single perspective. The contributors to this volume blend rigorous scholarship and objective standards with the special perspective of being close to the issues at hand.

All but one of the authors share the view that new thinking has represented a significant improvement over the former, Marxist–Leninist-based policy of the Soviet Union. Each, for one reason or another, views the changes in the region about which they write as a positive move toward normalization. In this, the authors represent the views of many peoples and states in the world. On the other hand, new thinking has complicated and made more difficult the situations of those who have seen the Soviet Union as an alternative to the power of the United States and to a Western model of development, one which emphasizes market economies and trade dominated by multinational corporations. Zafar Imam articulates this view clearly in chapter 11. The other contributors – including the editors – ascribe to a Western, non-class-based view of international relations; and they watch with concern the move to the right in Soviet politics. At the same time, as their chapters make clear, their analysis leads to the conclusion that it is not possible for old thinking as we knew it to replace new thinking and that many of the foreign policy changes that have taken place in the past few years will perforce survive into the post-glasnost era.

Part I

The Soviet Union and the international political system

1 Soviet reform in international perspective

Deborah Nutter Miner

The extraordinary changes in foreign and domestic policy initiated by the Soviet Union in the past six years under Mikhail Gorbachev have left all but a very few statesmen and scholars in the West perplexed and unsure of the foundation of their assumptions about policy toward that great half-Western/half-Eastern giant. The years since the death of Chernenko have been filled with contradictory trends, as the forces of conservatism and reform have engaged in a competition with one another. The events in the USSR have been both unprecedented and deeply rooted in the Russian and Soviet past – unprecedented because of the depth and abruptness of the turnaround in both domestic and international affairs, and deeply rooted in the recurrent problems with which the Russian and Soviet leaderships have been forced to deal since the advent of Imperial Russia under Peter the Great.

Because the dramatic shifts in the foreign policy of the USSR have had a direct and critical impact on the foreign policy of the United States, as did the hostility between the two countries which preceded these shifts, it has been the job of scholars since 1985 to probe carefully into the origins, goals, and future of the new political thinking about international relations in the Soviet Union and the foreign policy based on it. Three interrelated sets of questions cluster around these issues at this critical juncture in Soviet history, as Mikhail Gorbachev faces diminishing support for his reforms and appears to be moving toward the right in an effort to retain power. (1) What are the features of the international environment that led to new political thinking? Are these features likely to change in the future or remain the same? (2) What have been the goals of new political thinking in the international arena? Is it merely old political thinking – i.e. Russian or communist expansionism – in new ideological garb? Is its purpose merely to gain time for internal reform, as many conservatives fear? Has it, on the other hand, presaged a revolution in foreign policy with its talk of mutual security and the common interests of mankind transcending class interests, as some others in the West hope? Or is it something between these two poles, an adjustment to new political realities, constituting a policy of what might be called "enlightened realism" for the Soviet Union? Finally, are its tenets, as has been argued recently, so required by the international environment that new political thinking would survive the end of internal reform in the USSR?[1] (3) How does new political thinking fit in with the Russian and Soviet past? Is it a marked departure? What are the antecedents in Russian/Soviet history that can help us better understand its likely future? What can the results of the past efforts at reform reveal about the ability of the current reforms to survive and perhaps even deal with the recurrent problems of border insecurity, the fear of internal chaos, and the issue of nationalities that have always pulled the Russian and Soviet leadership back toward autocracy and repression whenever it has attempted reform?

The struggle to find even partial answers to these difficult questions may lead to a better sense of the future contours of Soviet foreign policy and perhaps a better sense of how the United States and other Western allies should or are apt to respond to it. The following three sections of this chapter address these three clusters of questions about the origins, goals, and future of new political thinking, followed by a conclusion that radical Soviet economic and political reform is a *sine qua non* of great power status, which has been and remains a culturally important goal for the Soviet leadership. Economic success in today's international economy increasingly demands liberalization, market mechanisms, and free flow of information, unlike the requirements for success in previous economic periods. However, the linking of the nationality problem (and the possible break-up of the union) with political liberalization by important leaders in the reform movement, particularly Boris Yeltsin, President of the RSFSR, and Stanislav Shatalin, a former economic adviser to Gorbachev and author of the Shatalin economic plan, has made reform questionable. It has given the military, until recently uncomfortable with but supportive of reform, reason to doubt the outcome of Gorbachev's reform movement and its stake in it. This has made possible the formation of a conservative coalition of the military high command, the KGB, party loyalists, and governmental bureaucrats opposed to new political thinking. Eventually, however, the decreasing ability of an economically and politically unreformed Soviet Union to hold its internal empire together and to assert its influence in international affairs in a multipolar, economically oriented, and technologically sophisticated world will make reform once again a viable option for major groups in the Soviet leadership and society. Until that time, a conservative coalition will be unable to return to a pre-Gorbachev foreign policy, however much it would like to, but it is likely to pursue a less cooperative, more region-oriented foreign policy based on protection of its borders and the securing of aid and investment from countries other than the United States.[2]

The sources of new political thinking

The pressures for the current period of reform in the Soviet Union did not originate within the Soviet Union itself. Although important changes had occurred in both the sociological and psychological make-up of Soviet society and its political elite previous to the initiation of economic and political reform by Mikhail Gorbachev, the demands of the changed and changing international environment, both economic and political, have been the major determinants of Gorbachev's new foreign and domestic policies as they have evolved since 1985.

When Gorbachev took over the reins of leadership from Brezhnev, Andropov, and Chernenko, he was presented with an international environment in which the Soviet Union was faced with increasing difficulty in maintaining its superpower status. Perceptive analysts both within and without the Soviet Union were already making these arguments and had been doing so for some time,[3] and any well-connected and politically knowledgeable traveller, as they all were, from the Soviet Union to the West had to question the previously prevailing view that the Soviets were making gains on the West. Leonid Brezhnev served as General Secretary of the Communist Party of the Soviet Union in a period with a decreasing rate of economic growth. In fact, the rate of growth of industrial output declined steadily throughout his tenure in office. Although it is difficult to trust any figures on Soviet economic growth, it is instructive that both Soviet and American official sources reported this decline. Soviet statistics reported average rates of growth of 10 percent in the 1950s, 7 percent in the 1960s, less than 5 percent in the 1970s, and about 3 percent in the early 1980s; and the CIA estimated percentage growths in Soviet GNP of 5.5 percent in the period 1951–55; 5.9 percent in 1956–60; 5 percent in 1961–65; 5.3 percent in 1966–70; 3.7 percent in 1971–75; and 2.7 percent in 1976–80.[4]

Yet, in spite of this downward trend in the growth of GNP during the Brezhnev period, guns prevailed over both butter and investment in national spending priorities. Throughout this entire period, the Soviets, with a markedly lower per capita GNP than that of the United States – at least one-half if not one-third – put approximately twice the percentage of GNP into the military sector as did their rival. This over-investment in the military sector allowed the Soviets to struggle for and then reach strategic parity with the United States in the late 1960s, recognized and symbolized by the SALT I accords; but it also contributed to the corrosion of the economic strength of the country, already weighed down by the problems of over-centralization and the lack of the market mechanism and individual incentive.[5]

During the late 1960s and early 1970s, the Soviet leadership assumed, as Marxist–Leninist doctrine indicates, that as the correlation of forces – a broader, more encompassing term, which includes socio-political forces, which the Soviets use in place of the balance of power – changed in favor of the Soviet Union, the United States would become more accommodating of Soviet power.[6] They had what they could consider evidence of this in the willingness of the United States to negotiate the SALT I agreement and ABM Treaty. Hence, the Soviet leadership, underestimating American political and military resolve, went forward with the deployment of two new heavy, MIRVed intercontinental ballistic missile (ICBM) systems, the SS-18s and SS-19s, that theoretically had the capability to wipe out the US ground-based ICBMs. Although the United States still retained a deterrent force in its submarines and bombers, conservative strategic thinkers in the United States feared a Soviet move toward superiority and posited a Soviet capability for nuclear blackmail.[7] These concerns multiplied and led to the formation in November 1976 of an organized American voice, the Committee on the Present Danger, arguing for a military build-up. President Carter did initiate such a build-up at the end of his term following the Soviet invasion of Afghanistan, and President Reagan expanded it. The MX and Midgetman missiles, the Trident submarine with the D-5 warhead, cruise missiles, the B-2 and Stealth bombers, and improved command and control as a group promised to turn the tables on the Soviets and to lead them to another, more difficult, round in the arms race.[8]

The Strategic Defense Initiative, announced unexpectedly by Reagan in March of 1983, compounded the military problems confronting the Soviets and signaled that they had lost the technology race. As ill-conceived and technologically impossible as SDI was, it made clear to the Soviets the technological and economic gap between them and the Western world. Although they accurately pointed out that they could successfully negate a US strategic defense with inexpensive and technologically crude countermeasures, and produced a scientifically impressive report demonstrating this fact,[9] such a response was not befitting a superpower any more than minimum deterrence would have been a legitimate superpower response to the strong offensive nuclear threat of the 1960s and 1970s. Prestige and credibility demanded the construction of an equally capable strategic defense. The Soviet leadership knew that its current capabilities for strategic defense were inferior, as evidenced by the outdated technology used in the Krasnoyarsk radar. If the nuclear arms race continued unabated, the Soviets would have to engage in a new and costly round of that race with an adversary that had demonstrated that it had leapfrogged into the post-industrial revolution and was enjoying its benefits in the military sphere.[10] The post-industrial or information-age revolution, based in large part on the effective integration into the economy of breakthroughs in physical processes and the information sciences, has drawn a line between the East and the West akin to the North–South line separating those states that have industrialized and those that have not. The old East–West line is becoming a line drawn not between states with different political and economic organizations, but between societies with different levels of industrialization.[11]

To make matters worse for the Soviets, the technological spin-offs of SDI were heralded to be large, and thus SDI stood as a symbol of future technological progress by a West that had always amazed and impressed the Russian and Soviet rulers by its scientific know-how. And, finally, Western Europe, Japan, and even the newly industrialized countries of East Asia also had left the Soviets behind in this new technological race in the civilian economy, changing the whole international economic game, making Soviet products uncompetitive and unattractive in a world market and making the quality of life as important as territorial integrity and political independence for a state to maintain and protect.

Gorbachev, then, has been looking at a world in which the rules of the game have changed: at a world in which the United States, with a GNP at least double, if not three or more times, that of the USSR, is talking about decline or at least relative decline;[12] at a world in which the Japanese GNP has pulled ahead of that of the USSR; at a world in which the European powers are joining together in an integrated economic community with a potential combined GNP greater than that of the USA; at a world in which even China had achieved an average growth rate of approximately 8 percent before the events in Tiananmen Square of June 1989; at a world in which the newly industrialized countries are stronger traders than the USSR. During the Brezhnev era Soviet foreign and military policy had gone beyond the bounds of what was economically sustainable at a time when those very bounds were changing to the disadvantage of the USSR. Brezhnev's over-investment in the military sector may have led to strategic parity with the United States, but the victory had been Pyrrhic. It had only contributed to a lopsided and technologically backward economy, incapable of technological sophistication, at a time when the possession of advanced technological capabilities had become the *sine qua non* of national power.

The emerging international order is also one in which military power, the Soviets' great strength, will be of decreasing utility. Instead of the Soviet–American military axis acting as the major determinant of international relations, as has been the case since the end of World War II, the Japanese–American–West European economic axis will very likely fulfill this role. The economic means of foreign policy, such as the ability to fund the economic and political transformation of Eastern Europe, increasingly give states more influence than does military capability. This will become only more the case in the 1990s and beyond, as advances in biosciences, such as our means of developing bacteria-produced drugs, disease and weather-resistant plants, and bacteria designed to clean up pollutants, join those in the physical sciences to make the protection and furtherance of human survival and the quality of life central goals and means of foreign policy.[13]

For the Soviets this is not a very pleasant prospect. Soviet military power, already built on a very weak, over-extended economic foundation, is at risk because the Soviet Union, with its centralized economy and strict censorship of information, is in a particularly weak position to participate in the technological revolution that is the basis of modern industrial capacity and which in turn determines the ability of a state to be an effective player in international trade. As important, or more important, is the fact that the Soviet ability to participate in the international economic order is similarly limited. Both of these limitations feed on one another in a downward spiral.

Why is this so? Why are the Soviets in such a weak position technologically? And why is it so hard for them to "play catch-up"? The reasons are many and complex, and by now fairly common knowledge to us all. In part the reason is cultural. There is a need for an entrepreneurial spirit, for risk-taking, for an attention to detail, and for an openness that neither the Russian nor the Soviet tradition provides. There are also political and economic reasons: there is a need for at least a mixed economy with a strong market mechanism, for a strong civilian economy with adequate research and development support, for a consumer market that demands improved products, and for the decentralization of decision making. There is also a need for involvement in the world economy, for relatively free trade with other countries and for the competition that brings. These are not easy accomplishments for an insecure country afraid of foreign influence. Furthermore, there is a need for better information flow – more photocopy machines, more personal computers, and computer networks – all of which are currently circumscribed by Soviet paranoia about security. Finally, there is also a need for strong applied, as opposed to theoretical, science – in the

Soviet Union the applied sciences are looked down upon and are poorly equipped – and for unimpeded contact with the international scientific community. Without all of this, there can be no self-propulsion in the various areas of a technological society.

The decline in the Soviet share of world power, then, is not likely to reverse itself easily or soon. In fact, optimistic analysts, of whom there are fewer and fewer, see a world of five potential great powers in the twenty-first century – Western Europe, Japan, the United States, the Soviet Union, and China – with the Soviets in the difficult position of next-to-last or last among equals.[14] The Soviets are unlikely to be better than fourth in the pecking order, and if the Chinese are able to save their economic reforms, in spite of the tragic events of June of 1989, the Soviets may not fare even that well.

More disturbing to the Soviet leadership must be the prospect that without radical and immediate economic reform and progress, their country may cease to be a global power altogether and may instead at best become a regional power in Europe and Asia, with a limited ability to compete with a united Germany and an integrated European Economic Community for influence in Europe, and with China and Japan for influence in Asia. Already the Soviets have largely retreated from Afghanistan, Africa, the Caribbean, and Central America. This is a sea-change from the days of the 1970s, when Soviet, East European, and Cuban troops served in Africa, and Soviet arms and aid flowed in increasing amounts to client states and created fears of Soviet ascendancy in the Third World.

Perestroika and glasnost are the domestic solutions designed to avert the downward slide in the Soviet Union's place in the international pecking order. Without internal reform, this slide cannot be reversed; and even with reform the task is daunting. Russia was late in coming to the first industrial revolution, following Great Britain, France, Germany, and the United States, but once it began its industrialization in the late nineteenth century, it was able to make remarkable progress, outpacing other European states in its rate of growth.[15] But the technological and societal infrastructure required by the information revolution of the second half of the twentieth century is infinitely more complicated and specialized. And it demands the development of a critical mass of technological sectors to produce the synergism needed to continue to compete successfully. Because this economic revolution is undergoing change at an exponential rate, the later one enters the race, the more difficult this task. Without the continuation and acceleration of internal reform, the Soviet Union's prospects as a great power are grim indeed.

The elaboration and implementation of new political thinking

As noted previously, the foundations of new political thinking developed in the civilian think tanks of the USSR's Academy of Sciences, particularly the Institute for the Study of the USA and Canada and the Institute of the World Economy and International Relations, during the latter years of the Brezhnev–Andropov–Chernenko era. Scholars in these institutes had access to Western political science, had the opportunity to study and travel abroad, and had begun to struggle to develop more adequate explanations of international events than those provided by Marxism–Leninism.

The first hints of Gorbachev's new political thinking appeared in December 1984 in a speech made on his now famous trip to Great Britain before he was elected General Secretary. Its key points were gradually elaborated in subsequent statements on foreign policy by Gorbachev and Shevardnadze, and in articles by scholars in such journals as *Kommunist*, *Mirovaia ekonomika i mezhdunarodnye otnosheniia*, and *SShA*. Briefly, new political thinking argues that in today's world the concept of security has changed such that national security must now be mutual security, and that an adversary's security is as important as that of one's own state. Force is a less useful, as well as less legitimate, means for securing foreign policy objectives than the political and diplomatic means of foreign policy. Arms control at all levels between the superpowers is critical for the deterrence of nuclear war, more critical than the possession of superior military capability. Regional disputes must be settled peacefully on the basis of the interests of all concerned parties. In December 1988, Gorbachev, in a speech to the United Nations, discussed regional disputes and declared that the United Nations is the best forum for the settlement of such issues, and that the Soviet Union would henceforth cooperate fully in its security activities. New political thinking also draws on developing nations of interdependence, arguing that international "interdependence" calls for cooperation by all to solve ecological and other problems. Most significantly, Gorbachev has said that the common interests of mankind have transcended class interest as the basis of international relations. The new thinking further holds that states may pursue different paths to and from socialism and that difference in economic and political systems does not constitute grounds in and of itself for foreign policy disputes.

Gorbachev's enunciation of and support for new political thinking eventually led to foreign policies based on it: the moratorium on underground nuclear testing from August 1985 to February 1987; the freezing of the deployment of SS-20 missiles in Europe; the unilateral reduction of the Soviet armed forces in Europe announced in December of 1988; the INF agreement and the asymmetrical dismantling of all Soviet intermediate-range nuclear forces; the withdrawal of troops from Afghanistan; the support given to the United States and the United Nations in settling the Iran–Iraq war; and eventually the freeing of Eastern Europe in 1989, the reunification of Germany in 1990 within NATO, and most recently, support for US action in the Persian Gulf, as well as for UN-sponsored peace settlements in Cambodia and Angola.

Given these actions, it is difficult to argue any longer that new thinking is old thinking in new ideological garb. New thinking does, in fact, have a large propaganda component, with its talk of Soviet support for mutual security, interdependence, and the common interests of mankind, but it has clearly not been a hoax to lure the West into complacency; whether it is merely an attempt to gain space and time and reform is more difficult to assess. At the same time, it has not been a "revolution" in foreign policy presaging the end of the pursuit of self-interest by states, and the end of conflict, as some in the West would like to think. While Gorbachev's ideas may sound similar to those of Western political scientists writing about global humanism and world order, they are not the same. Gorbachev clearly does have a "bottom line" when it comes to Soviet interests and has not gone beyond it in order to accommodate the needs of other states or groups. His conception of security is liberal, but it is not nonexistent.

Instead, his is a sophisticated conception of self-interest and security appropriate to a multipolar, economically interdependent world. It makes a great deal of sense to see Gorbachev's foreign policy not as a revolution, but as an erratic evolution – an evolution by fits and starts from the time of Lenin until today when the Soviet Union has finally come to see itself as a "normal" state in the interstate system. New political thinking appears to mark the end of the revolutionary goals of Soviet foreign policy and involves an acceptance of a state-centered, non-ideological world in which all states accept the legitimacy of other states. For a state to accept the legitimacy of other states which are "different" economically or politically requires a degree of self-confidence and trust not previously seen in Soviet foreign policy and not common in that of tsarist Russia. Observers and scholars have often noted the sense of isolation, inferiority, and paranoia associated with Russian and Soviet foreign policy. New thinking has none of these traits and reflects a more open and tolerant view of international affairs, a view shorn of the insecurity of the past, allowing the Soviet leadership to be both hard-nosed and pragmatic, on the one hand, and cooperative and trusting on the other. It has served several goals, each of which is more important to some groups in the Soviet leadership than others: (1) to gain space and time for reform and the Soviet game of "catch up"; (2) to lessen the defense budget; (3) to rearrange spending priorities among guns, butter, and investment; and (4) to appear "responsible" and non-ideological in order that the Soviets can assume a place in international trade and in those international organizations that set the rules of trade.

Seen in this light, Gorbachev is what Western scholars refer to as a neo-realist, or enlightened realist, if realism is understood to mean an active concern with the distribution of capabilities and power among states. Gorbachev is intensely concerned with the Soviet power position and wishes to improve it. At the same time, as a neo- or enlightened realist, he understands that the world is moving toward some form of multipolarity, as well as increasing economic interdependence and that in this new world the game will be played differently in some respects. The pursuit of self-interest, and the resulting disagreement and conflict, will remain the underlying dynamic of international politics in a world dominated by trade and other economic issues and in which many problems will demand cooperative solutions and still others will be amenable to such solutions. Gorbachev's plans call for the Soviet Union to be in a position of strength in this new world.

This emerging world of interdependence will remain state centered. While states will be intimately connected through trade and finance, states will pursue their self-interest within those bounds. Interdependence in Europe works because it serves the economic interests of the states involved; and if there ever is a United States of Europe, it will be because those states chose this course as in their best interests. Enlightened self-interest in a multipolar world does not deny the satisfaction of the interests of the state; it merely sees the interest of that state as tied to the satisfaction of the interests of other states. It seeks a shared view of international relations, the legitimacy of the great powers, and cooperation in solving problems, on the idea of a concert system akin to that of the early nineteenth century in Europe or what Gulick has called the balance of power system.[16]

New thinking, then, is both transitional and permanent – transitional in that it is geared to the period when the Soviet Union is playing catch-up, and permanent in the sense that many of its tenets make sense in the multipolar, economically interdependent world most scholars expect to emerge in the twenty-first century. We should, then, expect that both now and in the future the Soviets will continue to be protective of their interests and their security, as has in fact been the case under Gorbachev. He has been careful to protect the security interests of the

Soviet Union. The INF treaty, despite asymmetrical Soviet cuts, does not jeopardize Soviet interests in Europe, and his START proposals are in accord with the current plans of the Soviet military to move the Soviet nuclear arsenal away from vulnerable fixed, land-based ICBMs to mobile ICBMs and submarines. If the Soviet Union is able to improve its international position, it will be more inclined to play a leadership role and to exert its influence on global issues. In the meantime, it is "hunkering down" to deal with its internal reform.

A good example of "enlightened self-interest" is the Soviet attitude toward the United Nations. In December 1988 Gorbachev spelled out a reversal of past Soviet policy toward the United Nations and advocated a larger role for the UN and the Security Council in particular in solving international disputes. Since the Soviet Union has one of five permanent seats with a right of veto on the Security Council, an increased Security Council involvement in peaceful settlement would give the Soviet Union influence in disputes it might not otherwise have. This is an effective way of achieving influence over US foreign policy at very little cost.

Interestingly, Gorbachev has been able to secure military and KGB acceptance of new political thinking, most likely for what they see as its transitional nature and because of the need during this transition to create an international environment favorable to reform. Such an environment will allow the Soviet Union to resume its place in the international pecking order. The more "enlightened" parts of new thinking have always occasioned criticisms by some of the military and KGB High Command, although Gorbachev has been able to outmaneuver them.[17] During 1989 and 1990, middle-ranking military officers and the High Command have been increasingly disturbed by a Soviet foreign policy that allowed the revolutions in Eastern Europe, the dissolution of the Warsaw Pact, and the reunification of Germany and its membership in NATO; that has supported the United States in the Persian Gulf; and that has reduced significantly the size of the army and has subjected the army to harassment and danger in the republics of the Soviet Union. This leads to the question of whether new thinking is the *only* workable foreign policy option for the Soviets in today's world. Scholars have recently argued that this is the case, that Gorbachev's foreign policy would survive the fall of Gorbachev or a turn by Gorbachev to the right, both of which options appear increasingly probable.[18] The foreign policy differences between the military and Gorbachev give a sense of what would be a possible alternative to Gorbachev's new thinking.

It is true that Soviet foreign policy cannot return to the pre-Gorbachev era because the Soviet Union does not have the capability to function as a global power, which would mean competing in a major technological arms race with the United States or in a foreign aid race with Western Europe or Japan. However, it would be possible for the Soviet Union to pursue a European and Asian regional policy that would be less "enlightened" and more willing to work against the interests of the United States. The Soviet Union could seek agreement with Germany whereby the Soviet Union stays out of Eastern Europe, but retains its current Western borders, and for which Germany in return is generous in aiding and trading with the Soviets. The Soviet Union could also reach accommodation with Japan, although this is admittedly more difficult, by returning the Northern Islands to Japanese sovereignty and similarly seeking Japanese aid and trade. The Soviet Union could at the same time return to a less cooperative policy toward the United States, reverting to a perception of the United States as threatening because of its military capabilities. Such a Soviet policy would be more willing to champion anti-American forces in the Third World, and less willing to support American-led coalitions such as the one in the Persian Gulf. Had the Soviets not supported the United States in the Security Council resolutions creating the embargo against Iraq and allowing the use of force in the Gulf, a US-led coalition against Iraq would have been problematic, particularly since China might have been bolder in expressing its concerns about the operation.

In short, Soviet foreign policy could work to frustrate US goals and could seek to split the US–Western European–Japanese alliance, all the while depending on Western Europe and Japan for economic aid. A multipolar world does not have to be cooperative, although it can be, and there has been every reason to be hopeful that the relations among the great powers in the emerging world order will be cooperative. But, as happened in the nineteenth century, multipolar systems can lead to concert-type arrangements that promote cooperation among the great powers or to confrontational systems filled with mistrust, anxiety, and conflict. After several decades of an operating concert among the great powers, Britain and France feared the power of Russia after its participation in ending the revolutions in 1848; this led to the Crimean War of 1853–55. And, in turn, defeat in the Crimean War led Russia to become a revisionist state and to break with the idea of a concert, which in turn favored the nineteenth-century unification of Germany,[19] the subsequent growth of which was destabilizing to the European order.

Soviet policy, out of fear of US power, then, could return to a more distrustful mode, concerned to protect its borders by alliances with strong neighbors and to frustrate US foreign policy globally by not supporting US goals in the Third World. Such a policy would be workable in a period of internal reaction, might very well be capable of procuring economic support for the Soviet state without its full transition to a market economy, and at the same time allow the Soviets to attempt to deal with their restive nationalities. It would certainly not allow the Soviets to reform and to improve its technological competitiveness quickly. It might, however, very well be a satisfactory compromise to the military high command and other conservative forces.

The return to Russian conservatism?

The international environment has always played a critical role in determining not only the foreign but also the domestic policy of the Russian-Soviet state. It bears remembering that at various times in its history, it has been subject to threats from without, starting with the threat of a powerful Mongol empire in the East and continuing with threats from powerful states to the West: the Poles and Lithuanians, the Swedes, the French, and the Germans. These experiences have generated the Russians' unusual concern with their relative power position; and a centuries-old sense of cultural, economic, and political inferiority relative to the West has made them even more insecure and intent on achieving and then retaining international rank and prestige.

The Russians, from the time of Peter the Great, have been determined to secure a position of power in the European world. Part of the social contract between Stalin and his successors, on the one side, and the Soviet people on the other, is that the Soviet Union be *powerful*. The strength of the neo-Stalinist group in the Soviet Union is based in great part on this. Through his rapid industrialization policy of the thirties and forties, Stalin made Russia the great power it had not been since the time of the Congress of Vienna after the defeat of Napoleon, when Russian power was at its height. From 1814 until its defeat in the Crimean War of 1853, Russia was considered the most powerful state in Europe. The defeat in Crimea demonstrated that the Russian economic and social systems were anachronistic and could not compete with those of Western Europe. Following reforms such as the abolition of serfdom and the reorganization of the financial system by Alexander II in the second half of the nineteenth century, the industrial revolution took hold, only to be interrupted by the revolutions of 1917, themselves in part the result of the important but diluted reforms put in place to reposition Russia in the world. It was not until Stalin's revolution, as horrendous as it was, that the Soviet Union reclaimed its place as a great power.

This desire to be a great power is deeply engrained in the Russian-Soviet psyche. The problem has always been Russia's backwardness relative to the West. Peter first raised the issue of reform on a Western model and the issue has been a contentious one since that time. It was raised most consistently and articulately in the nineteenth century by critics and revolutionaries and pervades Soviet thinking to this day.

The period following the Crimean War was one of the most dramatic occasions when Russia faced the prospect of being a weak state internationally and turned toward internal modernization and reform to reverse the situation under Alexander II. Although his abolition of serfdom did not solve the problem of land reform, this in addition to his financial reforms and his encouragement of railway-building and industrialization led to an impressive average annual rate of growth of 8 percent in industrial output. Interestingly, this reform period coincided with a period of what was known as *recueillement* in foreign affairs, based on the realization that for a number of years Russia would have to play a less active role in international affairs and avoid "foreign adventures" while concentrating on internal reform.

Another era of comparable reforms was the period of Lenin's New Economic Policy following defeat in World War I and a costly victory in the Civil War. The reforms of Alexander II and of Lenin are interesting benchmarks for the current reforms. In neither case were the reforms completed. Gorbachev and Soviet scholars themselves refer back to Lenin and the period of the New Economic Policy as they struggle to reform. Lenin, the great pragmatist, knew that the Soviet state was relatively weak and needed to reform internally, as well as to pursue a more moderate policy internationally, particularly with regard to trade. All of these reforms were followed after Lenin's death by Stalin and his policies of rapid industrialization and enforced collectivization, which has made many observers, both Soviet and Western, skeptical and fearful for the outcome of the present reforms. Such a brutal reaction did not follow Alexander's reforms, but they, too, ended in reaction.

Alexander's reforms were slowed down and essentially stopped by internal resistance. The opposition was able to use the threat of internal rebellion to bolster its argument that political reform was dangerous and destabilizing. The Polish insurrection of 1863, the attempt on Alexander's life in 1866, and the growth of revolutionary movements in the country slowly turned the tide away from reform until the assassination of Alexander II and the advent of the reign of the intensely conservative Alexander III ended reform altogether.[20] Lenin's reforms may have been less a reform than a tactical retreat that was quickly reversed. However, a comparison of the reforms of Alexander II and Lenin with those of Gorbachev can lead to another, not wholly pessimistic conclusion. The Soviet Union after the Civil War was weak and needed trade, credits, and diplomatic recognition to strengthen itself in the world. Lenin was responding primarily to signs of political instability resulting from desperate conditions at home. His policy of relaxation of internal political and economic controls and of improvement in relations with the capitalist powers was designed to save the Bolshevik regime. Foreign policy concerns had to come second. But the international economic system did not demand full participation in order for a state to survive and prosper, and it was possible to cope with this political instability without fully opening up to the rest of the world. Hence, Stalin's plan of economic autarky, political isolation, and rapid industrialization was a viable alternative to Lenin's policy, an alternative that offered, among other things, both growth and power. Lenin's policy was not the only policy, in fact was probably not the best policy that could offer the Soviet Union a quick return to the great power club.

In the case of Alexander III, the situation was similar in this regard. Although Russia's international position could have been improved by more internal economic and political reforms, the country was able to advance its position dramatically under Alexander III and even under Nicholas II. By 1914 it was the fourth largest industrial power in the world. Russia's hidden backwardness hurt it, but did not keep it from steady industrial progress, and its leaders were able to believe that the lack of reform would *not* lead to its exclusion from the club of great powers, even though we now know that the antiquated structures of the tsarist regime were unable to cope with the long-drawn-out war that was to come. As A.J.P. Taylor points out, the other great powers expected Russia eventually to outdistance Germany in industrial power: "The British were right to suppose after 1905 that their weight was needed to hold Germany in check; but also right in their belief that, if the struggle could be postponed, the growth of Russia could prevent it altogether."[21]

Similarly at the time of Khrushchev's reforms, the Soviet Union was growing at an adequate pace and could reasonably expect to continue to grow and conceivably to outstrip the West. Brezhnev's more conservative policies could thus be seen as no more risky, perhaps even less risky, than those of Khrushchev. Brezhnev did institute more openness than had his predecessors in foreign policy, but he did not bring the Soviet Union into the world economy. No one in the Soviet leadership would have expected him to do so, as it still seemed possible to sustain growth and maintain superpower status without such participation.

Yet it was during this period that the world was changing in such a way that this self-imposed isolation meant a dramatic decline in Soviet economic strength, putting at risk the Soviet international position. Some Soviet scholars and policy makers realized this, as the rate of economic growth took a sharp downturn. Andropov tried a reform based on improving the efficiency of the old system, but it was bound to fail. The Stalinist system, no matter how efficient, was no longer a viable alternative. Soviet scholars during the Brezhnev era had come to realize this, as did, we assume, Gorbachev and other members of the top leadership. Gorbachev's policies, although they are focused on domestic and foreign policy reform, are dictated by the international environment, with its technological and economic demands, and by the Soviet Union's deep-seated desire to remain a great power. These goals have until recently been shared or at least accepted by the major decision-making groups in the USSR, including the military. That the military has allowed the drastic changes in foreign policy that have occurred is testimony to how seriously they view the problem. For the military and other conservative groups more than for Gorbachev and his advisors, new thinking has most likely been regarded as a *transitional* phenomenon – in the vein of Lenin's one step backwards, and akin to the numerous Russian and Soviet reverses of the past.

In the past two years, however, the military has had more and more difficulty seeing Gorbachev's new thinking as a positive step toward Soviet renewal in foreign policy. New thinking has come up against the nationality problem. Gorbachev and his intellectual advisers were slow to recognize the impact of this difficult and potentially unsolvable issue. As the various republics have demanded autonomy and independence, as in the Baltics and Georgia, as the conflict erupts between ethnic groups as in Central Asia and the Caucasus, as old ties with other nations reassert themselves as in Moldavia, reform becomes dangerous to the very survival of the Soviet Union and the question of its global position becomes more abstract. In the past year, the military has been subjected to attacks and harassment in the republics, and it has had the added indignity of its retiring ranks facing homelessness. Perestroika, glasnost, and new thinking are not likely to make sense to an institution whose mission and capabilities are both threatened at home.

The defeat of the Shatalin 500-day plan for radical economic reform in the Fall of 1990 is symptomatic of this.[22] The Shatalin plan not only called for privatization but also gave economic sovereignty to the republics, with the Soviet Union retaining only those economic powers delegated to it by the individual republics. It was this aspect of the plan – its economic decentralization and the potential political consequences – that made it unacceptable. It can be argued convincingly that this is the only solution to the crisis of the Soviet empire. Ideally, such a plan would create a situation similar to that of the emerging European community: a group of states voluntarily cooperating for their individual and combined good. It can also be argued persuasively that the only alternatives to this are repression and coercion, which will render impossible economic reform and international power. But the sad truth is that the Soviet Union is not the economic magnet that the European Community has become. On the contrary, one can most accurately describe the forces between the Union and the republics as magnetically repulsing, not attracting. The republics, and in some cases the autonomous republics, are pushing away from what they realistically see as an economic morass and are drawn instead to other, more economically secure neighbors, as the Baltics look toward Scandinavia and Germany, or to ethnically similar neighbors, as in the case of Moldavia.

Conservative forces, then, have two unpalatable choices: (1) new thinking, which has allowed Eastern Europe to go free and has encouraged the desire for independence in the Soviet Union itself; and has reduced the size, influence, and prestige of the army, all for the long-term goal of economic equality with the West or (2) less internal political and hence economic reform in order to hold the Union together. The link-up of the republics and the democratic forces in the RSFR under Yeltsin and Gorbachev's own unwillingness to contemplate the break-up of the empire have pushed even Gorbachev away from the first option and into alliance with the military and other anti-reform forces in the Communist Party and the bureaucracy.

The costs of this policy are high – delaying the information revolution in the USSR, slipping lower in the international pecking order and out of the ranks of the great power club and into the ranks of secondary or regional status, and risking membership in the IMF, World Bank, and GATT. But the alternative, the break-up of the Union, is as of now even more unpalatable. What is needed is the confidence to let the republics go, even though the risks of this are at the present incalculable and threatening and hence impossible to accept. A new thinking of the nationality problem must come before radical internal reform and new thinking in foreign policy can survive. The Soviet Union under a less reformist leadership cannot return to political hostility and economic isolation, but it will probably not be the cooperative, internationally minded Soviet Union of the 1987–90 era.

Notes

1 Allen Lynch, "Does Gorbachev matter anymore?" *Foreign Affairs*, vol. 69, no. 3 (Summer 1990), pp. 19–29.

2 This conclusion revises one I have previously expressed, most recently in Deborah Nutter Miner, "The Soviet Union confronts an interdependent world," in *La Politique étrangère sovietique à l'aube des années 90* (Quebec: Centre Québécois de Relations Internationales, Collection Choix), 1990, pp. 1–8.

3 For a detailed and insightful discussion of the development of new political thinking in the Soviet Union before Gorbachev, see Allen Lynch, *Gorbachev's International Outlook: Intellectual Origins and Political Consequences* (New York: Westview Press, 1989).

4 Cited in Paul Dibb, *The Soviet Union: The Incomplete Superpower* (Urbana: University of Illinois Press, 1986), pp. 67, 72.

5 The problem of the lack of market mechanism in the Soviet Union has been analyzed fully by such scholars at Anders Åslund in *Gorbachev's Struggle for Economic Reform* (Ithaca, *NY*: Cornell University Press, 1989), Ed A. Hewett in *Reforming the Soviet Economy* (Washington, D.C.: Brookings, 1988), and Marshall Goldman in *USSR in Crisis: The Failure of an Economic System* (New York: Norton, 1983).

6 This argument is put forward in Peter H. Vigor, *The Soviet View of Disarmament* (London: Macmillan, 1986).

7 Colin S. Gray was the most outspoken and articulate proponent of this theory. See, for example, his article, "The Strategic forces triad," *Foreign Affairs*, vol. 56, no. 4 (July 1978), pp. 771–89.

8 The strategic situation faced by the Soviet Union in the early 1980s is clearly spelled out in Robbin F. Laird and Dale R. Herspring, *The Soviet Union and Strategic Arms* (Boulder, CO: Westview Press, 1984), especially pp. 139–52.

9 Yevgeni Velikhov, Roald Sagdeev, and Andrei Kokoshin, *Weaponry in Space: The Dilemma of Security* (Moscow: Mir Publishers, 1986).

10 Daniel Bell refers to three industrial revolutions: the first based on the steam engine and factory machine production; the second on electricity and chemistry; and the third on computers and telecommunications. See Daniel Bell, "The world and the United States in 2013," *Daedalus* vol. 116, no. 3 (Summer 1987), pp. 1–21.

11 A clear picture of these "lines" is found in Gerard Chaliand and Jean-Pierre Rageau, *Strategic Atlas: A Comparative Geopolitics of the World's Powers* (New York: Harper and Row, 1990), p. 183.

12 I will not go into the debate on decline, except to note that this chapter is influenced by the arguments of both Paul Kennedy, *The Rise and Fall of the Great Powers* (New York: Random House, 1987), and Joseph S. Nye, Jr., *Bound to Lead: The Changing Nature of American Power* (New York: Basic Books, 1990).

13 Miles Kahler explores the impact of these advances in "Science and technology," *Foreign Affairs*, vol. 69, no. 4 (Fall 1990), pp. 123–38.

14 See Kennedy, *The Rise and Fall of the Great Powers*, pp. 488–514, especially p. 513.

15 A.J.P. Taylor in *The Struggle for the Mastery of Europe 1848–1918* (Oxford: The Clarendon Press, 1957) is more impressed by Russian industrial growth between 1890 and 1914 than is Paul Kennedy. But both recognize its existence. See Taylor's introduction, pp. xxx–xxxi, and Kennedy, *The Rise and Fall of the Great Powers*, pp. 488–514.

16 Edward Gulick, *Europe's Classical Balance of Power* (New York: W.W. Norton and Company, 1955).

17 See Bruce Parrott, "Soviet national security under Gorbachev," *Problems of Communism*, vol. 37, no. 11 (November 1988), pp. 1–36.

18 See Lynch, "Does Gorbachev matter anymore?"

19 Norman Rich in *Why the Crimean War? A Cautionary Tale* (Hanover, NH: University of New England Press, 1985) discusses the end of the concert idea and its result in the Crimean War, as well as making some interesting comments in his conclusion about the choice of a concert or "grouping" policy. The standard account of Russian foreign policy in the nineteenth century which discusses the breakdown of the concert system and its impact on Russia is found in Barbara Jelavich, *A Century of Russian Foreign Policy 1814–1914* (New York: J.B. Lippincolt Company, 1964).

20 Michael Karpovich provides an overview of the reforms in *Imperial Russia, 1801–1927* (New York: Henry Holt and Company, 1932). Fuller accounts are found in Nicholas V. Riasanovsky's standard *A History of Russia* (New York: Oxford University Press, 1984) and Hugh Seton-Watson, *The Decline of Imperial Russia* (Boulder, CO: Westview Press, 1985).

21 Taylor, *The Struggle for the Mastery of Europe*, p. xxxii. Taylor goes on to argue that the British failed to understand the implications of the growth of the United States: "They failed to realize that, if they quarrelled, America might step in to knock their heads together – and would be strong enough to do so." *ibid.*

22 See Ed A. Hewett, "The new Soviet plan," *Foreign Affairs*, vol. 69, no. 5 (Winter 1990–91), pp. 146–66; also see John Tedstrom and Philip Hanson, "The economics and politics behind Shatalin's plan for an economic union," *Report on the USSR*, vol. 2, no. 42 (October 19, 1990).

Part II

The Soviet Union and Europe

2 The changing Soviet–East European relationship

Mette Skak

One of the most fascinating aspects of the democratic revolutions in Eastern Europe in the latter half of 1989 was Soviet behavior.[1] Not only did the Soviets applaud the overthrow of authoritarian socialist regimes, they actively intervened against them on several occasions and thereby totally reversed the familiar pattern of Soviet intervention in Eastern Europe. The USSR has relinquished the old principle of communist one-party rule. This is a revolutionary development which signifies that hegemony is being replaced by normal interstate relations in the Soviet–East European relationship.

The final step in the radicalization of Soviet policy toward Eastern Europe was taken in August 1989 in connection with the negotiations on the establishment of a Solidarity-led Polish government. Throughout the summer, the Soviet Union was somewhat ambiguous in its pursuit of pan-Europeanism and self-determination in Eastern Europe. Indeed, this ambivalence culminated in a campaign against reformers in Hungary and Poland that lasted until about 12 August.[2] Soviet foreign ministry spokesmen warned against attempts at "destabilization" and criticized the "maneuvers" of Solidarity thereby pressuring Solidarity to offer the Polish Communist Party, the PZPR, the crucial ministries of the interior and defense. Afterwards, the Soviets displayed loyalty toward Solidarity and put pressure on the PZPR instead. On 22 August, a few days after Tadeusz Mazowiecki had been nominated prime minister, Gorbachev devoted a 40-minute phone call urging Rakowski to join the Solidarity-led government.[3] The night of 22 August was equally historic, as it was the night when Hungarian Foreign Minister Guyla Horn decided to let the East German refugees use his country as an escape route to West Germany. Before making that decision, which meant breaking a treaty with the GDR, Lászlo Kovács of the Hungarian foreign ministry had obtained Soviet approval.

The exodus from the GDR, in turn, was a decisive catalyst for the collapse of the Honecker regime. Gorbachev already had warned Honecker, in connection with the fortieth anniversary of the GDR in early October, that "he who comes too late will be punished by life itself." When hundreds of thousands went into the streets in Leipzig on 8 October, the Soviet ambassador, Kochemasov, issued a directive to the commander-in-chief of the Soviet forces in the GDR, Snetkov, not to intervene. As for Peter Mladenov's palace coup against Todor Zhivkov of Bulgaria on 9 November, diplomats insist that Mladenov had talked to Gorbachev in advance about removing Zhivkov. Whether this is true or not, Gorbachev already on 10 November, the day of the Central Committee meeting confirming Zhivkov's dismissal, sent a telegram to Mladenov stating that the USSR would stand by as he implemented radical reform.

Soon after the events in the GDR and Bulgaria came the Czechoslovak "Velvet Revolution" triggered by police violence against 3,000 young demonstrators on 17 November; rumors had it that one student was killed. The enormously popular Civic Forum and the Public against Violence gradually emerged as the leaders in the Czechoslovak uprising.[4] Soviet leaders warned the Czech government that they would not tolerate violence, and on 16 November Moscow summoned chief party ideologist Jan Fojtik to say that the Soviet Union publicly would denounce its 1968 invasion of Czechoslovakia.

The Kremlin claimed that it "foresaw" the overthrow of the Ceauşescu regime in Romania, and many have speculated on an active Soviet role in this. But closer investigations do not confirm the Moscow conspiracy theory, which also would be surprising in view of the limited Soviet leverage over internal affairs in Romania. In a press conference on 25 December, Soviet Deputy Foreign Minister Ivan Aboimov stressed that the Warsaw Treaty members did not discuss a military intervention, although they did consult each other on the Romanian crisis.[5] But clearly Soviet sympathies were on the side of the anti-Ceauşescu forces, when the showdown finally came.

The pattern of Soviet behavior was that of pulling the carpet out from under orthodox communists in an attempt to pave the way for radical reform communism in Eastern Europe.[6] So, what actually happened and has happened since then went far beyond Soviet wishes. This makes the strict Soviet adherence to the Sinatra doctrine, i.e., the right of East Europeans to "do it their way," all the more striking.[7] Gone are the demands that communists should be heading certain ministries; instead, the Soviet leaders have let bourgeois governments take over in the GDR, Hungary, Poland, and Czechoslovakia.

Why did the Soviet Union intervene in support of democracy in Eastern Europe, and what has brought this volte-face in Soviet foreign policy? This is the first question addressed in the following analysis of the changing Soviet–East European relationship. I shall point to problems of hegemony and modernization and to developments at the level of actors as well as cognition. The second part of this contribution concerns how the Soviet–East European relationship is changing. The overall observations are that the Soviet Union is intent on maintaining close cooperation with Eastern Europe and probably would prefer a primacy-like position as the end result. The new Soviet–German economic axis provides the Soviet Union with some levers of influence. Generally, however, Soviet power and influence in Eastern Europe is declining, although developments are more contradictory than often perceived.

The analytical point of departure is Soviet interests, options and developments. For better or worse the USSR continues to shape developments in Eastern Europe, although the image of the Soviet Union as a monolithic actor is more misleading than ever. Before beginning the analysis, a historical introduction to the Soviet–East European relationship is warranted, since their relations were always very problematic.

Russia, the Soviet Union and Eastern Europe

Originally, the Russian approach to Eastern Europe built upon apprehension of security, e.g. in the era of the strong Polish–Lithuanian state (from 1386). The Polish intervention into Russian affairs during the Time of Troubles – for example, when the Poles ravaged Moscow in 1610 – contributed to the Russian perception of vulnerability. But at times Russia was an equally threatening power to East Europeans, especially following the establishment of the Russian Empire in 1721. Russia played a vital part in the partitions of Poland, and a strange mixture of Russian interventionism and Messianism toward Eastern Europe characterized the nineteenth century.

The first half of the century was the era of the Holy Alliance among Russia, Prussia and Austria, an arrangement that led to Russian military interventions in Poland in the winters of 1830–31 and 1863–64 and in Hungary in 1849 to crush nationalistic upheaval. For the Poles and the Hungarians, Russian behavior was an anticipation of Soviet interventions in the latter half of the twentieth century for the sake of preserving the socialist status quo.[8] The Balkan Slavs in particular came to feel the Messianic side of Russian political culture in the form of Pan-Slavism in the latter half of the century. But contrary to common perceptions, the Bulgarian–Russian relationship was not one of pure harmony, and Romania generally fell victim to Russian foreign policy.

As for the early Soviet period, the role of the Czechoslovak legion in the Civil War in 1918 and the Polish attack on Ukraine in 1920 could only add to the Russian mistrust of the East Europeans. According to Hugh Seton-Watson it was the February revolution of 1917 and not the October revolution that raised hopes among Eastern Europeans because they needed Russia's support against the Germans, the Austrians and the Turks.[9] Seen from Eastern Europe, the October revolution paved the way for German economic dominance in Eastern Europe because of the Bolshevik withdrawal from World War I. So motives of self-defense played a role when several East European governments later sided with Nazi Germany. For the Poles, Soviet conduct during World War II, particularly the massacre in the Katyn Forest and Soviet passivity during the 1944 insurrection in Warsaw, was traumatic.

The overall point here is that the Soviet–East European relationship was characterized by mutual apprehension and tension even before 1945 and the subsequent brutal Sovietization of Eastern Europe. The latter era marked the decisive poisoning of an already strained relationship. The politico-cultural impact of the history of the Soviet–East European relationship has been a Soviet perception of Eastern Europe as a target for the legitimate pursuit of hegemony – as an alternative to right-wing nationalism and bourgeois political influence if not outright aggression. East Europeans tend to see the Soviet Union as a reactionary, despotic, atheistic and un-European power.

Sovietization was preceded by excesses on the part of the liberating Red Army, and Soviet demands of war reparations and other economic arrangements crippled the economies of Eastern Europe. Sovietization meant the imposition of the Soviet totalitarian structure – with its extreme centralism, collectivization, purges, etc. – upon the Eastern European societies and the establishment there of an indigenous nomenklatura elite. But it also meant progress in terms of industrial development and modernization, and it introduced in Eastern Europe the educational revolution with its broad political impact. The expansion of education has been instrumental in creating the social and mental basis for the systemic change of 1989–90. As Bogdan Denitch has noted, "Increasingly large groups now exist that demand some of the amenities traditionally associated with middle-class European life, and the regimes are pressed to fulfil these needs in a number of ways."[10] Later in this chapter I shall elaborate upon the perspective of development dynamics introduced here.

Problems of hegemony and modernization

Why did the Soviets give up hegemony in Eastern Europe? A simple answer is that they had to concentrate on the mounting problems at home. While there is some truth in this view, it fails to account for the element of calculation and decision in Soviet behavior toward Eastern Europe. As shown above, the USSR was neither disinterested nor passive regarding the changes in Eastern Europe. The dynamics and problems of the Soviet–East European relationship reflect the hegemonic role of the Soviet Union *vis-à-vis* Eastern Europe. According to Hedley Bull, hegemony is defined as a medium type of dominance relationship, i.e. a soft type of dominance:

> Occupying an intermediate position between dominance and primacy there is hegemony. Where a great power exercises hegemony over the lesser powers in a particular area or constellation, there is resort to force and the threat of force, but this is not habitual and uninhabited but occasional and reluctant. The great power . . . will employ [force] . . . with a sense that in doing so it is incurring a political cost.[11]

The reason why the Soviet position in relation to Eastern Europe has been one of hegemony rather than outright dominance is that Soviet interests *vis-à-vis* Eastern Europe were always in conflict.

As James Brown has argued, the Soviet interest in cohesion within the socialist community clashed with the interests in viability, i.e. stable and efficient regimes.[12] The conflict between cohesion and viability is a conflict between Sovietization and modernization and a conflict between short-term and long-term interests, respectively. Thus, it is the challenge of adapting to a changing (modernizing) environment that is the ticking bomb under hegemonical systems.[13] Eastern Europe became a tremendous burden for the Soviet Union economically and strategically, and so "the empire struck back," as Valerie Bunce observed years ago.

The above reasoning hinges on the validity of the concepts of change and development. The Soviet withdrawal from Eastern Europe can be viewed as a function of development dynamics because what characterizes Soviet-type states is not only repression and a rigid power structure but the deliberate choice of industrialization and "scientific-technological revolution." This implies choosing the same kind of development dynamics that characterize pluralist societies, i.e. increasing complexity, international interdependence and the increasing saliency of non-military issues of security. Actually, the approach of modernization is well established as a Sovietological paradigm.[14]

When applied to Soviet-type societies, the approach of modernization emphasizes the unintentional aspects of development, because they may be transformed into structural hindrances to the maintenance of the economic and political structures of these societies, as well as into social and political forces behind social change. The educational revolution that paved the way for rising demands of participation, as cited above, is one example of this phenomenon. This hypothesis of "fundamental democratization" can be traced back to Karl Mannheim's monograph *Man and Society in the Age of Reconstruction* (New York, 1940) but has been reiterated in later contributions. For instance, Lewis A. Coser and Jerry Hough have pointed to the "mutual dependence of reforming forces from above and below."[15]

Sten Tellenbeck has drawn attention to the contradictions in the Soviet model of economic development, the built-in limits to growth:

> Whatever institutional structure an industrial society has, it seems to be imperative that a transformation from extensive to intensive growth presupposes a change from the mechanism of coercion to the mechanism of institutionalized conflict. This is so because intensive growth cannot be commanded, but can only be achieved by releasing potential human resources by the application of incentives congruent with existing value systems.[16]

In other words, there is a basic interdependence between economic and political reform – an observation that adds another dimension to the hypothesis of "fundamental democratization." Here lies the common ground between Robert A. Dahl and Mikhail S. Gorbachev. The need for political reform is not only related to problems of motivation and mobilization of innovative potential but has to do with the need to crush the power of the bureaucracy. Besides, a centralized and repressive political structure contains no mechanism to correct wrong decisions and, so, authoritarianism is a source of its own degeneration.

As for Soviet policy toward Eastern Europe, the point is that development dynamics narrow the margin for the politics of cohesion and Sovietization. A definitive switch to the politics of viability became an acute need to secure efficiency of cooperation at a more advanced stage of development. Years of ignoring the increasing need for economic and political reforms left the USSR with no other option than to provide for basic legitimacy, now that the unpleasant decisions have to be made. For this reason Moscow replaced its hegemony with a policy of letting East Europeans "do it their way."

The interplay between national and international forces of change is illustrated by the Soviet crisis, which is a crisis of the very "superpowerhood" of the Soviet Union. The Soviet economic crisis generally is seen not as an immediate problem of legitimacy but as the decisive determinant of Gorbachev's perestroika, and rightly so. But there also is a dimension of the crisis of legitimacy because of the effect of economic decay on the Soviet international position. The high-technological arms race launched by the Reagan administration, in particular the challenge of SDI, was arguably a most decisive factor in convincing Soviet decision makers, including the military, that something had to be done. As Paul Kennedy convincingly has shown, the structure of the Soviet superpower, as well as Soviet hegemonical practice, have been particularly self-destructive – a conclusion that is underscored by quantitative investigations into the burden of the Soviet empire.[17]

Other determinants and aspects of reform in the Soviet Union

The structural determinants of reform cited above are the long-term causal factors of change. However important they may be, they are not sufficient factors of change but have to interplay with conditional factors of change at the level of actors and the level of cognition. Some of these conditional factors are relevant to the Soviet–East European relationship. Soviet policy toward Eastern Europe used to be in the hands of Leonid Brezhnev, Mikhail Suslov, Boris Ponomarev, Oleg Rakhmanin, and others who are now either dead, "retired," or removed from a position of influence. Reform-minded people such as Vadim Medvedev, Aleksandr Iakovlev, Nikolai Shishlin, Giorgi Shakhnazarov, and Aleksandr Kapto have taken over. Moreover, academic foreign policy experts (*mezhdunarodniki*) have come to play a more direct role in foreign policy formulation, e.g. Oleg Bogomolov, Viacheslav Dashichev, Andrei Kortunov, and Sergei Karaganov.

The formerly independent East European office of the CPSU Central Committee, the Department for Liaison with Ruling Workers' and Communist Parties, has been relegated to the status of a subdivision within the International Department.[18] This change signals a development away from the "big brother" party-based relationship *vis-à-vis* the small Warsaw Pact partners toward a normal interstate relationship. Accordingly, the role of the Soviet Ministry for Foreign Affairs has been strengthened in East European affairs, and professional diplomats have been appointed ambassadors to East European states in lieu of the previous political ambassadors.

The implication of all this is an entirely different decision-making milieu, the advent of new points of view and values, and a more sober approach. A development toward democratization of the whole foreign policy process has taken place, accompanied by glasnost in the field of information and debate. True enough, this development will not necessarily settle all problems in relation to Eastern Europe, and it is possible that various, perhaps even rivaling, foreign policies of the seceding Soviet republics will evolve.

Soviet foreign policy doctrine also has undergone a revolution. New political thinking means a departure from the old dualistic approach to international relations, and this new approach gradually has been applied to Eastern Europe. The emphasis is now on universal human values and interests at the expense of class values and *partiinost*. On a more practical level, a development toward a more genuinely pan-European policy can be observed. Following the progressive undermining of the Soviet negotiating position because of internal weakness and the overwhelming need for Western economic intervention in Eastern Europe, Gorbachev neither can nor wants to dictate the framework for the "common European house."[19] So, it has become a concept that implies convergence on Western premises as described by the statement of the Bonn conference of the CSCE on economic cooperation of April 1990.

To summarize, the above model of explanation concerning why the Soviet Union has reoriented its policy toward Eastern Europe focused on the contradictions of hegemony, development dynamics, and the actual crisis of the Soviet superpower. Changes within the Soviet decision-making milieu and the actual adoption of new political thinking are important as well. The rest of the analysis deals with the specific changes of the Soviet–East European relationship beginning with general developments. Later, I shall discuss power relations, the Warsaw Pact, and economic cooperation, including regional cooperation.

The changing Soviet–East European relationship

The crushing of the 1968 Prague Spring can be seen as the specific historical background for the change in the Soviet approach to the Warsaw Pact allies. It led to an extremely depressing "normalization," which was the beginning of the end: a most bureaucratic conception of "real socialism," economic decline, and intellectual disillusionment. In retrospect it seems that here the Kremlin missed a historic chance of saving communism by not opting for reform communism.

The intellectuals resorted to "anti-politics," György Konrád's term for the alternative politics of civil society, culminating in the birth of Solidarity and the rebirth of KOR in Poland in 1980. According to Timothy Garton Ash, these "politics of social self-organization aimed at negotiating the transition from communism."[20] Accordingly, by 1989 reform communism was a non-starter. The Polish crisis of 1980–81 was interesting from yet another point of view: The Soviet leaders showed restraint, as if realizing that the problems could not be solved by military resolve. What followed was a very self-critical Soviet debate on "real socialism" that anticipated the Gorbachev revolution.[21]

The original approach of the Gorbachev leadership concerning the socialist community was a mixture of continuity and change, but eventually the stress came on democratization in Eastern Europe. In a speech in Kiev in early 1989, Gorbachev called for accountability of East European governments and, equally important, the official denouncement of the Brezhnev doctrine coincided with a new wave of reform in Hungary and Poland.[22] An absurd reversal of roles came in connection with the formation of the Polish Solidarity-led government in August 1989, when the Ceauşescu regime of Romania, hitherto an ardent anti-interventionist Warsaw Pact regime, called for an armed intervention in Poland.[23] But without the support of the Kremlin the struggle for the "protection of socialism" was merely pathetic.

Soviet behavior during late 1989 and 1990 marks the shift to a new Soviet policy in Eastern Europe building upon *laissez-faire* and the pursuit of a deideologized Soviet nationalist interest. This is to be elaborated below, but before that a few comments on the Soviet reaction to the "loss" of Eastern Europe are necessary. The meeting of the CPSU Central Committee in early 1990 was the first indication that the official Soviet line of restraint and accommodation was controversial.[24] The conservatives accused the Soviet leadership of having "sold out" the socialist community. At the Russian Party Conference in the summer of 1990 a top Soviet officer, Al'bert Makashov struck an extremely sarcastic tone on the withdrawal from Eastern Europe.[25] His views were reiterated by other officers who spoke of a "betrayal of Soviet interests."

This criticism would indicate that the new line lacks consolidation. On the other hand, the traditional Kremlinological view, namely that foreign policy disputes in the Soviet leadership are purely instrumental in the struggle for power, is not necessarily irrelevant when it comes to judging the actual significance of the heated debate of mid-1990. The conservatives have a point in speaking about the danger of Russia becoming isolated as the single remaining socialist bastion. Russian isolationism, which may lead to aggressiveness, has become a very real problem as the loss of the "internal empire," the Soviet republics, moves closer and adds to the loss of the external East European empire.

So far the Gorbachev leadership has pursued a non-interventionist East European policy. Official programmatic declarations on the policy toward this region are not frequent – probably a reflection of the internal disputes. The draft platform of the CPSU Central Committee for the 28th Party Congress spoke approvingly of the revolutions in Eastern Europe and declared Soviet willingness to cooperate with virtually all political parties in the region. But the final version adopted by the 28th CPSU Congress was vague on Eastern Europe and merely called for "new forms of cooperation."[26] Only Soviet *mezhdunarodniki* have given more specific hints of the contents of the new policy.

The first post-1989 attempt of formulating a new concept for Soviet policy toward the Warsaw Pact allies was launched by three employees of the Institute of USA and Canada.[27] They advanced the idea of partnership, which they contrasted to an ideologically based alliance. They argue that today's Soviet client in Afghanistan, the Najib regime, is a liability and therefore that "loosing one of yesterday's allies does not automatically weaken the international position of the USSR." They see an "objective basis for integration between the Soviet Union and Eastern Europe," citing the legacy from the common development since World War II, common problems in the field of foreign policy especially concerning the entry into the common European house, and common priorities in the field of military security.

Their article shows that the Soviet Union wants to maintain a relatively close cooperation with Eastern Europe, while simultaneously working on a closer relationship with the West. Karen N. Brutents, deputy director of the CPSU CC International Department, urged an East European policy building upon real, long-term national interests, which is not a truism after years of an ideologized foreign policy, and he presupposes cooperation in various fields.[28] Others add that Soviet influence in Eastern Europe is yielding and that the Soviet–East European relationship also will become one of competition in the economic field *vis-à-vis* Western Europe.[29]

Most likely, the USSR will pursue a differentiated policy in Eastern Europe and will focus primarily on East-Central Europe (Poland, Czechoslovakia, and Hungary). This region always has been a sphere of vital Soviet security and economic interests and will continue to attract the USSR because Western investments in Eastern Europe concentrate upon this region. In other words, the Soviet Union will choose East European partners capable of becoming partners in the modernization of the Soviet economy, just as it is now turning to newly industrialized countries like South Korea. Soviet relations with the individual countries of East-Central Europe as of 1990 can be summarized as follows: a new understanding between the USSR and Poland; restored confidence in the GDR after the defeat of the SED and eventually confidence in the reunified Germany; and, finally, a good relationship with Czechoslovakia as well. In contrast to this, the Soviet–Hungarian relationship has deteriorated slightly, as illustrated by the Soviet reaction to Hungary's decision to leave the Warsaw Pact. Prime Minister József Ántall alienated the Soviets by calling their country "the sick man of Europe" of today and a power that kept the world in fear for seventy years.[30]

Yet it is neither Hungary, nor Czechoslovakia nor Poland that is the cornerstone of the new Soviet policy in East-Central Europe, but unified Germany. The Treaty of Good-Neighborliness, Partnership and Cooperation between the Federal Republic of Germany and the USSR formed the framework of a new and more intimate Soviet–German relationship. It replaces the previous equally important Soviet–GDR and Soviet–FRG economic relationships. Both sides apparently want it to become an economic security partnership, and especially the Soviet side entertains great expectations:

> For the Soviet Union and Germany, the prospect of an economic space from the Rhine to the Urals is unfolding. Several promising types of cooperation could emerge including free economic zones, joint ventures and banks. The intimate coupling (*tesnoe perepletenie*) of German and Soviet economic potentials would not only radically change the economic features of the old continent, but also, in our view, be the best contribution to European security.[31]

Presumably the multiplicator effects from the new Soviet–German relationship will replace the old levers of influence and power *vis-à-vis* Eastern Europe that the USSR is now losing, as argued below.

Soviet levers of power in relation to Eastern Europe

East European democratization means a total reorganization of the old power structure, which implies abolishing the very structure of Soviet hegemony. Measures have been taken against the secret police, the riot police, the army, the nomenklatura system, and the communist parties throughout the region. Pace and types of measures vary, and the most radical dismantling of the old system has taken place in the countries north of the Balkans, leaving Romania at the bottom of the list. This is an interesting pattern because of the importance of the northern region, including Hungary, to the Soviet Union.

It remains unknown whether the KGB maintains its secret cooperation with the East European intelligence services,[32] and the reorientation of the armies toward genuine national goals entails loyalty conflicts. But Soviet troops are leaving the area and the Warsaw Pact does not seem to work in a military operational sense. The East European communist parties, the nerve-center of the Soviet exercise of hegemony, have been defeated in most countries, their properties are being confiscated, and party cells in the factories abolished. Even when allowing for the fact that the transformation is not a smooth one – as, for instance, the nomenklatura often has succeeded in turning itself into a capitalist elite – the overall conclusion is that the classic Soviet instruments of power are beyond Soviet control. And Moscow acquiesces.

This loss makes the economic levers of power and influence all the more focal. They are East European dependency on Soviet energy deliveries and East European dependency on the Soviet market as an outlet for industrial products. Regarding the former, the Soviet Union is losing control over its "energy weapon" because the Soviet production of oil is falling. This decline in production results from obsolete equipment, rising marginal costs as exploitation moves deeper into Siberia, and strikes. Production of oil for 1990 was expected to be 4.5 percent below target, and the Soviet Union has announced export cuts to Eastern Europe amounting to 7 million tons, or 10 percent of contracted exports. Soviet officials term this an "enforced oil embargo."[33]

The Soviet inability to increase oil production spells enormous problems for the East Europeans, in particular after the Gulf crisis that sabotaged their attempts to find new energy partners. Czechoslovakia did succeed in getting a special deal on extra oil deliveries from the USSR in the autumn of 1990. In connection with this, President Havel warned that Soviet violations of contracts might prompt Prague to be less considerate about Soviet interests in negotiations on the future of the Warsaw Pact and the new order in Europe.[34]

In other words, Soviet economic weakness undermines the Soviet negotiating position *vis-à-vis* the East Europeans, except, perhaps, in the area of imports. Traditionally, the USSR imports production equipment, other industrial goods and agricultural products from Eastern Europe, but they are not of a competitive quality, as far as industrial goods are concerned. The Soviet Union has announced that by 1 January 1991, Soviet trade with CMEA partners would be conducted in hard currency – a change that could prompt the Soviets to reconsider imports from Eastern Europe. The Soviets probably will turn to OECD countries for a significant part of the technological imports now that they will have to use their sparse hard-currency resources. If asked by East European governments to continue imports they may demand political concessions, or the East Europeans themselves may exercise self-censorship, as already has been seen.[35]

Warsaw Pact and economic cooperation

The problems of Warsaw Pact and CMEA cooperation reflected the dilemma between the Soviet desire for Sovietization and the pursuit of military and economic efficiency. The reliability of the East European armies of the Warsaw Pact always was questionable, and the Soviets began to recognize the need for fundamental reform. In the autumn of 1989 Gorbachev and Evgenyi Primakov expressed confidence in even the Finlandization of Eastern Europe.[36] But this attitude changed, particularly when the Hungarian leaders backed by the parliament in May 1990 decided to negotiate a formal withdrawal from the Pact.[37]

As the Soviets failed to dissuade the Hungarians from taking this step, they have lost the battle. But, on the other hand, the Hungarian debate on the question of leaving the Warsaw Pact revealed doubts and an awareness that the initiative could backfire if the Soviets are pushed too hard and their interests ignored. In case of armed clashes between Hungary and Romania, which became a loyal Warsaw Pact member, Hungary would find itself isolated from the residual Warsaw Pact.

The Warsaw Pact summit of June 1990 in Moscow showed that although the alliance might cease as a military organization, the Pact countries would continue to cooperate politically.[38] In 1990 Czechoslovakia actually took the lead in defining the Pact's future and adopted a more cautious and incremental approach to the dismantling of the organization than did Hungary. Czechoslovakia viewed the Warsaw Pact as a framework for negotiations on disarmament, as a necessary interim security structure until a new European security system has been established, and as an instrument in that process as well. Havel proposed a series of organizational reforms, and both Czechoslovakia and Poland were concerned about the possible counterproductive effects from the Hungarian approach.

So, the remaining Northern Tier countries of the Warsaw Pact and the USSR found common ground regarding the transformation of the Pact into a political forum. Gorbachev is believed to have declared at the June summit that any reform of the Warsaw Pact would be acceptable, except for its abolition. A substantial Soviet argument for maintaining the alliance was that it would counteract the threatened Balkanization of Eastern Europe as nationalistic and social tension increased.[39] Other arguments for preserving the alliance focused on the lack of institutionalization of the CSCE and on NATO's unwillingness to accept East European countries as members. Yet, the long-term prospects for the Warsaw Pact were gloomy because of the attraction of the West European systems of security and economic cooperation for the East Europeans. In fact, this process of Europeanization seems to be the general direction of change throughout the region, although it is a process confronting nationalistic and other challenges.[40]

The CMEA also was in severe crisis because of the built-in contradictions in the CMEA mechanisms of cooperation and the attraction of the EC. The Council Session of January 1990 in Sofia appointed a committee to work on organizational reform, and in March it was decided to drop plan coordination and multilateral cooperation, i.e. joint investments primarily in Soviet energy production.[41] In relation to CMEA cooperation the Soviets displayed a more radical attitude than the East Europeans, as reflected in the unilateral Soviet decision to switch to hard-currency trade by 1991. The Soviets wanted to create an entirely new, OECD-like organization, and it was suggested that the USSR might be the first country to leave the CMEA.[42]

In early 1990 all six East European CMEA countries made it clear that they wanted the future association agreements with the EC to provide for later membership, but the Community has tried to avoid exactly that.[43] It is the structural and institutional differences between the formerly centrally planned economies and the EC economies that create the main hindrance combined with the needs to work on the integration of the previous GDR into the Community. The Gulf crisis has served to make EC membership an even more faint possibility for the East European countries, and so strategies for regional economic cooperation come increasingly into focus. The most interesting example of this is the pentagonal cooperation among Hungary, Czechoslovakia, Italy, Austria, and Yugoslavia, a framework that is becoming more consolidated and begins to attract positive attention from the IMF and the World Bank as well as the EC itself.[44] The explicit purpose of pentagonal cooperation is to serve as a bridge to the EC, where Italy works as the direct link and a good link because of its ambitions in the field of *Ostpolitik*. Austria's participation is not a question of simple geographical necessity either. The USSR is "very interested" in the pentagonal, an indication perhaps that it would like to join the cooperation if it becomes an economic success.

Baltic or neo-Hanse cooperation, however, would be a concept of more direct relevance for the Soviet Union. This idea is beginning to attract serious interest from Northern Germany and Scandinavia – e.g. Pehr Gyllenhammar, director of the Volvo concern – in addition to the already keen interest of Estonia, Latvia, Lithuania and Poland.[45] In order not to alienate the Russians it is important to consider ways of linking the Western parts of Russia to the economic and cultural cooperation of the new Hanse. The economic free zones of Kaliningrad

(Königsberg) and Leningrad represent feasible and possibly the only solutions to this. Thus the reform-minded mayor of Leningrad wants to cooperate with the Baltic republics no matter what their future status will be.[46]

Conclusion

The rise of nationalism in the Soviet Union and the process of secession raise new uncertainties for the analysis of the Soviet–East European relationship as does the economic chaos in the USSR. Nevertheless, the present pragmatic policy toward Eastern Europe appeared relatively consolidated by late 1990. The Soviet government wants to maintain cooperation with Eastern Europe, and the national interest in a deideologized and economic sense is the key to Soviet conduct.

However, the previous two organizational frameworks for Soviet–East European cooperation have crumbled. The new Soviet–German economic axis may become a lever for Soviet (or later Russian) influence in Eastern Europe, and the USSR (Russia) will not cease to be an important economic partner for Eastern Europe. Regional cooperation adds a new dimension to East European affairs and may have a future impact on Soviet (Russian)–East European relations. But the developments inside the USSR have a more immediate impact, as recognized by the East Europeans themselves.

Notes

1 Throughout this contribution the term "Eastern Europe" refers to the GDR, Poland, Czechoslovakia, Hungary, Romania, and Bulgaria, which together with the USSR comprised the Warsaw Treaty Organization as well as the core of the CMEA.

2 V. Gerasimov characterized the Hungarian opposition as extremely anti-socialist and anti-Soviet, *Pravda*, 8 August 1989; Malchun suggested that Walesa acted irresponsibly, *Izvestiia*, 11 August 1989. See also Mette Skak, "Sovjetunionens politik over for Osteuropa," *Politica*, no. 1 (1990), p. 47.

3 *International Herald Tribune*, 15 January 1990. Where no other references are given, this newspaper's accounts of the East European revolutions are the main source.

4 Gerard Davies, "Czechs examine KGB role in revolt," *The Guardian*, 11 May 1990.

5 See "K sobytiiam v Rumynii" and "Zaiavlenie MID SSSR," *Pravda*, 26 December 1989. See also Michael Shafir, "Ceausescu's overthrow: popular uprising or Moscow-guided conspiracy?" *Report on Eastern Europe*, 19 January 1990.

6 This interpretation is confirmed by the late 1989 Soviet commentaries. See L. Shevtsova, "Stanovlenie sotsializma v Vostochnoi Evrope: Sovremennyi

vzgliad," *Kommunist*, no. 17, November (1989), pp. 124–27; interview with Peter Mladenov, *Pravda*, 4 December 1989.

7 The term "Sinatra doctrine" was invented by Soviet foreign ministry spokesman Gennadii Gerasimov, *New York Times*, 26 October 1989.

8 See George Konrad, *Antipolitics: An Essay* (London: Quartet Books, 1984), p. 51.

9 Hugh Seton-Watson, "Eastern Europe," in *The Soviet Union and World Politics*, ed. Kurt London (Boulder, CO: Westview, 1980), pp. 55f.

10 Bogdan Denitch, "The domestic roots of foreign policy in Eastern Europe," in *The International Politics of Eastern Europe*, ed. Charles Gati (New York: Praeger, 1976), p. 244. The point about education and "middle classinization" as a vital factor of societal change is repeated by Lucian W. Pye, "Political science and the crisis of authoritarianism," *American Political Science Review*, vol. 84, no. 1 (1990), pp. 7, 10.

11 Hedley Bull, *The Anarchical Society: A Study of Order in World Politics* (London: Macmillan, 1985, reprint), p. 215. For elaborations and further references to the theoretical literature, see Mette Skak, "The waning of Soviet hegemony in Eastern Europe," paper presented at the 11th Nordic Peace Research Conference, Elsinore, 21–23 August 1989 (Institute of Political Science, University of Aarhus, mimeo).

12 James Brown, "Relations between the Soviet Union and Eastern European allies: a survey," *RAND Report*, R-1742-PR, November 1975, Santa Monica, CA, p. 2.

13 Jan F. Triska, ed., *Dominant Powers and Subordinate States: The United States in Latin America and the Soviet Union in Eastern Europe* (Durham, NC: Duke University Press, 1986).

14 See, for example, Seweryn Bialer, ed., *The Domestic Context of Soviet Foreign Policy* (Boulder, CO: 1981); also, Robert O. Keohane and Joseph S. Nye, *Power and Interdependence: World Politics in Transition* (Boston: Little Brown, 1977).

15 Lewis A. Coser, "The intellectuals in Soviet reform," *Dissent* (Spring 1990), pp. 181–83; and Jerry Hough, "Gorbachev's politics," *Foreign Affairs*, vol. 68, no. 5 (Winter 1989–90), pp. 26–41. The Soviet Union and Hungary are cases in point on the interplay of forces of change. See also Lucian W. Pye's contribution cited in note 10.

16 Sten Tellenbeck, "The logic of development in socialist Poland," *Social Forces*, vol. 57, no. 2 (1978), pp. 452–53.

17 Paul Kennedy, *The Rise and Fall of the Great Powers: Economic Change and Military Conflict from 1500 to 2000* (London: Unwin and Hyman, 1988); Charles Wolf, Jr., "Costs of the Soviet empire," *Wall Street Journal*, 30 January 1984.

18 There are numerous sources for this and the following, including communications with top *mezhdunarodniki*.

19 This position was evident at the Malta summit. See Stephen Shenfield, "Between Moscow and Brussels," *Detente*, no. 15 (1989), pp. 7–8.

20 Timothy Garton Ash, "Eastern Europe: the year of truth," *The New York Review of Books*, 15 February 1990.

21 Jonathan C. Valdez, "Crises, contradictions, and Eastern Europe: Soviet

theoretical debates and reform, 1982–1986," paper presented to the 4th World Congress for Soviet and East European Studies, Harrogate, 21–26 July 1990 (University of Kansas, Department of Political Science, mimeo).

22 TASS, 23 February 1989. For details on the development of Soviet policy in Eastern Europe during the Gorbachev years, see Skak, "Sovjetunionens politik over for Osteuropa"; Mark Kramer, "Beyond the Brezhnev Doctrine: a new era in Soviet–East European relations?" *International Security*, vol. 14, no. 3 (Winter 1989–90), pp. 25–67.

23 Michael Shafir, "East European reactions to Polish developments," *RAD Background Report*, 16 October 1989.

24 Bill Keller, "Moscow looks nervously at East Europe tumult," *International Herald Tribune*, 8 February 1990.

25 Stephen Foye, "Military hard-liner condemns 'New Thinking' in security policy," *Report on the USSR*, 13 July 1990.

26 See "Towards humane, democratic socialism," TASS, 12 February 1990, and *Pravda*, 15 July 1990.

27 A. Bogaturov, M. Nosov, K. Pleshakov, "Kto oni, nashi soiuzniki?" *Kommunist*, no. 1 (1990), pp. 105–14.

28 Karen Brutents, "The continent's new landscape," *New Times*, no. 22 (1990), pp. 13–15.

29 Sergei Karaganov, "The problems of the USSR's European policy," *International Affairs* (Moscow), July (1990), p. 76; Andrei Kortunov, "Vneshnaia politika: prodolzhenie diskussii," *Kommunist*, no. 12, August (1990), pp. 116–17.

30 *Report on Eastern Europe*, 31 August 1990. Radio Moscow called the decision to leave the Warsaw Pact "emotional" and "devoid of statesmanship," views that were repeated by top Soviet officers; ibid., 6 July 1990.

31 S. Smol'nikov, "Novaia logika evropeiskogo razvitiia," *Kommunist*, no. 6 (1990), p. 28. For the Soviet–German treaty, see *Frankfurter-Allgemeine Zeitung*, 14 September 1990.

32 Vladimir V. Kusin, "The secret police: disliked and weakened, but not beaten yet," *Report on Eastern Europe*, 9 February 1990.

33 "Evropa bes SEV?" *Pravda*, 10 August 1990; Quentin Peel, "Soviet oil industry wins $1 bn deal from Moscow," *Financial Times*, 19 October 1990.

34 *Report on Eastern Europe*, 19 October 1990. On the terms of the oil deal, see Leslie Colitt, "Soviet oil supply deal averts trade row with Prague," *Financial Times*, 31 October 1990.

35 The Bulgarian government criticized a student demonstration in support of Lithuania in Sofia in April 1990, *Report on Eastern Europe*, 2 July 1990.

36 "Vystuplenie M.S. Gorbacheva," *Pravda*, 26 October 1989; *International Herald Tribune*, 30 October 1989.

37 For this and the following, see Alfred Reisch, "Government wants negotiated withdrawal from the Warsaw Pact," *Report on Eastern Europe*, 8 June 1990.

38 For this and the following, see Douglas C. Clarke, "Warsaw Pact: the transformation begins," *Report on Eastern Europe*, 22 June 1990. The prediction was confirmed by Marshal Sergei Akhromeev, Reuters, 4 October 1990.

39 Karaganov, "The problems of the USSR's European policy," p. 77.
40 For elaborations, see Mette Skak, *Sovjetunionen og Østeuropa. Fra Sovjetisering til Europaeisering* (Copenhagen: SNU, 1990).
41 "COMECON takes first steps to dismantle itself," *Financial Times*, 28 March 1990.
42 "Evropa bez SEV?"; "L'URSS pourrait quitter le COMECON," *Le Monde*, 24 September 1990.
43 For further details, see Skak, "Sovjetunionen og Østeuropa."
44 Vladimir V. Kusin, "The initiative from Venice," *Report on Eastern Europe*, 17 August 1990. See also Skak, "Sovjetunionen og osteuropa."
45 Skak, "Sovjetunionen og osteuropa"; see also Marion Gräfin Dönhoff, "Auf den Spuren der Hanse," *Die Zeit*, no. 43, 19 October 1990.
46 Timothy Frye, "A portrait of Anatoli Sobchak," *Report on the USSR*, 17 August 1990.

3 Soviet–Nordic relations in the era of perestroika and new thinking

Ole Nørgaard

Since the early 1960s the Nordic subregion has been an island of tranquility and stability, the result of structural and political developments in the international system initiated in the postwar years. Both in the military and the political spheres the confrontations between the Nordic countries and the Soviet Union as an emerging superpower were replaced by a relationship characterized by mutual accommodation between conflicting ideologies and interests.

This relatively calm and stable system is now in flux. All the pillars of the traditional system are changing. The immediate factor behind the changes is, of course, the revolution in Soviet domestic and foreign policy. But coalescing with this development are structural changes in the military, political, and economic environment of the region which have been underway for at least the last decade.

Perestroika and new political thinking in the Soviet Union as well as the dramatic changes in the international arena, especially the emergence of the Baltic republics as political actors, have swept away the traditional pattern of Soviet–Nordic relations and created a new one. The pattern has evolved from one characterized by Soviet dominance to one in which the Nordic countries have been able to support the Baltic republics without jeopardizing relations with Moscow. This chapter[1] attempts to grasp the contours of the emerging new Nordic system and especially those aspects which determine relations with the Soviet Union. The first part summarizes the main characteristics of the Nordic–Soviet relationship up to the mid-1980s. The second part analyzes the structural factors of change which have emerged gradually during the last decade and those which reflect the accelerating changes in Eastern Europe and the Soviet Union. The political responses to the changed environment of Soviet–Nordic relations are the subject of the third part, while the last part of the article considers three alternative scenarios for future Soviet–Nordic relations.

Soviet–Nordic relations, 1949–1985

The tranquility which characterized Nordic–Soviet relations from the early 1960s onwards followed a decade in which relations were "strained by harsh Soviet criticism, angry messages, and easy suspicions."[2] Soviet behavior can be seen as a reaction to the gradual Danish and Norwegian integration into the Western alliance, especially their acceptance of the rearmament of Germany, its accession to NATO, and – for Denmark – the resulting reorganization of the area command structure into COMBALTAP.[3] However, through this decade of mutual accusations, suspicion, and political maneuvering, a regional pattern gradually emerged. Denmark and Norway evolved into loyal but somewhat reluctant NATO members with self-imposed limitations on their military integration. Sweden developed a position of strongly armed – somewhat Westward-leaning – neutrality. Finland also settled for neutrality, but worked out a special relationship with the Soviet Union codified in the Treaty of Friendship, Cooperation and Mutual Assistance signed in 1948.

For some, this pattern of Nordic foreign policy affiliations signified a regional subsystem equilibrium epitomized in the concept of the "Nordic balance." As summarized by Janes, this arrangement essentially means "that moves by one superpower or its alliance in the region will lead to response from the opposing superpower or its alliance."[4] Finland, for obvious reasons, has been hesitant to acknowledge the existence of the Nordic balance. If the arrangement reflected reality, the Finns would have to accept that a closer Norwegian or Danish integration into NATO would be paralleled by a closer Finnish military and political cooperation with the Soviet Union. Instead, the Finns prefer to see relations between the Nordic countries and the Soviet Union as consisting of bilateral ties. Denmark's and Norway's limitation on their NATO participation is basically seen as a result of domestic political constraints.[5]

Soviet scholars and politicians persistently have rejected the concept of the Nordic balance. On the theoretical level they have argued that the tranquility in the Nordic subregion has been a result of the relationship between the two superpowers and hence cannot be ascribed to regional political forces. Politically, it has, at least until quite recently, been impossible for the Soviets to accept any theory which gives NATO credit for stability and peace.[6]

Whichever characterization best grasps the pattern of Nordic–Soviet relations, the Nordic area became for twenty years "the quiet corner of

Europe . . . existing in spite of the strategic location of the Nordic countries."[7]

The reasons behind this temporary stability and tranquility were numerous. At the international systemic level, the general lessening of international tension created a benevolent environment which made it possible to make the necessary accommodations between the perceived security interests of the individual Nordic countries and of the Soviet Union. Further, the accelerated Soviet military build-up promoted an increased Soviet international self-confidence that made it easier for the Soviets to come to terms with, especially, Danish and Norwegian participation in NATO.

The tranquility in interstate relations further was reinforced by domestic developments in the Soviet Union and the Nordic countries. In the Soviet Union the leadership change in 1964 installed a leadership much more incremental in political style than that of Khrushchev. This change in style was accompanied further by revisions in ideology, which – without departing from the revolutionary perspective – stressed the need to cooperate with allegedly "realistic" political forces in the West. The prime example of such "realistic forces" was provided by the Social Democratic parties which had a stronger position in the Nordic countries than elsewhere in the world (with the possible exception of the FRG).[8] After some initial skepticism, a stable majority of the Nordic populations gradually supported the new foreign policy relationships.[9]

A fragile balance

From the very beginning of the cold war the peace of the Nordic corner of Europe was jeopardized by factors some of which, ironically, were partly responsible for the stability in the first place.

One factor was the Soviet military build-up. An important part of this build-up was the political endorsement of a new Soviet maritime strategy perceived as the "optimum means to defeat the imperialist enemy, and the most important element in the Soviet arsenal to prepare the way for a communist world."[10] In the Nordic context the consequence of this strategy was that the military build-up on the Kola peninsula, which became the home base of the Soviet Union's Northern Fleet, became the major locus of the Soviet Union's strategic reserve force and heavily defended by SA missiles. Although the military capabilities installed on the Kola peninsula were not directed at the Nordic countries, they of course had implications for the security of the region. These implications were further reinforced as the United States responded to the Soviet naval build-up by the adaptation of the new advanced "Maritime Strategy."[11]

Second, the prospect of natural resource exploitation in the Barents Sea produced a territorial dispute with Norway over 45,000 square miles of the sea shelf.[12]

Third, in 1972 Denmark joined the EC – the only Nordic country to do so. Under the existing bipolar international system both Sweden and Finland regarded membership in the EC, which consisted only of NATO countries, as incompatible with their traditional neutrality. Norway's entrance into the community was blocked by the voters in an emotional referendum, epitomizing what has been termed the "Peer-Gynt-Mentality,"[13] the predominance of parochial and isolationist attitudes in the Norwegian polity. At that time, Denmark's entrance into the EC created a nascent suspicion, in Moscow and in the other Nordic countries, that Denmark was on its way out of the Nordic structure and instead heading for a tighter link with the West. For the Soviets this signaled a somewhat ambivalent position, as until recently they have opposed closer Nordic cooperation in the economic sphere.[14]

Fourth, the relationship between the Soviet Union and its Nordic neighbors was characterized from its very beginning by an inherent and unstable asymmetry, as noted by Lindahl.[15] The small, open and politically pluralized Nordic countries faced a superpower with a closed information system and a highly centralized foreign-policy-making structure. This asymmetry produced some obvious leverages for the Soviet Union in relation to the domestic politics of the individual Nordic countries. To what extent the Soviet Union exploited these possibilities, and especially made use of "agents of influence" in the Nordic public, is still a highly sensitive political question. The issue was revitalized by the publication of a book by a former KGB officer in Copenhagen, Oleg Gordievskii, in which he tells of alleged infiltrations of Danish parties and organizations.[16] Whatever their intentions, it seems fair to say today that Soviet attempts to influence the perception and attitudes of the Nordic public had no lasting influence.[17] Through the 1970s and 1980s a broad majority of political parties continued to support the established foreign policy of the individual Nordic countries.

Fifth, developments in the international system affected popular attitudes toward the Soviet Union in the Nordic countries. In Denmark, for example, periodic surveys since 1968 give a clear indication that the majority of the Danish population up to the beginning of the 1980s perceived the behavior of the Soviet Union as the major threat to world peace.[18] In Sweden the perception of a Soviet threat traditionally has been lower, but peaked in the early 1980s as a direct result of the submarine incidents,[19] and Soviet harassment of Swedish intelligence vessels in the Baltic Sea. However, from the mid-1980s and in conjunction with shifting views at the parliamentary level, a trend to a more positive Danish evaluation of the Soviet Union has emerged. This trend accelerated after Gorbachev's ascent to power. Hence, an opinion poll in Denmark in 1987 showed that 25 percent of those asked believed that the Soviet Union was more serious in its negotiations on arms control than the United States. Only 9 percent saw the United States as the most serious negotiator.[20]

This increasingly positive attitude toward the Soviet Union among the Danish population differs from Norway and Sweden. A study carried out for the USIA by Gallup illustrates some suggestive differences in the attitude to Soviet policies. The most significant difference is to be found toward the Soviet proposal for a Nordic nuclear-free zone. Forty-six percent of the Danes interviewed supported the Soviet proposal even if it was in conflict with NATO membership. In Norway only 32 percent spoke out in support of the proposal. The differences also reflected the various perceptions of the threats to national security which exist in the Scandinavian countries. For example, 66 percent of the interviewed Swedes and 46 percent of the Norwegians perceived the Soviet Union and the Warsaw Pact countries as the major threat. Only 24 percent of the Danes shared this opinion.[21]

Putting aside the question of Soviet manipulation of public opinion, these differences must be explained by at least three sets of factors. First, it is of obvious importance that the Soviet presence was felt much more acutely in Sweden and Norway, either because of submarine intimidations or, in the case of Norway, because of unresolved conflicts about borders in the Norwegian Sea. Second, Denmark, for historical reasons, has a much stronger pacifist tradition than the other Scandinavian countries. This tradition of pacifism fuels stronger political conflict about defense policy than exists in the other Nordic countries. Third, the consequences of the youth movement in the late 1960s and early 1970s probably have had a more lasting impact on political life in Denmark than is the case in most other European countries except the Netherlands and the FRG. Regarding security policy, the movement itself changed the focus of concern from an actor (the Soviet Union) to the anonymous structural threats inherent in the arms race itself, in pollution, or in the gap between North and South. At the same time, new groups with differing values and attitudes became active in the political struggle over ways to enhance national security.[22] These groups were, for example, women and people working in the caring professions. In this respect, it is illustrative that the strongest polarization in relation to security politics is felt between what has been termed the "fathers" (men over 40) and "daughters" (women under 40). It can be argued that these developments, which of course are common to most Western countries, have been more pronounced in Denmark.

All the above-mentioned trends presented danger to the stability of established Soviet–Nordic relations. And they individually produced a number of political initiatives and proposals. The Nordic nuclear-weapons-free-zone proposal proved to be the most controversial but also the most persistent since it was first introduced by Finnish President Urho Kekkonen in 1963.

The revolution in the Soviet Union and Eastern Europe

Compared to the landslide of events related to Soviet domestic and foreign policy, to Eastern Europe and to the general European system, each of the above-mentioned factors fades in significance. In the last year it seems that most of the parameters which produced the pattern of Soviet–Nordic relations have been swept away by the spiraling sequence of events.

Changes in the military sphere, political developments in Eastern Europe, the reunification of Germany and the withering away of the Warsaw Pact have changed the environment of the Nordic subregion. These changes have produced a yet unsettled controversy in the Nordic countries about the extent and type of linkage of events in the region to developments at the all-European level. On the one hand, proponents of the so-called "sausage theory" argue that the thinning out of the forces in the central European theater increases the importance of the periphery, i.e. the military capacity in the North. According to this argument, the CFE and START negotiations do not change the situation in the Nordic region, as neither naval forces (except strategic nuclear submarines) nor amphibious troops, are part of the negotiations.[23] On the other hand, it has been argued that the "sausage theory" and related arguments must be perceived as an excuse on the part of the Nordic security establishment to respond to the general improvement in East–West relations. A domestic conservatism, which in the individual countries is explained particularly by the perceived need to maintain consensus on foreign policy issues, is related to this view. Evidence of this failure to respond to all-European developments is the fate of the study group on the Nordic nuclear-weapon-free zone, composed of officials from the Nordic foreign ministries. The group was established in 1987 but has not yet managed to produce a report.[24]

In the political sphere the revitalization of the EC has increased its attraction for the Nordic countries, which seem to be heading for membership in the next decade. Entrance into the EC has been recommended strongly by Danish Foreign Minister Uffe Ellemann-Jensen as the only way to bolster Nordic values in an expanded community. The attraction of the European Community, especially for Finland and Sweden, is bolstered further by the fading of the bipolar structure of the European system. Until now concern for their neutrality has been the major obstacle to EC membership. But the concept of neutrality obviously loses its substance when there no longer exist adversaries in relation to whom the neutrality can be defined. Swedish Prime Minister Ingvar Carlsson recently argued along similar lines when he stated in the Swedish parliament that under the emerging circumstances it is possible "to combine a Swedish membership of the EC with neutrality."[25] For Finland it is of particular importance that the Soviet Union today does not seem to have any objection to future membership.[26] In Norway the syndrome of the 1972 referendum is still a vivid part of political life.[27] A further incentive for the non-member Nordic countries to reconsider entry into the EC is the reunification of Germany. A frequent argument in Nordic politics is that the only way to restrain the new Germany in European affairs is to tie the huge neighbor into a web of all-European institutions. For this purpose a reinforcement of the Nordic tier of the EC with Norway, Sweden, and Finland would be an obvious advantage.[28]

Fundamental changes in the Soviet domestic arena also have had ramifications for Soviet–Nordic relations. The more favorable Soviet perception of the international system and of Western societies has improved its relationship with the Nordic countries. The progressive role played by the social democratic parties, as now acknowledged in Soviet ideology,[29] has in some quarters in the Soviet Union made the "Scandinavian" (or Swedish) model equal to the imagined "third way" between capitalism and socialism.[30]

The foreign-policy-making process in the Soviet Union also has been changing. It is obvious that the former closed and centralized decision-making process no longer exists and that broader political groupings and movements have for some time had at least an indirect impact on the foreign policy line. The developments in the Baltic republics seem to give the Nordic countries at least rudimentary leverage in relation to the former closed and monolithic neighbor. We shall return to this point later.

As in the rest of Europe, the future configuration of East–West relations in the Nordic region is still in an embryonic phase. Politicians in the Nordic countries, in the Baltic republics, and in Moscow continuously are trying to catch up with events. But it seems as though the political initiatives are constantly several steps behind the initiatives of thousands of private citizens, organizations, and firms exploiting the new opportunities for contact and profit.

It is from this perspective that the next part of the chapter will examine the political initiatives which have appeared so far. Do they reveal any evidence as to what will be the future pattern of Soviet–Nordic relations?

From Murmansk to Vilnius: the politics of northern perestroika

Although perestroika and new thinking in foreign policy originated in the Soviet Union, the innovation in politics has created a momentum which demands political responses not only abroad but also within the Soviet Union. Hence, Soviet politicians have been faced with the task of implementing the new concepts and almost simultaneously of responding to the political dynamics ignited by the new foreign policy. These reactions in turn stem from two sources. First, inside the Soviet Union, the striving for independence primarily in the Baltic republics, itself a product of perestroika, has influenced greatly the prospects of a successful implementation of Gorbachev's perestroika in the region. Second, the reactions to the initiatives from the Nordic countries, in the Nordic Council and in the individual countries, also have contributed to the formation of the new pattern of Soviet–Nordic relations.

The Soviet–Nordic perestroika

Since Gorbachev's ascent to power in March 1985, Soviet policy toward the Nordic area has been the subject of two extensive attempts to formulate a coherent framework for the development of future relations: in Gorbachev's Murmansk speech in October 1987, and in his speech in Helsinki in October 1989.[31]

The visions and proposals in the Murmansk address partially reflected old proposals in the sphere of security politics but also applied the general principles of new political thinking to the problems of the Nordic area.[32] To the first category belong the proposals for a nuclear-free zone and limitations on naval activity in the Nordic seas. The first proposal has been favored by the Soviets since it was introduced by Bulganin in 1958 and later reintroduced by Finnish President Kekkonen in 1963. The second proposal touched the very core of the NATO strategy because it could increase the vulnerability of the transatlantic reinforcement route, the so-called GIUK-gap (Greenland, Iceland, UK). The last category included proposals for cooperation within spheres of high priority for the Nordic countries: exploitation of resources in the Nordic areas, arctic research, environmental protection, and navigation through the North–East route.[33]

Gorbachev further elaborated on his vision of the future pattern of Soviet–Northern relations during his official visit to Finland in October 1989.[34] In an attempt to construct what he called "the Northern wall and roof of the common European home" he announced Soviet initiatives to decrease military tension and introduced a host of old and new proposals for confidence-building measures and political cooperation in the region.

Regarding the military initiatives, he promised "a complete restructuring of the Soviet armed forces in the northern region during the 1990s." He stressed that nuclear systems on Soviet territory already were deployed in areas from which they could not reach Northern Europe. He announced the removal of the Golf-class submarines and the destruction of the remaining four by the end of the year and reiterated the idea of Finnish President Mauno Koivisto for confidence-building measures in northern maritime areas, including mutual notification of accidents on naval ships.

In the political sphere, while in Helsinki Gorbachev proposed to set up a parliamentary group of Nordic countries to discuss all problems of the region "ranging from security to human rights." This institutionalization also would include contacts between the Nordic Council and the Supreme Soviets of the Soviet Union and the union republics and autonomous republics "situated in the northern part of the USSR." The Presidium of the Nordic Council supported the suggestion for parliamentary contacts, and a number of meetings have taken place between parliamentarians from the Nordic countries and the Supreme Soviet.[35]

In a broader perspective, the principles of new political thinking led to the establishment of "a global framework into which the Europeanization could be fitted without jeopardizing Soviet security interests," as stated by Saeter.[36] The new approach in Soviet foreign policy also opens up a more active role for the Nordic countries within the CSCE process. And it "contributes to and stimulates and legitimizes an European reorientation on the part of the Nordic countries, including the neutrals." In this vein, some of Gorbachev's remarks during his visit to Finland could be interpreted as a Soviet endorsement of future Finnish membership in the EC. Hence, the Murmansk speech of 1987 and the Helsinki speech of 1989 became the events which linked the

Nordic region to the European process and the concept of "our common European home."

The Baltic factor

In his speech for nomination as chairman of the Latvian Supreme Soviet, Latvian communist politician Anatolijs Gorbunovs summarized his vision of the future position of the Baltic states in the international system:[37]

> Latvia, together with Lithuania and Estonia, as subjects of international law, must strive to establish contacts with political and economic structures in Europe and in the world, the Council of Europe, the Nordic Council, the European Economic community, the UN. . . . Actually, the essence of our foreign policy platform is a wish to realize our particular geo-political and cultural history situation – to build a bridge between West and East.

With this vision in mind and with regard to the geopolitical location of the republics, it is understandable that the leaders of the independence movements in Estonia, Latvia, and Lithuania have selected the Nordic countries as their first and major focus of foreign policy activity. The attempts to establish relations with the neighbors along the Baltic is not built on any naive assumption that balanced relations can be established immediately in the field of economic and security policy. In the economic field the interest seems more oriented toward Eastern Europe, based on the sound assumption that these will be the only realistic markets for products which the Baltic economies are able to produce at present.[38] In the field of security the Baltic republics also seem aware that they somehow have to find an accommodation with Soviet interests.[39]

But because of historical linkages across the Baltic and elements of a common cultural heritage, both leaders and citizens in the three Baltic republics seem to expect that the Nordic countries can act as their bridge to the Western world, which would allow them to escape the usual route through Moscow (in political as well as geographical terms).

Hence, it was not accidental that Lithuanian Prime Minister Kazimiera Prunskiene and Foreign Minister Algirdas Saudargas chose the Scandinavian countries for their first extensive trip abroad. The goal of the visit in late April 1990 was to seek possible economic and financial support after Moscow blockaded Lithuania economically. The trip, however, was somewhat of a sobering experience for the Lithuanian premier, who achieved political support but no concrete promises of economic assistance.[40]

However, while the official contacts may have netted little in tangible results, the number of other contacts between the Baltic republics and the Nordic countries has increased rapidly. After more than forty years of isolation, the populations in the neighboring countries are now in a process of rediscovering each other. As a result, relations are developing in almost all societal and political spheres. In sports events the Baltic participants are received almost as celebrities. In political gatherings, many Scandinavian parties are establishing contacts with prospective partners from the three republics.[41] And an increasing number of students are enrolled at Nordic universities supported by grants from the Nordic Council, governments, and individual universities.

The aspiration for independence in the three Baltic republics in conjunction with the possibilities opened by the principles of new political thinking also has changed the Soviet policy-making process in relation to the Nordic countries. The Baltic republics gradually are evolving their own policies in spheres which were previously the privilege of Moscow. And through their participation in Moscow politics and especially the increasing role of the Congress of People's Deputies and its commissions – and skillful exploitation of the principles of new political thinking – they have added a new set of political factors to the formulations of Soviet policy toward the Nordic countries.[42]

These changes in the foreign policy-making process reflect a contradiction between the socio-political dynamics of perestroika and the abstract principles of new political thinking in the Baltic region. That such a contradiction exists became obvious in April 1990 when a group of parliamentarians from the Nordic Council were denied access to Lithuania. This was a clear violation of the principles and commitments included in the Murmansk and the Helsinki addresses.[43] As a response to the Soviet cancellation of the visit to Lithuania, the Nordic Council in protest canceled the whole tour which should have taken the delegation to the other Baltic republics and to Moscow.

The Nordic reactions: reversal of the asymmetry

Inside the Nordic countries the previous political base of relations with the Soviet Union also has changed. First, Nordic perceptions regarding the possibilities of change and reform in the Soviet system have focused not on the Soviets' sincerity but on the question of their staying power.[44] In line with this both the majority of Nordic leaders and the public are reluctant to pursue politics which might threaten the internal political position of Soviet reformers.

Second, the political developments in the Baltic republics have had a stronger political impact in the Nordic countries than elsewhere. Due to historical reasons, their proximity, the emigrant communities (especially in Sweden), and the emotional identification with other small states living on the periphery of a superpower, the developments in the three Baltic republics have produced strong political and public reactions in all the Nordic countries. As early as March 1988 Swedish opposition leader Bildt called for Nordic initiatives to bolster the emerging Baltic independence movement.[45] And in March 1990 Danish Premier Poul Schlüter called for a strong protest against Soviet moves in Lithuania.[46]

However, the quest for Nordic action as a response to Soviet behavior toward the Baltic republics has been tempered by two factors. First, there has been broad, although not unanimous, political support behind the view that President Gorbachev finds himself in a delicate political situation. Too much foreign criticism might worsen his chances of success. This view was stated clearly, for example, during Swedish Foreign Minister Sten Andersson's visit to Estonia in November 1989. In order not to hamper perestroika's prospects, "the expansion of the Baltic republics' independence must take place within the framework of the Soviet Union," he said.[47] Second, the various international political partnerships of the individual Nordic countries until recently have made it impossible for the Nordic countries to find a common ground for action.[48] This became clear at the meeting of the Nordic Council on 22 April 1990 where the Nordic foreign ministers failed to agree on joint action to support Lithuania.[49] The communiqué issued from the meeting merely called on Moscow to refrain from violence against Lithuania. The semi-official explanation for the outcome, as it was leaked to the press, concerned the Finnish and Swedish hesitation to be involved in too strong a criticism of their Soviet neighbor. However, it seems that Denmark, in spite of its earlier call for stronger actions, had no reason to be unhappy about the outcome. The day before, the EC heads of states, during their meeting in Dublin,[50] also had refrained from strong action in response to the Lithuanian question for fear of undermining Gorbachev's position. Sweden also seems hesitant to voice criticism too strongly. Sweden was the only Nordic country to recognize the Soviet annexation of the Baltic states in the early 1940s, and as late as November 1989 the Swedish Foreign Minister is reported to have endorsed the view that the USSR is not an occupier in the Baltic states.[51]

The dilemma between wanting to give the Baltic republics political support and being reluctant to engage in behavior which might undermine Gorbachev's position has led to a new sort of officially sponsored but subnational foreign policy. The individual governments and the Nordic Council of Ministers have allocated relatively generous funds to promote relations between the Nordic countries and the Baltic states in the field of cultural, educational, and scientific cooperation. The Nordic Council of Ministers also has decided to open information bureaus in Tallin, Riga, and Vilnius, and the Baltic republics are in the process of opening bureaus in the Nordic capitals. The first joint information bureau of Denmark, Sweden, Finland, and Iceland is to start functioning in Vilnius next year.[52]

As a result of political initiatives, a spiraling number of low-level initiatives have been developed in relation to the Baltic states. Since early 1990 Nordic political parties, institutions, organizations, and even municipalities have been establishing and signing agreements with official authorities in the Baltic states. In practical terms this substate foreign policy implies that Nordic officials are trying to circumvent their reluctance to lend manifest state-to-state support to the Baltic republics through officially sponsored low-level initiatives which gradually are drawing the Baltic republics into a network of Nordic–Baltic cooperation. In turn this development is but one of many factors which are contesting Soviet-Russian hegemony in the Baltics.

In a wider perspective this course of action implies the prospect of a fundamental change in Nordic–Soviet relations. The asymmetrical relationship in which the monolithic superpower had vast opportunities to influence the policy-making process inside the Nordic countries now seems to have been reversed. Today the openness of the Nordic societies, their pluralized political systems, their small size and their relative insignificance in relation to Soviet global ambitions have become an asset in dealing with the superpower neighbor under the conditions of perestroika and new political thinking. It is those features which allow the Nordic countries to pursue their goals in relation to the Soviet Union, goals which consist of gradually undermining Soviet hegemony in the Baltic republics without engaging in state-to-state confrontation. For the time being such actions are perceived as a possible threat to the supreme goal of sustaining the reform process in the Soviet Union.

The future of Soviet–Nordic relations: three scenarios

The emerging pattern of Soviet–Nordic relations, as shown above, was molded by three major categories of factors: by a change of Soviet perceptions and policies, by the rise of the three Baltic states as emerging political actors inside the Soviet Union and internationally, and by the active Nordic policy in support of the new Baltic governments.

Any inquiry into the future of Soviet–Nordic relations has to follow the same lines of analysis. However, each of the three parameters are not to be considered as independent variables. They are themselves a product of developments inside the Soviet Union and at various levels of the international system. In particular, it can be argued that three categories of developments, each with its own dynamics, will determine the future pattern of Soviet–Nordic relations. For each of those developments a number of alternative subscenarios can be envisaged.

Global development. The crucial alternatives here will concern the extent to which the previous bipolar pattern of international relations will be replaced by a multilateral structure eliminating East–West confrontation. In Europe the question is still whether the existing bipolar pattern of European security will be replaced by multilateral security arrangements, e.g., within the framework of an institutionalized CSCE.

European development. The future development is here related to the two alternative prospects for the future of the European Community. One line of thought sees the future of the EC as a closed, highly integrated community with political, economic, and military functions. Others prefer an open community with an increasing number of European (including East and Central European) nations as members, but at the same time a community only concerned with economic affairs. In this view, political and military issues should be handled in other fora.

Reforms in the Soviet Union. At least three alternatives seem to exist. First, Gorbachev's internal program of reforms succeeds. Second, the general economic, social, and political decay results in a military *coup d'état.* Third, the Soviet Union in its present form disintegrates, and a number of independent republics with various economic and political systems are created.

It is the combination of each of these subscenarios which will set the environment for the future development of Soviet–Nordic relations. Of course this path of analysis requires a number of reservations. First of all, we clearly are talking in terms of ideal types. Perestroika will not completely fail nor fully succeed. Neither will the European pattern of security at one stroke change from the bipolar structure into multilateral arrangements nor will it be completely open or completely closed. Second, although the individual subscenarios have their own internal dynamic, they also are connected, making segregated analyses of each variable unproductive. For example, the success of domestic perestroika in the Soviet Union will to an unknown extent depend on international developments. And the prospects for the remaining Nordic countries to join the EC will depend on the future pattern of European security. This also implies that some of the theoretically possible combinations of subscenarios in the real world are unlikely to occur. It is, for example, hard to imagine a situation in which the security pattern in Europe will remain bipolar and Finland and Sweden will join the EC. These observations should direct our attention toward three possible scenarios setting the stage for future Soviet–Nordic relations:

Scenario 1: Failure of perestroika and restoration of the Nordic balance

In this scenario the reform process in the Soviet Union would fail. In internal affairs, this would not imply a complete return to the old system. Rather, economic reforms would continue but under the protection of a restored authoritarian state – a development which one Soviet analysis called "technocratic perestroika."[53] In such a regime the military likely would play an increased political role, but probably without establishing a military dictatorship. But at least in the short term the military would be able to hinder a further development toward independence in the union republics.

In foreign policy a development along these lines would imply a more conservative orientation with renewed stress on military strength. However, it would not imply a complete return to the two-camp approach, in a situation where a reestablishment of the old-time Warsaw Pact is clearly not possible. Rather, the Soviet Union still would pursue new security arrangements within the CSCE framework, but probably without too much success. The restoration of an authoritarian state would make the process of reform in Eastern Europe difficult, as these countries will in the foreseeable future be dependent on trade with their huge neighbor. In foreign policy the East European countries would be constrained heavily in their freedom of action and the best they could achieve probably would be a position not unlike Finland's. This would also make their future integration into an expanded European Community difficult and hence could be a stimulus to the "closed" version of the EC. Under such circumstances NATO would be unwilling to give up its present functions. In this scenario it probably would be impossible for Finland, and most likely also for Sweden, to enter the Community if the EC were to develop military functions. If, however, the EC were to remain exclusively a framework for economic cooperation, it could be argued that the Soviet Union would have such strong interests in economically healthy neighbors (and trade partners) that the Soviets would not object to a Finnish, Swedish, and possibly East European entry into the EC. For Norway, where the threat from the Soviet Union is also bilateral, and possibly also Iceland, this scenario presents further incentives to closer European integration. Under unstable European political circumstances, and with prospects of reduced American engagement in Europe, both countries would have strong inducements to improve their position *vis-à-vis* the Soviet Union through membership in the EC and possibly a revitalized WEU.

Under this scenario we would witness a resurgence of the established pattern of Soviet–Nordic relations. The Baltic states again would be firmly within the grip of Moscow. Finland would resume its place as a loyal neutral neighbor. Norway and Denmark would restate their commitments to NATO, and Sweden again would pursue a Westward-leaning neutrality.

Scenario 2: Russia as a regional power

The second scenario also assumes a failure of perestroika. At the same time, however, the Soviet empire would disintegrate into its constituent parts as the center would prove too weak to keep the national independence movements under control. Instead, the West would face the rise of various independent nations with various political systems. In Russia we could expect the development of some variant of authoritarianism, perhaps under the leadership of President Boris Yeltsin, whereas various types of democracies would develop in the Baltic republics.

In this scenario, the Soviet Union/Russia would lose its status as a global superpower but would remain a strong regional actor. Russia would have an even stronger interest in CSCE as a future framework for European cooperation, as it would lose its possibility to influence events in Europe through its relations with the United States. Under these circumstances, Eastern Europe would have a larger degree of freedom regarding economic and political development, which would be determined largely by internal factors. In foreign policy East European countries would be restrained by the interest of the new Russian neighbor. The relation to the EC would remain open and be determined by the future strategy decided upon by the EC institutions.

For the Nordic countries such a development would produce a mixed situation with new possibilities, but also persisting restraints. On the one hand, this scenario would increase possibilities for cooperation around the Baltic Basin. On the other hand, Russia would remain a strong regional and conservative power with its own national interests. Those interests could hamper Poland and the Baltic states from achieving closer cooperation with the West and could impede cooperation in the Baltic basin in the field of security. However, it also would slow the

Finnish and perhaps Swedish approach to West European economic and political cooperation. Finland, as the closest neighbor to Russia, would have to consider its position in any future conflict which might arise between Russia and the European Community. Sweden would have to weigh its interest in remaining neutral in future European conflicts against its wish to contribute to the containment of a unified Germany in a web of strong European institutions. The reduction of the Soviet Union/Russia to a regional power also could reduce the US naval presence in the Nordic waters, leaving Norway further exposed to Soviet/Russian intimidations. Hence, in this scenario there exist also powerful inducements for Norway to join West European foreign policy cooperation within the EC institutions. As a consequence, a sort of reconstructed Nordic Balance, which also would include the independent Baltic republics and Poland, could emerge.

Scenario 3: The Baltic basin as a new center, a new Hansa

This scenario assumes the success of Gorbachev's perestroika. Such a success also would mean the end of the Soviet system in its present form, as a number of republics would use their newly won freedom to gain partial or full independence from the Soviet Union. On the European level, expanded CSCE institutions would constitute the framework for an all-European security system, leaving the notion of a Nordic Balance a concept of the past.

This development would open the way for the remaining Nordic countries gradually to join the EC constituting the Nordic tier of an expanded community. Only Norway and Iceland for domestic reasons could choose to remain outside the community. This development also would open the prospect for the Baltic basin as a new political and economic zone. In its first stages this development would be hindered by the uncompetitive economies of the previous socialist states. In the longer perspective, and assuming that economic reforms in Eastern Europe and the Baltic states succeed, there should be prospects for "increasing political and economic cooperation in the Baltic basin between the Nordic countries, the emerging Baltic states, Poland, and possibly also the Soviet Union and Northern Germany."[54] Of course the attainment of this vision also would require that the EC choose the path toward open and expanded European economic cooperation. Regarding security policy, the establishment of a Nordic nuclear-free zone seems a probable outcome, supported by the independent Baltic states.[55]

In the real world, of course, none of the three scenarios outlined will be realized fully. However, considering development in the Soviet Union on the global and on the all-European level, Scenario 2 represents the most likely outcome at present. However, it also is the scenario which represents the most substantial uncertainties regarding the pattern of future Soviet–Nordic relations. And yet the fluidity of all the factors considered makes such a conclusion not much more than an educated guess.

Notes

1 I am grateful for useful critique and comments from my colleagues, associate professors Niels Amstrup and Steven Sampson and assistant professor Thomas Pedersen. Judgments and remaining errors are of course my sole responsibility.

2 Örjan Berner, *Soviet Policies toward the Nordic Countries* (Lanham: The Center for International Affairs, Harvard University, University Press of America, 1986), p. 105.

3 See Martin Heisler, "Denmark's quest for security: constraints and opportunities within the alliance," in *NATO's Northern Allies*, ed. Gregory Flynn (London: Rowman and Allanheld, 1985), pp. 66ff.

4 Robert W. Janes, "Moscow and the military build-up in Northern Europe," *Problems of Communism*, March–June (1989), p. 128.

5 Arne Olev Brundtland, "The Nordic balance," *Cooperation and Conflict*, II (1966), pp. 30–63; for a critical discussion of the concept, see Erik Noreen, "The Nordic balance: a security policy concept in theory and practice," *Cooperation and Conflict*, vol. 23, no. 1 (1983), pp. 43–56; Roy Allison, *Finland's Relations with the Soviet Union. 1944–1984* (New York: St. Martin's Press, 1985); and for a recent Finnish critique of the concept of "Nordic balance," see Pertti Joenniemi, "Europe changes; the Nordic system remains," *Bulletin of Peace Proposals*, vol. 2, no. 2 (1990), pp. 205–17.

6 For a summary of the Soviet stance, see Lena Jonson, "Soviet policy towards Sweden and the region of Northern Europe under Gorbachev," *Cooperation and Conflict*, vol. 25 (1990), pp. 10–11; see, also, her chapter 4, below.

7 Janes, "Moscow and the military build-up," p. 127.

8 Franklyn Griffith, "The sources of American conduct. Soviet perspectives and their policy implications," *International Security*, vol. 9, no. 2 (1984), pp. 3–50; and Ole Nørgaard, "New political thinking East and West: a comparative perspective," *Gorbachev and Europe*, ed. Vilho Harle and Jyrki Iivonen (London: Printer Publishers, 1990).

9 See Heisler, "Denmark's quest for security," pp. 66ff; and Arne Olev Brundtland, "Norwegian security policy: defense and non-provocation in a changing context," in *NATO's Northern Allies*, ed. Gregory Flynn (London: Rowman and Allanheld, 1985), p. 184.

10 Admiral Gorshkov as quoted in Finn Sollie, "The Soviet challenge in Northern waters. Implications for resources and security," *The Arctic Challenge*, ed. Kari Möttölä (London: Westview Press, Boulder), pp. 92–93.

11 For an introduction to the implications of the military developments in the far North, see Möttölä, *The Arctic Challenge*, and Clive Archer, *The Soviet Union and Northern Waters* (New York: Routledge, Chapman and Hall, 1988).
12 Sollie, "The Soviet challenge," pp. 92–93; Helge Ole Bergerse, Arild Moe, Willy Østreng, *Soviet Oil and Security Interests in the Barents Sea* (New York: St. Martin's Press, 1987).
13 "Norwegens Schwanken vor Europa," *Neue Züricher Zeitung*, 21 September 1990.
14 See Yurii Kommisarov, *Bezopasnost' i sotrudnichestvo. Opyt Evropeiskogo Severa* (Moscow: Mezhdunarodnye otnosheniia, 1989), quoted in Jonson, "Soviet policy towards Sweden and the region of Northern Europe under Gorbachev," p. 11.
15 Ingemar Lindahl, *The Soviet Union and The Nordic Nuclear-Weapons-Freezone Proposal* (New York: St. Martin's Press, 1988).
16 Christopher Andrew, Oleg Gordievskii, *The Inside Story* (Hodder, 1990).
17 Jørgen Dragsdal, "KGB ikke konkurrencedygtig," *Information*, 10 October 1990.
18 The surveys are carried out by *Observa* and published in *Jyllandsposten* and usually reproduced in *Dansk Udenrigspolitisk Arbog*.
19 "Styrelsen för psykologisk försvar," *Rapport 154* (Stockholm, 1989), table 10.
20 *Jyllandsposten*, 26 April 1987.
21 Reported in *Week-End Avisen*, 27 April 1988. This conclusion later was challenged in a study of the Institute of Political Science at the University of Aarhus. In this study, conducted in relation to the 1988 general elections, it was found that 69 percent of the voters would support a nuclear-free zone only if the establishment of such a zone would be approved by the NATO alliance and would not affect the East–West military balance. Nikolaj Petersen, "Sikkerhedspolitikken og 1988-valget," *To Folketingsvalg*, ed. Elklit and Tonsgaard (Aarhus, 1988). To which extent this result signified a general trend or only a transient effect of the election campaign is not yet clear. Recently a more comprehensive analysis of threat perceptions in the Nordic countries has been published in Nikolaj Petersen, Karin Lindgren, *Trussel eller tillid? Nordiske omverdensbilleder under forandring* (Nordsam, 1990).
22 Jørgen Goul Andersen, *Kvindelige vaelqere i bevaeqelse* (Center for Kulturforskning, Aarhus University, 1988); Mary Kaldor, "The concept of common security," *Policies for Common Security*, ed. Sipri (London, 1985); and Petersen, "Sikkerhedspolitikken og 1988-valget," p. 321.
23 See, for example, Bo Huldt, "Svensk neutralitet – historia och framtidsperspektiv," *Svensk neutralitet. Europa och EG*, ed. Ulla Nfordlöf-Lagerkranz (Utrikespolitiska Instituten, MH Publishing, Stockholm, 1990); and Gustav Hägglund, Pauli Järvenpää, *Finland's Present Strategic Position and Finnish Defense* (Utrikespolitiska Institute, Stockholm, 1990).
24 Joenniemi, "Europe changes: the Nordic system remains."
25 Quoted in *Neue Züricher Zeitung*, 21 October 1990.
26 Martin Saeter, "New thinking, perestroika, and the process of Europeanization," *Bulletin of Peace Proposals*, vol. 20, no. 1 (1989), p. 54.

27 But the collapse of the center-right government in October 1990 proves that membership of the EC is reentering the political agenda.
28 See, for example, Niels Andreń, "Neutraliteten, säkerheten och Europa," *Svensk neutralitet. Europa och EG*, pp. 76–92. For a further discussion of Nordic options in the economy of a future Europe, see Clive Church, "The politics of change: EFTA and the Nordic countries' responses to the EC in the early 1990s," *Journal of Common Market Studies*, vol. 25, no. 5 (June 1990), pp. 401–30.
29 See, for example, Aleksandr Sabov, "Shvedskaia spichka," *Literaturnaia gazeta*, 11 April 1990; B.K. Sepchagov, "Shvedskaia Model′: Tretii put′ razvitiia," *IKO* (1990), pp. 183–98.
30 "Evropeiskoe soobshchestvo, segodnia. Tezisy Instituta mirovoi ekonomiki i mezhdunarodnykh otnoshenii SSSR," *MEMO*, 12 (1988), pp. 5–18.
31 For the Murmansk speech, see *Pravda*, 2 October 1987; for the Helsinki speech, see *Pravda*, 27 October 1989.
32 For an extensive review of the Murmansk speech, see Arne Olav Brundtland, "Den nye sovjetiske nordpolitikken og mulige norske svar," *International Politik*, nos. 2–3 (1988), pp. 95–133.
33 "USSR Supreme Soviet Commission's appeal to northern countries," *TASS in Russian for Abroad 0610 GMT*, 12 February 1986. Reported by SWB, 15 February 1988.
34 *Pravda*, 27 October 1990.
35 See, for example, "The Soviet Union and Nordic Council plan closer contacts," TASS, 5 December 1989; and "Nordic foreign ministers want cooperation with Baltic states," SWB, 14 September 1990.
36 Saeter, "New thinking, perestroika, and the process of Europeanization," p. 54.
37 "Latvian Supreme Soviet Session: Gorbunovs' nomination," SWB, 7 May 1990.
38 Based on interviews with Baltic politicians.
39 See, for example, "Latvian premier supports Latvia's 'Finlandisation,' report on Gudmonis's speech in Latvian Supreme Soviet following his nomination for the premiership," SWB, SU/0762 3/1, 12 May 1990.
40 "Lithuanian premier's news conference on return from Scandinavia," *TASS in Russian for Abroad*, SWB, SU/0747 A1/1, 25 April 1990.
41 For an extensive account of the Baltic–Nordic relations, see Ole Nørgaard, "Northern Europe," *Yearbook of Soviet Foreign Relations*, ed. Alex Pravda (I.B. Tauris) (forthcoming).
42 This observation stems from interviews with Baltic officials.
43 As reported in Danish newspapers, 17–18 April 1990.
44 Ole Nørgaard, "Danish policies towards democratization in the Soviet Union," prepared for the APSA 86th Annual Meeting, San Francisco, August–September 1990.
45 "Swedish opposition leader Bildt proposes closer contact with Soviet Republic," Associated Press, 8 January 1990.
46 AP, 25 March 1990.
47 As reported by TASS and SWB, SU/0615 A1/7, 16 November 1989.
48 Denmark, Norway and Iceland are in favor of a strong defense of the Baltic

states' right to independence, whereas Sweden and Finland have shown more understanding of Moscow's position in the conflict. The official position of the individual Nordic governments' policy in relation to the Lithuanian declaration of independence and to Moscow's reactions is described in *Nordisk Kontakt*, 5 (1990), pp. 13–23.

49 AP, 22 April 1990, and as reported in Danish newspapers.

50 AP, 21 April 1990.

51 As reported in SWB, SU/0615 A1/7, 16 November 1989.

52 SWB, 15 October 1990.

53 Ia. Rakitskaia, B.V. Rakitskii, "Razmyshleniia o perestroike kak sotsial''noi revolutsii," *EKO* (1988), 5, pp. 3–28.

54 Nikolaj Petersen, *Denmark's Foreign Relations in the 1990s* (Institute of Political Science, Aarhus University, 1990).

55 "Estonian leaders appeal over relations with military" (text of "summary" of address to people of Estonia by Rüütel, Toome and Väljas), SWB, SU/0609 B/5. 10 March 1990.

4 Soviet signals to the Nordic countries during the Lithuanian crisis of 1990

Lena Jonson

At the beginning of 1990 Gorbachev and the Soviet leadership were confronted by the specter of Lithuania's becoming the first Soviet republic to declare its independence. In December 1989 the Lithuanian Communist Party, led by Algirdas Brazauskas, declared its independence of the Soviet Communist Party. Elections to the national assemblies of all republics were scheduled for March, and it was evident from the atmosphere in Lithuania that a newly elected parliament would declare the republic's independence. This is, in fact, what happened on 11 March 1990.

It was a matter of urgency for the Soviet leadership to prevent other states from recognizing such a declaration of independence. Making it clear to the world that Moscow would not accept an independent Lithuania thus became an important objective.

The aim of this study is to analyze Soviet signaling to the rest of the world in a bid to prevent recognition of Lithuanian independence. Although American reactions to events in Lithuania were undoubtedly of most interest to Moscow, the focus of this chapter will be on crisis communication between the Soviet Union and its small neighbors to the northwest. With their geographical proximity, historical ties, and groups of exiled Balts, the Nordic countries followed the course of events in the Baltic region with particular interest, and the stances they adopted were arguably not without political importance. Soviet policy toward the Nordic countries thus can be considered an important aspect of Soviet policy toward the West in general. This study is concerned with Soviet signaling to the Nordic area throughout this crisis, with particular attention focused on the largest country in the region – Sweden. The inquiry covers the period between January and the end of April 1990 – i.e. from shortly before until shortly after the Lithuanian declaration of independence.

The actors in this study are the Lithuanians, represented first and foremost by the Lithuanian government, the Nordic governments, and the Soviets, the latter being dealt with here as if they constituted a "black box." That is to say, the possible differences among the various Soviet actors will not be explained here.

This study is based exclusively on published material. The Soviet sources include the Communist Party daily *Pravda* – which at the time in question can be considered to have been the organ which best reflected the official stance – the Soviet news agency's selected overview of the press, *Soviet Press-Weekly Review*, and the news agency APN's Swedish news bulletin. The Nordic sources include the two biggest daily newspapers, the independent conservative *Svenska Dagbladet* and the independent *Dagens Nyheter*, as well as Foreign Ministry press releases from Sweden, Denmark, and Norway.

Tomas Cynkin has shown how the Soviet Union adapted signaling to the United States during the crises over Czechoslovakia in 1968 and Poland in 1981.[1] Cynkin characterizes Soviet signaling during the 1968 crisis as having been a

> subtle two-pronged policy of delicate signaling, intended to elicit whether there was much likelihood of such counter-measures, and designed moreover to diminish it. This began to be manifested in signals designed to bring pressure upon Dubcek and to indicate the Soviet leadership's resolve. Additionally, Moscow began to signal its desire for improving relations with the United States, apparently with the intent of detaching Washington's interest in developments in Czechoslovakia in order to allow the USSR a free hand.[2]

By the time of the Polish crisis in 1981 the West had learned its lesson of 1968, and the Soviet Union was unable to use a similar strategy with the same success as before.

The Lithuanian crisis differs from the earlier two crises mentioned here in several respects, above all in the fact that Lithuania already was incorporated in the Soviet Union. For Moscow, the problem was nevertheless a similar one, in that the task was to minimize any possible attempts by the West to influence the outcome of the conflict. In the case of Lithuania, it concentrated on preventing the West from recognizing Lithuanian independence. Moscow did this with the aid of direct and indirect signals that demonstrated to the West its sovereignty over the Baltic states.

Before proceeding with the analysis, a definition of the key concept – signaling – is in order. A signal may be defined as a statement or action, the meaning of which is established by tacit or explicit understanding among international actors.[3] "Signaling" in international relations is a very subtle and elusive phenomenon. What is meant here by "signal" is a statement or action that can be understood as a message or indication as to what Soviet intentions and policies are in a given issue. What exactly were Moscow's signals? Signals can be analyzed from the perspective of the receiver or that of the sender. They can be intentional or unintentional. A study of Soviet signals from the perspective of the receiver would be based on Swedish perceptions. The focus of this study is instead on the sender and thus the sender's intentional signals. This places the researcher in the peculiar intermediary position of trying to interpret the sender's intentional signals without doing so through the perceptions of the receiver.

Intentional signals need not be part of a strategy which has been consciously planned from the start of a given issue; decisions may have been made on an *ad hoc* basis. To this may be added the problem of the audience. To whom are the signals actually directed? Signals can be aimed expressly at a particular group of receivers within the country but at the same time contain signals to other audiences, including foreign ones. We cannot be sure whether or not the signals are sent intentionally to all the audiences; they can be aimed intentionally at one audience and unintentionally reach another one as well.

What are the possible effects of these signals? A causal connection between Soviet signals and Nordic behavior in the Baltic issue is, of course, impossible to establish. We shall have to rest content with ascertaining whether there is, in fact, a correspondence between, on the one hand, the behavior of the Soviet Union's external environment which Moscow signaled as being desirable and, on the other hand, the actual behavior of that environment, represented here by the Nordic countries and especially Sweden, in the Lithuanian issue. This will be done by studying the changes in Nordic behavior during the relevant period.

Soviet signals are classified here as "direct" or "indirect" depending on whether they are aimed expressly at the external environment or are aimed first and foremost at Lithuania. "Indirect" signals, in other words, are specifically aimed at Lithuania but at the same time can be construed as messages to the rest of the world concerning Moscow's intentions and determination with regard to Lithuania. Governments and foreign ministries in other countries carefully follow the unfolding of events, such as those in Lithuania and the USSR, and their reports form the basis of the official stances they adopt on the relevant issue.

Direct and indirect signals are classified as "declarations" and "sign signals" respectively, the former concerning substantive issues and comprising official and formal declarations or statements, and the latter having to do with signals which do not explicitly concern a given issue but which nevertheless provide a message of significance to that issue. The symbols can be "verbal" (verbal signals) or "non-verbal" (signals of a physical nature). Among the latter can be counted military maneuvers and economic sanctions.

Intentional Signals

	declarations	sign signals	
		verbal	non-verbal
indirect	1	3	4
direct	2	5	6

Declarations:
1 indirect, i.e. official statements on the actual issue aimed at Lithuania but also intended for the West;
2 direct, i.e. official statements on the issue aimed at the West.

Sign signals:
3 verbal and indirect, i.e. statements of significance to the issue and aimed at Lithuania but also intended for the West;
4 non-verbal and indirect, i.e. in the form of physical behavior of significance to the issue, aimed at Lithuania but also intended for the West;
5 verbal and direct, i.e. statements of significance to the issue aimed at the West;
6 non-verbal and direct, i.e. in the form of physical behavior aimed at the West.

Signals can contain two main types of message: they can be meant as a "stick" or a "carrot." These in turn can contain several subgroups. Warnings, demands, ultimata, and threats can be assigned to the "stick" category. What is meant here by "warning" is the pointing out of the serious consequences which would result from a given behavior on the part of the other side; "demands" comprise concrete demands made on the other side; "ultimata" stipulate measures the opponent must take within a given space of time; and, finally, "threats" indicate the measures Moscow would take were the opponent to fail to do as requested.

Among the "carrots" are, first and foremost, promises, both explicit and in their more obscure manifestation, whereby the prospect of something better is dangled in front of the opposite party's nose. Another "carrot" is encouragement in the form of words of appreciation for a policy pursued by the opposite party. This category also includes cooperative gestures, such as understanding the views of the other side and appealing to the opponent for a certain behavior.

The study will be presented as follows. The first two sections will comprise analyses of Moscow's indirect and direct signals to Sweden and the Nordic countries, respectively, on the Lithuanian issue. The third section will take up the Lithuanian and Baltic policies of the Nordic countries, and will be followed by a concluding section.

Indirect Soviet signaling

These signals were aimed at Lithuania and indicated exactly how Moscow stood on the issue of Lithuanian aspirations for independence. At the same time they can be considered indirect indications to the rest of the world as to the appropriate stance to adopt toward those aspirations.

Declarations

The announcement by the Lithuanian Communist Party in December 1989 of its independence from the CPSU resulted in a strong condemnation by the specially convened meeting of the Central Committee on 25–26 December. This condemnation, however, met with no response from the Lithuanians, and so, on 11 January, Gorbachev arrived in the Baltic republic to discuss the growing conflict between Moscow and Vilnius.

Gorbachev warned at the time that a rift in both the Communist Party and in the Soviet federation would threaten his policy of reform or perestroika as well as his own position.[4] At the same time he unexpectedly announced that a new draft law would be presented stipulating the mechanisms for the withdrawal of a republic from the union.

At the opening of the specially convened Congress of People's Deputies on 13 March, Gorbachev rejected all thoughts of independence talks because, as he put it, negotiations could be conducted only with foreign states. He said he considered the Lithuanian declaration of independence to be illegal and would not recognize it.

Two days later, on 15 March, the Congress announced that the Lithuanian declaration of independence was illegal and invalid and that Soviet law continued to apply in the republic.[5] At the same time, the Congress gave the president, the Supreme Soviet and the government authorization to "protect the legal rights of the individual" in Lithuania as well as "the rights and interests of the Soviet state."

One day later, on 16 March, Gorbachev gave Lithuanian leader Vytautas Landsbergis an ultimatum, demanding that he tell the Soviet president within three days how Lithuania would comply with the resolution of the Congress.[6]

On Monday, 19 March, Prime Minister Ryzhkov announced the measures the Soviet government would take against Lithuania. Soviet-owned firms would be run directly by the relevant ministry in Moscow; surveillance of "vital objects" such as nuclear plants would be stepped up; and the ministries for communications, the navy, fishing, and civil aviation would guarantee communication and transport facilities of importance to Soviet interests in Lithuania, the Kaliningrad area, and the Russian republic, as well as transit via the port of Klaipeda. The customs service, the Ministry of the Interior, and the KGB were assigned the task of enforcing standing customs regulations.[7]

On 21 March, the measures were stepped up with Gorbachev's presidential decree taking immediate effect. Gorbachev ordered the KGB to increase its controls on Lithuania's foreign borders and prevent violations of Soviet law. The sale of firearms was banned and citizens were ordered to turn those already in their possession over to the Ministry of the Interior within seven days. The interior and foreign ministries were instructed to tighten restrictions on visas and the arrival of foreigners in Lithuania.[8] In a telegram to Landsbergis on 22 March, Gorbachev demanded that all measures taken toward the establishment of a voluntary Lithuanian defense force should be discontinued immediately.[9]

The newly established Presidential Council and Federal Council assembled in the final days of March and approved the measures the president and government had taken against Lithuania.[10]

On 31 March, Gorbachev turned to the Lithuanian people and their parliament and urged them to change their policy, warning of the consequences should they fail to do so.[11] On 13 April, a further escalation was undertaken, with the joint statement to Lithuania by Gorbachev and Ryzhkov, in which they warned that if Lithuania did not respond within two days to calls to repeal laws and decisions that were not in accordance with Soviet law, an economic blockade of vital products would be imposed on the republic.[12]

Sign signals

Verbal signals. In spite of Moscow expressly condemning separatist tendencies concerning both the Communist Party and the union in this way, there were a number of indications that compromises could nevertheless be possible.

By the time the Central Committee was summoned to a special meeting on 25–26 December, Gorbachev was speaking in vague terms of "mutual concessions" and "compromises." When chief ideologue Vadim Medvedev visited Vilnius on 9 January, he softened his previously harsh characterization of the breakaway as "a blow against all of perestroika," saying instead that the Communist Party as a whole could benefit from increased decentralization.[13] As early as January, Ligachev said in an interview with the Swedish press that military force would not be used against Lithuania, but at the same time issued a stern warning of the consequences were a republic to secede from the union.[14]

The promise Gorbachev made during his January visit to Lithuania regarding a pending state treaty that could facilitate the secession of a republic indicated that compromise was not inconceivable. Gorbachev's demand during private discussions with Brazauskas in March that Lithuania pay 21 billion rubles in compensation can be considered a threat, indicating the economic costs of secession, but it also implied that secession could be negotiable.

After the Congress of People's Deputies on 15 March condemned Lithuania's declaration of independence, Gorbachev is reported as having said that a dialogue with Lithuania would of course be maintained, but that it would not be considered as negotiation on the independence issue.[15] In spite of the condemnation by the Congress, Gorbachev continued to intimate the possibility of dialogue and reconciliation. In private talks with Brazauskas in mid-March he said that if a referendum were carried out, a full dialogue would follow. He also had discussed with Brazauskas (on 17 March) Finland's relationship with the Soviet Union as a conceivable model for Lithuania.[16]

In this way, Moscow had, on the one hand, openly declared from the very start that Lithuanian emancipation would not be accepted. On the other hand, from the beginning of 1990 until the condemnation by the Congress in mid-March, there were certain indications – given in private talks or indirectly – that Moscow would be prepared to embark on a dialogue and to compromise. This willingness subsequently was replaced by clear dismissals of any thought of negotiations on the independence issue.

Moscow continued, however, even after the congressional condemnation, to emit unclear signals as to the extent of its determination to make Lithuania give in. Thus, Gorbachev issued the Friday, 16 March, ultimatum to Vilnius to respond within three days to the demands of the Congress, but the following Sunday when questioned by journalists at a Moscow polling station, denied that it was a question of an ultimatum.[17]

A review of articles on Lithuania published in *Pravda* during March and April shows that the newspaper was used for the purposes of signaling that a harder line was being taken on the issue in the most critical weeks. The study is based on 103 articles published in the two-month period, which has been broken down here into six ten-day periods.

The number of articles increased significantly between the point at which Moscow officially began to condemn Lithuania and the middle of April, when the economic blockade was imposed. The articles are divided according to issue area and publication date in Table 4.1.

Table 4.1 *Issues in* Pravda*'s reporting of Lithuania (no. of articles)*

	Period I 1–10 March	Period II 11–20 March	Period III 21–31 March	Period IV 1–10 April	Period V 11–20 April	Period VI 21–30 April
Declaration of independence; Lithuanian laws	1	9	10	7	1	5
Political situation in Lithuania	1	2	4	7	1	5
Military matters	1		9			
Border questions			4			
International consequences		1	3	7	1	1
Economic matters					2	4
Others	1				1	
TOTAL	4	12	30	28	9	10

Table 4.2 *Soviet and foreign actors and their signals in* Pravda*'s reporting of Lithuania (foreign actors in parenthesis) (no. of articles)*

	Period I	Period II	Period III	Period IV	Period V	Period VI
Carrot	1 (0)	1 (1)	3 (3)	5 (0)	0	1 (0)
Stick	0	4 (1)	18 (3)	15 (13)	4 (1)	4 (4)
Neutral	1 (0)	1 (0)	3 (1)	2 (1)	2 (1)	5 (2)
Soviet total	2	6	24	22	6	11
TOTAL	4	12	30	28	9	10

The articles represent behavior (in the form of words or actions) on the part of the Soviet actors which can best be characterized as belonging to the "stick" category. By "actor" is meant the main actor in the article, who could be "Soviet," "Lithuanian," or "foreign." The behavior of these actors is classified as brandishing the stick – i.e. they issue demands, warnings, ultimata or threats – or dangling a carrot, be it an appeal, understanding, encouragement, a promise or a "neutral" stance. A series of warnings was relayed via foreign actors in *Pravda*'s reporting. These are given in Table 4.2, together with Soviet actors' signals. Most of the Soviet "carrot" signals belong to the ten-day period prior to the announcement of the economic blockade decision. They were forwarded in the form of appeals by individual actors in *Pravda*.

Non-verbal signals. As early as January, Moscow had dismissed the thought of using military force against Lithuania. In spite of this, military means were used in the Baltic republic in individual actions for political aims. What was remarkable, however, was that it took until 17 March for the military to be used in this way. It was then that the news filtered through of military maneuvers with 150 tanks in southern Lithuania.[18] It was at first unclear whether the maneuvers were normal, and the uncertainty surrounding the military actions heightened the political effect. A series of individual actions followed in subsequent days. A military helicopter circled over the parliament building and scattered leaflets in Russian condemning both the independence declaration and the popular front or Sajudis.[19] On the following day, 18 March, lower-ranking officers openly took part in a pro-Moscow demonstration arranged by the Edinstvo organization.[20] There were recurrent individual military actions of a similar nature.[21]

When the military initiated its actions on 17 March, neither the president nor the government had issued any official directive or decree. All that existed were the condemnation by the Congress of People's Deputies and Gorbachev's "ultimatum," which was due to expire on 19

March, and which also contained nothing about what Moscow intended to do if Vilnius failed to comply with its demands. The military thus seemed at first to be acting on its own initiative, while at the same time signaling a determination on Moscow's part whch was not yet reflected in the decisions and signals of the political leadership.

Gorbachev's presidential decree of 21 March gave the military greater possibilities to act. As early as 19 March, plainclothes Soviet guards had, in accordance with the statement that day by the Soviet government, been deployed at the Ignalina nuclear power plant, and customs officers at five of Lithuania's border crossings were replaced.[22] On 23 March, TASS reported that the Ministry of the Interior and the KGB had taken measures in accordance with Gorbachev's decree. Border surveillance was stepped up. Lithuania's contacts with the outside world were obstructed by visa restrictions. The Soviet prosecution authorities sent a group of experts to enforce compliance with Soviet law in the renegade republic.

The establishment of voluntary Lithuanian forces, frontier outposts, and supervision of the customs services were serious tests of Moscow's sovereignty. The issue of surrendering firearms and the rounding up of deserters from the Soviet army concerned the military to the greatest possible extent, and its assistance in collecting weapons and deserters increased its possibilities to act as well as its room to maneuver. On 24 March, for the first time in the course of the conflict, a military demonstration of 100 vehicles, including tanks, was carried out in Vilnius. The military made a number of statements about the situation in Lithuania.

The presidential decree thus conveyed a considerable escalation of military means by Moscow. Troops in Lithuania were reinforced. On 25 March the military began occupying Lithuanian buildings and, two days later, had seized the party headquarters in Vilnius. Soviet crack soldiers stormed hospitals to arrest Lithuanian deserters. On 2 April the military seized the party's press building and on 5 April the premises of Lithuania's prosecution authorities.

Economic sanctions against Lithuania followed with the joint statement by Gorbachev and Ryzhkov on 13 April, at which time Moscow stopped deliveries of oil and gas to the republic. The blockade was the final step in the escalation of measures.

Summary: indirect signaling

Moscow's actions toward Lithuania can be divided into phases. The introductory phase extended until 15 March and the Congress of

People's Deputies' condemnation of the Lithuanian independence declaration. The second phase, which was characterized by continued indecision on the part of Moscow as to how to handle the Lithuanian situation, ended with the presidential decree of 21 March. The third phase began with the 21 March presidential decree and indicated a sudden and tardy determination to put an end to the Lithuanian struggle for independence. The fourth phase extended beyond the period included in this study. It began with the lifting of the economic sanctions in early summer, at which point Lithuania "froze" its independence legislation while refusing to withdraw its declaration, and a deadlock between Vilnius and Moscow was reached. In this respect, the Lithuanian crisis differed from those over Czechoslovakia and Poland, in which the Soviet Union succeeded in interrupting the liberation process.

Direct Soviet signaling

Background: Soviet policy toward the Nordic countries and Sweden since 1985

Under Gorbachev, Soviet policy toward Europe as a whole and Sweden in particular has entailed improved relations and the promise of better things to come. On the issue of military armaments in the region, however, little has happened since Gorbachev came to power. Ever since 1987, Soviet policy toward the Nordic countries has entailed a military initiative concerning disarmament in the northern region – one, however, deemed insufficient by the Nordic countries. In his speech in Murmansk in October 1987, Gorbachev presented proposals for confidence-building measures at sea and for naval disarmament. These were aimed first and foremost at the United States and NATO and not at the Nordic countries, which did not respond immediately – not even Sweden, which on the international level was advocating the initiation of talks on naval disarmament.

When Gorbachev was in Helsinki in October 1989, his speech contained few concrete offers relating to disarmament in the north European region. He emphasized instead that the strategic nuclear and naval forces in the area, which he conceded "alarmed our Nordic neighbors," would remain in place and could be reduced only through negotiations with the United States. He pointed out the significance of naval disarmament and confidence-building measures at sea and proposed naval agreements concerning northern Europe.

In the Baltic Sea region, a number of disarmament measures were carried out at the end of the 1980s, including the dismantling of old

Soviet medium-range missiles and a reduction of troops in the Leningrad area. The only concrete offer concerning the region made by Gorbachev in Helsinki was to remove five nuclear-armed submarines from the Baltic Sea. As the submarines already were obsolete, the offer really was nothing but a gesture. Soviet disarmament proposals in the northern region, i.e. including the northern seas, thus were very limited, and the Nordic governments consequently reacted with a "wait-and-see" attitude.

As early as the Murmansk initiative of 1987, the Soviet Union had presented proposals for cooperation with its Nordic neighbors. These can be considered attempts to find new ways of cooperating in the face of a lack of readiness to disarm. The Murmansk speech also contained invitations to the Nordic countries to cooperate on economic joint ventures, scientific and technological projects, environmental issues, and the extraction of minerals and natural resources on the Kola Peninsula and in the Arctic. One aspect of this cooperation was initiated under the label of "the Kola project."

Gorbachev also suggested in Helsinki in 1989 that the USSR and the Nordic countries establish more permanent discussion fora. He thus proposed that a permanent group of parliamentarians with participants from those countries be formed to discuss regional problems including everything from security issues to human rights. He also wanted to establish contact with the Nordic Council and suggested that a delegation from the Council meet with representatives from the Supreme Soviet for talks. At a later stage, he suggested, representatives from the parliaments in the Soviet republics and the autonomous regions would be able to participate. The latter proposal could only refer to the Baltic republics together with the autonomous areas of Karelen and Komi in northwestern Russia. In his speech he gave high priority to environmental cooperation.

Soviet researchers spoke at this time of a tendency in Europe toward increased regional cooperation. This gave nourishment to the ideas emerging in Sweden and northern Germany of a sort of new Hanseatic League, which in its modern manifestation would entail cooperation between all states bordering on the Baltic. According to the Nordic countries, the Baltic republics were to be included as an important component of future Baltic cooperation. Soviet legislation of November 1989 granted the republics greater economic autonomy and the possibility of extending cooperation with the Nordic countries.

Bilateral relations between the USSR and Nordic countries had improved since 1986. Although the desire for extended economic cooperation had been expressed clearly when Ryzhkov visited these countries in January 1988, no expansion of economic relations ensued. Several old conflicts had been resolved; others had been swept under the carpet.

The old dispute with Norway over the drawing of the border in the Barents Sea remained unresolved. Gorbachev's Helsinki speech of 1989, however, contained a promise to Norway to find a solution.

One of the thorniest issues dividing Sweden and the Soviet Union, regarding the borders of the economic zone in the Baltic Sea, had been solved by the spring of 1988. Of course, uncertainty continued to prevail in Sweden as to whether it was Soviet submarines that were violating Swedish territorial waters, but the issue had lost its urgency in Swedish domestic politics. Another major issue in bilateral relations was the Raul Wallenberg case,[23] and since the summer of 1989 the Soviets had shown a new attitude and intention to clarify what had in fact happened to the Swedish diplomat. No other major issues disturbed bilateral relations, which had improved considerably following Prime Minister Ingvar Carlsson's visit to Moscow in 1986.

In the Soviet domestic political debate, the "Swedish model" concept came to play a special role. An altered official view of Swedish domestic policy had begun to grow apparent as early as October 1987, when the Soviet ambassador to Stockholm, Boris Pankin, praised the Swedish model in the journal *Moscow News*. What the concept entailed, in his view, was above all an economic policy that resulted in an internationally competitive industry, relatively low unemployment, a social welfare system, and a readiness for political compromise.[24] In keeping with this Soviet interest in the Swedish model, discussions and seminars took place between Swedish and Soviet economists and politicians in 1989. In reporting from a Soviet parliamentary delegation's visit to Sweden the following February, the "Swedish model" was described as follows:

> This delegation's visit is yet another confirmation of the new phase in relations with the Social Democrats that Mikhail Gorbachev proclaimed last spring – a phase with "comparison of ideas and exchange of experiences." Of special interest to the Soviet Union are social democratic experiences of solving current political, social and economic problems. The Finnish and Swedish Social Democrats experienced this earlier than the other parties with which the Soviet Communist Party has traditionally had the most lively contacts.[25]

Swedish foreign policy was praised, as it had been previously, for being active in efforts to bring about disarmament, detente and international support for the Third World.[26] The Soviets praised even more strongly Sweden's neutrality policy. This emerged, for example, in Gorbachev's speech in Helsinki in October 1989, when he praised the contribution to stability and detente of the small Nordic states and expressed his high regard for the neutral countries in general.[27] In the Soviet press, Sweden was often pointed out as having a special role in international relations as a sort of international bridge-builder. Vice-Admiral Vladimir Zakharian, the vice-chief of staff of the Soviet navy, praised "Stockholm's cautious and well-considered behavior" when he criticized the RAND Corporation's submarine report in February 1990. It was his view that the Soviets and the Swedes could very well discuss all the issues of navigation in the Baltic Sea, in a spirit of mutual understanding, and appoint a preliminary expert commission to deal with all notifications of incidents near the Swedish coast.[28]

Moscow was clearly positive to increased exchange between Sweden and its neighbors across the Baltic – Latvia, Estonia, and Lithuania. The law stipulating economic self-government for the Baltic republics of November 1989 allowed and created real possibilities for direct exchange. At the same time, it emerged that the Soviets did not want to allow Sweden to develop cooperation exclusively with the Baltic republics; the Soviets pointed out that northwestern Russia was part of an area of natural cooperation. Pankin spoke in the summer of 1989 of "a zone of intensified cooperation in economic, scientific, technological and cultural respects" that embraced the Nordic countries, the Baltic republics and northwestern Russia. In an interview in November, Shevardnadze spoke of cooperation with the northwestern Soviet Union, which he defined as including Leningrad, the Baltic states, Karelen, Komi, and parts of the Russian interior.[29] He stressed that cooperation would have to take place on an interstate level, meaning that on the Soviet side it would have to be the union that acted. The republics, however, would be able to open trade offices in the countries with which they had developed cooperation, implying that Baltic trade offices could be established in Sweden. As areas in which cooperation could be developed, Shevardnadze named the economy, ecology, science and technology, and cultural exchange.

This is the general background against which Soviet signaling to the Nordic countries during the Lithuanian crisis in 1990 should be seen. This includes both those signals aimed at the West in general – which naturally includes Scandinavia – as well as those aimed specifically at the Nordic countries. As with those analyzed in the preceding section, the signals can be roughly characterized as belonging to the "stick" or the "carrot" category and as taking the form of declarations, verbal, or non-verbal signals.

Declarations

Declarations concerning Lithuania and aimed at the outside world in the first phase, up to the condemnation by the Congress of People's Deputies on 15 March, were the expression above all of warnings regarding the international consequences that would ensue should the West support Lithuanian aspirations.

Shevardnadze warned as early as the end of January not only of the consequences of Lithuania leaving the Soviet Union but also of support for and recognition of an independent Lithuania by other countries. Moscow considered the latter to be interference in internal Soviet affairs. In the first place, Shevardnadze said that "a withdrawal by one or another republic from the union would not only create further military-political and economic stress factors for their inhabitants, it would also lead to a serious destabilization of the existing international structure. No one has an interest in that." He continued by saying that "problems in interethnic relations are so fragile and sensitive that any involvement from outside in their process of development should be avoided. There could otherwise be unforeseen consequences."[30]

The day after Lithuania declared its independence, the spokesman for the Soviet foreign ministry, Gennadii Gerasimov, warned other countries not to support the republic. The warning was aimed above all at the United States because that country had urged the Soviet Union to recognize Lithuanian independence. "Whoever tries officially to dictate something to us is guilty of involvement in internal Soviet affairs," he said. He continued by saying that Moscow refused to comply with any dictate whatsoever, and added that the USSR did not expect any government would try to issue one.[31] A similar warning against involvement in internal Soviet affairs was aimed by the Soviet parliamentary committee for international affairs at the US Senate and House Committee on Foreign Affairs on 6 April.[32]

Similar warnings also were aimed at the West in the phase ending in the presidential decree and thereafter. When Gorbachev met Senator Edward Kennedy at the end of March, at the time that Moscow's conflict with Lithuania had progressed but the West's stance on the issue was not yet clear, Gorbachev reiterated his warning of the possibly negative international repercussions should the West try to support the renegade republic. According to an APN account, Gorbachev stated

> that the profound changes in the world are taking place with difficulty and in some places with pain. There are surprising turns of events and conflict and crisis situations occur. Now that the world has entered a watershed period, it has been repeatedly said in contacts with Western leaders that, in this complicated and

stormy process, attempts should be avoided to exploit it to the disadvantage of whoever it may be.

There seems to have been understanding for this, Gorbachev pointed out. But when complications arose, one began to forget and use the same old double standards: one's own actions were judged by one yardstick, other's actions in their own country with another yardstick, and "alarm" expressed.[33]

At the beginning of April, Gorbachev aimed words of warning at Britain's Foreign Minister, Douglas Hurd, saying that Lithuania's attempt to break away was damaging to international peace. The hazardous actions Lithuania had undertaken could be very costly, not just for the Lithuanian people but also for the Soviet Union and world peace, he said, according to Soviet television on 10 April.[34] Gorbachev also returned to the theme of possible repercussions on Soviet–American relations in his talks with US congressmen on 12 April.[35]

After having been in the United States with US Secretary of State Baker at the beginning of April, Shevardnadze expressed confidence that the government understood the Soviet leadership's problems with Lithuania.[36] The Soviets, however, judged Washington as being subjected to pressure by groups supporting Baltic independence.

In spite of Soviet unease, no Western government recognized the Lithuanian declaration of independence, and words of appreciation for this cautious restraint began to be heard from the Soviet Union. Because the West's stance could be judged as being neither stable nor predictable, Soviet appreciation also signaled encouragement to the West to continue pursuing a cautious policy on the Lithuanian issue. Foreign Ministry spokesman Maslennikov's words could be interpreted in this way when he made a statement about Western states not having recognized the Lithuanian government.

Because all countries on the official level show a certain restraint and try not to get involved in internal Soviet affairs, the Soviet government and president consider the Western stance to be satisfactory. And should individual groups of politicians, in the U.S. or elsewhere, pass resolutions that constitute interference in our internal affairs, our country will reject their attempts.[37]

Regarding the initiative by French President François Mitterand and West German Chancellor Helmut Kohl to mediate between Vilnius and Moscow, Vadim Perfiliev of the Soviet Foreign Ministry told a press conference on 27 April that his government read their suggestion as support for its policy, and he expressed his appreciation of "the leaders of Western countries making efforts to contribute to a dialogue on the Lithuanian issues." It was Perfiliev's opinion that one could perceive an understanding of the Soviet government's desire to find a solution to what had been put in motion by Lithuanian leaders.[38]

The warnings aimed at the United States and the West naturally applied to Sweden and the Nordic countries as well. No express warnings were aimed at the Nordic countries, however; rather, as was the case with Sweden, the Soviet Union only expressed its appreciation of their policies toward the Baltic republics. These appreciative words could be interpreted either as encouragement to continue the policy or as intimations of promising future developments.

Faith in Swedish behavior on the Baltic issue had emerged in an interview with Boris Pankin in the summer of 1989.

> The Swedish government's official policy is aimed at not doing anything which could destroy the favorable development of Gorbachev's version of perestroika. The fate of perestroika, or so they say in Sweden, is decided in Moscow. And in line with that, hotheads from the Baltic republics, who come to Sweden – so it seems – to get support and advice, are advised to strengthen ties with Moscow and with the leadership of our party and our state, who are on the driving end of perestroika. And this very strengthening of cooperation between the Baltic republics and Sweden is considered in the light of perestroika in the USSR. This is [the Swedish government's] policy and consensus prevails between all six political parties in the parliament on the issue.[39]

When the Soviets express confidence in or praise for a given policy, it also can be considered as encouragement to pursue the policy. In 1989, Pankin pointed out that the Soviet government was conscious of the fact that the Swedish government would do nothing to endanger perestroika or relations with Moscow. There was no comparable official assessment of the Swedish stance on the Baltic issue expressed during the period analyzed in this study. In an interview in the Swedish press in mid-May 1990, Ambassador Pankin expressed once again his confidence in the Swedish government *vis-à-vis* the Soviet Union, and thus also on the Lithuanian issue. Pankin quoted former Swedish Prime Minister Olaf Palme's phrase about "common security," saying that there could be no security when individual nations thought only of themselves; their neighbors' fears and security needs must also be taken into consideration. This, maintained Pankin, was what Sweden was seeking to do.[40]

Because of this orientation in Swedish foreign policy, Pankin said that Sweden played a role that the Soviet Union considered special. "It's also because of this that Sweden means considerably more to the Soviet Union than it would simply on the basis of the country's physical parameters, the size of its population or scale of production. It gives [Sweden] an added importance."

Sign signals

Verbal signals. Gorbachev's European policy contained prospects of continued detente and increased cooperation in Europe. The upheavals in Eastern Europe in the autumn of 1989 implied a disintegration of the postwar bloc pattern in Europe but nevertheless had been accepted by Moscow. Gorbachev declared himself willing to seek new patterns of cooperation and new security structures in Europe together with the West. Granted, there was conservative opposition to his European policy, notably at the Central Committee's meeting in February, but such critics did not appear to be in a position to influence foreign policy making.

Shevardnadze touched on the improved prospects for cooperation and detente in his new year forecast for APN, saying how it was "impossible to solve current global problems without processes of integration, without the formation of an all-European sphere, within the economy and all areas."[41] Some Soviets, for example, Shevardnadze in his January article in *Izvestiia*, talked of a future "European confederation."[42]

The Party daily *Pravda*, however, continuously contained warnings linked to the Lithuanian crisis and aimed at the West. The message was the same as that of the official declarations.

On the day before the Lithuanian declaration of independence, a commentator in *Pravda* thus warned of the international consequences should the West exploit the situation. In a larger analysis of the changes in Eastern Europe, Gennadii Vasilev warned those in the West who wanted to exploit the changes in the East and who saw one side's loss as another's gain that "it can indeed also be so that both sides either win or lose."[43]

The Soviet press used interviews with Western politicians to issue warnings of the risks of supporting Lithuania. *Pravda* above all exploited the comments of the West German Social Democrats to this end. Apart from the aforementioned argument about international destabilization, the following cautionary arguments by foreigners were reprinted in *Pravda*:

- Nationalist aspirations could risk or interrupt the policy of perestroika; Gorbachev's opponents could gain the upper hand and undermine his position.[44]
- The military and security-political balance of forces in the postwar period could be shaken unilaterally were Lithuania to break away, since it was unclear how the republic would design its foreign and defense policy.[45]

Borders could begin to be altered in Europe.[46]

The realization of a "common European home" might be jeopardized.[47]

Europe could become fragmented and consequently unstable. The chairman of the West German Bundestag, Rita Zussmut, for example, spoke out against Lithuania's secession from the Soviet Union and argued that a return to the nineteenth-century division of Europe into small nation-states outside the framework of federal structures would be a terrible thing.[48]

Lithuania had little chance of existing as a self-sufficient economic unit.[49]

Statements connected with Soviet military interests in the Baltic Sea, above all the military base in the Kaliningrad area but also the harbor in Lithuanian Klaipeda, were few and far between. Soviet Fleet Commander Vladimir Chernavin claimed in March that an independent Lithuania would undermine Soviet strategic interests. He said that an independent Lithuanian army would be much too weak to provide "a serious and reliable defence" against NATO's forces. An independent Lithuania, he continued, would cut the Soviet fleet off from its main base in Kaliningrad.[50] These are statements which probably were aimed above all at Lithuania but which doubtless also had the intended effect of alerting the West to the fact that the Lithuanian issue had military and security policy aspects of great sensitivity to Moscow.

Kaliningrad's status as part of the Russian republic was taken up in a major article in *Pravda* on 22 March. The article aimed accusations against those in Lithuania who were demanding that the Kaliningrad area should be surrendered to Lithuania and Poland, albeit with the right of access to a harbor in the area for Russians, White Russians and Ukrainians. The author of the article warned that similar thoughts would bring in their wake revision of not just the Soviet Union's borders but also Poland's eastern frontier and would affect the results of the Second World War in general.[51] The article was aimed at Lithuania but contained a clear message to the West as well of the danger of beginning to change postwar borders. The question of Lithuania's borders became topical in the White Russian Supreme Soviet as well, which on 29 March announced that it would demand territory from Lithuania which the latter had acquired in 1939 and 1940.[52]

The Soviet press also warned of the consequences should the Lithuanian issue, which had become controversial in, not least, US domestic politics, be manipulated by groups of exile Balts. The Soviets judged the US government as being subjected to pressure exerted by groups supporting Baltic independence. In mid-April *Pravda* carried a major article on the West's behavior and stance on the Lithuanian issue, in which the author opined that it would be thoughtless to cast East–West relations under the feet of Lithuanian nationalists.[53] The author, Tomas Kolesnichenko, wrote that the Lithuanian issue threatened US–Soviet relations and argued that strong forces were exerting pressure on President Bush. These were "right-wing forces" and "representatives of the military-industrial complex," the latter having been activated by developments in Eastern Europe. "And if anyone is truly interested in extreme measures in Lithuania, it is precisely those who insist on recognizing 'Lithuanian independence' straight away. I don't think it is necessary to emphasize yet again just how dangerous such a stance is, including for those who adopt it." Public opinion in the United States recommended, on the other hand, a more cautious line on the Lithuanian issue, Kolesnichenko wrote.[54] "From this it follows that restraint and understanding must be shown today not just by us but also by Washington." A worsening of relations also would affect the US side, he warned. On 26 April the newspaper reported that Bush had announced the United States would impose "no sanctions whatsoever" against the USSR because of the Lithuanian issue.[55]

During the entire episode, *Pravda* printed statements by Western politicians showing restraint and indicating that they did not want to recognize Lithuanian independence.[56] In a major article, *Pravda* made an issue of the fact that the United States and Great Britain had early on recognized the Baltic states' incorporation in the Soviet Union *de facto*. Thus, for example, several days after their incorporation on 6 August 1940, President Roosevelt extended the US–Soviet trade agreement of 1937.[57]

As with the declarations, the signals aimed at Sweden during the period discussed here were full of promise, encouragement, and appreciation for Swedish policy. No warnings were aimed specifically at Sweden.

At the end of March, however, *Pravda* assessed Deputy Foreign Minister Pierre Schori's words as to the position the West should adopt on the issue. *Pravda* wrote that in the countries of northern Europe and particularly those bordering on the Baltic Sea, developments on this issue were devoted great attention. The dominant tone of commentators, both politically and those active socially, wrote the newspaper, is caution and balance (*vzvesennost'*). Schori was quoted as having said, "I consider that observers should restrain themselves from making overly hasty statements before having acquainted themselves with the circumstances."[58]

The Soviet press has for many years quoted foreign voices to underline its own views. It also has been a part of this tradition to select that part of a foreign politician's statement which corresponds best with the Soviet stance. *Pravda*'s reporting of Schori's words thus can be considered an exhortation to Sweden to pursue a cautious policy.[59]

Non-verbal signals. The only non-verbal measures the Soviet Union took in relation to the Nordic countries were diplomatic. With the presidential decree of 21 March, Gorbachev attempted to isolate Lithuania. Visa restrictions for foreigners were tightened. On 23 March the Soviet Foreign Ministry ordered Western diplomats to return to Moscow. When the Swedish Foreign Ministry tried to get permission to send a representative to Lithuania on 23 March its request was denied by the Soviet authorities, who referred to "current conditions."[60]

The strongest move against Sweden came on 9 April when the Soviet Union turned down a visa application by a Swedish cultural delegation, led by Pierre Schori, hoping to visit Lithuania. The Soviet authorities explained this by saying it would be impossible to carry out the journey at that time. No further reasons were given.[61] The same thing happened to a group of parliamentarians from the Nordic Council, who were denied visas to Lithuania the same month.

Apart from this, no changes were apparent in the cooperation already planned with the Baltic republics in the form of air and ferry connections with Riga and Tallinn. Moscow allowed them to progress, and exchange between Sweden and the other two Baltic republics continued as well.

Summary: direct signals

During the first phase in 1990, up to the condemnation by the Congress of Peoples' Deputies on 15 March, and the second phase which ended in the presidential decree of 21 March, the Soviet Union warned the United States and the West of the international consequences that could transpire should the West recognize Lithuanian independence. This took the form of declarations, statements by Gorbachev, Shevardnadze, and foreign ministry spokesmen. The Soviets also aimed at the West some signals which best can be characterized as "carrots," containing as they did the prospect of continued detente and extended cooperation in Europe.

The warnings aimed at the United States and Europe naturally embraced the Nordic countries as well. No explicit warnings, however, either in the form of declarations or signals, were aimed directly at Scandinavia. The signals sent to Sweden, for example, were expressions of appreciation for and confidence in Swedish policy towards the Baltic republics. In this way Moscow encouraged and urged Sweden to continue with its earlier policy, which excluded recognition of an independent Lithuania. No Soviet criticism of Sweden's Baltic policy was expressed publicly.

The presidential decree of 21 March indicated a toughening of Soviet policy toward Lithuania as well as of its signals to the West. At this point, Moscow also sent non-verbal signals with the objective of cutting the West off from Lithuania and emphasizing Soviet sovereignty over the republic. This message was expressed most clearly to Sweden in the refusal to grant the deputy foreign minister a visa to Lithuania.

Nordic reactions to the Lithuanian crisis

Although the stances they had earlier adopted toward the Baltic republics differed, the Nordic countries reacted similarly to the Lithuanian crisis in 1990. The stance adopted by Denmark and Norway in the postwar period was characterized by a policy of "non-recognition"; neither country legally had recognized the annexation of the Baltic states by the Soviet Union in 1940. This meant that, as most other Western countries, neither Denmark nor Norway had any official contacts with authorities in the Baltic republics.

Sweden, on the other hand, had recognized Soviet power in the Baltic region at an early stage – and was, in fact, the only country to do so, with the notable exception of Nazi Germany. As early as August 1940, Stockholm accepted Moscow's assumption of diplomatic representation for the three Baltic states in Sweden. *De jure* recognition came on 30 May 1940, when Baltic debts to Sweden amounting to 20 million kronor were squared and agreements were signed between "the Swedish government and the government of the Union of Soviet Socialist Republics" aimed at "mutually settling economic claims concerning the Lithuanian, Latvian and Estonian republics."[62] Recognition of the situation by Finland came after the war.

Swedish recognition can be seen as having been forced on the country by the increasing pressing international situation that prevailed in 1940. But where Swedish sympathies really lay is obvious from Östen Unden's words to the Swedish parliament on 16 August 1940:

> It is natural that the events that have taken place in the Baltic Sea area affect us here in Sweden in a very special way. Three previously independent states have been liquidated in a matter of days. The apparently voluntary nature can fool no observer. . . . The remaining small states in Europe which are still free have had a new instructive object lesson in witnessing the tactic used against the Baltic states.[63]

When Nordic interest in contact with the Baltic republics was revived in 1988, Sweden – unlike other states, for the reasons mentioned above – had official channels open to them. This, however, resulted in problems, such as for example when Sweden began to discuss the establishment of a Baltic consulate in the autumn of 1988: how was Sweden to balance, on the one hand, consideration for Baltic independence aspirations with, on the other hand, consideration for the plight of Moscow, with which Sweden had diplomatic relations? What would the consulate's status be, and in what relation would it stand to Moscow? The solution finally chosen by the Swedish government in the spring of 1989 was to open only a branch office of Sweden's Leningrad consulate.[64]

The fact that Sweden recognized the Soviet annexation of the Baltic states has marked Swedish policy toward the region in the postwar era and entailed clear limitations on Sweden's official position.[65] Everything concerning the Baltic region has been politically sensitive to Swedish relations with Moscow. It must be noted, however, that neither Denmark nor Norway drew attention to Baltic affairs in spite of formally pursuing quite a different policy from Sweden and Finland; they too avoided raising and criticizing the situation there to any great extent. Because Moscow had broken the Baltic states' old ties with the rest of the world, and communication went instead via Leningrad, the Baltic republics were effectively isolated.

When the Baltic struggle for independence gathered speed at the beginning of 1988 and popular fronts formed in the republics that summer, interest in the region more or less exploded in the Nordic countries. A rapid expansion of contacts between the Nordic and Baltic states began in the autumn of 1989, with the Nordic governments supporting and encouraging contacts, exchange and cooperation to a great extent. This interest was reflected in the decision by the Council of Nordic Ministers in January 1990 to investigate the possibility of opening Nordic cultural and information centers in the three republics. At their meeting in Turku on 6–7 March 1990, the Nordic foreign ministers declared in a joint statement that their Nordic countries were prepared to extend exchanges with the Baltic republics.

By December 1989 the Swedish branch consulate in Tallinn was opened, to be followed by another in Riga which was opened *de jure* in March 1990 and began work *de facto* in May. Finnish branch consulates already had been established. A Danish cultural center opened in Riga in April 1990.

At the same time as Nordic governments offered encouragement and support to the Baltic republics, it was possible to perceive a certain caution and fear of the consequences of the growing conflict between

Vilnius and Moscow. An important role clearly was played in this respect by the concern that Gorbachev's position within the USSR would be weakened. At the same time, the tradition of caution exercised by the Nordic countries when dealing with large neighbors throughout the postwar period should not be overlooked.

Caution of this sort was in evidence when Swedish Foreign Minister Sten Andersson visited the Baltic republics in November 1989 and in a number of the statements he made the following spring, which raised a chorus of criticism from both Swedish and Baltic voices. The statements by Andersson differed, however, from those of the government, including those of the Advisory Council on Foreign Affairs (*Ultrikesnämnden*). The Foreign Minister urged Sweden on several occasions to take care not to provoke the USSR.[66] What exactly that meant, was not, however, entirely clear. In a speech to the Social Democratic Party in Stockholm at the end of April, Andersson elaborated on his assessment of the way in which Sweden could provoke the Soviet Union with its statements. His argument ran along the following lines. (a) The USSR could in this way be provoked into taking further coercive measures which, in the worst instance, could lead to the use of military force; (b) The enemies of perestroika would be strengthened; (c) Sweden could lose its chance of mediating between Moscow and Vilnius;[67] (d) Sweden's relations with the Soviet Union would deteriorate; (e) An escalation of measures on the part of the Soviets, Lithuanians or Swedes could lead to further measures being taken by the other side.[68]

The official reactions of the Nordic governments to the Lithuanian declaration of independence and to the increasing pressures exerted by the Soviet authorities were, as mentioned, very similar in spite of their historically different positions on Soviet sovereignty over the Baltic states.

The Swedish Advisory Council on Foreign Affairs assembled on 13 March, two days after the Lithuanian declaration. It issued a statement saying, "We assume that the legitimate rights of the Lithuanian people to national self-determination will be complied with in accordance with the stipulations and spirit of the Helsinki document."

At the same time it was clear that Sweden was not going to recognize Lithuanian independence. It thus invoked what is referred to as the "universality principle," whereby recognition demands that the would-be state fulfils such criteria as having a territory, a population, and a government that wields sovereign and effective control over the territory in question.[69] According to Andersson, the idea of recognition foundered on the last of these points.[70]

The initiation of military activities in Lithuania on 17 March occasioned no change in Swedish policy. After the Soviet authorities toughened their measures against Lithuania with the presidential decree of 21 March, the Swedish embassy in Moscow tried to send a representative to the republic. The Soviet Foreign Ministry turned down the request.[71]

On 28 March, the Council gathered for a new meeting. Prior to the meeting, the non-socialist parties had demanded a tougher stance on the part of the government. After a three-hour-long session, the parties and government reached agreement, saying in their joint statement that "all force or threats to use force are unacceptable. Intervention by the Soviet military risks worsening an already serious situation. The events of recent days thus give cause for alarm."[72] Facing the press, however, the prime minister declined to describe the statement as criticism of Soviet behavior and maintained that criticism would be leveled if the USSR took to methods which "we do not consider should be used." At the same time, the statement called for continued contact and exchange with the Baltic states.[73]

On 20 April the Council met to discuss, among other things, how Sweden should act now that the Soviet Union had increased pressure on Lithuania with the blockade. The Council's statement of 20 April was more strongly worded than previous ones. It noted that Soviet actions had made the situation in Lithuania worse and that it had caused problems for Swedish–Soviet cooperation. "Should Soviet actions continue in this way, further disruptions in our contacts in a larger perspective as well cannot be excluded."[74]

The Swedish attitude that can be read from the Council statements up to April 1990 expressed, on the one hand, increasingly strong Swedish criticism of Soviet actions against Lithuania and, on the other, a continuation of the Swedish tradition of caution in not recognizing Lithuanian independence. The Council statements stressed, moreover, the importance of developing contacts with the Baltic region. The Swedish government's interest in this seems to have intensified in the course of the crisis.

In his statement of 12 March, Danish Foreign Minister Uffe Elleman-Jensen referred to the fact that Denmark had never legally recognized the Soviet annexation of Lithuania. This, however, did not mean that the Danish government recognized Lithuanian independence; like all the other Western countries, the Danish government also refrained from taking that step. Instead, it urged negotiations between Moscow and Vilnius on the conditions for Lithuanian secession from the union.[75]

In a statement on 22 March, the Danish government appealed to the

Soviet Union to begin negotiations with Lithuania that were free from pressures and threats. In the statement, the government expressed support for "Lithuania's formally independent status achieving its full and actual content."[76]

In a speech to the Folketinget on 18 April, the Danish Foreign Minister summarized Danish policy on the Lithuanian issue as follows: to get the Soviet Union to keep its promise not to use force in Lithuania; to urge both Moscow and Vilnius to begin negotiations; and to extend and strengthen all useful contacts without establishing diplomatic relations yet.[77]

Danish policy thus can be seen to differ little from that of the Swedish government. The Finnish government was more cautious in its statements, but by and large its policy was the same as that of the other two. The policies of the Nordic governments pursued in 1990 can be said to have compensated for their failure to recognize an independent Lithuania by encouraging and supporting contacts and exchange between their countries and the Baltic states. Their policies can be characterized by what Ole Nørgaard describes as "a new sort of officially sponsored but subnational foreign policy."[78]

The policies of the Nordic countries during the 1990 Lithuanian crisis appear to have conformed to a largely uniform and consistent course of balancing between the Soviet Union and Lithuania. The changes which nevertheless arose in the spring of 1990 cannot be seen as consequences of Soviet signaling to the Nordic countries as to how they should react to the crisis. Their policies, on the contrary, changed to the advantage of the rebel republic, which was offered support even as Moscow was chastised for its behavior.

Conclusion

As argued earlier in the chapter, Moscow's signals to the West concerning its intentions and determination to maintain its sovereignty over Lithuania were not entirely unambiguous. Moscow declared that Lithuania was part of the Soviet Union while indicating that it could be prepared to negotiate and make compromises. It is possible that the signals were unclear because the balance of power in the top political leadership in Moscow was in the same ambiguous state. It also is possible to perceive an inability to deal with an entirely new situation entailing demands for national self-determination. It also is conceived that Gorbachev, by hinting at certain concessions, hoped that Lithuania would give in. It has been shown, finally, that Moscow's direct signals to the rest of the world were less ambiguous.

Was the Soviet Union then successful in its signaling – indirect and ambiguous or direct and clear – to the rest of the world, exemplified here by the Nordic countries? In the short term, it was, in that Moscow managed to prevent Vilnius from exercising its declared sovereignty. Furthermore, no Western state recognized an independent Lithuania – neither those governments which, like Denmark and Norway, had never acknowledged Soviet sovereignty over the Baltic states, nor those, like Sweden and Finland, which had accepted the state of affairs in the region *de jure* as early as the 1940s.

It is, however, impossible to say whether it really was Soviet signaling that was decisive for the decision of Nordic and other governments to not recognize Lithuania. It would seem reasonable to believe that in the Nordic case a long-established tradition of caution when dealing with powerful neighbors was important.

Considering 1990 as a whole, moreover, it is possible to state that the USSR was not successful in ending the Lithuanian crisis. Moscow achieved a deadlock situation at best without managing to force the Lithuanian government to capitulate. Western interest in the republic continued to grow, and the desire to develop contacts and cooperation intensified.

Times thus have changed since the Soviet Union succeeded in preventing the West from becoming involved in its conflicts to assert its ultimate sovereignty over Czechoslovakia in 1968 and Poland in 1981. It became increasingly apparent in the course of 1990 that the USSR could no longer enforce its supremacy over its erstwhile empire and that the West would no longer stand by and watch it try to do so. This new state of affairs was evident in the position of the Nordic countries, which while not formally acknowledging an independent Lithuania, openly supported its attempts to achieve autonomy.

Notes

1 Tomas M. Cynkin, *Soviet and American Signalling in the Polish Crisis* (London: Macmillan, 1988).
2 *Ibid.*, p. 18.
3 Robert Jervis, *The Logic of Images in International Relations* (Princeton, NJ: Princeton University Press, 1970), p. 20.
4 *Pravda*, 12, 13, 14 January 1990.
5 *Pravda*, 17 March 1990.
6 *Ibid.*
7 *Pravda*, 20 March 1990.
8 *Pravda*, 22 March 1990.
9 *Pravda*, 23 March 1990.
10 *Pravda*. 31 March 1990.

11 *Pravda*, 1 April 1990.
12 *Pravda*, 14 April 1990.
13 *Svenska Dagbladet*, 11 January 1990.
14 *Ibid.*
15 *Report on the USSR* (Radio Liberty), 23 March 1990; *Svenska Dagbladet*, 17 March 1990.
16 *Svenska Dagbladet*, 18 March 1990; *Report on the USSR*, 30 March 1990.
17 *Dagens Nyheter*, 3 March 1990.
18 *Svenska Dagbladet*, 18 March 1990.
19 *Ibid.*
20 *Dagens Nyheter*, 19 March 1990.
21 For example, leaflets in Russian were scattered from a military helicopter on 23 March (*Svenska Dagbladet*, 23 March 1990).
22 *Svenska Dagbladet*, 21 March 1990.
23 Raul Wallenberg was the Swedish diplomat who saved thousands of Hungarian Jews from deportation to German concentration camps at the close of World War II. He was arrested by Soviet troops in Budapest in 1945 for reasons that are still unclear. There has long been controversy as to the truth of the official Soviet claim that Wallenberg died in prison in 1947. The Wallenberg case was never an issue of serious contention between the governments of Sweden and the Soviet Union, but a new willingness to talk about the episode on the part of the Soviets in 1989 was viewed by the Swedes as an indication of a more general conciliatory attitude and willingness to discuss sensitive issues.
24 B. Pankin, "In Sweden," *International Affairs*, no. 7 (1989).
25 Igor Pavlov, APN, 6 February 1990.
26 *Ibid.*
27 "Speech by Mikhail Gorbachev at the Finlandia Palace on October 26, 1989," *Daily Review. Translations from the Soviet Press* (Novosti Press Agency, 27 October 1990); "Soviet–Finnish Declaration."
28 APN (in Swedish) 1 March 1990; *Pravda*, February 1990.
29 *Svenska Dagbladet*, November 1989.
30 Quoted in Associated Press, 28 January 1990; TASS, *Soviet Press Weekly Review*, 1990, no. 4.
31 *Svenska Dagbladet*, 13 March 1990.
32 *Pravda*, 7 April 1990.
33 APN (in Swedish), 27 March 1990.
34 *Pravda*, 11 April 1990.
35 *Pravda*, 13 April 1990; SP no. 16, p. 66.
36 *Izvestiia*, 9 April 1990.
37 *Komsomolskaia Pravda* (reprinted in APN in Swedish), 19 April 1990.
38 *Svenska Dagbladet*, 28 April 1990.
39 Pankin, "In Sweden."
40 *Dagens Nyheter*, 13 May 1990.
41 APN (in Swedish), 11 January 1990.
42 *Izvestiia*, 18 January 1990.
43 *Pravda*, 10 March 1990.
44 *Pravda*. 19 and 23 March 1990.

45 *Pravda*, 19 March 1990.

46 An SPD Bundestag representative and chairman of the Soviet–West German Friendship Union said, "We are interested in stability in the USSR for a dynamic development of perestroika. It is necessary that the Soviet Union is transformed so that small nations thrive, but this can only be achieved if they stay in the USSR and not the other way around. The loss of Lithuania is not just a loss for the Soviet Union but also for the Warsaw Pact." He also spoke out against new borders in Europe (*Pravda*, 24 March 1990).

47 The East German newspaper *Neues Deutschland* wrote about Lithuania (*Pravda*, 30 March 1990) that Lithuania is a stumbling block not just for perestroika in the USSR but also for the construction of a common European house. It said the situation in Lithuania jeopardized all the positive developments that had been achieved during the perestroika period in the USSR, Europe, and the entire world.

48 *Pravda*, 22 March 1990.

49 *Pravda*, 19 March 1990.

50 *RFE/RL Special*, 19 March 1990; *Report on the USSR*, 30 March 1990.

51 *Pravda*, 22 March 1990.

52 *Soviet Press-Weekly Report*, no. 15 (1990); *Selskaia zhizn*, 1 April 1990.

53 *Pravda*, 15 April 1990; compare *Dagens Nyheter*, 17 April 1990.

54 See also Gennadii Vasilev's assessment in *Pravda*, 4 April 1990.

55 *Pravda*, 24 April 1990.

56 *Pravda*, 5, 13, 21 and 26 April 1990.

57 *Pravda*, 26 March 1990.

58 Former Finnish Foreign Minister Kejo Korchonen said that when Finland declared its independence in December 1917, he immediately requested recognition from Sweden, but that government urged Finland to turn to St. Petersburg. Such a procedural order would also be sensible today in terms of Lithuania (*Pravda*, 23 March 1990).

59 Several Soviet journals turned their attention on Sweden and carried articles during the spring of 1990 that took up Swedish policy in individual issue areas. See, for example, *Argumenty i fakty; Literaturnaia gazeta*; and *Novoe vremia*.

60 *Svenska Dagbladet*, 24 March 1990.

61 *Dagens Nyheter*, 10 April 1990.

62 Wilhelm M. Carlgren, *Svensk Utrikespolitik 1939–45* (Stockholm, 1973), p. 225. Another school of international law experts maintains that the *de jure* recognition came only after the war – if then (Ove Bring).

63 *Ibid*.

64 *Svenska Dagbladet*, 15 and 25 April 1989.

65 Anders Kung, *Estland – En Studie i Imperialism* (Stockholm: Aldus/Bonniers, 1971).

66 *Svenska Dagbladet*, 23 March 1990.

67 The Swedish ambassador in Moscow had at that point succeeded in relaying contacts between leading Lithuanian politicians and Vadim Zagladin. *Svenska Dagbladet*, 23 March 1990.

68 *Svenska Dagbladet*, 23 April 1990.

69 Statement by Foreign Minister Sten Andersson following the meeting of the

Advisory Committee on Foreign Affairs on 13 March 1990. Press statement from the Foreign Ministry, 13 March 1990.

70 *Dagens Nyheter*, 14 March 1990.

71 *Svenska Dagbladet*, 23 March 1990.

72 *Dagens Nyheter*, 29 March 1990.

73 *Ibid.*

74 Statement by Prime Minister Ingvar Carlsson following the meeting of the Advisory Council on Foreign Affairs on 20 April 1990. Press statement, the Cabinet Office, 20 April 1990.

75 Udenrigsministerjet Pressemeddelelse, no. 43 (1990).

76 Udenrigsministerjet Pressemeddelelse, no. 50 (1990).

77 Reply by the Foreign Minister on 18 April 1990 in the Folketinget to question number 25 of 22 March 1990: "Which initiatives is the government undertaking to support Lithuanian aspirations for independence?"

78 See Ole Nørgaard, "Soviet–Nordic relations in the era of perestroika and new thinking," chapter 3, above.

5 Neutrality and new thinking

Stephan Kux

Analysis of the USSR's attitudes toward neutrality and the European neutrals has never ranked high in the study of Soviet international relations. The few works on the subject refer to the special nature of the USSR's behavior toward Austria, Finland, Ireland, Sweden, or Switzerland.[1] Some studies stress the consistency and continuity of Soviet policies and assume a deliberate strategy *vis-à-vis* the neutral states. Yet most analyses are either limited to the discussion of concepts of neutrality in the Soviet theory of international relations or the study of Moscow's relations with individual neutral countries. Few studies take a comparative perspective, analyzing the USSR's policies in the broader context of Soviet–European or East–West relations. In the absence of such an analytical framework, it is thus difficult to elaborate on distinctive patterns of Soviet attitudes toward neutrality and the European neutrals.

This is the more regrettable as the USSR's experience with neutrality may become more relevant for Soviet foreign policy. Gorbachev has pointed out that Soviet relations with the neutral states, particularly with Finland, serve as role models for the "common European home." The newly independent countries of East-Central Europe and the Soviet republics seeking more independence from Moscow also are considering the option of neutrality and non-alliance. At the same time, the revolutionary changes in Europe have profound implications for the position of the neutral states and the very meaning of neutrality. The objective of this chapter is to analyze the USSR's changing views on neutrality in the light of new thinking and recent developments in Europe. It starts with a brief discussion of Soviet relations with the European neutrals in the postwar period, continues with an assessment of the implications of new thinking on the USSR's attitudes toward neutrality, and ends with tentative conclusions regarding the changing relevance of neutrality for Soviet foreign policy in the 1990s.

Neutrality, in essence, describes the behavior of a state not participating in a war between third powers. Corresponding rights and obligations are codified in the 1907 Hague Convention on Neutrality in War at Land and on Sea. A neutral country is, for instance, obliged to deny the parties in conflict the use of its territory, sea or airspace for hostile acts or the transportation of troops and supplies. Other rules and disengagement apply. In the strict sense, neutrality thus only applies to a situation of war. Some states have committed themselves to stay permanently neutral. They are expected to follow a policy of neutrality making neutral conduct in a future war credible already in times of peace. First and foremost, this includes non-participation in military alliances, since membership in an organization of collective defense could hinder a country in remaining neutral in case of war. The maintenance of a credible defense should demonstrate the country's capability to defend its territory. In the case of Austria or Finland, additional security guarantees and restrictions apply based on bi- or multilateral agreements. Other expectations regarding neutral behavior, such as ideological neutrality or equidistance, have evolved over the years without finding approval by the neutral states or in international law.[2]

The evolving Soviet view on neutrality

The Soviet notion of neutrality

Soviet legal and political doctrine hardly accepted neutrality as a generally applicable, legally binding norm in international relations. Ideologically, neutrality was considered unacceptable; politically, at times, it proved to be useful. Neutrality and neutralization were not viewed as an end, but as a means in the zero-sum confrontation of the cold war. Yet Soviet perceptions of neutralization as a political weapon and of the neutral states as dominos in the East–West stalemate frequently are overstated. While Soviet literature refers frequently to neutrality as a dynamic notion, as a lever of change, the USSR soon came to realize that the neutrals formed an integral part of the postwar order, contributed to its stabilization and provided little potential for a shift in the alignment of forces (*gruppirovka sil*). It is precisely the relative continuity and predictability in the behavior of the neutrals and the irreversibility of their status that best suited the Soviet leadership. Given the neutrals' strategic location and their considerable economic and military potential, the USSR had more interest in preserving the situation than in provoking risky change. In this respect, the non-aligned countries of the Third World proved to be much more promising. Over time, the Soviet Union started to accept the existence of permanently neutral states in Europe and to treat them with benign, but watchful neglect. With few exceptions in the 1950s, the notion of neutrality never received much attention in Soviet academic and political literature. Relations with the European neutrals hardly ranked high in priority on Moscow's foreign policy agenda. Austria, Finland, Ireland, Sweden, and Switzerland were dealt with on a case-by-case basis at a subordinate level in the Central Committee or the Foreign Ministry.

While the European neutrals remained of limited importance for the achievement of central strategic objectives, they proved helpful on the operational and tactical level. Gorbachev conceded: "It is difficult to overestimate their importance to us at the height of the Cold War, when the Western world built a wall of alienation around us." And he emphasized that the neutrals "held out against all short-term anti-Soviet tempests."[3] In the confrontation of the cold war, they proved to be reliable, predictable partners serving as honest brokers for diplomatic initiatives and as bridges for trade and other contacts helping the USSR and its allies to overcome the isolation of containment.

Austria, Ireland, Sweden, and Switzerland

During most of the postwar period, relations with Austria, Ireland, Sweden, and Switzerland were mixed, at times contradictory, following the cycles of East–West relations. There probably has never been an official line toward these countries. Commentaries on the neutral states and their relations with the USSR seldom appeared in the Soviet press. Yet the few that were written were read carefully in Berne, Dublin, Helsinki, Stockholm, and Vienna, since they were considered to convey a clear message on the policies the Soviet leadership approved or disapproved. On the one hand, Soviet commentators expressed their satisfaction with the state of bilateral relations. On the other hand, they sharply criticized a certain behavior of the neutral states. "Spy mania," overarmament or suspicious contacts with NATO were among the most frequent "misdemeanors." Such criticism continues, even during the Gorbachev period, with almost predictable regularity.[4]

The USSR thus clearly projects expectations regarding appropriate neutral behavior. It obviously claims a certain *droit de regard*, or at least the right to intervene in case the neutrals act against Soviet interests. While it is difficult to establish patterns of signaling, these official and unofficial communications nevertheless reflect elements of calculation and decision on the part of the USSR. Soviet signaling is probably not only the result of a carrot-and-stick policy, but an expression of genuine irritation over the notion of neutrality in general, and the behavior of the neutrals – often perceived as "erratic" and "irrational" – in particular. Yet at times the USSR not only had difficulty in accepting the independent, self-interested behavior of neutral states, but of most small- and medium-sized countries in its neighborhood.

Finland: neutrality plus

Soviet–Finnish relations, in contrast, are of a special nature. They provide a particular example of the logic of the USSR's attitude toward neutrality. The legal basis of Finland's neutrality is the 1948 Treaty of Friendship, Cooperation and Mutual Assistance with the USSR, in which Helsinki expressed its "desire to remain outside the conflicting interests of the Great Powers." In 1983, the Treaty was extended for another twenty years. Finland repeatedly has stated its commitment to permanent neutrality and gained broad international recognition. Yet starting in the early 1970s, Soviet officials and commentators became increasingly reluctant to refer to Finland as a neutral state. At best, it was conceded that the Finns were "striving to exercise a peace-loving neutral policy." Commentators pointed at the relatively weak legal foundations of Finnish neutrality, questioned the very wisdom of such a posture and emphasized the priority of Finland's bilateral commitments to the USSR over other international obligations.[5] From a Western point of view, this understanding drastically narrows the essence of Finnish neutrality. In the Soviet perception, the Finnish combination of restraint, "good" behavior toward the USSR, security guarantees, and classical neutrality represents a more advanced, more progressive posture of neutrality. As Gorbachev stressed during his visit to Finland in October 1989, the 1948 Treaty and Finland's neutrality "are not at odds, but rather reinforce each other." "Neutrality plus," or conditional neutrality limited through bilateral commitments, makes Finland a more predictable, more reliable partner than Sweden or Switzerland. It forms the role model for other small- and medium-sized Western countries. During his visit to Helsinki in October 1989, President Gorbachev nevertheless removed any ambiguities regarding Soviet acceptance of Finland's status. He conceded that "Finnish neutrality, as the neutrality of all countries with such a status for that matter, has its peculiarities, but I would like to state with all certainty that the Soviet Union unreservedly recognized Finland's neutral status and will continue to fully observe it."[6]

The case of Finland illustrates the dilemma between too high Soviet expectations regarding the neutrals and the realities of their independent, self-interested behavior. While there seems to be a considerable degree of pragmatism and tolerance in Soviet attitudes toward

Sweden or Switzerland, there is much more sensitivity and nervosity in the USSR's perception of Finland and – to a lesser degree – Austria. While Moscow continues to be extremely positive about the state of its relationship with Helsinki, it notices the slightest twist and turn in Finland's domestic politics or foreign policy with seismographic exactitude. The higher the expectations, the greater the chances of disappointment.

Neutrality and new thinking

New thinking in the USSR's foreign and security policy has profound implications for the Soviet view on neutrality. Probably the most important development of new thinking for the European neutrals is the recognition that all states – large and small, socialist or capitalist – have a right to sovereignty and self-determination. Each nation, it is recognized, has legitimate, genuine interests of its own and acts accordingly. Gorbachev's commitment to the primacy of international law in interstate relations also reinforces Soviet understanding of neutrality, which has a strong legal connotation. On a practical level, the USSR started to show greater interest in the European neutrals and to demonstrate more sophistication in relations with them. In 1985, Soviet *mezhdunarodniki* started to discuss a new category of actors in international relations, the "small countries in Western Europe," among them Denmark, Greece, the Netherlands, and the European neutrals.[7] In the assessment of Iurii Melnikov, an expert on Europe at the Institute for World Economy and International Relations (IMEMO), the "small countries" have to be taken more seriously given their considerable economic and political weight. At a 1988 scientific conference of the Foreign Ministry, participants stressed the need to step up dialogue with the neutrals and other small countries in Europe.[8] The small European countries in general, and the neutral states in particular, have experienced a renaissance in Soviet foreign policy. Bilateral relations have improved substantially; consultations and high-level contacts take place on a regular basis. Commentators also stress the role of the neutral and non-aligned countries in the Conference on Security and Cooperation in Europe (CSCE).

Soviet experiences with the neutral states also influence discussions on the "common European home." Relations with the European neutrals are praised as "models for good-neighborly relations in a common European home" and as "trailblazers in international affairs." In particular, Soviet commentators stress a certain stability, predictability, and reliability in the behavior of the neutrals; good relations not based on ideological commonalities, but on mutual respect, common interests, and political affinities; a certain cooperation and coordination in foreign affairs and arms control; and certain security guarantees and commitments relating to the neutrals' declared intention to stay out of a future conflict. Relations with the European neutrals, particularly with Finland, serve thus as prototypes for relations in the "common European home."

An important element of the neutrals' trailblazer role is their "active, peace-loving foreign policy." In Gorbachev's view, there are vast opportunities for cooperation between the USSR and the neutral states in removing the threat of war. "Points of coincidence" include the neutrals' support for nuclear-free zones, the dissolution of blocs or disarmament proposals resulting in a certain congruity with the USSR's foreign and security policy agenda. These common denominators are codified in numerous joint statements and mutual commitments. The USSR is thus not so much interested in the neutrals' commitment to stay out of war, but in their attitude toward essential questions of Soviet interest. As one observer stresses, what is important is the essence of a country's policy and not the label or status attached to it.[9]

Neutrality after the cold war

The changing strategic position of the European neutrals

The radical changes in the economic, military, and political situation in Europe have profound implications for the meaning of neutrality, the condition of the neutral states and the USSR's relations with them. At this point, it is difficult to assess the full extent of these changes. Soviet observers have hardly addressed the issue. Given the importance of the issue, a tentative assessment is nevertheless in place. With the disappearance of the Central Front and the withdrawal of all Soviet forces from the GDR, Hungary, and Czechoslovakia by 1994, Austria and Switzerland will become strategic hinterland comparable to the position of Ireland. Conversely, the strategic importance of the neutral and non-aligned countries on the USSR's northern and southern flank is likely to increase – at least in relative terms. Soviet military experts long have stressed the fact that the "Strategic North" is becoming more important for the defense of Europe and the global equation of forces. Soviet planners particularly are concerned about the nuclear and conventional firepower deployed on NATO ships in the Baltic and North Sea.[10] Military deployments and activities in this region have increased markedly over the last decade. Evidence of the USSR's increasing interests in the northern flank seem to be the continued incursions of submarines into Swedish waters.[11] More recently, the USSR has moved ground and air forces from East-Central Europe to the Nordic region. In May 1990, for instance, a Soviet air regiment with forty Mig-27s was redeployed from Debrecen in Hungary to the Kola Peninsula. These movements have a significant impact on the regional balance of forces. The loss of air and naval bases in the GDR and on the Baltic shores could render Finland's and Sweden's airspace and territorial waters more important, at least hypothetically. The European neutrals and the East-Central European countries could face increasing pressure from the USSR and NATO to improve their naval and air defense capabilities in order to prevent the utilization of their territory by either side.

The neutrals and the European Community

The second important change in the condition of the neutral states is the progressing economic and political integration of (Western) Europe. The European neutrals have started to redefine their relationship with the European Community (EC). This is most visible in the case of Austria and Finland. In recent years, Finland, which for many years remained at the fringes of European integration, has revolutionized its relations with the EC and other institutions of European integration. At the same time, Helsinki's barter agreement with Moscow, which includes the exchange of Finnish industrial products, ships, and consumer goods for Soviet oil and gas, is likely to be abandoned soon. This "Europeanization" results in a loosening of traditionally close economic and political ties with the USSR, in a virtual *renversement des alliances* in the pattern of Finland's foreign relations. Austria constitutes a similar case. In 1989, Vienna submitted its application for full membership in the EC. The other neutrals are contemplating similar steps.

Given Moscow's more realistic appreciation of European integration, Soviet reactions to these developments have been mixed. The Soviet leadership is aware that it has no alternative to the European Community to offer the European neutrals. While Soviet trade with most West European countries experienced a dramatic decline in the last years, the neutral states were hit particularly hard. Thus the USSR expresses understanding that the neutrals seek to participate in the benefits of the EC. On some occasions, however, Soviet concerns over the dynamics of European integration and its band-wagoning impact on the postwar order have become visible. At the 19th Party Conference in July 1988, the then Soviet ambassador to Bonn, Iulii Kvitzinskii, warned that "more and more European states may begin to be sucked into the EEC and via the EEC into NATO – that is, there may be the construction of an all-European branch of NATO and no development in the direction of equal and constructive cooperation of the two systems on an all-European basis."[12]

Similar concerns are reflected in Moscow's ambiguous attitude toward Austria's application for EC membership. In August 1989, the Soviet leadership submitted an *aide-mémoire* to the Austrian government. While not explicitly speaking out against Austria joining the Community, the note states that "the Soviet government is convinced that a permanently neutral state's membership in such an organization as the EC would result in the loss of its concrete opportunities to implement its policy of neutrality." The *aide-mémoire* calls for a "strict and complete adherence to the [1955] State Treaty and the law on Austria's permanent neutrality."[13] The reason for these reservations is not that Moscow has suddenly a more orthodox interpretation of the legal provisions of neutrality than the neutrals themselves. The USSR rather starts to view the neutrals, which together with Norway belong to the European Free Trade Association (EFTA), as important allies in strengthening Moscow's weakening bargaining position *vis-à-vis* the EC. Vladimir Shenaiev, director of the European Department of the USSR Academy of Sciences, explains the USSR's trilateral approach toward building the economic pillar of the "common European home":

> I think it would be best for the future of Europe if the common home were to include all three integration organizations: EC, EFTA, and CMEA. To eliminate EFTA and CMEA for the benefit of the EC – or even weakening EFTA – would disturb the construction of the common home. . . . If Austria joins the EC . . . it will not be conducive to the common home. . . . Together, and within EFTA, the neutral countries can do much more for the future of Europe, as long as they act jointly and not individually.[14]

Soviet economists started to study the experience of the EFTA countries as an example for the USSR's own relationship with the EC or as a model for revamping the Council of Mutual Economic Assistance (CMEA).[15] In his speech to the Council of Europe, Gorbachev suggested a "deeper relationship" with EFTA, and during his visit to Finland he proposed the promotion of trilateral interaction between the EC, EFTA and the CMEA in order to promote a common European economic space.[16] Soviet experts express a similar interest in improving relations wth other European institutions apart from the EC such as the Nordic Council, which includes the NATO members Denmark, Iceland, and Norway and the neutrals Finland and Sweden, or the Council of Europe, in which the neutral and non-aligned countries hold approximately half of the seats and chair important commissions and committees. During the period of transition toward a new European architecture and the subsequent period of operation of pan-European institutions, the neutral and non-aligned countries thus are viewed to be of great importance to the USSR as potential trailblazers, allies, and counter-weights against the growing hegemony of the EC and NATO in European politics. As Gorbachev explains, "The movement toward a new Europe will be a lengthy and difficult process, and I believe . . . that we cannot do without the constructive contribution of states such as Finland and other neutral and non-aligned states."[17] After all, they currently constitute one-third of all European nations.

German reunification and neutrality

German reunification and the renunciation of the Four Powers' special rights in Europe also have an important impact on the status of the neutral states and their relations with the USSR. At least in the case of Austria and Finland, neutrality is related directly to the postwar order and the status of the Four Powers. Many restrictions on Austria's and Finland's sovereignty have been explained by the need to contain Germany and its former allies. Finland's 1947 Paris Peace Treaty, for instance, sets limits on the size and composition of Finnish armed forces and prohibits armament purchases from Germany. The 1948 Treaty of Friendship, Mutual Assistance and Cooperation directly refers to Germany as a potential aggressor. With German reunification and the termination of the Four Power regime, central assumptions of these treaties have become outdated. In Austria and Finland, pressure is growing to revise certain provisions limiting national self-determination or to renunciate these bi- and multilateral commitments altogether. In September 1990, the Finnish government unilaterally made a "Decision on the Provisions of the Paris Peace Treaty Relating to Germany and the Limitations on Finnish Sovereignty" stating that the postwar restrictions on sovereignty are "outdated also in the case of Finland." In a formal statement, President Koivisto declared that the reference to Germany in the 1948 Treaty with the USSR "is factually not valid anymore." Austria has made similar declarations.[18] These adjustments are of a formal nature and have little immediate implications for the two countries' status of permanent neutrality or their relations with the USSR. The unilateral renunciation of postwar restrictions and commitments nevertheless could induce fears on the part of the Soviet leadership that Austria and Finland could redefine their status and return to a fully independent foreign policy, similar to the one during the pre-war period, which might not always be as predictable and beneficial toward the USSR as under current arrangements.

Neutrality after alliance

The "Finlandization" of East-Central Europe

The newly independent countries of East-Central Europe and the Soviet republics and states seeking more independence from the center have expressed their interest in neutrality and non-alignment. With Gorbachev's renunciation of the Brezhnev doctrine of limited sovereignty and the recognition of the former satellites' right to national self-determination, Soviet attitudes toward the requirements of bloc membership have started to change. At least theoretically, the postulated "freedom of choice" (*svoboda vybora*) implies the possibility that some countries could leave the Soviet bloc and become non-aligned. In an interview with the West German weekly *Die Zeit* in May 1985, then Politburo member Aleksandr Iakovlev actually suggested "that many of the Eastern rooms in the common European home could be furnished in the Finnish style." Other experts in Gorbachev's entourage also hinted that some of the USSR's lesser allies such as Hungary or the CSSR could become neutral.[19] These statements were, however, made before the dramatic developments of fall and winter 1989.

For the USSR, neutrality first became an issue in the context of the rapid developments in the GDR. In February 1990, once Gorbachev understood that German reunification was inevitable, he tried to prevent NATO membership of the reunited Germany in a last-ditch effort. Stalin's historic proposal "unification versus neutrality" was on the table again. Gorbachev did not elaborate on the specific provisions of neutrality in terms of Germany's rights and obligations. Like Stalin, he equated neutrality with neutralization and non-alliance. At the meeting between President Gorbachev and Chancellor Kohl in July 1990, the Soviet leadership finally abandoned neutrality as a condition for German reunification. This does not necessarily mean, however, that the USSR has abandoned fully the option of neutralizing Germany. Soviet observers do not exclude such an outcome either as a result of a change of power in Bonn or of a transformation or dissolution of NATO.

In the meantime, neutrality had become a major issue in the former socialist camp and even within the Soviet Union. The newly elected leaders started to cash in on Gorbachev's promises and demanded a change in the former unequal treaties, the abolition of the imperial institutions, and the total withdrawal of the Soviet troops from their territories. Exercising their newly gained freedom of choice, most Warsaw Treaty Organization (WTO) members have expressed their intention to reduce their commitments to or withdraw altogether from the pact. On 26 June 1990, for instance, the Hungarian parliament passed a resolution charging the government to freeze Hungary's participation in the WTO's military organization and to begin talks on the country's withdrawal from the pact by the end of 1991. The resolution formally reestablishes Imre Nagy's unilateral declaration of neutrality of 1 November 1956.[20] Alliance with the USSR is not considered anymore as *conditio sine qua non* for achieving security. Few observers believe that the WTO will survive at all. Other bloc members are, however, more cautious in order not to provoke the USSR. So far, the Soviet leadership has hardly reacted to these attempts to leave the WTO. As Foreign Minister Shevardnadze emphasized, it will be up to the individual country to choose its future status; the USSR does not intend to impose models on its neighbors or to limit their newly gained sovereignty and independence.[21] Officials only express their expectation that the process of disengagement would be based on negotiations and managed in an orderly way. There are few warnings that changes in bloc membership would result in a dangerous shift in the "alliance of forces." Most statements are limited to pledges to renew and transform the WTO into a democratic, political alliance of equal partners.

So far, the USSR seems to have no specific concepts for future relations with its East-Central European neighbors. Notions of "Finlandization" or "neutralization" of East-Central Europe are more popular among Western observers than Soviet officials.[22] In a rare reference to "Finlandization," Gorbachev emphasized:

> We and Finland have fulfilled and are fulfilling pioneering work . . . and this experience – what used to be called Finlandization – must now be called an asset and a large contribution toward building new relations in Europe. I think that there is a very great deal that is useful here. Europeans, all of us together have to think about it. . . . What was once the object of criticism and all kinds of speculation is now standing up as an example, as a reference point, showing what relations can be like.[23]

Gorbachev actually might have thought of "Finlandization" as a model for reshaping the USSR's relationship with its neighbors to the West. In this context, it is of interest that the Soviet leadership's profile of relations with the newly independent East-Central European countries has a lot in common with its profile of the European neutrals over the past twenty years. Gorbachev and his advisors refer to a "new type" of relations with East-Central Europe, to a "really civilized, equal relationship" built on "voluntary participation, reciprocity, respect, and cooperation."[24] As one observer explains, the USSR's relations with Finland have been more stable and beneficial in this respect than those with the former allies, despite the fact that Finland "is remote from us in terms of social structure."[25] Finland and the other neutral states provide the USSR with important experiences in dealing with countries "belonging to a different social system."

The newly independent East-Central European states are expected to behave in a similar way to the neutrals. In the words of Genadii Ianaev, the new Politburo member in charge of international affairs, the USSR is ready to cooperate "with all progressive, democratic parties and movements in Eastern Europe which seek to create equitable relations between our countries and a climate of trust on the continent."[26] The East-Central European countries are expected to share a minimum of Gorbachev's interests and perspectives, namely to promote partner-like, good-neighborly relations with the Soviet Union, to avoid the USSR's isolation from the process of European cooperation and integration, and to support some of the Soviet foreign-policy initiatives.

While the comparison with the case of the European neutrals has various flaws, the "neutralization" or "Finlandization" of its East-Central European neighbors would have distinctive advantages for the USSR and could encourage it to distinguish between genuine security concerns and ambitions to preserve the crumbling empire. The East-Central European nations, quasi-neutralized and semi-demilitarized, have become nobody's friend and nobody's foe. Poland and its neighbors are sandwiched between two sides, a Soviet Union in turmoil and a reemerging Germany anchored within NATO and the EC. Western and Soviet observers are concerned that with the gradual disengagement of military potentials in the center of Europe, a new strategic vacuum will emerge in East-Central Europe. In the view of Igor Malashenko, an expert in the CPSU Central Committee's International Department, geopolitics teaches that there will always be a struggle for control of the rimlands bordering on the heartland no matter what the ideological dimensions of the conflict are.[27] The East-Central European nations thus will have to address some security interests of their neighbors to the East and to the West. Their armed forces will have to perform functions in order to honor certain explicit or implicit security guarantees, such as the defense of national airspace or territory against use by a third power. In this context, the notion of a buffer state and buffer zone could become more important, i.e. the commitment of a certain area or region to a set of well-defined rights and obligations whose primary function is to disengage two conflicting parties and thus reduce the likelihood of military conflict. The Hague Convention on Neutrality in War at Land and on Sea, of 1907, which specifies such rights and obligations, could serve as model. The Hague Convention is, however, increasingly outdated and limited in its application to neutral countries in case of war. For the East-Central European countries, a more appropriate, universal codex of mutual rights and obligations of European armed forces in times of peace, crisis, and war might be more appropriate. Yet Pavel Baiev, a historian at the Institute for Europe, rejects the idea of transforming East-Central Europe into a "buffer zone." It would bring Europe forward toward a system of collective security. Moreover, "such a scheme has, just as the idea of neutrality, a double ceiling, since it covers up the possibility of transforming the 'buffer zone' into a zone of unlimited German influences."[28] Some East-Central European countries have already started to show growing interest in closer ties with NATO. In this context, neutralization could assume its classical function of denying a potential opponent new allies – especially since it might be more attractive for the USSR to have a predictable, stable, neutral neighbor rather than a dissatisfied, rebellious ally torn between extreme positions.

Thus the USSR's experiences with the neutral states might become more relevant in shaping relations with former allies. The theory and history of neutrality offer a variety of options: (1) a "Finnish solution," i.e. a combination of non-alliance, good-neighborly relations and specific security guarantees toward the USSR in form of bilateral treaties of friendship, cooperation and mutual assistance ("neutrality plus"); (2) an "Austrian or Swiss solution," i.e. unconditional neutrality based on a unilateral declaration or a multilateral agreement without specific security guarantees toward the USSR; (3) a "Greek solution," i.e. continued, but loose membership in the WTO combined with active efforts to weaken the pact's military and political integration (internal neutralization).

Differentiation will be necessary, not only between different East-Central European countries, but also between different dimensions of security and cooperation. The meaning of "Finlandization," for instance, can be interpreted widely depending on the periodization of Finnish–Soviet relations. Until 1956, for instance, the USSR maintained a naval base in Porkkala near Helsinki. Such an arrangement could allow Soviet troops to remain in Poland, while Warsaw formally leaves the Warsaw Pact. A related problem is the interpretation of the provisions of the 1948 Treaty on Friendship, Cooperation and Mutual Assistance. It is, for instance, unclear whether Article 2 requires the coordination or integration of Finnish and Soviet air defenses in times of crisis – in the context of the WTO a highly relevant problem. Thus there is not one, but various models of "Finlandization," models which reflect the unique situation and experience of Finland in a given historic period. Moreover, the term is rooted in the period of the cold war. It is historically tainted and politically stigmatized. Exactly for these reasons, it is doubtful whether the East-Central European countries are willing to sacrifice their newly gained independence for limited sovereignty, conditional neutrality, and a Treaty of Friendship, Cooperation and Mutual Assistance with the USSR.

Neutralization and disengagement within the USSR

With the Baltic states' declarations of independence and the rapid disintegration of the USSR's state structure, the issue of neutrality has gained an important domestic dimension. At stake is the future military-political status of the independence-minded republics and the military integration within the USSR. The status of the Soviet Army in the Baltic region will form an important issue in the negotiations between the Baltic states and the USSR. Formulating their independent security policies, Baltic leaders seem to take into account the USSR's difficult situation and strategic interests in the region. Lithuania's President Vytautas Landsbergis explains that while independence itself is not an issue for negotiations, the conditions and the period for achieving it can be discussed:

> Lithuania is willing to take Soviet security interests into account and to guarantee the transit routes to the sea of Kaliningrad as well as the use of the port of Klaipeda by the Soviet Navy. Concluding a treaty on the preservation of Soviet bases in an independent Lithuania seems conceivable. However, the strength and the duration of the stay of Soviet forces in Lithuania must be discussed.

Lithuanian Prime Minister Kazimiera Prunskiene also concedes that the Soviet government is already overburdened with the exit of troops from Eastern Europe and concludes that troop withdrawals from Lithuania would not occur before the Soviet Army has withdrawn "from states more to the West."[29] In the long term, however, the Baltic states envisage a restoration of their security arrangements in the nineteenth century and the interwar period.

The Ukrainian parliament has been more straightforward declaring the Ukraine's "intention of becoming a permanently neutral state that does not take part in military blocs and that adheres to non-nuclear principles." The Belorussian parliament followed suit declaring "the aim of the Belorussian SSR of making its territory a non-nuclear zone, and the republic – a neutral state."[30] Both republics intend to remain part of the USSR, but proclaim the right to their own armed forces, internal troops, and organs of state security. Other republics pursue less confrontational strategies. Refusals to implement the military draft and other acts challenging the center's prerogatives in foreign and security policy can be considered as attempts at neutralization from within. Demilitarization, denuclearization, and neutralization obviously serve as means to an end, i.e. the military and political disengagement from the Soviet empire. They have to be seen in the context of negotiations on the redistribution of powers between the center and the constituent republics.

The Soviet leadership's reactions to these developments are much more categoric than in the case of East-Central Europe. The center insists on its right and the strategic necessity to draft and mobilize soldiers and to deploy troops on the entire territory of the union. Soviet politicians nevertheless concede the necessity to address issues of military alignment in the context of the new Treaty of Union. Ideas include the conclusion of a "Vilnius Pact," i.e. a multilateral military alliance within a future Soviet federation or confederation. While "Finlandization" might not be an appropriate model for reshaping Soviet–East-Central European relations, it could serve as a yardstick for security arrangements within the USSR.

Conclusion

Soviet relations with the neutral states are far from unique. While the European neutrals perform certain useful functions at the tactical and operational level, they are hardly of strategic importance to the USSR. As Gorbachev explains, "Given all the changes that take place in small states, the world has nevertheless not changed."[31] Soviet observers also see fewer and fewer differences in the behavior of the European neutrals and other "small- and medium-sized countries" such as Denmark, Greece, or Hungary. Recent treaties with Germany set new standards for bilateral relations which go beyond what the USSR has achieved in its ties with the neutrals. The normalization of European relations and the emergence of new varieties of neutrality or quasi-neutrality in East-Central Europe thus lead to the erosion of the Soviet view of permanent neutrality.

Neutrality, in the classic sense, does not exactly transcend East–West structures, but is very much a part of the status quo. With the shift toward a multipolar European order and the creation of pan-European institutions, the very notion of neutrality is losing its meaning. In Gorbachev's view, all states will become neutral once the blocs are dissolved and the "common European home" is constructed – at least the small and medium-sized countries. For Valentin Falin, head of the CPSU Central Committee's International Department, in turn, the notion of neutrality will lose its meaning altogether once the military alliances are eliminated, Europe is unified and all countries enjoy equal security.[32] The "common European home" seems to envision a highly integrated, regulated Europe with supranational institutions and majority rule. Similar to American, British, or Soviet attitudes after 1945, every state is expected to participate in the "united nations of Europe"; solidarity leaves little room for non-participation and neutrality.[33] Soviet tolerance toward the particularities of the neutral states is likely to decline.

Neutrality thus is not necessarily an attractive notion for the East-Central European states. They are not seeking non-alliance, segregation, and isolation, but realliance, cooperation, and integration. And especially for relations with the EC, neutrality is a liability rather than an asset. To be not aligned, i.e. not a member of a military alliance, does not necessarily require to be non-aligned or neutral. With changing notions of alliance, integration and cooperation, there are more attractive models for asserting a state's sovereignty and independence than classic neutrality.

Notes

1 Cf. H. Fiedler, *Der sowjetische Neutralitätsbegriff in Theorie und Praxis* (Cologne: Verlag für Wissenschaft und Politik, 1959); P.H. Vigor, *The Soviet View of War, Peace and Neutrality* (London: Routledge and Kegan Paul, 1975); Margot Light, "Neutralism and non-alignment: the dialectics of Soviet theory," *Millennium: Journal of International Affairs*, no. 1 (1987), pp. 79–92; Curt Gasteyger, "The neutrals, the Soviet Union, and the West," in *The Missing Link, West European Neutrals and Regional Security*, eds. R. Bissell, C. Gasteyger (Durham: Duke University Press, 1990), pp. 136–49.

2 For a discussion of the concept of neutrality, see D. Frei, *Dimensionen neutraler Politik* (Geneva: Graduate Institute for International Studies, 1969); H. Hakovirta, *East–West Conflict and European Neutrality* (Oxford: Oxford University Press, 1988).

3 M. Gorbachev, speech at Finlandia Hall, *Pravda*, 27 October 1989, pp. 1–2.

4 For a discussion of Soviet signaling, see Lena Jonson, "Soviet policy towards Sweden and the region of Northern Europe under Gorbachev," *Cooperation and Conflict*, no. 2 (1990), pp. 1–19; and, Lena Jonson, "Soviet signals to the Nordic countries during the Lithuanian crisis of 1990," chapter 4, above.

5 Cf. Iu. Komissarov, *Liniia Paasikivi-Kekkonena. Istoria, sovremennost', perspektivy* (Moscow: Mezhdunarodnye otnosheniia, 1985); Y. Bartenev, Iu. Komissarov, *Tritsat' let dobrososedstva. K istorii sovetsko-finliandskikh otnoshenii* (Moscow: Mezhdunarodnye otnosheniia, 1988). See also Roy Allison, *Finland's Relations with the Soviet Union, 1944–84* (London: Macmillan, 1985); B. Petersson, "Soviet commentators and the vexing case of

Finnish neutrality," *Nordic Journal of Soviet and East European Studies*, no. 4 (1987), pp. 49–60.

6 M. Gorbachev, speech at Finlandia Hall, p. 1.

7 L.S. Voronkov, "Malye strany zapadnoi evropy v mezhdunarodnykh otnosheniiakh," in *Malye strany zapadnoi evropy*, ed. Iu. Iudanov (Moscow: Mysl', 1984), pp. 338–57; I. Melnikov, "Malye strany zapadnoi evropy v mezhdunarodnykh otnosheniiakh," *Mirovaia ekonomika i mezhdunarodnye otnosheniia*, no. 2 (1986), pp. 89–92; Iu. Karelov, "The smaller countries of Europe in the modern world," *International Affairs* (Moscow), no. 2 (1986), pp. 65–71.

8 *International Affairs* (Moscow), no. 10 (1988), p. 63.

9 L.S. Voronkov, *Non-Nuclear Status to Northern Europe* (Moscow: Nauka, 1984), p. 24.

10 See V. Pavlov, " 'Arctic Option' and its alternative," *Krasnaia zvezda*, 11 March 1989, p. 5; K. Voronov, "Create a new Hanseatic League in the Nordic area," *Svenska Dagbladet* (Stockholm), 16 May 1990, p. 13; Northern Fleet Commander F. Gromov, "Common sense," *Krasnaia Źvezda*, 22 July 1990, p. 5.

11 In 1985, when Gorbachev came to power, eighteen violations were reported according to a RAND study. Since then, the number has jumped to an average of nearly three violations a month, or more than thirty a year. See G. McCormick, *Stranger Than Fiction* (Santa Monica, CA: RAND Corporation, 1990).

12 *Pravda*, 3 July 1988, p. 2.

13 *Aide-mémoire* submitted by Soviet ambassador G. Shikin to Chancellor F. Vranitzky on 10 August 1989, in *Die Presse* (Vienna), 11 August 1989, p. 2.

14 V. Shenaiev, interview, *Wochenpresse* (Vienna), 1 September 1989, pp. 42–43.

15 Cf. "Posledstviia formirovania edinogo rynka evropeiskogo soobshchestva (Material podgotovlen otdelom zapadnoevropeiskikh issledovanii IMEMO AN SSSR)," *Mirovaia ekonomika i mezhdunarodnye otnosheniia*, no. 4 (1989), pp. 38–44; I. Frantseva, "Difficult return to Europe," *Izvestiia*, 23 July 1990, p. 5.

16 *Pravda*, 11 July 1989, p. 2.

17 M. Gorbachev, news conference, TASS (English), 26 October 1989.

18 *Neue Zürcher Zeitung*, 26 September 1990, p. 4.

19 A. Iakovlev, *Die Zeit*, 12 May 1989, p. 5; O. Bogomolov, quoted in *New York Times*, 11 February 1989, p. A13; former chief-of-staff Marshal S. Akhromeev, quoted in *Frankfurter Allgemeine Zeitung*, 31 July 1989, p. 12. Akhromeev and Bogomolov subsequently both denied that they had referred to neutrality.

20 For a discussion of the Hungarian debate on neutrality, see A. Reisch, "Hungarian neutrality: hopes and realities," *Radio Free Europe Report on Eastern Europe*, no. 10 (1990), pp. 11–28.

21 E. Shevardnadze, interview, *Ogonek*, no. 11 (1990), p. 3.

22 See H. Timmermann, "The Soviet Union and Eastern Europe: dynamics of 'Finlandization,' " *Radio Liberty Report on the USSR*, no. 33 (1990), pp.

15–18; M. Kerner, S. Stopinski, "Finnlandisierung als Perspektive?" *Osteuropa*, no. 3 (1990), pp. 255–71.

23 M. Gorbachev, news conference, TASS (English), 26 October 1989.

24 M. Gorbachev, report to the 28th CPSU Congress, *Pravda*, 3 July 1990, p. 3; E. Shevardnadze, speech to the 21st Party Conference of the USSR Foreign Ministry, *Vestnik Ministerstva Inostrannykh Del SSSR*, no. 5 (1990), p. 10.

25 M. Antiasov, "Eastern Europe: times of change," *Izvestiia*, 31 July 1990, p. 5; cf. A. Bogatyrov, M. Nosov, K. Pleshakov, "Kto oni, nashi soiuzniki?" *Kommunist*, no. 1 (1990), pp. 105–14.

26 Interview, *Pravda*, 13 August 1990, p. 1.

27 Chief-of-staff M. Moiseev, report to the 28th CPSU Congress section on the CPSU's international activities, in *Krasnaia zvezda*, 7 July 1990, p. 1; S. Karaganov, "The problems of the USSR's European policy," *International Affairs* (Moscow), no. 7 (1990), pp. 72–80; I. Malashenko, "Russia: the earth's heartland," *International Affairs* (Moscow), no. 7 (1990), pp. 46–54.

28 Pavel Baiev, "Across the limits of atlanticism," *New Times* (in German), no. 27 (1990), p. 25.

29 V. Landsbergis, reported in *Neue Zürcher Zeitung*, 9 August 1990, p. 4; K. Prunskiene, interview, *Izvestiia*, 21 August 1990, p. 3.

30 Article IX of the Declaration of Sovereignty, *Pravda ukrainy*, 17 July 1990, p. 1; Article X of the Belorussian Declaration on Sovereignty, reprinted in *Argumenty i fakty*, no. 31 (1990), p. 2.

31 M. Gorbachev, speech in Odessa Military District, *Pravda*, 19 August 1990, p. 1.

32 M. Gorbachev, meeting with K. Grosz, *Pravda*, 25 March 1989, pp. 1–2; V. Falin, interview, *Uj Forum* (Budapest), 28 July 1989, pp. 21–23.

33 Cf. M. Amirdzhanov, M. Cherkasov, "Etazhi obshcheevropeiskogo doma," *Mezhdunarodnaia zhizn*, no. 11 (1988), pp. 29–42; G. Vorontsov, "Ot Khel'sinki K 'Obshcheevropeiskomu Domu,'" *Mirovaia ekonomika i mezhdunarodnye otnosheniia*, no. 9 (1988), pp. 47–54.

Part III

The Soviet Union and the developing world: global trends

6 From new thinking to the fragmentation of consensus in Soviet foreign policy: the USSR and the developing world

Roger E. Kanet, with Garth T. Katner

In the spring of 1985, when Mikhail S. Gorbachev assumed the leadership of the Communist Party of the Soviet Union, relations with developing countries were still at the center of Soviet foreign policy. Despite growing evidence of a reconsideration of this emphasis among Soviet analysts, the USSR remained deeply involved in regional conflicts across the entire spectrum of the Third World – from Cambodia and Afghanistan in Asia to the Horn and Angola in Africa and Nicaragua and El Salvador in Central America. Western analysts asserted that the role of the Soviet Union as a global power was based almost exclusively on its military capabilities, including both command over ever more sophisticated nuclear and conventional armaments and expanding military involvement in Third World regional conflicts. Moreover, in their view, the military stalemate in US–Soviet relations had deflected Soviet superpower aspirations toward the Third World.[1]

After 1985 the Soviet Union underwent revolutionary changes in both its domestic and its foreign policy. In the foreign policy area the initial focus of these changes emphasized the reduction of conflict with the West, especially the United States, as an essential element of the overall reform of Soviet society. The result was a series of agreements on arms limitations and a dramatic improvement in the international political atmosphere. In addition, developments in the Soviet–East European relationship throughout 1989 and 1990 were of historic importance and resulted in the collapse of Soviet-imposed Marxist–Leninist regimes in East-Central Europe and the emergence of independent states, as well as structural changes in the entire political-security balance in Europe.

Changes of great importance have also occurred in Soviet policy in Asia, where relations with the People's Republic of China and with the Republic of Korea have been normalized. Although changes in Soviet policy toward and relations with developing countries have been less

The authors wish to express their appreciation to Deborah Nutter Miner and Paul Marantz for their perceptive critiques of an earlier version of this chapter.

dramatic than those in Europe, they have nonetheless been of very visible and growing importance. During the first six years after Gorbachev's rise to political prominence Soviet troops were withdrawn from Afghanistan, the USSR supported and actively encouraged the withdrawal of Vietnamese and Cuban troops from Cambodia and Angola respectively, and Soviet support for the Nicaraguan elections of spring 1990 facilitated the shift of political power in that country. In brief, without abandoning its chief Third World partners, the Soviet Union initiated far-reaching shifts in its perceptions of the place of the Third World in international politics, of its long-term objectives in the region, and of the costs that it is able and willing to bear in pursuing those objectives.

It is the purpose of this chapter to examine the shifts in Soviet policy toward the Third World that have occurred since 1945, with special consideration given to Soviet involvement in regional conflicts.[2] The gist of the argument presented is that the Soviet leadership has recognized its basic inability to mold the international environment to meet its own objectives. Soviet new thinking concerning the Third World since about 1987 and Soviet behavior in the Third World since approximately 1989 indicate that much of what in the past was called the "Soviet Grand Design" has been abandoned in official policy. The demands of domestic economic and political reform and the failures of earlier Soviet foreign policy activities are at the root of the changes that have occurred. This applies to shifts in policy toward the Third World, including regional security conflicts, as well as in policy toward the USSR's erstwhile enemies in the industrialized world.

The Soviet Union under Mikhail Gorbachev has been in the process of entering the international political-economic system from which it had attempted to isolate itself and to whose overthrow it was committed ever since the Bolshevik Revolution of 1917. It is abandoning its decades-old commitment to a "class-based" foreign policy which has proven to be dangerous, largely ineffectual, and inordinately costly. An integral part of this shift in Soviet perspective and policy on international politics involves a shift in perspective and policy concerning the developing world in general and Third World regional conflicts in particular.

However, at the very time that these new interpretations and objectives emerged in official Soviet policy, the "consensus" that underlay Soviet foreign policy visibly eroded. Throughout 1990, for example, former Foreign Minister Eduard Shevardnadze responded most vehemently to those within the Soviet hierarchy who charged him and President Gorbachev with virtual capitulation to the West and to "giving away" Soviet positions in Eastern Europe and throughout the Third World.[3] The current lack of unity in foreign policy perspectives in the USSR and the dramatic moves away from reform by President Gorbachev by early 1991 make it far more difficult to project likely future Soviet policy. Without this ability to predict the specific directions which might be followed it becomes especially important to examine the general tendencies which may influence future Soviet policy toward the Third World, as well as the West.

The Brezhnev legacy and the Gorbachev reforms

At the height of the Brezhnev era in the mid-1970s optimism peaked concerning both the direction and pace of international developments and prospects for the expanded role of the USSR. Developments of the prior decade tended to support this viewpoint. The Soviet Union had closed the strategic nuclear gap with the United States and had achieved strategic parity. This parity, and by extension Soviet equality as a global power, had been recognized in a series of agreements negotiated at Vladivostok, Moscow, and Helsinki. The conventional forces of the Soviet Union in Europe, as well as its expanded ability to project military power beyond its immediate borders, had been enhanced by the modernization of Warsaw Pact forces and by the creation of an ocean-going navy and long-distance air transport capabilities.

The West's acceptance at Helsinki of the postwar status quo in Europe, the *de facto* defeat of the United States in Vietnam, and the coming to power of self-proclaimed Marxist–Leninist national liberation movements throughout the Third World – often with direct Soviet support – gave further evidence of the expanded role of the Soviet Union in world affairs. In the international economic realm the Soviets envisaged the establishment of a socialist international division of labor that would first counter and eventually replace the dominant capitalist world market.[4] Domestically, economic growth rates, though they had slowed since the immediate postwar period, still enabled the Soviet leadership to fulfil its promises to meet growing consumer demands and simultaneously to maintain the expanding military and economic commitments necessitated by its new role as a global power.

Despite this Soviet optimism of the early 1970s and the apparent reality that underlay it, a decade later the Soviets found themselves increasingly on the defensive internationally. The detente with the West, especially the United States, had collapsed into a new cold war complete with economic embargo, revitalized US military spending, and a new US assertiveness in foreign policy. Despite Soviet blustering,

West European NATO states had agreed to the deployment of intermediate-range nuclear weapons, and the Reagan Administration had committed itself to the development of the Strategic Defense Initiative (SDI, or "Star Wars"). In short, a new round in the postwar arms race had begun.

In the Third World the USSR had been, in effect, frozen out of participation in key developments in the Middle East, and a number of its new allies/clients (Afghanistan, Angola, Ethiopia, Kampuchea, and Nicaragua) had failed to create stable political-economic systems and were increasingly challenged by domestic insurgencies supported by the United States and others. The result was a growing demand for Soviet military and economic support, including the direct takeover by Soviet troops of responsibility for the security of the Marxist–Leninist regime in Afghanistan. Along with this came criticism of Soviet intervention by a large number of developing countries themselves. In yet another area the Soviets found that the political attractiveness of their socio-economic-political model had weakened dramatically. The unity of the Soviet-led World Communist Movement had shattered long ago. In Western Europe communist parties had either lost domestic support or had asserted their independence from Moscow – or both. In the Third World a growing number of Marxist regimes – e.g. those in Benin, Guinea-Bissau and Mozambique – were modifying their commitment to socialism and reestablishing or strengthening economic and political ties with the West. These problems arose at the very time when the weaknesses of the Soviet economy were becoming most apparent. By the beginning of the 1980s economic growth rates had, in the words of General Secretary Mikhail Gorbachev, "fallen to a level close to economic stagnation." The technological gap between the Soviet economy and the economies of its major competitors, including a number of newly industrialized countries (NICs), was expanding.[5] After decades devoted to catching up with the West in a wide range of fields and of establishing themselves as a global power, the Soviets now faced the prospect of stagnation and decline.

Briefly, the situation inherited by Brezhnev's successors was one filled with contradictions. Although the Soviet Union had emerged as a global superpower with wide-ranging interests and capabilities, this position was based largely on military power. The nuclear stalemate with the United States, the renewed activism of US policy, and the expanding role of other countries in global affairs, however, precluded turning this enhanced military position into effective political gains. The weaknesses of the Soviet economy raised questions about the possible over-extension of international commitments and limited the relevance of the USSR for many of the most pressing of international problems – economic development, international trade, and hard currency debts.

After assuming leadership of the CPSU, Mikhail Gorbachev spoke repeatedly of the domestic and foreign policy problems facing the USSR. He committed himself to a major reform of the entire Soviet socio-economic-political system as a means of resolving those problems. The basic argument that he presented initially to support this reform can be summarized briefly as follows. First, the economic problems of the Soviet Union and the technology gap between the Soviet Union and the West were expanding and implied a decreasing ability of the Soviet economy to support the legitimate needs of the population or to insure the military security and global standing of the Soviet state in the twenty-first century. Second, economic reform within the framework of socialism was essential, in order to overcome the economic problems and technological weaknesses that threatened to undermine the USSR's international status; required, as well, as a precondition for economic reform is a reform of the political process which will make officials more responsive to the needs of economic rationality.[6] Third, to overcome entrenched bureaucratic forces within the Soviet Union which would resist change, a more open but still controlled political system that encourages criticism and "rationality" in support of reform was required. Finally, policies were needed which would permit the Soviets to benefit more fully from advances in the international economy and to accomplish, by means other than primarily military, major Soviet foreign policy objectives. In other words, soon after coming to power Gorbachev and his advisors laid out the justification for perestroika, glasnost (or openness) and democratization of the political process; they also noted the interdependence of domestic reform and changes in Soviet foreign policy.

In sum, the primary objectives of Gorbachev's campaign of perestroika and glasnost were based on the recognition that the position of the USSR in the world depended upon a dramatic improvement in the functioning of the Soviet economy. In his report to the 27th Party Congress in early 1986 he expressed this point most forcefully: "In a word, Comrades, acceleration of the country's economic development is the key to all our problems; immediate and long-term, economic and social, political and ideological, domestic and foreign."[7] Perestroika became Gorbachev's call for major reform with the goal of revitalizing the economy, closing the technology gap, and turning the USSR into a fully competitive global superpower – not, to use Paul Dibb's term, the "incomplete superpower" lacking virtually all but military power as an instrument to influence world developments.[8]

As is clear from the vantage point of early 1991, the expectations of General Secretary Gorbachev and his advisors concerning their ability to turn around the Soviet economy have not been fulfilled. The economy has continued to deteriorate, glasnost and democratization contributed both to the opening up of Soviet domestic politics and to the possible disintegration of a unified Soviet state and are now under relentless attack from conservative political elements. In the foreign policy area, although Gorbachev and his former Foreign Minister Eduard Shevardnadze accomplished many of their objectives of improving relationships with the United States, Western Europe, and China, these goals have been accomplished at times at substantial political cost. They have also resulted in widespread opposition on the part of more conservative elements within the Soviet political system of the kind that resulted in Shevardnadze's resignation. In the remainder of this chapter, we shall examine the evolution of Soviet policy toward the developing world from 1985 to 1991.

Gorbachev's Third World policy: from new thinking to foreign policy fragmentation

Between Gorbachev's rise to power in 1985 and 1991 Soviet policy toward the developing world went through three basic stages. In the first period, which can be labeled "the period of great expectations" and lasted from 1985 until approximately 1988, the promotion of new political thinking did not really coincide with a comparable change in policy or behavior. The dominant Western response during this period was that new thinking was largely tactical and did not represent a break with the "grand design" that had underlain Soviet policy in the past.

The second period, which was characterized by a flurry of new foreign policy initiatives from Cambodia in Southeastern Asia to Nicaragua in Central America, lasted from 1988 until mid-1990, or so. It was during this period that the reality of the structural changes in Soviet policy in the Third World was increasingly recognized in the West – as well as the reality of changes in other aspects of Soviet foreign and domestic politics.

The third period of Soviet Third World policy began in 1990 and continues to the present. In effect, this is the period in which any consensus on Soviet foreign policy has fragmented, in which individual republics of the Soviet Union have attempted to assert their autonomy, and in which the Soviet leadership has been forced to focus almost exclusively on domestic, as opposed to foreign policy, concerns. Although new thinking continues to dominate official policy statements, growing evidence has emerged of substantial opposition to various aspects of the new foreign policy, including that in the developing world. The resignation of Foreign Minister Shevardnadze in December 1990 and the hard-line anti-Western attack on Western banks by the new prime minister, Valentin S. Pavlov, in February 1991 were evidence of this shift away from the roots of new thinking.[9]

The period of great expectations

Before beginning our assessment of the implications of current developments in Soviet domestic and foreign policy for future Soviet behavior in the Third World, it is essential to trace in more detail the evolution of Soviet policy during the three periods since Gorbachev's selection as head of the CPSU in March 1985. Although President Gorbachev dramatized the problems facing the Soviet Union in both the domestic and the international arenas, he was neither the first nor the only important Soviet personality to outline the need to turn the USSR around.[10] Already in his report to the 27th Party Congress in February 1986 Gorbachev gave some indication of the content of new political thinking when he raised issues seldom, if ever, discussed publicly by Soviet political leaders in the past. The major points that he mentioned included recognition of the existence of "global problems, affecting all humanity" that required "cooperation on a world-wide scale," explicit stress on the interdependence of states, the argument that "it is no longer possible to win an arms race, or nuclear war for that matter," and strong criticism of the "infallibility complex" that had characterized previous foreign policy.[11]

New political thinking in the foreign policy area, as interpreted early in the Gorbachev era, contained three basic components. The first was a revitalization of Soviet foreign policy by rejecting the rigidity and the aggressiveness of Brezhnev's foreign policy and by appealing for greater flexibility in the implementation of policy and the reduction of the role of ideology in determining policy. The second was the introduction of new concepts or issues on the agenda of the top leadership: e.g., global problems and interdependence. Third was a reevaluation of the sources of national security which led to the conclusion that (1) military, especially nuclear, parity would soon cease to be a factor of political-military restraint; (2) national and international security had become indivisible; (3) a multi-faceted approach to problems of international security was required; and (4) international security was mutual, or "positive-sum" in nature.

Gorbachev's views drew heavily on those of academic analysts who already in the 1970s had begun discussing most of the issues that were to be placed on the agenda of the top political leadership after 1985. New thinking, as these views were termed by Gorbachev, became an integral element of Soviet assessments of developments in and policy toward the Third World. While the 1961 Party Program had spoken with great optimism about prospects for liberation and the role of the USSR in supporting the national liberation struggle, the 1986 Program emphasized the revitalization of neo-colonialism and imperialism in the Third World and referred only to the fact that the "CPSU supports the just struggle waged by the countries of Asia, Africa and Latin America against imperialism . . ." Progressive states were informed that the tasks of building a new society were primarily their own responsibility, although the Soviet Union would continue to render assistance where possible.[12] The three major concerns raised about the Soviet involvement in the Third World related to the escalating costs borne by the Soviet Union in supporting clients, the poor record of those clients after independence in creating stable political systems and functioning economies, and the negative impact that involvement in the Third World had on other Soviet policy concerns – in particular, relations with the United States.

Thus, by early 1986 the apparent official Soviet intention to reduce direct Soviet commitments to Third World clients was evident. In addition to raising the issue of the cost of supporting Third World allies, the Soviets now questioned the long-term viability of some of their client states and increasingly criticized the policies of some of these states. Even such a strong supporter of the model of "revolutionary democracy" as Rostislav Ul'ianovskii, long-time Deputy Director of the International Department of the CPSU, now emphasized the extended and tortuous path that the building of socialism would entail.[13] This new concern about Soviet policy in the Third World had an important impact on a reconceptualization of regional conflicts and the most appropriate Soviet response to those conflicts. In the past Soviet analysts and politicians had charged that Western imperialism was the primary source of regional conflict. The Soviets themselves, it was argued, had an obligation to support progressive groups throughout the Third World who were opposed to domestic opponents supported by the United States and its allies.

Early in the Gorbachev era a new interpretation began to dominate official Soviet interpretations. Gorbachev himself argued that "regional conflicts in Asia, Africa and Latin America are spawned by the colonial past, new social processes, or recurrences of predating policy, or by all three." The objective, according to Gorbachev, is to find a political, not a military solution to these conflicts.[14] Gorbachev went on to argue that every country has a right to determine its own political orientation and that neither of the superpowers should intervene in domestic conflicts.[15]

Thus, new thinking in relation to the Third World, as it emerged early in the Gorbachev era, implied: (1) the demilitarization of regional conflicts and the search for political solutions to those conflicts; (2) the deidealization or secularization of interstate relations and the basing of those relationships on mutual interests; and (3) refraining from violating the sovereignty of other nations including interference in domestic political debates.

The initial Western reactions to new thinking as it applied to East–West relations, as well as to Soviet policy in the developing world, was one of "wait and see," of cautious optimism. For example, Francis Fukuyama, who wrote extensively on this topic, was very cautious in his conclusions about the long-term implications of the new rhetoric that was applied to Soviet foreign policy.[16] The dominant initial Western interpretation of new thinking about the Third World could be summarized as follows: at the level of public debate Soviet academic analysts and highly placed officials presented a much less optimistic and more complex interpretation of the Third World than that which had characterized expectations expressed during the Brezhnev years; yet, the question remained whether this reassessment represented more than a mere tactical modification of Soviet doctrine, or whether it could be interpreted as the external manifestation of a learning process in which the Soviet leadership was increasingly aware of its basic inability to mold the international environment to meet its often expressed objectives. The question raised by most Western analysts, therefore, concerned the actual implementation of policy initiatives by the Soviet leadership that would move away from past policy.

By 1987 the intellectual foundations for a shift in Soviet policy had been established; however, the question that then arose concerned the degree to which that new assessment influenced actual Soviet behavior. It is necessary, therefore, to provide a brief assessment of the second period in Gorbachev's foreign policy toward the Third World, that in which the USSR engaged in a flurry of activity that resulted in a significant retrenchment of Soviet involvement and commitments. Throughout 1988 and 1989 the Soviet leadership initiated a number of important modifications in Third World policy aimed at (1) reducing areas of conflict with the West; (2) limiting the drain on Soviet resources; and (3) extricating the USSR from regional conflicts in which the prospects for success seemed virtually nonexistent. During this period there was seemingly widespread support within the USSR for the implementation of new policies – at least, there did not exist overt criticism of new thinking or of the modification of foreign policy behavior associated with new thinking. Politically, the new interpretation maintained that Brezhnev's policy in the developing world had perpetuated confrontational elements in US–Soviet relations and had, thereby, contributed dramatically to the deterioration of the superpower relationship.[17] Secondly, there was general agreement that Soviet commitments to client states throughout the Third World had resulted in escalating costs that contributed to the overall financial problems challenging the very foundations of the Soviet economy.[18]

During 1988 and 1989 the Soviets moved forcefully on a variety of fronts to modify important elements of their past policy throughout the Third World. Chief among these changes were the reassessment of security and economic commitments to radical Marxist–Leninist regimes – such as those in Afghanistan, Angola and Ethiopia – which were challenged by internal opposition (often supported by the United States), as well as of the economic assistance that had been committed to radical governments without seemingly having any positive impact on long-term economic growth. Finally, questions were raised about the long-term benefits to the USSR – or to recipients, for that matter – of the major arms transfer programs of the Soviet state.

New foreign policy behavior

We turn now to a brief examination of the actual changes in Soviet–Third World policy that occurred during 1988–89. By far the most dramatic and significant of the changes in Soviet involvement in the Third World was the decision, made in early 1988 and implemented by spring 1989, to withdraw Soviet combat troops from Afghanistan. After initial efforts to pacify the country by conquest and to exert greater pressure on Pakistan to accept the new "status quo" in the region it soon became clear that the communist government of Afghanistan, despite massive Soviet economic and military support and the direct involvement of well over 100,000 Soviet troops, was not capable of defeating the anti-communist rebels. The costs involved – both the military and the political costs, as the USSR attempted to normalize relations with both the United States and China, and growing unrest at home in the face of escalating Soviet casualties – contributed dramatically to the decision to withdraw. It must be noted, however, that the Soviet Union did not abandon the government of Najibullah, which it considered capable in the long term of stabilizing its control. The communist government of Afghanistan has continued to receive large amounts of economic and military support and has managed to stabilize its position for two full years after the departure of Soviet troops.[19]

In Southeast Asia, the Soviets contributed to the Vietnamese decision to withdraw combat troops from Cambodia by late 1989.[20] In Angola the Soviets have contributed to the resolution of the conflict. For example, they played an important behind-the-scenes role in the negotiations which resulted in the Cuban decision to withdraw more than two-thirds of their troops from Angola.[21] Initially, as in Afghanistan, the Gorbachev leadership had apparently hoped for a military solution to the civil war. However, when it became obvious that the MPLA was unable to assert full control over Angola, the Soviets pushed strongly for the negotiations that resulted in the ceasefire and the significant reduction of Cuban troops in Angola.[22]

To a substantial degree, Soviet policy in Ethiopia paralleled that in other Marxist–Leninist states where civil war challenged the central government authorities. Although Soviet military aid to Ethiopia was not significantly reduced as of early 1991, Soviet officials had announced their intention to reduce their involvement in the Ethiopian civil war.[23]

In Central America, there occurred a parallel development, as the Soviets first encouraged the Sandinistas in Nicaragua to permit an open and competitive election and, later, accepted what for them were the very negative results of that election.[24] Overall, during 1988 and 1989 the Soviet Union either encouraged or accepted a series of developments in relationships with Marxist–Leninist client states throughout the Third World that resulted in their military withdrawal, the beginnings of a negotiated solution to a long-standing conflict, or the reduction of their overall military and economic commitment to a client regime.

In many respects the parallels to developments in Eastern Europe are striking. Moreover, the motivations for the shift in Soviet policy parallel those at work in Eastern Europe. First, the decision had been made by the Gorbachev leadership that the costs of empire – that is the economic and political costs of maintaining a dominant position in Eastern Europe and/or areas of the Third World simply outweighed the benefits to be achieved. This motivation for permitting the collapse of communist regimes in East-Central Europe was made clear by former Foreign Minister Eduard Shevardnadze.[25] The motive has also been evident in relations with Third World clients, which were among the weakest and least stable of governments throughout the developing world. Moreover, continued involvement in regional conflicts are now viewed as one of the key inhibiting factors to a normalization of relations with the industrialized West and the entrance of the USSR into the international political and economic community. The latter has been viewed by

Soviet reformers as an essential element of the overall reform process and the revitalization of the economy.[26]

Closely associated with the shift away from strong support of and major involvement in regional conflicts, has been the questioning of the cost and long-term value to the USSR of both the military and economic relationships that have been established ever since the mid-1950s. For example, an editorial in *Izvestiia* in early 1990 provided specific information on the size and nature of the debt to the USSR. Of the total 85.8 billion rubles owed to the Soviet Union through 1 November 1989, 37.2 billion was owed by socialist developing countries and an additional 42 billion rubles by other developing countries.

Table 6.1 *Outstanding debts owed to the USSR as of 1 November 1989 (in millions of rubles)*

Total outstanding debt	85,845.6
of which	
Socialist countries	43,805.9
of which	
Socialist developing countries[a]	37,156.8
Developing countries	42,039.7
of which	
Progressive countries[b]	9,469.8
Major non-socialist developing countries[c]	25,783.6

[a] Cuba, North Korea, Laos, Mongolia, Vietnam
[b] Angola, Afghanistan, Benin, Cambodia, Ethiopia, Guinea-Bissau, Mozambique, Nicaragua, South Yemen
[c] Algeria, Egypt, India, Iraq, Libya, Syria
Source: "Unikal'nyi dokument," *Izvestiia*, 1 March 1990, p. 3

The article made clear that the amounts owed to the USSR were not likely to be repaid quickly enough to help the Soviet economy. Another Soviet author, writing in *Izvestiia* in mid-1990, noted that the amount owed to the USSR was the result of "economic, ideological, and military-political miscalculations." This author was highly critical of past Soviet policy and interpreted a July 1990 decree of President Gorbachev, calling for the implementation of the principles of mutual advantage in economic relations of the Soviet Union with all partners, as a move in the right direction.[27]

There have been those who have, for all practical purposes, argued that the USSR should abandon virtually all commitments throughout the Third World and focus exclusively on the solution of domestic problems. This is the position taken, for example, by Andrei Kolosov, who has complained that, although Soviet partners tend to be authoritarian political leaders not committed to the peaceful resolution of conflict, they continue to receive Soviet political, military, and economic backing. Kolosov concludes that the USSR must encourage these leaders to negotiate the settlement of internal conflicts, and should also move away from relying almost exclusively on military support to Third World clients and establish relationships in which "economic expediency, not ideological and political preferences, should become the determinant for developing economic ties with the Third World as well."[28]

On the other hand, there are those who strongly criticize the extreme position of Kolosov and others. For example, Andrei Urnov, Deputy Chief of the International Department of the Central Committee of the CPSU, criticizes Kolosov for his extreme position and argues that, although one might criticize past aspects of Soviet foreign policy, one simply cannot accept Kolosov's view that all Soviet allies are venal or that their opponents (such as Pol Pot in Cambodia, RENAMO in Mozambique, or the Eritrean separatists in Ethiopia) are morally superior.[29]

In sum, from 1988 until sometime in early 1990, the Soviet Union pursued a number of policy changes which resulted in a reorientation of its policies in key conflict regions throughout the Third World. It began, as well, to reduce commitments to some of its established allies. New thinking had indeed evolved into new behavior patterns. But, were these behavior patterns really that new? Can one really argue that the Soviet Union was on the verge of withdrawing from the Third World? In responding to these questions, one must take into account the fact that the apparent foreign consensus on foreign policy that characterized the USSR in the first two periods of the Gorbachev era broke down during 1990 and has been immersed in the increasingly vitriolic debates that have characterized Soviet political processes, whether they concern economic reform, constitutional changes, ethnic relations, or virtually any other aspect of domestic politics in the Soviet Union.

Fragmentation of foreign policy consensus

It is ironic that at the very time when the USSR could expect to begin benefiting from the changes which it had initiated in its foreign policy, the domestic consensus on that policy had already begun to fragment. Soviet policy in Asia, Africa, and Latin America during the last years of the 1980s resulted in a rapid reassessment in the West of the nature of Soviet foreign policy and the prospects for the USSR's entering the international community as an equal and beneficial contributor to the emergence of a new international order. While political leaders and political analysts in the West praised the Gorbachev leadership for its pragmatic and beneficial approach to regional conflicts and other foreign policy concerns – witness, especially, the early stages of the Persian Gulf conflict – voices emerged in the Soviet Union which condemned Gorbachev, his Foreign Minister Eduard Shevardnadze and other reformers for a foreign policy of capitulation. Thus began the third stage of Gorbachev's policy toward the Third World: a period of growing internal confrontation within the USSR itself and a period of division concerning the very roots of foreign policy and of a gradual weakening of the position of reformers that, prior to the end of 1990, resulted in Shevardnadze's resignation.

Throughout 1990 the debate on Soviet foreign policy became extremely vocal and heated. Shevardnadze, the architect of much of this new foreign policy, was the target of extremely critical comments by those who charged him and Gorbachev with having abandoned the security interests of the USSR in Central Europe by permitting, even encouraging, the demise of Marxist–Leninist regimes and unilaterally committing the Soviet Union to the withdrawal of its troops from the region. Elsewhere, Shevardnadze and Gorbachev were accused of abandoning the interests of their allies throughout the Third World.

The conservative attacks on Gorbachev's internal domestic and foreign policy reforms that emerged by early 1990 did not signify a unified opposition. Rather, they derived from a variety of groups whose interests did not always coincide, except increasingly in the fact that they opposed the reforms being considered or implemented in domestic economic and political relations, as well as in the foreign policy arena. To a substantial degree, Gorbachev and the reform leaders ignored the initial and sporadic offensive of the conservatives – those who opposed domestic decentralization and democratization, the emergence of political pluralism, the reduction of Soviet international commitments, and the decrease in Soviet military capabilities.[30] By 1990, however, these attacks became so frequent and all-encompassing that responses were required. Aleksandr Iakovlev, one of Gorbachev's three primary lieutenants, noted that the primary danger to the successful introduction of perestroika came from the conservatives.[31] Shevardnadze responded that the conservative criticisms of Gorbachev's foreign policy had the objective of discrediting the entire leadership and undermining the foundations of reform in the USSR.[32]

This opposition to new political thinking and Gorbachev's foreign policy has fallen into three broad groupings.[33] The first, who can be called "statists," consist of members of the party apparatus and the dogmatic wing of the party, as well as some senior military officers and writers. A second group, the "national-Bolsheviks," also find their supporters in the party apparatus and within the military. The third group, the "Russian nationalists," includes members of the Russian intelligentsia who range from moderate nationalists to the extremists associated with the right-wing organization "Pamiat." Though none of these groups has a well-developed, integrated foreign policy perspective or program nor an organizational structure, they are highly critical of recent developments in Soviet foreign policy – in particular of the collapse of Marxist–Leninist regimes in Eastern Europe and the implications that this might have for the erosion of internal authority within the USSR itself. The views of all three groupings are influenced both by positive perceptions of the Russian/Soviet imperial past and by fears of the dangers to Russia/USSR that emanate from the outside world.

In fact, from the very beginning there were within the party apparatus some who did not accept the underlying principles or assumptions of new thinking. For example, there were those within the party apparatus who opposed the replacement of class interests with universal human values as a basis for the foreign policy of the USSR.[34] While the earlier criticism occurred at the level of Marxist philosophy and ideology and appeared in specialized publications, more recently the criticisms by noted Russian writers of new thinking and behavior in the foreign policy area has occurred in the mass circulation press. For example, one Soviet writer sees in the concept of general human values a "terrible mistake" that contributed to the dangerous developments in Eastern Europe.[35] Another has argued that new thinking abandoned the interests of the socialist state and abandoned efforts to oppose bourgeois imperialist expansion throughout the Third World. The idea of integration into Europe is presented as dangerous for the very existence of the USSR.[36]

In response to the charge that the USSR was abandoning the Third World, Foreign Minister Shevardnadze noted in an interview in spring 1990 that it was true that the Soviet Union was in the process of reducing the intensity of some of its Third World contacts. He argued, however, that without solving its domestic economic problems, the Soviet Union would be in no position to help developing countries in the future. He noted, as well, that in most of the regional conflicts to which the USSR had been a party, military solutions simply did not exist.[37]

Shavardnadze's resignation, announced at a meeting of the Congress of People's Deputies on 20 December 1990, brought to an end what two well-known and influential Soviet analysts have called the "creative destruction stage of Gorbachev-era foreign policy."[38] Once again Shevardnadze responded to the attacks of conservative critics who charged him with contributing to the demise of socialism, though he also noted his concerns about the erosion of democracy and reemergence of dictatorship within the USSR.[39] In responding earlier in the year to charges by CPSU conservatives that Gorbachev's policies had resulted in the "loss of Eastern Europe," Shevardnadze had stated: "Perestroika is not responsible for the destruction of the political structure of Europe. It was destroyed by the will of peoples no longer willing to put up with oppression. The undermining of faith in socialism based on suppression and violence began in the 1940s, not in 1985."[40]

By 1990 the debilitating problems of a deteriorating economy, a chaotic society, and the inability of government or party to deal with either resulted in growing attention on the part of Gorbachev to domestic developments. At the same time, the consensus on foreign policy, in so far as it had existed, began to fragment. No longer was there agreement on the goals of Soviet foreign policy or the means by which to implement them.[41] In addition to the divisions on foreign policy noted above, there emerged autonomous foreign policy constituencies and actors, such as the autonomous union republics that by 1990 had begun to pursue their own foreign policy interests – often at odds with those of the all-union government. In addition to the foreign policy activities of the union republics, various branches of the bureaucracy and the armed forces began to express their idiosyncratic concerns, as these related both to domestic and foreign affairs.[42]

It is essential to recall that two forces have driven the Soviet Union to its current impasse in the foreign policy area, including its policies toward the Third World. The first is the growing domestic crisis which requires Gorbachev and the leadership increasingly to disengage from the international arena, particularly throughout the Third World, in order to concentrate more time and resources on internal problems. The key element of Gorbachev's response has been his gradual shift to the right, as he has searched for supporters among conservative elements within the party and state apparatus. Secondly, the forces of glasnost and perestroika which were initially unleashed by Gorbachev to provide solutions to deep-seated economic and political problems, have increasingly fragmented the domestic and foreign policy process. This, in turn, has eroded Gorbachev's ability to formulate and implement coherent and consistent foreign policy. A good illustration of the shift in Soviet policy can be seen in the USSR's position on the Gulf crisis – from whole-hearted support for the US-led international coalition in August 1990 to more conditional support and the effort to pursue autonomous policies by the time that actual fighting broke out in January–February 1991.

Future prospects of the USSR's Third World policy

The end of the cold war, the substantial reorientation of Soviet foreign policy over the last three years, as well as the internal political and economic upheavals within the USSR and the fragmentation of the consensus on foreign policy, all make it extremely difficult to provide any specific projections about likely developments in Soviet policy over the next decade, and beyond into the next century. However, several issues appear to be relatively clear as they impinge upon Soviet foreign policy, including that toward the countries of Asia, Africa, and Latin America. First, the collapse of an internal consensus on foreign policy and the reemergence of extremely conservative voices of those who view the policies of the recent past largely as a form of capitulation and self-initiated defeatism do not augur well for a continuation of the type of cooperation in US–Soviet relations that emerged during 1989–90. In the wake of the Gulf War, for example, there have been those within the Soviet military establishment who have advocated a significant increase in the commitment of Soviet resources to weapons development to counter the apparent superiority of US and Western weapons systems to Soviet weapons, at least when employed by Iraqi military forces. Moreover, there have been those who have argued that former Foreign Minister Shevardnadze tied Soviet interests far too closely to those of the United States. In his first months in office Aleksander Bessmertnykh, Shevardnadze's successor, attempted to distance himself and the USSR from such close association with the US – especially in the Gulf War.

Do these and related developments imply that the Soviet Union is on the verge of entering into a new round of active and expansionist involvement throughout the Third World or, more generally, that the USSR may well reemerge over the next decade as a direct challenger to US and Western interests, as it had been for more than forty years after the conclusion of World War II? The answer to this question is by no means clear. Yet there are factors that seem to mitigate against a renewal of large-scale Soviet support for radical regimes and revolutionary movements throughout the Third World. First, the political conditions in the Third World itself do not appear conducive to prospects for Marxist revolution on a level with what occurred during the 1970s. European colonialism, a primary contributor to past revolutionary activities, has largely disappeared. Moreover, the socialist model of socio-economic development has lost its appeal, given the fact that it has failed to accomplish its objectives anywhere in the world. Moreover, economic privatization and political democratization are attracting more support throughout the developing world that they have in the past. Thus, the political conditions throughout the Third World at the beginning of the 1990s do not seem conducive to the reemergence of radical Marxist movements on a broad scale.

A second set of issues that will influence Soviet foreign policy concerns the state of relations between the USSR and the United States. So long as the Soviet leadership is committed to a policy of economic revitalization which depends heavily upon cooperation in the economic realm with the United States and other Western industrial countries, widespread support for radical movements in the Third World is highly unlikely. The demise of the cold war has meant that regional conflicts are not likely to lead to increased US–Soviet tension and the detente in US–Soviet relations has been viewed as an essential element in the overall revitalization of the Soviet economy. Cordial relations – or at least non-hostile relations – with the West, and the United States in particular, should remain an essential component of an overall foreign policy strategy of any Soviet government over the next decade, as the USSR attempts to bring its domestic economic and political situation under control. Thus, it would appear that no Soviet leadership – even a conservative one – would be interested in pursuing a policy that would result in a dramatic deterioration of East–West relations or the possibility of a reemergent cold war.

A third set of developments that will greatly influence Soviet foreign policy during the 1990s, including that toward developing countries, will be the political and economic situation within the USSR itself. Presently political fragmentation and economic collapse must be the primary factors on which any Soviet leadership will concentrate. Involvement in overseas adventures will be highly unlikely, given the attention and resources that must be devoted to rebuilding the Soviet state – if the continued existence of that state is still a possibility. This does not mean that, should a hard-line conservative faction come to power within the Soviet Union, relationships with the West might not deteriorate. What it does mean is that even a hard-line conservative Soviet government would likely not have the resource base in the foreseeable future from which to reinitiate the kind of expansionist and aggressive policies that characterized Soviet policy in the last decade of the Brezhnev period.

Thus, the overall conclusion that we reach is that domestic and foreign "costs" will continue to enter seriously into considerations whether or not to pursue particular "opportunities" for the pursuit of Soviet interests overseas. Given the present domestic crisis, four types of opportunism are envisaged. First, "low cost, high return opportunism" involving behind-the-scenes efforts to resolve conflicts, to pressure allies or clients to join the bandwagon of international opinion, and to establish new relations with states that can promote Soviet domestic prosperity without alienating traditional allies or clients who remain valued assets. To some extent the Soviet efforts during the Gulf crisis to maintain ties with Iraq, to strengthen relationships with the government of Iran, while still providing general support for the UN coalition seem to fall into this category. A second category might be termed "no cost, high profile opportunism," in which the USSR would pursue global and regional initiatives or calls geared to peace and cooperation. The mediating role that the USSR played at the conclusion of the Indo-Pakistani War of 1965 is an illustration of this type of policy.

There is also a question of "lost opportunities" if the Soviet foreign policy process continues to fragment in terms of both domestic participants and the orientation of Soviet foreign policy. It is important to recognize that this process of fragmentation could result in a foreign policy process akin to that of the United States, where pluralism leads to compromise and consensus. On the other hand, it could also result in anarchy and chaos and in the overall undermining of the authority of any unified Soviet state. In either of these two cases, however, the issues to be decided will involve whether or not new thinking in the foreign policy area can offer a viable alternative to the old Soviet "Grand Design." Finally, there will be "opportunities that the Soviet leadership simply will not be able to ignore," because they will contribute directly and clearly to strengthening the national sovereignty of the Soviet state or they represent opportunities to be gained with little or no cost.

It appears evident that throughout the Soviet political spectrum, almost independent of political orientation, there exists a recognition that future Soviet involvement in the Third World must be more cost-effective and must contribute directly and immediately to the interests of the USSR. Even those within the Soviet establishment who have opposed the call for virtually complete Soviet withdrawal from the Third World, recognize the inordinately high costs of past Soviet involvement and the modest returns that the USSR has derived from those involvements.

The USSR will not likely make commitments to revolutionary movements or regimes throughout the Third World on a par with those made in the past. However – and this is a point that must be kept in mind – even during the high point of new thinking during 1988–89, the USSR did not abandon all of its Third World commitments. Although the Soviet leadership has reassessed its Third World commitments, it has not abandoned fully formed Leninist governments, such as those in Vietnam, Afghanistan, and Ethiopia. Soviet military and economic support has continued to flow to these regimes, although direct involvement has been reduced (especially in Afghanistan).[43] What the USSR has done is reduce its commitments to regimes considered unlikely to achieve any degree of stability, especially in situations where continued direct involvement and support was likely to undermine the attempt to improve relations with China and/or the United States.[44]

In conclusion, the position from which the USSR will pursue its interests in the Third World has changed dramatically since the period in the 1970s when the Soviet Union appeared to hold a significantly advantageous position versus the United States because: (1) revolution was rampant throughout the Third World; (2) the United States was immobilized in the aftermath of its disastrous experiences in Vietnam; and (3) the acquisition of nuclear military parity by the Soviet Union created an environment that contributed to a strengthening of Soviet expansionist drives.

In all of these areas the situation has changed dramatically for the USSR. The 1990s will likely see the Soviet Union – whether directed by political leaders committed to a continuation of domestic reforms or by a more hard-line leadership attempting to restore central controls over both the economy and the polity – pursuing policies of modest involvement that will contribute to the strengthening of the domestic Soviet economy.

Notes

1 See, for example, Paul Dibb, *The Soviet Union: The Incomplete Superpower* (Urbana: University of Illinois Press, 1986), passim.

2 Two recent publications that trace these developments in detail are Edward A. Kolodziej and Roger E. Kanet, eds., *The Limits of Soviet Power in the Developing World: Thermidor in the Revolutionary Struggle* (London: Macmillan; Baltimore: Johns Hopkins, 1989) and Roger E. Kanet and Edward A. Kolodziej, eds., *The Cold War as Cooperation: Superpower Cooperation in Regional Conflict Management* (London: Macmillan; Baltimore: Johns Hopkins, 1991). Substantial recent literature exists that examines aspects of Soviet involvement in Third World conflicts. Among these are: Roy Allison and Phil Williams, eds., *Superpower Competition and Crisis Prevention in the Third World* (Cambridge–New York: Cambridge University Press, 1990); Bertil Dunér, *The Bear, The Cubs and The Eagle: Soviet Bloc Interventionism in the Third World and the US Response* (Aldershot, UK–Brookfield, VT: Gower, 1987); Karen A. Feste, ed., *American and Soviet Intervention: Affects on World Stability* (New York–London: Crane Russak, 1990); Francis Fukuyama, *Gorbachev and the New Soviet Agenda in the Third World* (Santa Monica, CA: RAND Corporation, 1989); Galia Golan, *The Soviet Union and National Liberation Movements in the Third World* (Boston–London: Unwin Hyman, 1988); Jiri Valenta and Frank Cibulka, eds., *Gorbachev's New Thinking and Third World Conflicts* (New

Brunswick, NJ–London: Transaction Publishers, 1990); and Jeanette Voas, *Preventing Future Afghanistans: Reform in Soviet Policymaking on Military Intervention Abroad* (Alexandria, VA: Center for Naval Analyses, 1990).

3 See, for example, the comments of Foreign Minister Shevardnadze "Vystupleniia na plenume TsK KPSS," *Pravda*, 8 February 1990, p. 3. See, also, recent articles by Andrei Kortunov, Director of the Department of General Problems in Foreign Policy of the Institute for the Study of the USA and Canada. A. Kortunov, "What is meant by state interests in foreign policy," *Literaturnaia gazeta*, 11 July 1990, p. 14 (translated in the current *Digest of the Soviet Press*, vol. 42, no. 30, 1990, pp. 9–11) and A. Kortunov and A. Izyumov, "Clarifying our national interests," in *The Literary Gazette International*, vol. 1, no. 14 (October 1990), pp. 20–21.

4 Alexei Kosygin, "Direktivy XXIV S″ezdu KPSS po piatiletnemu planu razvitiia narodnogo khoziaistva SSR na 1971–1975 godu," *Pravda*, 7 April 1971, p. 6. For comprehensive discussions of the place of national liberation movements in Soviet Third World policy see S. Neil MacFarlane, *Superpower Rivalry and Third World Radicalism: The Idea of National Liberation* (Baltimore: The Johns Hopkins University Press, 1985); Golan, *The Soviet Union and National Liberation Movements in the Third World*; and Wayne P. Limberg, "Soviet military support for Third-World Marxist regimes," in Mark N. Katz, ed., *The USSR and Marxist Revolutions in the Third World* (Cambridge–New York: Cambridge University Press, 1990), pp. 51–118.

5 Mikhail S. Gorbachev, *Perestroika: New Thinking for Our Country and the World* (New York: Harper and Row, 1987), p. 19. See also the analysis of Abel Aganbegyan, Gorbachev's Chief Economic Advisor in 1986–87, in *The Economic Challenge of Perestroika* (Bloomington–London: Indiana University Press, 1988), pp. 1–3. Aganbegyan argued that growth actually ceased in the period. See also Kazimierz Ponanski, "Competition between Eastern Europe and developing countries in the Western market for manufactured goods," in *Joint Economic Committee, Congress of The United States, East European Economies: Slow Growth in the 1980s*, vol. 2, *Foreign Trade and International Finance*, ed. John P. Hardt and Richard F. Kaufman (Washington: US Government Printing Office, 1986), pp. 162–90.

6 Two well-known Soviet analysts have developed precisely this argument. See Alexei Izyumov and Andrei Kortunov, "The USSR in the changing world," *International Affairs*, no. 8 (1988), pp. 46–56.

7 Mikhail S. Gorbachev, "Politicheskii doklad Tsentral′nogo Komiteta KPSS XXVII S″ezdu Kommunisticheskoi Partii Sovetskogo Soiuza. Doklad General′nogo Sekretaria TsK KPSS Tovarishcha Gorbacheva M. S. 25 fevralia 1986 goda," *Kommunist*, no. 4 (1986), p. 29.

8 Dibb, *The Soviet Union: Incomplete Superpower.*

9 See Francis X. Cline, "Kremlin accuses banks in West of plot," *New York Times*, 13 February 1991, p. 13.

10 In the foreign policy area analysts such as Karen Brutents and Evgenii Primakov, and others, had questioned the assumptions of Soviet policy; in the domestic area the need for dramatic reform was noted by Abel Aganbegyan, Tatiana Zaslavskaia, and others. See, for example, Elizabeth K. Valkenier, *The Soviet Union and the Third World: An Economic Bind* (New

York: Praeger, 1983), p. 26; the article by Tatiana Zaslavskaia that was first published as "The Novosibirsk Report," *Survey*, vol. 28 (1984), pp. 88–108. See, also, the discussion of early calls for reform in Ed A. Hewett, *Reforming the Soviet Economy: Equality versus Efficiency* (Washington: The Brookings Institution, 1988), pp. 256–302.

11 Gorbachev, "Politicheskii doklad," pages 18–19, 36, and 41. For authoritative elaborations on new thinking see A.N. Iakovlev, "Dostizhenie kachestvenno novogo sostoianiia sovetskogo obshchestva i obshchestvennye nauki," *Vestnik Akademii Nauk SSSR*, no. 6 (1987), pp. 51–80; and Eduard Shevardnadze, "Report by Member of the Bureau of the CPSU Central Committee, Minister of Foreign Affairs of the USSR Eduard Shevardnadze at the Scientific and Practical Conference of the Ministry of Foreign Affairs," *International Affairs*, no. 10 (1988), pp. 3–34; A. Dobrynin, "Za bezìadernyi mir, navstrechu XXI Veku," *Kommunist*, no. 9 (1986), esp. pp. 22–25; E. Primakov, "Novaia filosofiia vneshnei politiki," *Pravda*, 10 July 1987, p. 4; and A. Bovin, "Novoe myshlenie – novaia politika," *Kommunist*, no. 9 (1988), pp. 115–25.

12 "Programma Kommunisticheskoi Partii Sovetskogo Soiuza," *Pravda*, 2 November 1961, p. 3; and "The Programme of the Communist Party of the Soviet Union. A new addition," *New Times*, no. 12 (1986), p. 43.

13 Rostislav Ul'ianovskii, "O natsional'noi i revol'iutsionnoi demokratii: puty evol'iutsii," *Narody Azii i Afriki*, no. 2 (1984), p. 16.

14 Gorbachev, *Perestroika*, pp. 173–74.

15 *Ibid.*, pp. 117, 187. Evgenii Primakov, a key foreign policy advisor to Gorbachev throughout the entire period since 1985, warned against viewing regional conflicts through a "prism of American–Soviet confrontation." Evgenii Primakov, "XXVII S″ ezd KPSS i issledovanie problem mirovoi ekonomiki i mezhdunarodnykh otnoshenii," *Mirovaia ekonomika i mezhdunarodnye otnoshenii* (hereafter *MEMO*), no. 5 (1986), p. 12.

16 See, for example, Francis Fukuyama, "Gorbachev and the Third World," *Foreign Affairs*, vol. 64, no. 4 (1986), pp. 715–31. The present author was also cautious in conclusions which he drew from the on-going debate. See Roger E. Kanet, "Reassessing Soviet doctrine: new priorities and perspectives," in Kolodziej and Kanet, eds., *The Limits of Soviet Power in the Developing World*, pp. 416–17.

17 See, for example, Viacheslav Dashichev, "Vostok-Zapad. Poisk novykh otnoshenii: o prioritetakh vneshnei politiki Sovetskogo Soiuza," *Literaturnaia Gazeta*, 18 May 1988, p. 14.

18 See, for example, Charles Wolf *et al.*, *The Costs of Soviet Empire* (Santa Monica, CA: The RAND Corporation, 1983), p. 19. See, also, Boris Ponomarev, "Real socialism and the liberated countries," *Slovo Lektora*, no. 3 (1984), translated in *Foreign Broadcast Information Service* (FBIS), *Soviet Union*, no. 3, 14 June 1984, pp. 2–6 (annex) and comments by then Politburo member Gaidar Aliev during a visit to Hanoi. See "Pravdnik narodov-pobratimov: miting Sovetskogo-V'etnamskogo druzhby," *Pravda*, 1 November 1983, p. 5.

19 For a discussion of this issue, see Marvin G. Weinbaum, "Superpower cooperation in Southwest Asia," in Kanet and Kolodziej, eds., *The Cold War as Cooperation*, pp. 310–40.

20 For details on recent Soviet policy in Southeast Asia see Sheldon Simon, "Superpower cooperation in Southeast Asia," in Kanet and Kolodziej, eds., *The Cold War as Cooperation*, pp. 341–68. See, also, Suzanne Crow, "Will the Moscow–Hanoi alliance survive aid and arms cutbacks?" *Report on the USSR*, vol. 2, no. 45 (1990), pp. 14–17.

21 See "Kubintsy ukhodiat iz Angoly," *Izvestiia*, 3 September 1990.

22 See Richard Weitz, "Moscow and its African allies," *Report on the USSR*, vol. 3, no. 6 (8 February 1991), pp. 8–11. See also Vladimir I. Dikhomirov, "The USSR and South Africa: an end to 'Total Onslaught'?" *Africa Report*, vol. 34, no. 4 (1989), pp. 58–61.

23 See, for example, Richard O'Regan, "Soviets fed-up with bickering, will quit arming Ethiopian war," *The Atlanta Journal and Constitution*, 5 March 1990, p. A-9; Jane Perlez, "Ethiopian government seen as fighting to survive," *The New York Times*, 17 April 1990, p. A-5.

24 See, W. Raymond Duncan, "Superpower cooperation in the Caribbean and Central America," in Kanet and Kolodziej, eds., *The Cold War as Cooperation*, pp. 245–46.

25 See, for example, Shevardnadze, "Vystupleniia na plenume TsK KPSS," p. 3.

26 For a discussion of changing perceptions of the USSR on regional conflicts see, among others, Andrei I. Kolosovskii, "Regional'nye konflikty i global'naia bezopasnost'," *MEMO*, no. 6 (1988) pp. 32–41; and Aleksandr K. Kislov, "Novoe politicheskoe myshlenie i regional'nye konflikty," *MEMO*, no. 8 (1988), pp. 39–47.

27 Elena Aref'eva, "Miloserdie ili vse zhe ideologiia?" *Izvestiia*, 24 July 1990, p. 1.

28 Andrei Kolosov, "Reappraisal of USSR Third World policy," *International Affairs*, no. 5 (1990), pp. 34–42, citation from p. 41.

29 Andrei Urnov, "The Third World and the USSR," *International Affairs*, no. 8 (1990), pp. 69–73. See also L.Z. Zevin and E.L. Simonov, "Pomoshch' i ekonomicheskoe sotrudnichestvo SSSR s razvivaiushchimisia stranami: uroki, problemy i perspektivy," *Narody Azii i Afriki*, no. 2 (1990), pp. 5–17. Zevin and Simonov see good prospects for the expansion of beneficial economic relations for the Soviet Union in trade with developing countries and argue that it would be foolish for the USSR to isolate itself from the long-term benefits possible from these relationships.

30 To be sure, there were those who criticized the Gorbachev leadership for moving too cautiously in reforming both domestic and foreign policy.

31 See the interview with Aleksandr Iakovlev in *Literaturnaia gazeta*, no. 1, 3 January 1990.

32 Eduard Shevardnadze, "V mire vse meniaetsia s golovokruzhitel'noi bystrotoi: interv'iu na bortu samoleta," *Izvestiia*, 19 February 1990, p. 5.

33 The following discussion benefits from Olga Alexandrova's "Konservative Opposition gegen das 'neue politische Denken,'" *Aktuelle Analysen*, no. 22/1990, 21 March 1990, Bundesinstitut für ostwissenschaftliche und internationale Studien.

34 See, for example, I. Usachev, "Obshechechelovecheskoe i klassovoe v mirovoi politike," *Kommunist*, no. 11 (1988), pp. 109–18.

35 Anatolii Saluzkii, in the discussion "Kakoi byt' Rosii?" *Sovetskaia kul'tura*, no. 8 (24 February 1990), p. 4.

36 Aleksandr Prokhanov, "Tragediia centralizma," *Literaturnaia rossiia*, no. 1 (5 January 1990), pp. 4–5.

37 "Press-konferentsiia E.A. Shevardnadze," *Pravda*, 27 March 1990, p. 5.

38 Alexei Izyumov and Andrei Kortunov, "The end of 'New Thinking'," *Newsweek*, 31 December 1990, p. 54.

39 "Shevardnadze resigns at 20 Dec. Congress session," Moscow Radio domestic service in Russian, 1200 GMT, 20 December 1990, translated in *FBIS-Sov*, 20 December 1990, pp. 11–12.

40 Shevardnadze, "Vystupleniia na plenume TsK KPSS," p. 3.

41 See, for example, Kortunov and Izyumov, "What is meant by state interests in foreign policy."

42 For a discussion of the fragmentation of Soviet foreign policy constituencies see Tamara J. Resler, "National assertiveness and foreign policy in the USSR," unpublished paper presented at the annual meetings of the International Studies Association, Vancouver, BC, 19–23 March 1991. See, also, Jan Arveds Trepans, "Baltic foreign policy in 1990," *Report on the USSR*, vol. 3, no. 2 (1991), pp. 15–18.

43 See Janus Bugajski, "*Perestroika* in the Third World," *The Fletcher Forum of World Affairs*, vol. 15, no. 1 (1991), pp. 93–110. Bugajski concludes "that the disintegration of communist regimes throughout the Third World cannot be considered either universal or inevitable" (p. 103). For similar conclusions see Marian Leighton, "Moscow's Third World empire," *Global Affairs*, vol. 5, no. 2 (1990), pp. 133–56, esp. pp. 152–53; and William E. Griffith, "Gorbachev's policies toward the Third World," in Mark N. Katz, ed., *The USSR and Marxist Revolutions in the Third World* (Cambridge, New York: Cambridge University Press, 1990), p. 142.

44 On the issue of continued Soviet support to established Marxist–Leninist regimes see S. Neil MacFarlane, "L'URSS et les régimes marxistes–léninistes au Tiers Monde, en Afrique Subsaharienne et en Amérique Latine," in *La Politique étrangère soviétique a l'aube des années 90*, ed. Claude Basset (Quebec: Centre Québecois de Relations Internationales, Collection-CHOIX, 1990), pp. 128–36.

7 Soviet new thinking on national liberation movements: continuity and change

Anuradha M. Chenoy

In the recent past the Soviet government has been critically reviewing its earlier world view. This rethinking of the theory and practice of foreign policy has included a radical overhaul of the theory of national liberation movements which has formed the framework of Soviet policies toward the Third World. These new formulations, however, retain some elements of continuity. In order to ascertain Soviet policies toward the Third World, it is necessary to understand both the changes and continuities in this new political thinking.

Debates and controversies about the national liberation movements have existed among Soviet analysts and official policy makers since the establishment of the Communist International in early 1919, the most famous being the Lenin–M.N. Roy debate concerning the possibility of an alliance between the national bourgeoisie and local communist parties. Though the process of debate was halted at the time of Stalin, even then Eugene Varga, the Soviet Hungarian economist who believed that capitalist encirclement had been weakened, argued against the official position on the relationship between the colonies and the metropole.[1]

From the 1960s onwards a growing debate occurred on the assessment of Third World societies. Some Soviet scholars questioned aspects of the models being evolved and initiated debates on the subject,[2] but the official Soviet position remained dominant. Scholars thus have noted that "the basic outlines of Soviet doctrine on the Third World have remained quite stable since the death of Stalin."[3]

In the early 1980s, the Soviets used theories of national liberation with some degree of flexibility to explain varying situations. The dominant trend favored the continuation of an alliance with national liberation movements and continued to use old theoretical models with slight modifications. But, as a prominent scholar of the subject has pointed out, one could "discern one relatively consistent theory of an orthodox or conservative nature and several other fragmented theories of a more sophisticated and realistic nature."[4]

Under the Gorbachev regime opinions about the Third World have increased in complexity, and divergences in opinion have increased. The debate on these issues is more open than ever before, although there is a dominant trend in Soviet academic thinking which coincides with official statements. National liberation movements continue to be related to the overall Soviet world view, and the Third World remains an important element of Soviet strategic and social activity. But the new approach appears to be an important epistemological break with the past in several important respects.

Characterizing historical periods

A traditional task established by Lenin and continued by every Soviet leader at the beginning, as well as at other crucial points, of his regime has been to define the nature of imperialism, to relate it to the nature and role of the socialist world, and thereby to describe the characteristic features of his period. It is in this context that Soviet regimes have evaluated the position of the colonized and less developed countries. Overall Soviet strategies and foreign policies were shaped by these assessments of the characteristic features of each historical period and then linked to the dynamics of the national liberation movements and consequently to the perceived tasks of Soviet foreign policy.

In keeping with this tradition, Mikhail Gorbachev criticized the aggressive nature of imperialism in his speech at the 27th Party Congress in February 1986. He noted the contradictions between competing capitalist states and the possibility of the emergence of new power centers. Several things, however, were different in Gorbachev's approach to imperialism and capitalism. One was the lack of impending "doom" or "deepening crises" predicted for the capitalist system, which earlier Soviet leaders had prophesied. On the contrary, Gorbachev stated that the general crisis of capitalism not only did not "rule out possible growth of the economy and the emergence of new scientific and technological trends," but in fact allowed for the sustenance of specific economic, military, and political positions, although at the cost of various social conditions.[5] Gorbachev also dropped the formulation "third stage of the general crisis of capitalism" which had been developed in the Brezhnev period. He focused on new contradictions facing the contemporary world, such as those affecting the environment and natural systems and world cultures. These, he argued, necessitate common solutions and point to the obvious interdependence of the world.

Furthermore, in the 27th CPSU documents, the definition of peaceful coexistence between states with different social systems no longer was linked with specific forms of class struggle. Thus, class confrontation was no longer considered a primary objective in international affairs. This definition was a significant break from the past. Stalin characterized the dominant trend in his epoch of world development as being one of "irreconcilable antagonism" with the West. Khrushchev and later Brezhnev classified their period as one of competition and struggle against imperialism during the transition from capitalism to socialism.[6] Gorbachev, except for remarking that the "post-World War II phase" was over, has not characterized the current period.

The Soviet belief in the struggle against imperialism from the 1960s onwards had been accompanied by appeals for a united front against imperialism within the framework of peaceful coexistence. This broad front was to include the international socialist system, working-class movements, and forces of national liberation. Gorbachev has dropped this formulation and, while retaining a relatively mild, sophisticated, and generalized critique of imperialism, the focus of his new thinking has shifted to the development of the Third World as the responsibility of all mankind. In this new view the great powers and the Third World must engage in a common effort to achieve global economic development.

Further theoretical shifts for understanding the Third World were initiated after the 27th CPSU Congress. It became clear, as a number of scholars noted, "that the Third World is no longer given the central position in overall Soviet foreign policy that it received under Brezhnev."[7] The economic and political costs of alliance with unstable Third World regimes had become too great to justify Soviet support.

The revised edition of the party program, which emerged after the debate in the 27th Party Congress, repeated some aspects of the traditional understanding of imperialism and capitalism in that it linked the internal contradictions of these systems to their eventual decline. The new program, however, did not harp on class struggle in international relations.[8] This document evidently appeared as the compromise position accepted after conservative elements criticized the new formulations by the Gorbachev group. Bolder changes in Soviet new thinking on the Third World started appearing only after 1987, most likely following the Soviet–US Summit and INF Treaty of 1987. It is from this juncture that new thinking in foreign policy appeared to reach a point of no return. The main trends in the Soviet conceptualization of national liberation movements and their ideas on the Third World follow this new line, although the tug of war between positions is by no means over.

Even though debates on the nature of capitalism and imperialism existed in the early 1980s and scholars pleaded for realistic appraisals, the official position remained a reiteration of earlier stances. Thus Andrei Gromyko stated that the USSR would not allow the United States to achieve dominance. Soviet scholars worked within this framework until the Gorbachev era. His position that "continuity in foreign policy has nothing in common with a simple repetition of what has been done, especially in tackling problems that have piled up,"[9] set the stage for the necessary rethinking in Soviet praxis on East–West relations.

Rethinking ideology

New thinking is based on a reassessment of the vitality of capitalism. As Soviet scholars during the Gorbachev era have pointed out, the "capitalist system has managed to adapt to new circumstances. It has survived despite the emergence of the socialist community and has withstood the collapse of the colonial system."[10] This new realization of the viability and adaptability of capitalism has been accompanied by the acceptance of the obsolescence of the existing Soviet model of socialism.[11]

In acknowledging the development of capitalism, separating the military-industrial complex from political forces, and recognizing the pluralistic nature of other societies, new thinking has led to a debate among Soviet analysts over ideology. The need to separate political positions from "ideological intolerance" was introduced by Gorbachev into new thinking almost immediately after the Geneva Summit and INF Treaty. His statements that "ideological differences should not be transferred to the spheres of interstate relations" and that foreign policy should not be subordinated to ideology were extended to the theoretical formulation for the need for "deideologization."[12] Georgii Shakhnazarov and other theorists have pleaded for the deideologization of state-to-state relations, including those between the Soviet Union and the Third World.

A number of analysts have put forward the view that in the past the Soviet analysis of the Third World had been colored by ideological spectacles, which needed to be discarded in order to restore a realistic picture of events in the developing world. These scholars argued that this approach had resulted in myopic assessments of a variety of alternate world views and developments and that the previous identification of national interest with "anti-imperialism" had led to a confrontational approach, which in turn had led to a massive arms buildup by Third World states. Although some Soviet scholars have been critical of the manner in which the role of ideology is being downplayed,[13] official documents have adopted a deideologized approach, as is evident from most official documents currently coming out from the Soviet Union.

Debate on neo-colonialism

National liberation movements traditionally were identified as anti-colonial movements and later as movements of the ex-colonies likely to develop along independent paths. Soviet strategists perceived such movements as important allies of the socialist world at a time when the socialist bloc faced a Western anti-communist alliance. Once these movements had completed the task of overthrowing colonialism, the main task of these states was perceived as one of averting "the maneuvers of neo-colonialism."[14] Thus, during the debates of the 1960s and 1970s, Soviet analysts agreed that possibilities existed for the national liberation movements to move toward "pro-socialist paths of development."[15] While a plurality of interpretations existed among Soviet scholars on their assessment of Third World societies at the micro-level, the macro or grand theory continued to lay emphasis on neo-colonialism as a crucial factor in Third World problems.

With glasnost in Soviet scholarship, various views on the phenomenon of neo-colonialism and its relationship to the Third World have now been voiced. Most Soviet scholars agree that except in a limited number of areas such as Palestine and South Africa, the wave of national liberation movements is over. Some analysts believe that, even if contradictions between developing countries and Western imperialist powers exist, the developing countries are not interested in defeating imperialism, but merely in fighting for a place within the "world capitalist family."[16] This argument strengthens the new dominant Soviet view of the interdependent nature of the world system.

A debate in Soviet journals on the question of the capitalist system's dependence on neo-colonialism reveals that some analysts believe that barely any traces of colonialism exist in the period after the 1980s and that therefore the concept of neo-colonialism is outdated.[17] In their view, neo-colonialism is seen as having existed only during the period when the former colonial countries were in a transitional stage of breaking away from their colonial links. Other scholars differ with this outright rejection of neo-colonialism. Vadim Medvedev, for instance, argues that while capitalism has survived and stabilized, "it has sought compensation in various forms of neo-colonialism and latterly technological exploitation of the developing countries. Capitalism has found sufficient resources to widen its scientific and technological revolution and has used economic growth to blunt class struggle and increased its scope for social maneuvering."[18]

A related debate has centered around the theory of non-equivalent exchange, which until recently was a popular concept in Soviet thinking on the relationship between the West and the developing countries. Popov and Volkov, for instance, reject the theory of non-equivalent exchange and believe that the Soviets should draw lessons from the West, especially on methods of trade.[19] Other scholars, such as Karen Brutents, continue to hold more traditional views. He contends that the position of the developing countries in the international system has changed little because of their indebtedness to imperialist states and the pressure exercised on them by transnational corporations and private capital.[20] Writers such as R. Avakov, Georgii Kim, etc., take similar positions. Nidori Simoniia, well known for his works on the nature of capitalist development in the Third World, has intervened in this debate, arguing that militarism and exploitation of people are not necessary elements of developed capitalism. Current conditions have shown that subjugation and exploitation of other peoples proves unprofitable and dangerous. Thus, it is important to separate the military-industrial complex from the national economy and society. These forces, Simoniia believes, limit imperialism from being a monopoly or a dominant trend. Neo-colonialism, he argues, should be viewed in this light.[21] Although these ideas have been criticized by several Third World analysts who feel that Soviet scholars are condoning neo-colonialism, the dominant thrust in current Soviet scholarship is one of acknowledging neo-colonialism as a limited factor in international relations.

Developmental models

Lenin advocated support for national movements in the colonies if they were led by the national bourgeoisie. Although Stalin dropped this approach, Khrushchev adopted Lenin's thinking on this issue.[22] This led to an alliance between the Soviet Union and some countries of the Third World in the 1950s and 1960s.

The Third World, beset with problems of survival, development, and security, scorched by colonial memories, and frustrated by the increasing gap between West and East, was looking for models of development and strategies for growth. On the international plane, the American intervention in Southeast Asia, the Western alliance against Egypt, the liberation wars in North Africa, growing instability in Latin America, and other such issues sharpened the polarization of the world into blocs. The instability of the Third World regimes, the popularization of anti-imperialist slogans, and the Soviet Union's need for international alliances led to the growing Soviet association with Third World countries, particularly those in the non-aligned movement. The growing relationship between the Soviet Union and the Third World was especially evident in the United Nations and other international forums, where they acted as an effective lobbying group.

During this period Soviet analysts conceptualized models of development for ex-colonial nations. Intended essentially as a heuristic device, the model of the "non-capitalist path" soon was integrated into dominant trends of Soviet thinking on the Third World.[23] The non-capitalist path envisaged the transition from feudal and precapitalist social formations into non-capitalist systems as a prelude to socialist type systems.[24] The leading characteristics of a "progressive" system in the national democratic states were, for instance, a focus on a larger state economic sector, land reforms, ideological affinity with the socialist bloc, leadership by "revolutionary democrats," which included alliances with the local communist party, and a progressive anti-imperialist foreign policy.

While a few scholars were on occasion critical of this concept,[25] most analysts used it in some form or another. Non-capitalist development often was used synonymously with the concept of "socialist orientation" which envisaged a Soviet-type development model. The cases cited as examples for this model were Soviet Central Asia, Mongolia, Yemen, Ethiopia, and Burma. Soviet analysts gave this laudatory label sometimes to pro-Soviet regimes without careful study of the complexities of the societies thus labeled. Scholars questioned this model in the 1960s and 1970s, but this dominant ideological approach served to legitimate official policy, which sought to ensure that the so-called socialist-oriented states remained in the pro-Soviet, anti-imperialist camp. Soviet military assistance, economic support, aid, and trade policies coincided with the approaches laid down in the model (e.g. support to the state sector, and greater support to non-capitalist regimes). A number of Third World regimes, through the 1960s and 1970s thus were able to rely on Soviet assistance.[26] Moreover, Soviet assistance was used by the Third World countries to improve their negotiating positions *vis-à-vis* the United States and other Western countries.

The official patronage that theorists of the socialist orientation and non-capitalist path received, despite mounting criticism by some Soviet analysts, ensured the popularity of this theoretical trend until the early 1980s. During the Andropov interregnum this concept was used much less frequently[27] and doubts about the utility of the model increasingly were raised, although a number of analysts continued to use the concept.

The 1986 revised program of the CPSU still contained the formulation on socialist orientation. It continued to point to the possibility of the rejection of capitalism by ruling revolutionary democratic parties if they opposed feudal reaction internally and imperialist monopolies externally. The theoretical shift in the 27th CPSU Conference signaled the decline of such models. Because of the reinterpretation of the phenomenon of neo-colonialism under Gorbachev, analysts such as R.M. Avakov, Nidori A. Simoniia, V.L. Shenis, V.G. Khoros, and Georgii Mirskii, among others, are critical of this model, although a few scholars such as Gleb B. Starushenko, Rostidav A. Ul'anovskii, and Vladimir G. Solodovnikov, consider this model viable if some changes are incorporated.[28]

Scholars opposed to the concept of socialist orientation reject it as an illusion which tried to universalize the transition to socialism in a number of countries in an artificial manner. They contend that this model led to myopic perceptions of Third World states, political errors in bilateral relations and unjustified expenditures. Instances such as that of Egypt, which under Sadat turned against the USSR despite the latter's economic and military assistance, and Somalia, are cited in support of this contention. These theorists argue that the Soviets were led into supporting dictatorial regimes under the guise of "revolutionary democratic" leaders, just because they mouthed socialist slogans. These regimes while propagating anti-imperialism fanned local, ethnic, and communal tensions.[29] The trend which rejects these models of development is currently the dominant one. This trend is reflected in official documents which contain little or no reference to the non-capitalist path or to socialist orientation. The realism introduced by new thinking has led to the decline of this type of conceptualization and changed the theoretical discourse on national liberation movements.

Wars of liberation to regional conflicts

The Soviets traditionally have backed the right of national liberation movements to wage violent struggles against imperialism. It is true that the Soviet position diverged from that of the Chinese after the 1960s on the necessity of armed conflict, because the Soviets stressed the possibility of a non-violent path to socialism in the context of peaceful coexistence. Yet the Soviets were involved in almost all conflicts in the Third World, especially where they felt imperialistic or pro-imperialistic forces were involved. Soviet assistance came in the form of military, economic, or political support.[30] Thus, the Third World was the stage for military antagonism and rivalry between the great powers. (This is not to say that Third World states did not have their own political stakes or ideological preferences.)

The Soviets based their classification of national liberation wars on Lenin's formulations. Thus, a liberation war was a "just war" if the context of the war was anti-imperialist. However, after most colonies achieved independence the Soviets continued to classify several regional wars in the Third World as wars provoked by "imperialist and domestic reactionaries." Many wars were categorized on the basis of the pro-Soviet or anti-imperialist nature of the regimes involved.

Currently, in the context of new thinking, the key role ascribed to imperialism in the earlier analysis of the wars in the Third World has been toned down and the very relevance of "just" and "unjust" has been questioned. It now is argued that regional wars should be analyzed independently of the concept of "just" wars.[31] Some Soviet scholars have attempted to classify regional conflicts within conventional categories: (a) frontier and territorial claims, e.g. territorial disputes between Morocco and Mauritania in the 1960–69 period, conflicts in the Horn of Africa, and the dispute between Libya and Chad; (b) conflicts based on political, ideological, and communal motives, e.g. those between Iran and Iraq, and between India and Pakistan; (c) conflicts due to economic, ethnic and separatist concerns, e.g. Ethiopia and Eritrea; (d) a mix of these issues, along with problems due to colonial legacies, territorial disputes, historical issues, and bilateral problems.[32]

Such deideologization has paved the way for a new view of great power involvement in Third World conflict, particularly those conflicts that have the potential to escalate into confrontations involving great powers.

Soviet scholars have stressed that regional conflicts should not be viewed through the prism of the Soviet–American rivalry. In fact, some analysts believe that, given the complexity of these conflicts, resolution should be carried out by the parties directly involved, and great power assistance should be restricted to "localizing" these conflicts or providing the atmosphere for political solutions. In fact, some scholars have advocated that Soviet assistance in facilitating resolution of regional conflict even by political efforts be viewed cautiously as this might involve economic obligations. Thus, Soviet peace efforts currently are characterized as involving a "balance of interests" on all sides.[33]

The Soviet experience in regional conflicts – such as in Southeast Asia and the Middle East, but especially in Afghanistan – has influenced markedly recent Soviet thinking on the issue of regional wars. Soviet withdrawal from Afghanistan, after some 100,000 Soviet troops were unable to provide long-term stability to a radical regime, was seen as a confirmation of the argument that revolution cannot be exported and that war should not be an extension of politics. The material and human costs involved and the damage to the Soviet reputation and international prestige were also important influences on Soviet thinking. The Geneva settlement of the conflict in Afghanistan, where the United States and Soviet Union stand as guarantors, has been cited repeatedly as an important precedent for conflict resolution.

Similarly, the Soviet position of restraint in the resolution of the Angolan conflict and the independence issue in Namibia highlights the flexibility of their current methods of conflict resolution. In this case, the Soviets could have chosen to capitalize on their long years of support to the Namibian independence struggle. They could have attempted to polarize the frontline states and offer modest military support. But Soviet policy makers chose the option of not offering socialist models and paths of development. They maintained a studied neutrality even in the face of criticism from their old allies in the national liberation movements. Anatolii Adamashin, in fact, called the Namibian resolution a breakthrough as significant as the INF Treaty and a method of international cooperation which could be used as an example in other regional conflicts.[34]

The Soviet formula of national reconciliation which envisages the strategy for creating the widest possible political alliance for the resolution of local or regional conflicts differs from earlier united front tactics, mainly because it is based on the deideologization approach. Negotiations and alliance with all groups, including anti-communist forces, form the basis for this strategy.[35]

On the international plane the Soviets have advocated joint Soviet–US efforts to alleviate regional conflicts. Some analysts have put forward the view that the West has a stake in political stability in the Third World and is not interested in continuing conflict situations.[36] Thus, some moves were made even to bring together the opposing Pakistani and Indian sides, currently in the stage of a low-intensity conflict over Kashmir, in negotiations with US–Soviet representatives, a move not accepted by India.

The acceptance of the general assessment that in the coming decades most conflicts are likely to occur in Third World countries has led the Soviets to reiterate that conflict resolution should be carried out by the United Nations or through regional organizations and commissions. The logic of this argument is based not only on the current emphasis on international peace but also on a consideration of the costs of conflict and its aftermath. At a time of their own great resource crunch, the Soviets would like to keep their international commitments to a minimum.

The Soviets responded to the recent Gulf crisis by condemning Iraq's aggression against Kuwait and by supporting the US call for a United Nations arms embargo, and eventual military operation. Foreign Minister Eduard Shevardnadze, in a speech to Egypt's National Democratic Party in February 1988, put forward a formula for resolving the regional crisis in the Gulf. He advocated a dialogue through intermediaries such as the United Nations, withdrawal of forces by the countries involved, and guarantees by the superpowers and the United Nations.[37] This formula has been the basis of Soviet involvement, which has emphasized the necessity of negotiations and put forward the possibility of an Arab solution as an alternative to unilateral military intervention by a superpower.

A number of Soviet scholars have considered Soviet policy toward Iraq as a departure from earlier times, since in the past Soviet policy makers would have endorsed Iraq's action as an overthrow of a "reactionary monarchist regime in Kuwait." These analysts concede that "this turn in Soviet attitude may be interpreted in the Arab world as a betrayal of an old friendship."[38] However, most commentators agree that the Soviet position on the Gulf crisis was in keeping with their national interests and present realities. The September 1990 Helsinki summit was thus a reiteration of the Soviet–US agreement on regional crises and an endorsement of the Soviet role in the multilateral effort required in resolution of regional conflicts. This policy of resolving regional conflicts through compromise is especially important for the Soviets because it is a method of easing confrontation with the West, which is currently the main emphasis in their foreign policy.

Questioning economic assistance

Soviet policy makers and analysts have been raising questions about the economic aspects of their support for national liberation movements. They have discussed problems regarding trade policies with the Third World and sought methods of improving trade relations. In recent debates in the Congress of People's Deputies on the Soviet economic crisis, some speakers advocated cuts in Soviet aid to the Third World as part of the solution. The question of debts owed by developing countries and aid offered by the Soviet Union have been raised repeatedly.[39]

Statistics show that Soviet aid figures always have been less than 1 percent of their GNP. The amount of assistance planned for the Third World states for 1990 was 1.6 billion rubles. The total debt, including that for unpaid military supplies, owed by developing countries in 1989 amounted to 42.039 billion rubles of which 61.9 million rubles were written off and 7.812 billion rubles deferred.[40] Some social scientists raised the question of Third World debt during the Brezhnev period and appealed for measuring the costs and benefits of Soviet assistance.[41] However, the question is posed currently to show that Third World debt is a burden on the Soviet economy. Some analysts also consider this debt to be a consequence of earlier political and economic miscalculations. Soviet economic assistance also is criticized as supportive of regimes resisting democratization and restructuring.[42] Thus, a plea is being made that friendship with inbuilt losses give way to commercially viable credit and assistance policies.

Conclusion

As the foregoing analysis has shown, the new political thinking and consequent changes in Soviet foreign policy are clearly a major departure from earlier practice. In many significant ways these changes are more profound and far-reaching than those initiated during the Khrushchev years, particularly after the 20th Congress of the CPSU. While major components of new thinking clearly are based on preexisting trends and opinions in the Soviet foreign policy establishment, academia, the CPSU and fraternal parties, the overall package appears to be a major innovation in Soviet thinking and policy. It is significant that there is little use of the earlier mandatory phrase, Marxism–Leninism, these days.

Despite, and indeed partially because of, the very favorable response by the West to the new thinking and the new policy initiatives, there is considerable disquiet about the new Soviet policy among individuals in the Third World. The current Soviet stress on the integral world, universal human values, and deideologization – the key concepts that underpin new thinking – is viewed with some apprehension, if not suspicion, by many Third World leaders, including those of Cuba and Vietnam. It is felt that in its determined quest for peace and the deescalation of tensions, the Soviet leadership is tending to compromise on issues vital to the future of Third World states. Even the emphasis on a "common European home" is taken as evidence of a Eurocentrism in Soviet new thinking, where security and economic interests in Europe have overridden the earlier commitment to the national liberation movements in the East and South.

Events, however, do not bear out the above criticism. The decline of cold war tensions consequent on the new Soviet initiatives has led to progress in the settlement of several long-standing conflicts in the Third World, in Afghanistan, Nicaragua, Angola, and Namibia – and negotiations toward settlement in Cambodia and Southeast Asia. The negotiated settlements have involved compromise from all powers concerned but also have enabled the best possible deal for the Third World, given the present balance of forces.

It is clear that there has been a paradigmatic shift in the Soviet theory of national liberation. The theoretical quest for more or less uniformly applicable development models such as the "non-capitalist path" or "socialist-orientation," virtually has been abandoned. The focus is now on mutually beneficial bilateral relations.

In conclusion, it may be argued that at the root of these unprecedented and paradigmatic shifts there is a changed assessment of the developed capitalist countries on the one hand and the socialist or socialist-oriented countries on the other. Soviet theorists have recognized that developed capitalism is not "moribund" but indeed has stabilized and is expanding. It is the so-called socialist bloc which is in crisis, and their economies are admitted to be stagnant and socially inefficient. In face of this stark reality old theoretical precepts had to be modified radically, if not jettisoned, in order to relate to existing realities. The terms of discourse had to be, and have been, changed and will change further. This is evidently what the Soviet new thinking is all about.

Notes

1 Evgenii Varga, *Izmeniia v ekonomike kapitalizma posle vtoroi mirovoi voini* (Moscow, 1946), p. 219; also in the debate in *Voprosy ekonomiki*, no. 8 (1949), pp. 65–110.

2 A number of scholars have shown the plurality of trends among Soviet scholars since the 1960s. Robert B. Remnek, *Soviet Policy Towards India* (New Delhi: Oxford and IBH Co., 1975); Elizabeth K. Valkenier, *The Soviet Union and the Third World: An Economic Bind* (New York: Praeger, 1983); Anuradha M. Chenoy, "Soviet theorists on national liberation: with special reference to Soviet attitudes in the United Nations, 1945–65," unpublished Ph.D. thesis, Jawaharlal Nehru University, New Delhi, 1987.

3 S. Neil MacFarlane, *Superpowers' Rivalry and Third World Radicalism: The Idea of National Liberation* (London: Croom Helm, 1985), p. 185.

4 Galia Golan, *The Soviet Union and National Liberation Movements in the Third World* (London: Allen and Unwin, 1988), p. 253.

5 Mikhail S. Gorbachev, "Political Report of the CPSU Central Committee to the 27th Congress of the CPSU," February 1986, *Soviet Review* (March 1986), p. 17.

6 "Declaration of the Communist and Workers Parties of Socialist Countries," Moscow, 14–16 November 1957, in *Basic Documents of the Moscow Meetings of Communist and Workers Parties, 1957–1960–1969* (New Delhi: CPI Publications, 1972), p. 1.

7 Roger E. Kanet, "The Soviet Union and the Third World from Khrushchev to Gorbachev: the place of the Third World in evolving Soviet global

strategy," in Roger E. Kanet, ed., *The Soviet Union, Eastern Europe and the Third World* (Cambridge: Cambridge University Press, 1987), p. 14.

8 *The Programme of the Communist Party of the Soviet Union, a New Edition* (Moscow: Novosti, 1986), pp. 24–25.

9 Andrei Gromyko, interview, *International Affairs*, no. 2 (1985), p. 13; Gorbachev, "Political Report," p. 71.

10 Vadim Medvedev, "Velikii Oktiabr': Sovremennii mir," *Kommunist*, no. 2 (1988), p. 6.

11 Abel Aganbegyan, *The Challenge: The Economics of Perestroika* (London: Hutchinson, 1988).

12 Mikhail S. Gorbachev, *Perestroika: New Thinking for our Country and the World* (London: Collins, 1987), p. 147; also, Georgii Shakhnazarov, in *Kommunist*, Supplement, no. 5 (1989), p. 4.

13 "Foreign policy: lessons of the past," *International Affairs*, no. 6 (1989), p. 83; D. Yevstafiev, "Arms in the Third World," *New Times*, no. 34 (1990), p. 13; and "Openness in politics," *International Affairs*, no. 6 (1989), pp. 123–24.

14 Vasilii Vakhrushev, *Neo-colonialism: Methods and Maneuvers* (Moscow: Progress, 1975); see also L.L. Klochkovsky, *Economic Neocolonialism* (Moscow: Progress, 1975); and Peter Ivanovich Polshikov, *Capital Accumulation and Economic Growth in Developing Africa* (Moscow: Progress, 1981).

15 Soviet journals of the 1960s and 1970s published various articles on this issue. See, for instance, Karen N. Brutents, "Certain peculiarities of the national-liberation movement," *Voprosy filosofii*, no. 6 (1965), pp. 26–37; translated in *JPRS*, no. 31, p. 351; also, Nadori Simoniia, in *Kommunist*, no. 9 (1965), pp. 121–23.

16 Georgii Mirskii, "The USSR and the Third World," *International Affairs*, no. 12 (1988), p. 144.

17 Nikolai Volkov, and Vladimir Popov, "Has an era of neocolonialism materialized?" *International Affairs*, no. 11 (1988), p. 107.

18 Medvedev, "Velikii Oktiabr'," p. 6.

19 Volkov and Popov, "Has an era of neocolonialism materialized?"

20 Karen Brutents, "Osvobodivshiesia strany i antiimperialisticheskaia bor'ba," *Pravda*, 10 January 1986; R. Avakov, Georgii Kim, *et al.*, *New Thinking for a Secure World* (New Delhi: Allied Publishers, 1988), p. 35.

21 Nadori Simoniia, in a round table conference, *Narody Azii i Afriki*, no. 5 (1988), and *Pravda*, 2 January 1989.

22 Nikita Khrushchev, *Report of the Central Committee of the CPSU to the 20th Congress* (Moscow, 1956), pp. 26–29. "Statement of the Meeting of Representatives of the Communist and Workers' Parties," *Basic Documents of the Moscow Meetings* (Moscow: 1960), pp. 44–46.

23 Kim Tsagolov, "USSR and the Third World," *International Affairs*, no. 12 (1988), p. 145; also, S.W. Edginton, "The state of socialist orientation: a Soviet model for political development," *Soviet Union*, vol. 8, pt. 2 (1981), p. 250.

24 Georgii Kim and A. Kaufman, "Non-capitalist development: achievement and difficulties," *International Affairs*, no. 2 (1967), pp. 70–76; Rostislav A.

Ul'anovskii, "Osvoboditel'naia bor'ba narodov Afriki," *Kommunist*, no. 11 (1969), pp. 3–7; and Viktor Solodovnikov and K. Bogoslovskii, *Non-Capitalist Development: A Historical Outline* (Moscow: Progress, 1975), p. 4.

25 V. Ostrovitianov, "The working class and the national liberation revolution," in *National Liberation Movements: Vital Problems* (Moscow: Novosti, 1965), pp. 110–11; also, Evgenii Varga, "Ob ekonomiki poslevoennogo kapitalizma," *Kommunist*, no. 4 (1956), pp. 12–32.

26 *International Affairs* (editorial), no. 6 (1956), p. 63; and Vassil Vassilev, *Policy in the Soviet Bloc on Aid to Developing Countries* (Paris: OECD, 1969), pp. 4–15.

27 See David E. Albright, "The USSR and the Third World in the 1980s," *Problems of Communism* (March–June, 1989), p. 57.

28 Aleksei Kiva, "Sotsialisticheskaia orientatsiia: teoreticheskii potentsial; kontseptsii i prakticheskie realii," *Mirovaia ekonomika i mezhdunarodnye otnosheniia*, no. 11 (1988), p. 64.

29 Andrei Kozyrev and A. Shumikhin, "East and West in the Third World," *International Affairs*, no. 3 (1989), p. 6; Elena Arefeva, *Izvestiia*, 10 July 1989; Georgii Kim, *Narody Azii i Afriki*, no. 5 (1988), pp. 4–5. Kim specifies that the friendly relations of some Third World countries with the USSR had a big influence on labeling them as socialist-oriented, though he still considers socialist orientation as an "objective reality."

30 Resolution, 17 June 1969, *Conference of Communist and Workers' Parties* (Moscow), June 1969; *Marxism's New Horizons: Documents of the 22nd CPSU Congress* (New Delhi: Bookman, 1962), pp. 121–22; *Two Different Lines on the Question of War and Peace* (Calcutta: Editorial Department, Red Flag and People's Daily, Vanguard Publishers, 1963), p. 20; and Mikhail A. Suslov, "The struggle of the CPSU for the unity of the world communist movement," *Information Bulletin of Peace and Socialism*, of Prague, nos. 8–9 (1964), p. 304.

31 Andrei Kokoshin, "Alexander Svechin: on war and politics," *International Affairs*, no. 11 (1988), p. 126; also, Viktor Kremeniuk, "USSR and the Third World," *International Affairs*, no. 12 (1988), p. 137.

32 Vladimir V. Benevolenskii, "Problems of cooperation and unity in nonaligned movements," *Soviet Oriental Studies Annual 1986* (Moscow, 1986), pp. 232–34; also, Yurii Galin, *et al. Regional Conflicts: Causes and Effects* (New Delhi: Allied, 1987), p. 3.

33 Evgenii Primakov, "Novaia filosofiia vneshnei politiki," *Pravda*, 10 July 1988.

34 Anatolii Adamashin, Deputy USSR Minister for Foreign Affairs, *New Times*, no. 52 (1989), p. 34. Some analysts were convinced that Soviet policy makers were "wary of any political settlement in Namibia and continue to encourage the armed struggle there." Kurt L. Campbell, "Southern Africa in Soviet foreign policy," *Adelphi Papers*, Winter (1987–88), p. 25.

35 Gorbachev's emphasis on the necessity of building new relations with groups and parties of "different ideological orientations" gave much impetus to this policy. Mikhail S. Gorbachev, *Report at the 19th All-Union CPSU Conference* (Moscow: 28 June 1988).

36 Kozyrev and Shumikhin, "East and West in the Third World," p. 9.

37 TASS, 23 February 1988.

38 Leonid Mlechin, "The friends we did not choose," *New Times*, no. 34 (1990), p. 6; also, Andrei Okitskii, "The Arab world: a dynamite keg," *Moscow News*, no. 33, 26 August 1990; and Aleksandr Belonogov, Deputy Foreign Minister of the USSR, interview, *New Times*, no. 33 (1990), p. 5. The Gulf crisis led to rethinking on the concept of military cooperation with the Middle East. The Soviet Union recently established diplomatic ties with Saudi Arabia.

39 *Izvestiia*, 10 July 1989; *Izvestiia*, 1 March 1990; and *Soviet Land*, no. 4 (1990), p. 10.

40 USSR government reply to a question raised in Soviet Parliament.

41 See, Valkenier, *The Soviet Union and the Third World*, p. 148.

42 See, Elena Arefeva, senior researcher, Institute of World Economy and International Relations, interview, *Izvestiia*, 10 July 1989; and *Izvestiia*, 1 March 1990. Other analysts have questioned Soviet aid to Cuba and other developing countries. See, for example, Alexander Makhov, "The other Cuba," *Moscow News*, no. 38 (30 September 1990). See, also, the comments of Elena Gorovaia who argues: "The billions sent to Cuba and other Third World countries are not the USSR's only or its most hopeless losses. But why justify less losses with great ones?" Elena Gorovaia, "The twilight of ideology," *Moscow News*, no. 36 (16 September 1990).

Part IV

The Soviet Union and the developing world: regional and country case studies

8 Soviet policy in Central America during the Gorbachev period

Jan S. Adams

Western observers tend to give major credit for positive developments in Central America, such as the democratic transfer of power in Nicaragua in 1990, to regional factors – the role of the Contras, US aid, and various Central American peace plans. A factor seldom mentioned, but one whose importance scarcely can be over-emphasized, is the remarkable turnabout in Soviet foreign policy under the regime of Mikhail Gorbachev.

The initial source of change in Soviet policy – Gorbachev's new political thinking – contains three broad prescriptions for superpower behavior toward regional conflicts. First, this chapter identifies these guidelines, briefly surveys their restatement in operational terms by Soviet "scholar-explicators," and uses Central America as a case study illustrating their impact on a specific region of the world. To present a balanced view of today's Soviet–Central American policy, the continuing effect of some enduring components of theory and practice also are explored – reflections of great power conflicts of interest and continuing echoes of Marxism–Leninism that run counter to the new directions.

Second, it analyzes how glasnost and perestroika continue to change the *context* of foreign policy making in the Soviet Union in ways that are affecting Soviet relations in Central America and elsewhere. Three major factors are examined: the greater freedom of "secular investigation" enjoyed by foreign-policy experts and other social scientists who now provide input to policy makers, the greater number and growing influence of scholars who have begun to occupy policy-making roles in the new government, and the reshaping of the policy-making machinery, which enables USSR legislative bodies to discuss foreign policy issues and influence decisions.

It should be noted that the impact of the research of the "secular-investigators" discussed in this section goes beyond the deductive work of the "scholar-explicators" engaged in drawing out the policy implica-

The author would like to express appreciation for the support of the Mershon Center, Ohio State University, in the preparation of this chapter.

tions of Gorbachev's broad premises. While much of the explicators' policy advice follows quite logically from Gorbachev's broad premises, increased freedom in investigative methods opens inductive avenues of thought which are not so predictable. As one secular-investigator put it, the social scientist's new methodology is no longer "a pounding of accepted formulas in a scholastic mortar."[1] Soviet analysts now apply the Socratic method of investigation to their respective fields in ways and to a degree hitherto virtually denied them. Significant consequences of the work of the secular-investigators already are visible in Soviet relations with Central America and portend greater changes in the future.

Third, we consider how the frank acknowledgment of the failure of the Soviet economic and political model – made in the full glare of glasnost and convincingly illustrated by the East European revolutions of 1989 – has affected Soviet relations with Central American and other Third World countries through a number of ripple effects, including the restructuring of relations among the Comecon countries.

The accumulated impact of the changes of glasnost and perestroika, reinforcing the thrusts of Gorbachev's new thinking, has produced a new kind of Soviet foreign policy in Central America less threatening to US interests militarily and ideologically than policies of the past, and one which, by its demonstrated readiness to enter into bilateral and multilateral cooperative actions, has helped to create a favorable context for the solution of many regional problems.

The new directives

Gorbachev's prescriptions for superpower behavior toward regional conflicts may be stated as three broad directives: (1) demilitarize regional conflicts and seek political solutions based on a balance of interests; (2) secularize (deideologize) interstate relations; in other words, stop viewing regional conflicts through a prism of East–West, ideology-guided confrontation; and (3) refrain from violating the sovereignty of another nation; hence, oppose the export of revolution (or counterrevolution).

Demilitarize regional conflicts

In Gorbachev's words: "Regional conflicts in Asia, Africa, and Latin America . . . are spawned by the colonial past, new social processes, or recurrences of predatory policy, or by all three. . . . The main thing here is to take the interests of all sides into consideration and . . . search for a just *political* settlement."[2]

Soviet analysts have stated this more concretely. The prominent academician Evgenii M. Primakov, in an article intended to guide Soviet researchers and published shortly after the 27th Congress of the CPSU in 1986, called for "a joint search [by the USA and USSR] for a way to solve regional conflicts – in the Near East, in Central America, in South Africa – everywhere where breeding grounds exist for a military threat."[3] Accordingly, in August 1987, when five Central American presidents signed the Guatemala accord initiated by President Arias of Costa Rica, Soviet scholars hailed this signing as "unquestionable evidence of the acceleration of elements of new political thought on the [American] continent, a step toward the beginning of a perestroika of subregional relations."[4]

Another specialist in international relations, V.P. Sudarev, noted in late 1987 that "the call of the Soviet Union to restructure international relations on the basis of the principles of new political thought and the positive progress in Soviet–American relations have facilitated the creation of more favorable conditions for beginning a process of settling a series of regional conflicts." Sudarev listed five concrete steps the superpowers should take to end regional conflicts: "Limit direct military presence, halt the supply of weapons to crisis regions, refrain from any kind of acts to destabilize the fragile processes of political regulation, take on international obligations to guarantee the implementation (of these regulations), and finally purposefully pressure their allies with the aim of hastening the settlement of conflicts." He called these steps "constituent parts of a great power 'code of conduct' in regional conflicts."[5]

Sudarev's code has been reflected in a number of Soviet actions in Central America, the most dramatic of which was the announced cutoff, in January 1989, of Soviet weapons shipments to Nicaragua. Supporting the arms cutoff, the Soviet General Staff claimed in February 1989 that the USSR had only seventeen military specialists in Nicaragua, "in the servicing of military hardware"[6] (which, however, begged the question of how many Cuban advisors remained).[7]

Pressuring its allies to negotiate, the USSR systematically, openly, and emphatically urged Cuba and Nicaragua to participate in political talks to settle military crises. Thus, Article 7 of the Soviet–Cuban Friendship Treaty signed in Havana during Gorbachev's visit in April 1989 pointedly stated: "(the two parties) will spare no efforts in making the principle of rejecting the use or threat of use of force a universal norm of conduct in interstate relations and *fostering the settlement of conflicts between states solely by peaceful and political means.*"[8] And Moscow consistently applauded Nicaragua's unilateral cease-fire declarations in 1988–89, urging (with less than complete success) a cutoff of weapons to El Salvador's insurgents. As Foreign Minister Eduard Shevardnadze put it, Nicaragua's "original, innovative approach . . . fully accords with the spirit of the new political thinking and with modern progressive tendencies in international policy and . . . substantially contributes to a just political settlement in Central America."[9] Further reflecting the spirit of Sudarev's code, the USSR called for the use of multinational forces to police demilitarized areas.[10]

Meanwhile, "old political thought" also characterized Soviet theory and practice. Fancied or real obstacles to the implementation of Gorbachev's new thought continued to be blamed by Soviet analysts on the United States and explained in terms of familiar Marxist doctrine. Sudarev's stricture against military intervention meant US troops were viewed as the interlopers in Central America, and US military aid to El Salvador, Honduras, and the Contras was blamed for keeping the military conflict going.

The US military presence in Panama and Honduras was interpreted by some Soviet spokesmen, especially when addressing audiences in Latin America, as a deliberate military aggression against all of Latin America. Radio Moscow labeled the US invasion of Panama "an act of blatant international terrorism," and TASS international service said, "It seems Washington will continue to regard the countries of Latin America as its backyard and impose its orders on them by fire and sword."[11] *Pravda*, in an article entitled, "Recurrence of imperial thinking," asserted that the real US motives for the intervention were "maintaining military bases on Panamanian soil and control of the Panama Canal, wanting to teach a lesson to other Latin American countries."[12] And the well-known political commentator Alexander Bovin blamed the "President's imperial ambitions and willingness to put personal dislike [presumably of Noriega] above state interests," explaining further that "the Americans revel in strength and power in what they regard as their own 'backyard.' "[13]

Far less destructive than similar criticism of US policies in the past, however, such commentary was not sufficient to deter the generally positive impact on political events in Central America of Soviet efforts to play down force and play up political settlements in the region.

Secularize interstate relations

Gorbachev expressed this new ideological position succinctly: "I have often encountered leading Western politicians who regard the very existence of regional conflicts as the product of 'Kremlin conspiratorial activity,' " and he countered, "The Soviet Union, on the other hand, holds that these conflicts should not be used to engender confrontation between the two systems, especially when they involve the USSR and the USA."[14]

Echoing Gorbachev, Primakov's advice to scholars based on the new line of the 27th Party Congress warned against "viewing ongoing events in different regions through a prism of American–Soviet confrontation." He added, "in the present conditions, hostility between capitalism and socialism objectively can proceed exclusively in forms of peaceful competition and peaceful rivalry. Foreign policy in such conditions must not be a sphere of ideology."[15] Foreign Minister Shevardnadze agreed: "The struggle between the two opposing systems can no longer be considered a leading tendency of the contemporary era."[16]

Gorbachev's advisor Georgii Shakhnazarov, in a February 1989 article entitled, "East–West: on the question of deideologizing state-to-state relations," soundly denounced the "thesis about the fatal confrontation (and resulting implacable hostility) of socialism and capitalism," suggesting that, "a better means of dealing with an enemy is to turn him into one's friend, or at the worst, into an ordinary neighbor."[17] He argued:

> it is basically false to liken the relations between states or groups of states to relations between systems. That which can be called "intersystem" relations is wholly related to the sphere of ideology, of theoretic and political principles. The relations between states are material. States carry on talks between themselves and conclude agreements; systems cannot do this; they are not in a condition to exchange memoranda and to search for compromises. In essence, the concept "social system" is a high level of abstraction and to transfer it to the ground of political struggle means to do violence to reality.[18]

This view has very different implications in the Central American setting depending upon which superpower is being judged "ideological" or "non-ideological." For the USSR, non-ideological, secular behavior is linked closely with Gorbachev's third directive condemning the export of revolution; its goal is the achievement by the USSR of a new image as a country capable of cultivating diplomatic and trade relations with a broad spectrum of countries, of becoming the "ordinary neighbor" of countries throughout the world. In the past, the extensive political efforts of the International Department of the CPSU to develop ties with communist parties and liberation movements, while crowned with stunning success in Cuba, Nicaragua, and (until 1983) Grenada, hindered Soviet diplomatic efforts to establish normal ties with governments like Guatemala, Honduras, and El Salvador, which felt threatened by the party activity.[19] Recently, still lacking diplomatic ties with these three Central American countries, Moscow initiated exchanges of legislative delegations with Guatemala and Honduras, hoping to develop more lasting, open, and "secular" relations in the future.[20] Similarly, the USSR pressed Castro to play down revolutionary rhetoric and seek to normalize relations with his Latin American neighbors.[21]

Despite this new tack on the part of Soviet government organs, the CPSU did not abandon its ideological partners in the region nor foreswear all anti-imperialist rhetoric. In September 1988, the first deputy chief of the CPSU's International Department, Karen Brutents, visited in Panama with both the communist and the ruling parties, and in November, Moscow Radio Peace and Progress, broadcasting in Spanish, provided a forum for the leader of the People's Party of Panama, Ruben D. Souza, to call for a united front with General Noriega and other "patriotic forces" to resist US oppression.[22]

Some Soviet analysts condemned the United States for injecting an East–West confrontation and ideological debate into regional conflicts. A writer for the Soviet military press accused US Vice-President Daniel Quayle of illustrating the legacy of the previous administration's relations with Latin American countries when Quayle talked about the "worldwide contest between the USSR and the US" and "ways to achieve 'victory' in it." Ending his attack with an unexpected turn of humor, the Soviet journalist said,

> Grenada was trampled in the name of "combating communism." There was no hesitation in deceiving Congress for the sake of providing weapons to the contra formations. In general, the former administration's activity may be compared with those "Boy Scouts" who, wishing to earn credit, escorted an old lady across the street in threes. When asked why three were needed for this, they answered: "She put up a lot of resistance."[23]

On balance, the Soviet effort to pursue a new diplomacy with all Central American states, regardless of their political systems, was making slow, but steady headway. Its eventual success was closely linked to Gorbachev's third guideline.

Respect a nation's freedom of choice

Gorbachev has flatly denounced the concept of the export of revolution: "U.S. right-wing forces and propaganda portray our interest in Latin America as an intention to engineer a series of socialist revolutions there. Nonsense!" And he argued, "Every nation is entitled to choose its own way of development, to dispose of its fate, its territory, and its human and natural resources. International relations cannot be normalized if this is not understood in all countries."[24]

The advice of the 27th Party Congress in 1986 was similarly emphatic on this point: "Marxism–Leninism always assumed that it is useless and intolerable to instigate a revolution from outside. At the same time no one is able artificially, by means of the export of counterrevolution to preserve the social-political status quo in the world."[25] Primakov reinforced this thought a year later: "Back at the dawn of Soviet power, V.I. Lenin spoke out resolutely against the transformation of the first state of victorious socialism into an exporter of revolution to other countries, limiting its international influence to the framework of setting an example. Excluding the export of revolution is an imperative of the nuclear age."[26]

A particularly important corollary of this perspective was pointed out in 1989 by Karen Brutents, the leading spokesman on Third World affairs of the International Department of the CPSU Central Committee: "Every regional conflict has its specific origins. If compromises are needed to resolve them, they must be acceptable to all sides so that they can subsequently be respected by all. *They cannot be imposed.*" Brutents contrasted this with the situation under Brezhnev which "was based on a rationale of force and blocs," while today the settlement of regional conflicts requires "fastidious respect for each people's right to choose their own path and to forge their own destiny without external intervention."[27]

In terms of opportunities and costs this message offers the superpowers two quite different scenarios in Central America. For the USSR and its allies in the region the mandate calls for an end to the spread of revolution. Gorbachev, in his speech to the Cuban National Assembly on 5 April 1989, used it forcefully to wave Castro away from revolutionary adventurism when he denounced "any theories and doctrines that justify the export of revolution," and called for the "cessation of [the supply of] military arms to Central America from any quarter."[28] This was an unequivocal warning to Castro on his home turf that the Soviet Union opposed aggressive revolutionary activity as unlawful interference in the affairs of another nation. At the same time, avowing "non-interference" in Cuban affairs, Gorbachev could claim he was not trying to push Cuba in the direction of Soviet reforms. For Castro, nevertheless, the signal was clear. Ultimately dependent on Soviet oil and other economic support, he should avoid openly stoking revolutionary fires in Central America. As for the Soviet military presence, Gorbachev told the Cuban National Assembly, "The USSR does not have and does not intend to have naval, air force, or missile bases in Latin America."[29] And Iurii Pavlov, head of the Soviet Foreign Ministry's Latin American Department, asserted that "neither the USSR nor Cuba is exporting revolution. Nor should the United States suspect the USSR of trying to use its Latin American relations to undermine U.S. – or Western–Latin American relations."[30]

Applied to the United States, the principle of non-interference means no US intrusion into Central American affairs, especially for the purpose of maintaining the status quo and reversing revolutionary movements. It provides the Soviets with a convenient moral basis for attacking the Monroe Doctrine and championing the rights of Central American countries. Thus, the public affairs chief of the Soviet Foreign Ministry, Gennadii Gerasimov, titled an article about the US armed intervention in Panama, "Displaying the Monroe Doctrine to the world."[31] Some other commentators felt justified in referring to the actions of the "Gringos" in pejorative terms clearly intended to appeal to a Latin American audience. Radio Peace and Progress beamed a report in Spanish claiming that it was on orders of the "Yankee government" that "U.S. soldiers ravaged the headquarters of the People's Party of Panama [communist], destroying its archives. The same type of destruction was also carried out in the offices of other parties that advocate the return of the Canal Zone to the Republic." And the radio commentator, Aleksei Pavlov, concluded: "Those who continue to hang on to the old political idea of using force risk being paid with the same token. The confirmation of this possibility is the following information: Several extremist organizations in Chile and Colombia have announced that they would attack U.S. facilities in those countries. The first outbursts have already occurred."[32]

Moscow's support for the sovereignty of Latin American states finds ready sympathy among Central American countries, of course, and while this sympathy does not translate automatically into pro-Soviet support, it does permit the USSR to occupy a moral high ground in its relations with these countries. On the whole, however, despite echoes of old orthodoxies and practices, and appeals to revolutionary or nationalist values, current Soviet policy is based firmly upon the principle of cooperation between the US and USSR. And the forceful application by Soviet leaders of policies shaped by Gorbachev's guidelines clearly has contributed to an inevitable realignment of forces throughout Central America and the Caribbean.

The impact of glasnost and perestroika

In addition to the Gorbachev directives, glasnost and perestroika are significantly affecting Soviet foreign policy and the policy-making process. Three factors are most important: first, the ideological unshackling of social science research, which enlarges the range of policy advice and input from experts; second, the growing role of academic specialists in policy-making positions in the central party and government apparat; and third, the restructuring of the machinery of government affecting the foreign-policy establishment and the policy-making process in ways that give the new legislative bodies influential input into foreign-policy decisions.

Refreshing as the work of the Soviet "explicators" over the past four years has been, the process of drawing out specific policies that follow from the broad premises of Gorbachev's new political thinking remains essentially a familiar kind of scholasticism. Destined to be even more significant in the long run is the joint challenge of glasnost and perestroika to social science researchers not to portray reality as a reflection of some accepted line but to approach it in as scientifically neutral a manner as possible. Shakhnazarov, pinning down one aspect of this process, said it means overcoming an old cleavage in the sphere of scientific knowledge: "If with us the epithet 'bourgeoisie' was applied to the social sciences, it meant that this was not science at all, but a magic trick or even charlatanism, while on 'that other side' the same kind of connotations were given to the concept 'Marxist.' Both sides suffered losses, but most of all science itself."[33]

While some social scientists have been attacking old orthodoxies since the early 1960s,[34] the new openness, combined with severe official criticism of the Soviet model of economic development, has broken down ideological barriers that previously corseted thought, action, and policy. Meanwhile, the processes of perestroika have set off lengthy critical discussions of the socialist model, challenging "the original claims to infallibility and to the scientific nature of socialism,"[35] and redefining and exploring new directions for socialist development.

The difference between today's thought and that of two decades ago is suggested by two strikingly different works of the same author, R.M. Avakov. In 1974 Avakov, a specialist on the economics and politics of developing countries, served as chief editor of a book on dependent capitalism among Third World countries, a book which was criticized wryly by Jerry Hough as "capable of real simplicity." It advanced the following theory: "The greater the tie with state-monopoly capitalism, as a rule, the greater the dependence. The greater the dependence – in the final analysis – the greater the relative backwardness, which leads in turn to greater dependence, and so forth."[36]

In a 1987 article, the same R.M. Avakov launched a far from simplistic attack upon certain scholars studying socialist-oriented Third World countries, criticizing their antiquated notions and "declarative and ceremonial statements." Scolding them for "ideological myopia" (a criticism, as Avakov was doubtless aware, applied to his 1974 work), he charged that "the quantity of publications on problems of socialist orientation is inversely proportional to the level and quality of the studies." The reason for this, he explained, was that for Soviet social scientists it had become "nearly a ritual analysis in the case of countries of socialist orientation having crises and other negative processes, including failure in the economy and in domestic and foreign policy, to substitute sacramental phrases of the type 'they ran into difficulties,' 'they had to overcome the opposition of internal reaction and the remnants of colonialism,' etc." He added, "Difficulties, reactionary resistance, and the intrigues of imperialism do exist, of course. But there are other phenomena demanding objective study, such as contradictions inherent in development along the path of socialist orientation, intraparty struggle, degeneration of a leadership and regime, violation of the norms of good neighborliness and international law, etc." (Avakov cited Nicaragua as a case where Soviet readers had not been adequately informed about the many sides of the actual domestic political situation.)[37]

Examples of this sort demonstrate that a new and welcome era has opened for Soviet social scientists. This is especially important for the future Soviet foreign-policy process because the experts are now called upon for analysis of social affairs, not to prove an ideological point, but to contribute to a broad, international, scientific pool of knowledge. These conditions challenge the secular-investigators, scholars no longer bound by communist strictures, to provide national and international policy makers and the Soviet public with increasingly sound and realistic appraisals of foreign and domestic affairs, as well as a broader range of policy choices, including alternatives earlier precluded for ideological reasons.

A second factor shaping the foreign-policy process in new ways is the growing involvement of academic experts in policy making. Much scholarly analysis of international affairs now is designed specifically by its authors to influence policy decisions.[38] In mid-1987, academician Primakov, doctor of economic science, then director of the Institute for World Economics and International Relations (MEMO), told a Western reporter that the institutes "are closely involved in the formulation of foreign policy" and that his institute "receives assignments from the leadership and itself raises issues."[39] Subsequently, Primakov assumed government posts allowing him to affect policy even more directly. In 1989 he became chairman of the restructured Supreme Soviet Council of the Union, and in April 1990 he joined Gorbachev's Presidential Council. Similarly, his predecessor as director of MEMO, Aleksandr Iakovlev, became Central Committee secretary for international affairs on 5 March 1986, a full member of the Politburo on 26 June 1987, head of the party's Commission for International Affairs, 30 September 1988, and a Presidential Council member in 1990. The prominence of such scholars in Gorbachev's party–state apparatus,[40] the hearings given to academic experts by the new Soviet legislature (where the advice can be very specific and policy-oriented), and the appearance in the Ministry of Foreign Affairs of consultative councils, in which, according to the eminent historian, V.I. Dashichev, "scholars participate and at which various foreign-policy problems are freely discussed,"[41] indicate that with respect to the shaping of policy the opinions of the analysts today do indeed matter to a far greater degree than at any time in the past.

A third major factor portending far-reaching changes in Soviet foreign policies is the rapidly evolving context of the policy-making process resulting from the restructuring of the nation's political system. The new Congress of Deputies and the restructured Supreme Soviet are assuming unprecedented importance in foreign-policy decisions and already have begun to question how the USSR is spending its budget for foreign assistance. Thus the maiden address of the noted economist, N.P. Shmelev, on 8 June 1989, before the Congress of USSR People's Deputies, dealt specifically with the question of Soviet foreign aid to Cuba. Said Shmelev,

> It is reasonable to ask whether anyone has ever thought how much our interests in, for instance, Latin America cost us. According to professional U.S. estimates it is $6–8 billion every year. A considerable amount of that in hard currency. And, bafflingly, we spend a considerable proportion of this sum on, for instance, paying four times the going rate for Cuban sugar (compared with the world price). . . . This source alone would be enough to keep the consumer market in balance for the few years we need in order to turn ourselves around somehow and really embark on the road to reform.[42]

In a later article, E. Aref'eva, of the Institute of World Economics and International Relations, scolded the legislators for not reacting more forcefully to Shmelev's criticism of the foreign aid budget and for having refused to examine it more closely: "I think that even a cursory discussion in the Supreme Soviet of the structure of expenditure on economic aid would cast doubt on the advisability of a substantial proportion of this expenditure."[43] Such comments, echoed in legislative chambers and the press, illustrate the kinds of pressures deputies increasingly can be expected to exert toward limiting financial and military aid abroad, and in particular, aid to such countries as Cuba, which remains a bastion of Stalinist orthodoxies now discredited in the USSR.

Ripple effects of failure of the Soviet model

In addition to affecting Soviet foreign policy directly, glasnost and perestroika are having a practical impact on Soviet domestic and foreign affairs wth ripple effects around the world, whose full significance can be revealed only over time.[44] Already, however, the failure of the Soviet socialist model and the ebbing of East–West confrontation have had dramatic repercussions in the Third World. Thus, the kaleidoscopic political changes in Eastern Europe through 1989 raised earnest questions in India, where many intellectuals had in the past defended the Soviet model. A Madras journalist admitted, "The deep alienation in Eastern Europe came as a big shock to many here." And India's Foreign Minister declared that due to changes in the East–West confrontation, the non-alignment movement was now "irrelevant" and needed to be redefined. Of more immediate concern, by early 1990 hard economic questions were being asked in New Delhi about how much India could depend on traditional Soviet support in the form of continuing barter trade agreements.[45] Cubans and Nicaraguans were asking themselves the same questions.

In fact, well before 1990 there were unmistakable signs that economic and political restructuring in the USSR was creating difficulties in Soviet–Cuban relations. During Gorbachev's visit to Havana the heat of the two leaders' denials that Soviet perestroika was causing economic, political, and ideological rifts between their countries only served to draw greater attention to the two countries' diverging paths and the reasons for divergence. One cause of difficulty in Soviet–Cuban trade relations was that with the decentralization of Soviet industrial enterprises these firms found it more profitable to seek hard currency deals in Western Europe for goods promised to the Cubans. Castro himself provided ample evidence of a trade slowdown by complaining about delayed shipments and alleged inequities in Soviet–Cuban trade exchanges. A good example of this was an *Izvestiia* report of Castro's remarks in the Spanish newspaper *El Independiente* that "if the USSR continues its inequitable trade exchange with Cuba – selling its goods at increasingly higher prices and buying Cuban agricultural produce and raw materials at lower prices – this will amount to the same policy which the United States is implementing in respect of developing countries. Thus the USSR . . . will ultimately join the U.S. blockade of Cuba."[46]

In 1989, Castro's verbal attacks on the East European members of Comecon indicated his growing certainty that, because of their reorientation, they would not honor past, unfulfilled fraternal trade commitments to Cuba. He was particularly bitter about the restructuring of Comecon that began in late 1989 in ways that isolated Cuba from the other members.[47] In 1990, as East European independence grew, any chance faded that the earlier promise of Comecon nations – to support Cuba's forced development to bring its economy to the level of the most developed Comecon members – could ever be honored.[48] Meanwhile, the prospects of future East European trade and support to both Cuba and Nicaragua dimmed as the East European nations abandoned past barter/credit trading practices and sought hard currency markets in the West. In early 1990, Hungary, which had been selling trucks and other vehicles to Cuba, "informed the Cubans that future business transactions will be conducted with hard currency only."[49]

The lessening of East bloc assistance weakened the ability of Cuba and Nicaragua to maintain their economic independence from the capitalist world. As economic pressures and the fading luster of the revolutionary model pushed both countries toward greater accommodation with the capitalist West, Cuba resisted, while Ortega's Nicaragua embraced economic reforms reputedly condemned by Castro as "the most right-wing policy in Latin America."[50] The shift from East–West confrontation to cooperation between the superpowers and Moscow's direct advice to both Cuba and Nicaragua to normalize relations with the US put further pressure on these countries to seek a *modus vivendi* with the capitalist world. Thus, a ripple effect of perestroika helped to produce a sea of change in Soviet relations with its Central American partners.

Conclusion

Although events shaping Soviet domestic affairs could, under new leadership, force a change in the Soviet foreign-policy direction, the nation's economy could ill sustain a bold policy reversal or a return to the kind of military expansionism that, as glasnost revealed, cost the Brezhnev regime dearly and robbed the nation of its ability to achieve superpower status in the economic, technological, or social spheres in the immediate future. Meanwhile, Gorbachev's restructuring of the government machinery means that future foreign policy, because some of its input will be coming from a popularly elected legislature, will reflect domestic concerns, strengths, and weaknesses to a far greater extent than has been true in the past. Thus, for the near term the present policy directions seem assured.

In Central America and the Caribbean, Soviet policy under Gorbachev's leadership has been radically transformed. The USSR has renounced its former role of bankroll, model, and inspiration for Latin American leftist groups and disclaimed any intention to constitute a military threat in the US backyard. To the United States, therefore, the threat of a growing Soviet military presence in the Caribbean, argued so forcefully by the Reagan Administration, has receded. With the lowering of tension between NATO and a virtually defunct Warsaw Pact alliance, the military significance of wartime nuisance attacks on vital Caribbean sealanes aimed at cutting off the US supplies of oil from abroad or diverting US forces to protect Gulf port shipments to Western Europe decreased further. The vulnerability of the Panama Canal to attack became more of a commercial hazard to Japan and other nations using it for business than a crucial weakness in a vital US lifeline. In the resulting political climate even Soviet access to electronic surveillance capabilities and air and sea facilities in Cuba appeared benign.

In sum, by 1990 the cold war had ended in Central America; confrontation was replaced by a superpower partnership committed to settling local conflicts. Understating the dramatic implications of this point, Iurii Pavlov, the USSR Foreign Ministry's leading expert on Latin American affairs, said shortly before the 1990 Nicaraguan elections, "The very fact that the U.S. and USSR have changed from confrontation in the region to attempts to promote interaction exerts a favorable impact on the situation in Central America."[51]

This does not mean that the USSR will not be trying to expand its relations in Central America and the Caribbean at the expense of its US partner. Indeed, an expansion of "normal," non-ideological, and commercial relations is very much on the Soviet agenda, and this kind of presence in the region can be expected to grow. But the US and USSR will face off in an unequal economic competition in Central America, because Soviet efforts to expand trade and commerce in the region are not likely soon to challenge the US position effectively. Up to the present, as Nicola Miller has shown convincingly, except for the case of trade with Cuba (swapping oil for sugar), "there is not a single instance of lasting and mutually satisfactory economic convergence between the Soviet Union and a Latin American country."[52]

Nor does Moscow's attempt to become some kind of "ordinary neighbor" in the region mean that politically the Soviet leaders have given up their belief in the superior values of socialism in some yet-to-be-evolved form that may facilitate the winning of friends and influence with nations in Latin America. Viewing various cooperative actions taken by the Central American nations (Contadora, the Guatemala accord, plans for a Central American market, parliament, etc.), Soviet writers consistently support arrangements that might strengthen the leverage of these nations in dealing with the United States. A possible culmination of this development which Moscow views as promising is the wedding of various integration processes in Latin America with an integration of socialist movements in the hemisphere.[53]

In the post-cold war era, while Moscow carries on a kind of low intensity fencing and continues to view itself as a champion of American victims of US bullying, the maintenance of the newly forged partnership with the United States remains in first place on the Soviet national security agenda. As for the future, the regional impact in Central America and elsewhere of the critical US–Soviet linkage has only begun to unfold.

Notes

1 R.M. Avakov, "Novoe myshlenie i problema izucheniia razvivaiushchikhsia stran," *Mirovaia ekonomika i mezhdunarodnye otnosheniia* (hereinafter cited as *MEMO*), no. 11 (1987), p. 62.
2 *Perestroika: New Thinking for Our Country and the World* (New York: Harper and Row, 1987), pp. 173–74; emphasis added.
3 "XXVII s″ezd KPSS i issledovanie problem mirovoi ekonomiki i mezhdunarodnykh otnoshenii," *MEMO*, no. 5 (1986), p. 12.
4 Editor's column, "Tsentral′naia Amerika: na puti k miru, demokratii i razvitii," *Latinskaia Amerika*, no. 10 (1987) p. 5.
5 V.P. Sudarev, "Regional′nye konflikty: problemy razblokirovaniia," *Latinskaia Amerika*, no. 1 (1989), pp. 9, 13.
6 *Pravda*, 12 February 1989, p. 6.
7 Concerning the Cuban potential for military support, Georges Fauriol noted that "Moscow continued to supply Havana with sophisticated weapons (most recently sustaining an upgrade of air capabilities to MiG-29 from MiG-23 jet fighter aircraft)"; *Foreign Affairs*, vol. 69, no. 1 (1990), p. 131.
8 TASS, 5 April 1989; trans. in *Foreign Broadcast Information Service, Daily Report: Soviet Union* (hereafter cited as *FBIS-SOV*), 5 April 1989, p. 50 (emphasis added).
9 *Pravda*, 25 March 1989, p. 4; *FBIS-SOV*, 27 March 1989, pp. 31–32.
10 *Ibid.*, p. 32.
11 TASS, 30 December 1989; *FBIS-SOV*, 2 January 1990, p. 35; TASS, 4 January 1990; *FBIS-SOV*, 5 January 1990, p. 8.
12 8 January 1990; *FBIS-SOV*, 9 January 1990, pp. 15–17.
13 *Izvestiia*, 10 January 1990, p. 5; *FBIS-SOV*, 11 January 1990, pp. 59–60.

14 Gorbachev, *Perestroika*, pp. 173, 176.
15 Primakov, "The 27th Congress," p. 13.
16 *Vestnik Ministerstva inostrannykh del SSSR*, 15 August 1988, p. 34.
17 "Vostok-Zapad. K voprosy o deideologizatsii mezhgosudarstvennykh otnoshenii," *Kommunist*, no. 3 (February 1989), pp. 72, 75.
18 *Ibid.*, p. 68.
19 On the International Department, see Jan S. Adams, "Incremental activism in Soviet Third World policy: the role of the International Department of the CPSU Central Committee," *Slavic Review*, vol. 48, no. 4 (Winter 1989), pp. 614–30.
20 Soviet parliamentarians visited Honduras for the first time 2–6 August 1989; the first visit of Honduran legislators to the USSR was in August 1988; *FBIS-SOV*, 7 August 1989, p. 40. Soviet legislators first visited Guatemala 31 October–3 November 1989; *FBIS-SOV*, 9 November 1989, pp. 34–36.
21 E.S. Dabagian, "Integratsionnye protsessy – velenie vremeni," *Latinskaia Amerika*, no. 12 (1988), pp. 12–15.
22 *Pravda*, 20 September 1988, p. 4; Moscow Radio Peace and Progress, 23 November 1988; *FBIS-SOV*, 28 November 1988, pp. 40–41.
23 *Krasnaia zvezda*, 12 March 1989, p. 3; *FBIS-SOV*, 16 March 1989, p. 11.
24 Gorbachev, *Perestroika*, pp. 177, 187.
25 Primakov, "XXVII s″ezd," p. 13.
26 E.M. Primakov, "A new philosophy of foreign policy," *Pravda*, 10 July 1987, p. 4; *Current Digest of the Soviet Press*, vol. 39, no. 28, p. 2.
27 Karen Brutents, *L'UNITA*, 16 February 1989, p. 2; *FBIS-SOV*, 28 February 1989, p. 5 (emphasis added).
28 "Mikhail Gorbachev's speech to the Cuban National Assembly," *News and Views from the USSR* (Washington, D.C.: Soviet Embassy, Information Department, 6 April 1989), pp. 10, 13.
29 TASS, 5 April 1989; *FBIS-SOV*, 5 April 1989, p. 47.
30 *Rabotnicheskoe delo*, 30 March 1989, p. 4; *FBIS-SOV*, 3 April 1989, p. 31.
31 *Sovetskaia kul'tura*, 26 December 1989, p. 7; *FBIS-SOV*, 9 January 1990, pp. 56–57.
32 *FBIS-SOV*, 8 January 1990, p. 39.
33 Shakhnazarov, "Vostok-Zapad," p. 78.
34 See Elizabeth Kridl Valkenier, *The Soviet Union and the Third World: An Economic Bind* (New York: Praeger Publishers, 1983), and Jerry F. Hough, *The Struggle for the Third World* (Washington, D.C.: The Brookings Institute, 1986).
35 Cynthia Roberts and Elizabeth Wishnick, "Ideology is dead! Long live ideology?" *Problems of Communism*, vol. 38 (November–December 1989), p. 58.
36 R.M. Avakov and others, eds., *Razvivaiushchiesia strany: zakonomernosti, tendentsii, perspektivy* (Moscow: Mysl', 1974), p. 41, in Hough, *The Struggle*, p. 87.
37 Avakov, "Novoe myshlenie," pp. 54–55.
38 Thus, Avakov scolded officials for failing to implement the advice of economic experts in a timely fashion; "Novoe myshlenie," p. 60.
39 Paul Quinn-Judge, "Soviet shift in world policy," *Christian Science Monitor*,

16 July 1987, p. 10; see also, Ilya Prizel, *Latin America through Soviet Eyes: the evolution of Soviet perceptions during the Brezhnev Era 1964–1982* (Cambridge: Cambridge University Press, 1990), pp. ix–x.

40 Other examples include: Leonid I. Abalkin, doctor of economic science and former director of the Economics Institute in Moscow, now deputy chairman of the USSR Council of Ministers; Georgii Shakhnazarov, chairman of the Soviet Association of Political Science since 1974, a Gorbachev aide since March 1988, and many outstanding scholars elected to the Congress of People's Deputies, such as Gavril Popov, former editor of *Voprosy ekonomiki*, and Oleg Bogomolov, director of the Economics of the World Socialist System Institute, and eleven deputies representing the USSR Academy of Sciences.

41 *Komsomol'skaia pravda*, 19 June 1988, p. 3; and see Vernon V. Aspaturian, "The role of the International Department in Soviet foreign policy process," *The International Department of the CC CPSU Under Dobrynin*, Department of State Publication 9726 (Washington, D.C.: Foreign Service Institute, September 1989), pp. 14–16.

42 *Pravda*, 9 June 1989, p. 2; *FBIS-SOV*, Supplement, 9 June 1989, p. 28.

43 *Izvestiia*, 10 January 1990, p. 5; *FBIS-SOV*, 16 January 1990, pp. 18–20.

44 R.M. Avakov says: "a new sphere of Third World studies whose significance is impossible to estimate" is the "exceptionally interesting question about the impact on regimes of socialist orientation of the current processes of perestroika in the USSR and the decisive democratization of Soviet society." Such studies, he says, are only being talked about. "Novoe myshlenie," p. 56.

45 Barbara Crossette, "Policy of 'nonalignment' is re-examined in India," *The New York Times*, 14 March 1990.

46 *Izvestiia*, 23 January 1990, p. 1; *FBIS-SOV*, 26 January 1990, p. 27.

47 On CEMA's restructuring see *Pravda*, 11 January 1990, p. 6; and for Castro's response see *Pravda*, 30 January 1990, p. 4.

48 *Izvestiia*, 12 January 1990, p. 4.

49 Jacquiline Tillman, "Cuba's revolution is coming," *The Washington Post National Weekly Edition*, 8–14 January 1990, p. 25.

50 Mark Uhlig, "Cuba loses allure for Nicaraguans," *New York Times*, 18 January 1990, p. 9.

51 TASS, 16 February 1990; *FBIS-SOV*, 12 March 1990, p. 40.

52 Nicola Miller, *Soviet Relations with Latin America, 1959–1987* (Cambridge: Cambridge University Press, 1989), p. 220.

53 Dabagian, "Integratsionnye protsessy," pp. 12–14.

9 The Soviet reassessment of socialist orientation and the African response

Pierre du Toit Botha

Since Mikhail Gorbachev became Secretary General of the Communist Party of the Soviet Union (CPSU) in 1985 and the concepts of new thinking, openness, and restructuring were added to the Soviet lexicon on international relations, many interesting debates have arisen among Soviet academics and politicians about international politics in general and relations with the Third World in particular. The latter will be the main focus of this chapter.

Naturally, Gorbachev did not initiate this debate, and neither are debates about international relations anything new in the Soviet Union. What is new is the fact that Gorbachev's policies have lent a new dimension to these debates and have opened for discussion aspects previously considered outside the parameters of permissible academic debate. To the extent that Soviet social scientists responded to the new openness several key doctrinal concepts of the past, based on Marxist–Leninist philosophical assumptions, have been questioned. One of these was the concept of "non-capitalist development" (also referred to as "socialist orientation") for Third World countries.

The amendments made to the latter will be examined, first, within the broader context of the recent Soviet reevaluation of international relations theory, whereafter the discussion will focus on the adaptations to and the eventual demise of the theory of socialist orientation in Soviet literature. In conclusion the African response to the reassessment in the Soviet Union will be briefly addressed.

The Soviet leadership on the necessity for ideological change

In his speech during the 27th CPSU Congress in February 1986, Gorbachev described the "stagnation" in the country and stated that the USSR had reached a "turning point not only in internal affairs but also in external affairs."[1] At a Ministry of Foreign Affairs conference three months later Gorbachev criticized "stereotypes and cliches of the past" in Soviet foreign policy.[2] In his book entitled *Perestroika: New Thinking for our Country and the World*, Gorbachev emphasized the need to "rid our policy of ideological prejudice."[3] In a later publication he referred to a "rejection of the ideologization of inter-state relations"[4] and indicated that he was in favor of a "deideologization" of the latter.

The dysfunctional nature of ideology also has figured strongly in the speeches and publications of Eduard Shevardnadze, Vadim Medvedev, and Evgenii Primakov. They have all on occasion stated that Soviet foreign policy should be conducted on a "more profitable" and less ideological basis.[5]

The revision of international relations theory

The changes which have taken place in Soviet perceptions of socialist orientation as a model for the developing world should be viewed in a broader context and against the background of the general revision of theoretical concepts associated with the Soviet theory of international relations.

It should first be noted that the Soviet concept of "peaceful coexistence" has been amended, with most scholars and politicians no longer regarding it as a form of class struggle. The "principal contradiction" in the world is also no longer seen as the confrontation between capitalism and socialism.[6] Furthermore, instead of the previously dichotomous Soviet world outlook, the existence of universal values and the common interests of mankind are today being emphasized and the theme of an integral, interconnected, and interdependent world is frequently found in Soviet theoretical literature on international relations.[7] Closely related is the new emphasis on global problems which require international cooperation to be solved successfully.[8] This new view of the world places the emphasis squarely on *unity*. As three prominent writers recently stated:

> Every Marxist knows the dialectical formula of the unity and the struggle of opposites. Bias in any direction strips this formula of its dialectical nature and essentially transforms it into dogma or incantation. Let us say candidly, that in the recent past, we emphasized the struggle of opposite systems while clearly underestimating the fact that this struggle is taking place in the whole world.[9]

Another aspect which has changed in the Soviet Union since new political thinking was introduced is the perception of concepts such as the "world revolutionary process," the "nature of the epoch," and the "correlation of forces," which are related closely to peaceful coexistence. An analysis of these concepts provides some insight into Soviet perceptions of the prospects for revolutionary change in the world and the propensity for revolutionary activism in the USSR's foreign policy.

Recent Soviet writings dealing with these concepts have deviated remarkably from the previously optimistic view prevalent during the Brezhnev era that the correlation of forces had shifted in favor of socialism and that the historical process is leading mankind to socialism. This observation is based on the lengthy coexistence between the two social systems now envisaged in Soviet publications.[10] Furthermore, the criticisms in the press of the deficiencies of the components of the world revolutionary process,[11] as well as the rejection of the idea that violence is the "midwife of history,"[12] are also indicators of a more realistic view and new thinking in the Soviet Union.

Also noteworthy are the changes that have taken place in Soviet perceptions of the nature of imperialism and the dogma of the terminal general crisis of capitalism. Not only is the contemporary relevance of Lenin's *Imperialism, The Highest Stage of Capitalism* and the "terminal crisis of capitalism" questioned, but the whole idea of the aggressive nature of imperialism also has been reconsidered.[13] The previously unthinkable idea of a possible convergence between the two systems has become a topic of heated and enthusiastic debate in the Soviet Union.[14]

It is against this broader background that the recent debates in the USSR dealing with the prospects for socialism in the Third World should be viewed.

The theory of non-capitalist development

The theory of the "national democratic state" and "non-capitalist development" was created in the late 1950s to serve as a theoretical justification for Khrushchev's policy of supporting revolutionary nationalist movements in the Third World. Two definite phases of liberation were visualized, namely, political independence and economic liberation from imperialism. The latter was seen as synonymous with socialism.

According to the literature at the time countries in the Third World had a choice between non-capitalist/socialist-oriented development allegedly leading to economic independence from imperialism or capitalist development which was equated with slavery. Socialism also was depicted as a phenomenon of growing attraction in the Third World.[15]

The theory of non-capitalist development and the national democratic state, was finally incorporated in the documents of the 1960 Moscow Conference of 81 Communist and Workers' Parties. During the meeting a national democracy was defined as

> a state which consistently upholds its political and economic independence,

fights against imperialism and its military blocs, against military bases on its territory; a state which fights against the new forms of colonialism and the penetration of imperialist capital; a state which rejects dictatorial and despotic methods of government; a state in which the people are ensured broad democratic rights and freedom (freedom of speech, press, assembly, demonstrations, establishment of political parties and social organizations), the opportunity to work for the enactment of an agrarian reform and other democratic and social changes, and for participation in shaping government policy.[16]

Furthermore, the documents of this meeting contained clear policy prescriptions which these states were expected to implement – the consolidation of political independence, the carrying out of agrarian reform in the interest of the peasantry, the elimination of the vestiges of feudalism, the uprooting of imperialist economic domination, the restriction of foreign monopolies and their expulsion from the national economy, the creation and development of national industry, the improvement of living standards, the democratization of social life, the pursuance of an independent and peaceful foreign policy, and the development of economic and cultural cooperation with socialist and other friendly countries.

The notion of non-capitalist development was based on a vague statement made by Lenin during the Second Comintern that backward countries could bypass capitalism with the aid of the victorious proletariat. He said:

Are we to consider as correct the assertion that the capitalist stage of economic development is inevitable for backward nations now on the road to emancipation and among whom a certain advance towards progress is to be seen since the war? We replied in the negative. If the victorious revolutionary proletariat conducts systematic propaganda among them, and the Soviet governments come to their aid with all the means at their disposal – in that event it will be mistaken to assume that the backward peoples must inevitably go through the capitalist stage of development.[17]

To lend credence to their model, Soviet authors have since the 1960s propagated the idea that the viability of the theory had been proved by the historical process itself. It was argued that the Soviet Central Asian republics, Kazakhstan, and Mongolia had skipped the capitalist phase of development within a generation with the aid of the USSR. It is important to note that economic aid from the Soviet Union was from the start depicted as the crucial factor in non-capitalist development.[18]

In the 1960s Khrushchev described Algeria, Burma, Ghana, Guinea, Mali, and the UAR as national democracies on the road to socialism via the non-capitalist path of development on the basis of the anti-Western rhetoric and policies of the leaders of these states. By the mid-1960s

Soviet theorists had the problem of finding an explanation and solution to the political instability and the incidence of *coups d'état* in these states. The solution was seen to be the creation of Marxist–Leninist vanguard parties (MLVPs) because the underlying reason for the instability was identified by scholars as an inadequate institutionalization of the revolutionary process.[19] The argument in favor of MLVPs was based on the Leninist assumption that a strict selection of class allies with a high level of class consciousness and a thorough knowledge of Marxism, and a party in which the Leninist principle of democratic centralism was applied, would necessarily succeed in gaining complete control over the people and eliminate all factionalism.[20]

This prescription of the creation of MLVPs was generally adhered to by the "second generation" of revolutionaries who came to power starting in the mid-1970s in countries such as Afghanistan, Angola, Benin, Cape Verde, Ethiopia, Guinea-Bissau, Kampuchea, Laos, Mozambique, Nicaragua, and the PDRY.

Socialist orientation reassessed

As mentioned earlier, Gorbachev's new political thinking did not initiate the Soviet reassessment of socialism in the Third World but merely accelerated an existing process. However, new political thinking did open up a whole range of previously forbidden topics for discussion. In the early 1980s only the ineffectual application of the policy prescriptions of the socialist orientation model and the internal shortcomings of Third World regimes started surfacing in Soviet political literature.

The "external factor"

The whole question of Soviet economic aid to socialist-oriented regimes, which was central to the whole formula for bypassing capitalism, and which was known as the "external factor" of development, was amended as early as 1983 by Iurii Andropov when he shifted the emphasis to the "internal factor" and said that an "own effort" on the part of these regimes is required for building socialism.[21] He also described Soviet aid as merely an additional factor that may accelerate development. It should be noted that by the early 1980s the Soviet Union had come under tremendous pressure from the second generation of socialist-oriented regimes, which came to power during the mid-1970s, to bankroll their development efforts on ideological grounds.

Shortly after Andropov's statement the idea that the USSR's influence on the revolutionary process is *not* determined by aid to the components of the process, but rather by the force of example and the demonstration effect that effective growth in the USSR exerts on the process, became a general theme in Soviet writings, although nobody yet explicitly questioned the principle of granting aid to these regimes.[22]

During the last three years a qualitative change in the debate has occurred. On the one hand, Soviets have criticized the earlier ideological motives underlying Soviet aid programs, the impulse to undertake worthless prestige projects, the precedence which military aid enjoyed over economic aid and the unsuitability of Soviet machinery for the climatological conditions in the Third World. One Soviet writer even went so far as to describe previous Soviet–Third World economic relations as "planned loss-making friendships."[23] On the other hand, the socialist-oriented regimes have been criticized for opportunism, for the failure to fulfill their obligations and repay loans and for their inability, due to their backwardness, to assimilate the aid.[24]

The debate on aid was not confined to self-criticism and an attack on allies. It also focused on whether aid still should be given at all. Divergent opinions still exist concerning this issue. One school of thought argues that the USSR's economic crisis is of such a nature that scarce resources should not be wasted in the Third World. Other writers believe that aid should be continued but under totally different conditions. This debate is certainly not comforting to the USSR's allies. Still less can the new emphasis in the literature on cost-effectiveness and profitability be welcomed in socialist-oriented regimes. Andrei Kolosovskii recently proposed "normal economic relations" with developing countries, but added that the USSR needs primarily partners who are solvent or possess resources needed by the USSR.[25] This would necessarily place socialist-oriented regimes such as Benin, Congo (Brazzaville), Ethiopia, and Mozambique very low down on the new prority list of the Soviet Union.

Prospects for socialism in the Third World

Not only has the role of the external factor been downgraded and even questioned in Soviet literature, but a growing number of analyses have focused on the inability of these regimes to ever achieve socialism. The inventory in political literature of what is lacking in these regimes has grown over time. The idea propagated for some twenty years in Soviet political literature that non-capitalist development "transforms a backward country into an industrial country within the lifespan of one generation"[26] has since the 1980s regularly been replaced with more realistic assessments. Even such an optimist as Rostislav Ul'ianovskii had to concede in 1982 that the model "encompasses a long epoch of transition to socialism."[27] Another Soviet scholar, Rachid Avakov, possibly considering the prevalent economic stagnation in countries such as Angola, Benin, Congo, Ethiopia, and Mozambique, said, "Societies of a socialist orientation have been in existence for decades now. In our fast-moving age this is an entire era. In the countries of socialist orientation many generations are surely not destined to see the end of the transition and the establishment of socialism there in full."[28]

Some scholars argue that this process *is longer* than was previously believed because the transitions to socialism in Central Asia and Mongolia were unique cases. According to Georgii Kim "mechanistic" attempts to duplicate the Mongolian and Central Asian experiments could lead to serious errors in practical policy.[29] The reason given why the above mentioned cases are no longer seen as of direct relevance for Third World regimes is that Central Asia made the transition to socialism within the framework and as an integral part of the Soviet Union, while Mongolia's geographic proximity to the USSR and the latter's economic aid facilitated the building of socialism.[30] Neither of these so-called "beneficial factors" are viewed today as relevant to the situation in which the socialist-oriented regimes happen to find themselves. The quantitative increase in the number of "progressive" regimes especially during the mid-1970s strengthened the belief in the USSR that the revolutionary process was irreversible. Socialist orientation was depicted as an ever-expanding phenomenon with a steadily increasing number of regimes opting for socialism. However, the recent Soviet reassessment of the developing world admits that the revolutionary process was in fact *reversible*. Euphemisms such as "zigzags, veerings and retreats," "degenerations," and a "retracing of steps" were subtly used to describe the revolutionary process.[31]

Besides this, one seldom finds references today to the bright prospects of socialist-oriented states. Terms such as complex problems and serious difficulties have since the 1980s been used more frequently to describe the socialist experiments in the Third World.[32]

Another aspect of the Soviet reassessment of the revolutionary process in the Third World is the open admittance that socialism is in fact not gaining ground in the world but is losing the race against capitalism. According to Kim Tsagolov, "The eighties showed that the highest wave of the national liberation movement was over for both the world revolutionary process in general and socialist orientation in particular."[33]

The previous tendency in Soviet political literature to ascribe all negative phenomenon in the socialist-oriented regimes to imperialist meddling has been replaced with more realistic analyses of the internal deficiencies of these regimes themselves. One Soviet writer has said that the papering over, in the past, of internal defects could be ascribed to the existence of "prohibited zones" not open for critical evaluations. According to him:

> It has become a ritual virtually to substitute for an analysis of the crisis and other negative processes in countries of socialist orientation, including failures in the economy and domestic and foreign policy, sacramental [*sic*] phrases such as "they are encountering difficulties" and "they are having to overcome the resistance of internal reaction and the consequences of colonialism." Although difficulties, the resistance of reaction and the intrigues of imperialism admittedly do exist, there are also other phenomena requiring objective study. These are for example the contradictions inherent in development along the path of a socialist orientation, intraparty struggle, degeneration of the leadership and the regime, violations of the rules of good-neighbourliness and international law.[34]

Third World socialism and world capitalism

Another element indicative of the Soviet new thinking regarding socialism in the Third World has been the more sober perspective of a number of prominent scholars on the position and role of these states in the world capitalist economy. The former view of Soviet scholars, as well as of Western dependency theorists, that the developing countries are dominated and exploited by the industrialized Western states and are destined to remain an underdeveloped periphery of the latter if a "delinking" from that system cannot be accomplished has been abandoned.

Victor Sheinis, a senior comparativist at IMEMO, has explicitly denied that states such as Brazil, Argentina, and Mexico are trapped in a vicious circle of underdevelopment and dependence and has argued that they may even join the ranks of the medium developed countries such as Greece, Portugal, and Spain in the next decade.[35]

The Orientalist Nodari Simoniia has criticized the one-sided emphasis in Soviet literature on the negative consequences of capitalism in the Third World. In sharp contrast with the traditional view, Simoniia argued that capitalism in the Third World was really a historically specific model of capitalist development and wrote that independent development could not take place through a "de-linking" from the capitalist economy but only through a growing integration in this system on an equitable basis. He also believed that some of the leading countries in the Third World are on the threshold of achieving economic independence.[36]

Another prominent author Evgenii Primakov has referred to a number of "subimperialist foci" in the Third World wanting to create a special place for themselves in the world capitalist economy. In this group of countries he included NIC's such as Brazil, the Philippines, South Korea, Singapore, and the OPEC countries, which all have their own mini-TNCs and export capital to the Third World. His view was that the latter group has succeeded in moving away from one-sided dependence on the West toward a situation of asymmetric interdependence.[37]

In short, prominent Soviet scholars recently have acknowledged that capitalist development in the Third World is an objective process leading to economic progress and that Third World regimes never really had any choice of paths of development. Mirskii has argued:

> Whoever has made a conscious effort to overcome capitalist, that is spontaneous, development, has executed a choice in the full sense of the word, thrown down a challenge to chaos and inertia and swum against the tide. . . . It could only have been – and is now – a question of a greater or lesser degree of independence within the framework of the world capitalist system and of a "place in the sun."[38]

Vanguard parties

The traditional Soviet view since the 1970s that the creation of MLVPs subscribing to scientific socialism would serve as a solution for all political vacillations, internal instability, and attempted counterrevolutions in radical Third World regimes, has in recent years been revised. The civil wars and armed insurrections in places like Angola, Afghanistan, Ethiopia, Kampuchea, Mozambique, Nicaragua, and South Yemen, are where MLVPs began. Client states' inability to win these wars, plus the political and military costs incurred by the Soviet Union by propping up these regimes, most probably served as a catalyst for the Soviet reassessment of the thesis that MLVPs in the Third World automatically lead to political stability and a consolidation of the revolutionary process.

During the initial stages of the Soviet reassessment in the early 1980s, scholars only went so far as to point subtly to the differences between "revolutionary democratic MLVPs" and genuine communist parties and also questioned whether all the parties in the Third World that have laid claim to MLVP status are in fact genuine MLVPs. The leaders of Mali and Afghanistan were, for example, accused of ultra-leftism and running ahead of events by claiming to have created MLVPs. The message that Soviet authors explicitly conveyed was that these parties are neither brought into being by anybody's will nor are they a reflection of the imperatives of revolutionary theory.[39]

As strange as it may seem, an aspect that also has been criticized severely is the homogeneous social nature of MLVPs which has been identified as the principal reason for the poor communication between the ruling elites and the masses as well as the absence of revolutionary enthusiasm of the latter for the regimes' policies.[40]

A qualitative change has in recent years been made to the previous MLVP approach to political development in the Third World progressive regimes. Gorbachev's emphasis on the peaceful resolution of Third World conflicts through a process of national reconciliation and some form of accommodation of opposition forces in the political processes in the conflict-ridden socialist-oriented regimes, is clearly in contradiction with the former MLVP approach with its unambiguous emphasis on the exclusion of opposition (non-Marxist) forces.

Shortcomings and faulty policies

Numerous other factors have since the early 1980s been identified in Soviet scholarly literature as the reasons for the stagnation found in these regimes. The public sectors in the socialist-oriented Third World states have been criticized for being "poorly managed, with incompetent, corrupt technocrats in charge" and have been described as models of "mismanagement and objects of plunder." According to Alexei Kiva, these negative phenomena have discredited the very idea of social justice and socialism in the Third World.[41]

The rapid collectivization of the agricultural sectors in these regimes after Marxist–Leninist inspired elites came to power has been identified as a factor having had an extremely negative effect on production. Anatolii P. Butenko has declared unequivocally that: "Today – and this is obvious to any educated Marxist – the practice of the 'hasty socialization' of the small-scale producer (the peasant and craftsman) and the elimination of the petty and middle merchants has completely demonstrated its invalidity."[42] Furthermore, the previous emphasis on the promotion of heavy industry gradually has been replaced with an emphasis on the value of the agricultural sector and small-scale industries. Lenin's NEP has been proposed as a sound model of development that ought to be implemented in the Third World.[43]

Finally, another significant aspect of the Soviet reassessment of socialism in the Third World has also been the emphasis placed in recent years on the negative effects of "non-class factors" such as ethnicity, traditionalism, and religion, as causes of conflict, underdevelopment and instability in the Third World.[44]

The end of a theory

As mentioned earlier, the Soviet reassessment of socialist orientation as a development model for the Third World went through two distinct phases. The discussion above briefly dealt with the most important earlier amendments to the theory of non-capitalist development. Since 1987, however, a new dimension was added to Soviet Third World debates when the theory, previously considered above suspicion, became the focus of attacks.[45] Writers such as R. Avakov, Iu. Alexandrov, Iu. Gavrilov, A. Kiva, V. Khoros, V. Maximenko, G. Mirskii, V. Sheinis, and N. Simoniia have argued that the theory of socialist orientation amounted to wishful thinking and that it could never have worked in practice.

One of the most devastating attacks on the theory was an article written by Viktor Sheinis, a chief research fellow at IMEMO. After analyzing the poor economic performance of socialist-oriented regimes compared to capitalistic countries, he came to the conclusion that capitalism was a vehicle for progress in the Third World. In effect what he did was to return to Marx's Asiatic mode of development and to the classic Marxist interpretation of the progressive nature of capitalism, *vis-à-vis* feudalism. Furthermore, Sheinis said, "The overwhelming majority of the developing countries has been pulled into the process of capitalist development." That change makes the whole question of "bypassing capitalist development" meaningless. He also added, "It has to be acknowledged that the non-capitalist path on the periphery of the world capitalist system has not become and will hardly become in the foreseeable future an alternative which is of impressive dimensions and sufficiently convincing."[46]

Georgii Mirskii, a senior researcher at IMEMO, recently argued that Lenin foresaw revolutions breaking out in Metropolitan Western Europe and because the latter never materialized, the whole idea of bypassing capitalism proved to be false because the USSR cannot serve as a substitute for Western aid.[47] Although the revisionist attack on the theory of socialist orientation provoked counterattacks from orthodox writers such as Ul'ianovskii, Kaufman, and Agaev,[48] it is clear that the theory of non-capitalist development has been so discredited and ridiculed in the last few years that one can rightly refer to the death of the theory.

The African response

An interesting development is the impact that the Soviet reassessment has had on the policies of the African socialist-oriented regimes. While not all the changes that have taken place in the Marxist regimes in Africa in recent years should be ascribed to the reassessment of socialist orientation and new thinking in the USSR and may in fact merely be the result of a process of learning from past mistakes, there are nevertheless a whole range of factors pointing to some relationship between the Soviet rethinking described above and current trends in Africa.

This is evident first from the fact that at least five African Marxist regimes have stated explicitly that they could not remain indifferent to current changes in the Soviet Union and Eastern Europe and that policies more in tune with world trends will have to be adopted in the future. Angola's President Eduardo dos Santos in January 1990 referred to the late-1989 events in Eastern Europe and said, "It is important that we take into account the experiences by other peoples following the same political and ideological policy as ours, who have already had the opportunity to face, in practice, a series of problems and difficulties we could avoid if we are aware of them, adopting appropriate solutions."[49]

Similarly, Congolese President Sassou-Nguesso said in December 1989 that the ruling party in the Congo "will have to evolve with a pragmatism that accepts a liberal democracy."[50] The Stalinist regime of Mengistu Haile Mariam of Ethiopia, as well as the leaders of Guinea-Bissau and Cape Verde, have made similar statements regarding the collapse of communism in Eastern Europe.[51]

Secondly, it is also clear that there is a relationship between the USSR's new emphasis on the political resolution of Third World conflicts and national reconciliation, and the events that led to the Cuban withdrawal from Angola and the political independence of Namibia. Although the conflicts in Angola, Ethiopia, and Mozambique are still continuing, the fact that peace talks have taken place from time to time *with the encouragement of the Soviet Union* is a sign that the new Soviet thinking also has influenced African leaders.

Third, in the light of the theoretical attacks since 1987 on the theory of socialist orientation itself, it is likely that the renunciation of Marxism–Leninism as the official ideology by Benin and Mozambique is somehow related to the demise of the theory.[52]

Fourth, every Afro-Marxist regime today has adjusted at least some of its policies in accordance with the new prescriptions (some predating the Gorbachev era) found in Soviet writings or with the new policies and models that the USSR and East European countries themselves are trying to implement. Political aspects such as the adoption of new constitutions, the redefinition of the role of the ruling parties in society and multipartyism have been placed on the agenda. In Angola, Mozambique, Guinea-Bissau, Madagascar and Sao Tome and Principe, the ruling parties have lifted the former ban on opposition parties.[53]

In recent years all the Marxist regimes also have changed their economic policies. Soviet suggestions in this regard, of course, predate Gorbachev's coming to power. To a greater or lesser extent these countries have all implemented liberalization measures such as the denationalization of unprofitable state enterprises, the adoption of new investment codes, the greater use of market forces, and the acceptance of IMF restructuring programs.

Conclusion

It is quite clear that the revision of doctrinal concepts of the Soviet theory of international relations encouraged and accelerated the reassessment of socialist orientation as a model for the Third World. Although all the aspects of new thinking are not actually new and in some cases only amount to a subtle redefinition of philosophical assumptions, this is not the case with the theory of socialist orientation. In the last few years Soviet Third World scholars have chipped away at this theory to such an extent that nothing of it remains today. One of the possible implications of the Soviet reassessment is that it may endorse an eventual systematic disengagement from radical Third World regimes. Another aspect is that economic rather than ideological factors will take precedence in Soviet Third World relations. The new Soviet emphasis on solvent partners, profitability, and mutual benefit probably has led to a downgrading of the socialist-oriented regimes on the USSR's new priority list.

The Soviet reassessment and especially the more recent attacks on the theory must have been somewhat of a shock for the political elites in these regimes. It could not have been pleasant to hear that the theory in which they believed, to which they had affixed their hopes and which they had tried to implement in practice, could never have worked from the start and that the theory, as a result of the recent reinterpretation of Lenin, was in the first place never even applicable to their cases.

The fact that countries such as Benin and Mozambique recently renounced Marxism–Leninism and that there is currently a trend in the majority of socialist oriented regimes toward multipartyism and economic liberalization can hardly be a coincidence.

Notes

1 M.S. Gorbachev, report to the 27th CPSU Congress, in *Joint Publications Research Service-UKO-86-011*, 23 July 1986, p. 6.
2 *Foreign Broadcast Information Service, Daily Report: Soviet Union [FBIS-SOV]*, 2 September 1987, p. 23.
3 M. Gorbachev, *Perestroika: New Thinking for our Country and the World* (London: Collins, 1987), p. 250.
4 *FBIS-SOV-88-033*, 19 February 1988, pp. 57–58.
5 *FBIS-SOV-89-077*, 24 April 1989, p. 9; *FBIS-SOV-89-212*, 3 November 1987, p. 88; and *FBIS-SOV-88-244*, 20 December 1988, p. 12.
6 See "Address by E.A. Shevardnadze to a conference of the USSR Ministry of Foreign Affairs, June 25–27, 1988," in *Soviet Law and Government*, vol. 28, no. 2 (1989), pp. 21, 22, 25.
7 V.A. Medvedev, "Toward cognition of socialism," in *JPRS-UKO-89-005*, 2 March 1989, p. 5; N. A. Borisova, I.I. Lunev, and N.M. Shatskaia, "New political thinking and the world communist movement," in *JPRS-UIA-89-008*, 8 May 1989, p. 2.
8 M. Gorbachev, *October and Perestroika: The Revolution Continues* (Moscow: Novosti Press Agency Publishing House, 1987), p. 59.
9 E.M. Primakov, V.A. Martinov, and G.G. Diligenskii, "Certain problems in the new thinking," in *JPRS-UWE-89-011*, 5 October 1989, p. 2.
10 V.A. Medvedev, "The Great October and our time," in *JPRS-UKO-88-007*, 4 April 1988, p. 2; A.V. Nikiforov, "Peaceful coexistence and new thinking," in *JPRS-USA-88-006*, 5 July 1988, p. 2; A. Bovin, "October and peaceful coexistence," in *FBIS-SOV-88-217*, 9 November 1988, p. 11.
11 G.G. Diligenskii, "Revolutionary theory and the present day," in *JPRS-UIA-88-014*, 24 August 1988, p. 12; A. Bovin, and V.P. Lukin, "On the threshold of a new century," in *JPRS-UWE-88-004*, 19 May 1988, p. 28.
12 A. Iakovlev, *The Great French Revolution and the Present Time* (Moscow: Novosti, 1989), p. 15; A.A. Galkin, "New political thinking and problems of the workers' movement," in *JPRS-88-010*, 6 October 1988, p. 22.
13 Diligenskii, "Revolutionary theory," p. 9; Bovin, and Lukin, "On the threshold," p. 71; Primakov, Martinov, and Diligenskii, "Certain problems," p. 9.
14 Y.V. Shishkov, "Perestroika and the signs of convergence" in *JPRS-UIA-89-009*, 22 May 1989; S.V. Pronin, "Ideology in an interconnected world," in *JPRS-UWE-89-003*, 10 February 1989, pp. 2–11. See also Georgii Shakhnazarov's comments on Moscow Television in *FBIS-SOV-89-047*, 13 March 1989.
15 V.G. Solodovnikov, *The Present Stage of Non-Capitalist Development in Asia and Africa* (Budapest: Center for Afro-Asian Research, 1973), p. 12; Y. Zhukov, *et al.*, *The Third World: Problems and Prospects*, Moscow: Progress Publishers, 1970, p. 21.
16 "Statement of the meeting of representatives of the communist and workers' parties," *New Times*, Supplement to no. 50, 1960, p. 11.
17 V.I. Lenin, *Speeches at Congresses of the Communist International* (Moscow: Progress Publishers, 1972), p. 59.

18 V. Solodovnikov and V. Bogoslovskii, *Non-Capitalist Development: An Historical Outline* (Moscow: Progress Publishers, 1975), pp. 36–84.
19 N. Kosukhin, "Some features of the vanguard parties of the working people," *Asia and Africa Today*, no. 3, 1983, p. 5; A. Kiva, "Revolutionary-democratic parties: some trends of development," *Asia and Africa Today*, no. 4, 1978, p. 44.
20 Kosukhin, "Some features," p. 10.
21 Iu. Andropov, 1983 speech at the plenary session of the CPSU CC, in *The Current Digest of the Soviet Press* [CDSP], vol. 25, no. 25, 20 July 1983, p. 8.
22 Iu.S. Novopashin, "The influence of real socialism on the world revolutionary process," in *CDSP*, vol. 35, no. 43, 23 November 1983, p. 9.
23 B. Pikiatskin, "A bitter pill is the best medicine," in *CDSP*, vol. 41, no. 25, 1989, pp. 29–30; A. Kupriianov, "The close and distant Third World," in *FBIS-SOV-88-190*, 30 September 1988, pp. 4–6; B. Sergeev, "Help, but within one's means," in *FBIS-SOV-89-137*, 19 July 1989, pp. 10–11.
24 See sources cited in note 23 *supra*.
25 A.I. Kolosovskii, "Regional conflicts and global security," in *JPRS-UWE-88-011*, 14 October 1988, p. 15.
26 See "The programme of the Communist Party of the Soviet Union: 1961," in T.P. Whitney, ed., *The Communist Blueprint for the Future* (New York: E.P. Dutton and Co., 1962), p. 146.
27 R.A. Ul'ianovskii, "National and revolutionary democracy," in USSR Academy of Sciences, Institute for African Studies, *Africa in Soviet Studies: Annual 1986* (Moscow: Nauka Publishers, 1987), p. 22.
28 R. Avakov, "The new thinking and the problem of study of the developing countries," in *JPRS-UWE-88-003*, 22 February 1988, p. 31.
29 G. Kim, "Socialist orientation: theory and practice," *Socialism: Principles, Practice, Prospects*, no. 7, July 1988, p. 23.
30 Iu. Popov, *Essays in Political Economy: Socialism and Socialist Orientation* (Moscow: Progress Publishers, 1987), pp. 197–198; A. Kaufman, "Historical importance of socialist orientation," in *Socialism: Principles, Practice, Prospects*, no. 8, August 1986, p. 29.
31 Kim, "Socialist orientation," p. 23; K. Brutents, "The liberated countries at the beginning of the 1980s," in *JPRS-UKO-84-009*, p. 123; Avakov, "The new thinking," p. 25.
32 G. Mirskii, "The question of the choice of path and orientation of the developing countries," in *JPRS-UWE-87-009*, 22 September 1987, p. 80.
33 "The USSR and the Third World," *International Affairs*, December 1988, p. 146.
34 Avakov, "The new thinking," p. 27.
35 See P. Bellis, "Third World review," *Detente*, nos. 9/10, 1987, p. 42.
36 N. Simoniia, "Dialectics and interrelations," in *JPRS-UWE-85-007*, 28 June 1985, pp. 120–33.
37 E.M. Primakov, *The East after the Collapse of the Colonial System* (Moscow: Nauka Publishing House, 1983), pp. 42–48.
38 Mirskii, "The question," p. 72; A.M. Vasilev, "Liberated countries: realities and paradoxes of development," in *JPRS-UKO-88-001*, 11 July 1988, p. 81.

39 Iu.V. Irkhin, "Formation of the vanguard parties of the working people in socialist-oriented countries," in *JPRS-UPS-85-059*, 30 July 1985, p. 10; Ul'ianovskii, "National," p. 23; N. Simoniia, "The present stage of liberation struggle," *Asia and Africa Today*, no. 3, 1981, p. 4.
40 A.V. Kiva, "Socialist orientation: reality and illusions," *International Affairs*, July 1988, p. 85.
41 *Ibid.*, p. 83.
42 A.P. Butenko, "Some theoretical problems in the transition to socialism in countries with an underdeveloped economy," in *JPRS*, no. 1393, 29 March 1983, p. 73.
43 Kim, "Socialist orientation," p. 24.
44 V. Lee and G. Mirskii, "Socialist orientation and new political thinking," *Asia and Africa Today*, no. 4, 1988, p. 69; Mirskii, "The question," p. 71.
45 S. Woodby, "The death of a dream: Gorbachevist revisions of Marxism–Leninism for the Third World," unpublished paper, November 1988, pp. 21–24.
46 V.L. Sheinis, "The developing countries and the new political thinking," in *JPRS-UWC-87-003*, 9 December 1987, p. 10.
47 Mirskii, "The question," p. 22. See also Kiva, "Socialist orientation," pp. 78–86.
48 A. Kaufman and R. Ul'ianovskii, "The question of socialist orientation in liberated countries," in *JPRS-UIA-88-013*, 5 August 1988, pp. 20–26; S.L. Agaev, "Political realities of the developing world and social dialectics," in *JPRS-UWC-88-002*, 5 April 1988, pp. 1–10.
49 See President dos Santos' speech in *Angop Document*, no. 66, 6 February 1990, pp. 1–2.
50 British Broadcasting Corporation, *Summary of World Broadcasts* (*SWB*), *SWB ME/0633*, 9 December 1989, p. B5.
51 *Africa Research Bulletin* (*Political*), March 1990, p. 9865; *SWB ME/0673*, 27 January 1990, p. B6; *Keesing's Record of World Events*, February 1990, p. 37239 (hereafter cited respectively as *ARB(P)* and *KRWE*).
52 *KRWE*, February 1990, pp. 37238–39; *SWB ME/0635*, 9 December 1989, p. 2; *ARB(P)*, 15 January 1990, pp. 9514–15; Mozambique Information Office, *News Review*, no. 159/160, 1 August 1989; *ARB(P)*, 15 August 1989, pp. 9343–44.
53 See *SWB ME/0668*, 22 January 1990, p. B1; *News Review*, no. 171, 25 January 1990; Mozambique News Agency, *Mozambique File*, no. 165, April 1990, p. 7, and no. 166, May 1990, p. 12; *SWB ME/0736*, 11 April 1990, p. B8; *ARB(P)*, 15 May 1990, pp. 9653–54; *ARB(P)*, 15 December 1989, p. 9520 and *SWB ME/0729*, 3 April 1990, p. B5; *ARB(P)*, 15 January 1990, p. 9510.

10 Soviet policy in the Middle East: Gorbachev's imprint

Carol R. Saivetz

When Mikhail S. Gorbachev became General Secretary of the Communist Party of the Soviet Union in March 1985, the USSR was enmeshed deeply in Afghanistan, the Arab–Israeli dispute appeared both treacherous and stalemated, and the then five-year-old Gulf War presented increasingly serious problems to the Soviet Union. In 1985, the Soviet leadership was unwilling to consider withdrawing from Afghanistan, despite the war's rising costs. In the Arab–Israeli arena, the business-as-usual rhythm of siding with the Arabs against US-backed Israel was broken by the Camp David Accords and the Egyptian–Israeli peace treaty. Although Arab enmity toward Egypt provided Moscow with the initially strong rallying point of "rejectionism," in the long run this position left the Soviets with client states that were more or less peripheral to the central Middle East concerns. In the Gulf region, the Iran–Iraq War forced Moscow to play a careful balancing act between its military/political links with Baghdad and its hoped-for ties with anti-American Iran. Moreover, the war's divisive effects on the Middle East scuttled Soviet attempts at rallying Arab forces against the United States and Israel.

These events, in a nutshell, formed the Brezhnev (and Andropov and Chernenko) legacy to Mikhail Gorbachev. In contrast, the past five years have shown clearly that Gorbachev's priority, unlike that of his predecessors, is domestic reconstruction. This look inward required a different kind of foreign policy, one conducive to perestroika at home. In this light, the new General Secretary has demonstrated a willingness to use new approaches to the several overlapping Middle East conflicts. The following list is but a bare outline of Gorbachev's policy initiatives in the Middle East: Soviet troops have withdrawn from the protracted conflict in Afghanistan; the USSR opened diplomatic communications with Israel; Gorbachev apparently pressured both Syrian President Hafiz al-Assad and Palestine Liberation Organization Chairman Yasir Arafat to recognize Israel; and finally, the Kremlin has pursued a closer political, economic, and perhaps military relationship with Teheran.

These departures from previous Soviet policy in the Middle East are supported by a far more sophisticated understanding of Third World dynamics and by the new political thinking that constitutes the new Soviet world view. Yet, Soviet policy in the Middle East raises several important questions. Have Soviet objectives changed? What is the blend of old and new – despite new thinking – in Soviet policy toward the Middle East?

This chapter will analyze the innovations in Soviet Middle East policy in the Gorbachev era with a view to answering these questions. The first section will briefly examine Soviet policy in the Middle East in the era of perestroika. The second section will assess the features of Gorbachev's imprint and speculate on the future of the USSR's Middle East policy. And finally, the chapter will look briefly at the Soviet response to the Iraqi invasion of Kuwait.

Gorbachev and the Middle East

As described elsewhere in this volume, the new political thinking indicates new trends in foreign policy. In the simplest terms, because of the Soviet Union's pressing domestic problems, Gorbachev is seeking a respite from international tensions. It can also be argued that the new Soviet leadership found the costs of an empire too great. An end to the arms race, the withdrawal from Afghanistan, and an end to over-commitment in the Third World would facilitate expenditure of much needed rubles to rebuild and refurbish the domestic economy. Finally, the USSR, in search of capital investments, new technology, and a new role in the world, must appear less threatening so as to be admitted to the World Club.

These significant changes in the Soviet approach to international relations form the background to Gorbachev's imprint. A more nuanced and sophisticated understanding of superpower involvement in Third World politics underlies the specific changes in policy to be described below.

Perhaps the most telling indicator of the new Middle East policy has been the Soviet withdrawal from Afghanistan. At the 27th Party Congress in February 1986, Gorbachev proclaimed the five-year-old Afghan war a "bleeding wound." Later, in Vladivostok in July 1986, he announced the token withdrawal of six divisions from Afghanistan. Simultaneously, the new Afghan Communist Party Secretary Najibullah moved to broaden the base of his regime by proposing a six-month cease-fire and establishing a government of national reconciliation.

According to Soviet spokesmen, this vague formulation was designed to ensure communist control, but through a coalition government.[1]

The increasing costs of the counterinsurgency struggle, especially after the US decision to supply the mujahideen with Stinger anti-aircraft missiles, ultimately forced the USSR to call for an end to the war.[2] In February 1988 Gorbachev announced that a Soviet withdrawal from Afghanistan could begin 15 May, if a United Nations sponsored agreement among Afghanistan, Pakistan, the United States, and the USSR could be reached by 15 March. Although the original deadline was not met, the Soviets continued to seek a way out. Finally, after an April mini-summit between Najibullah and Gorbachev in Tashkent, the two announced agreement on the terms of a withdrawal. The UN sponsored settlement called for a Soviet withdrawal by 15 February 1989, and the resettlement of refugees. In addition, the USSR loosened the link between its prestige and the fate of the Afghan government.

While Moscow's attention was focused perhaps on Afghanistan, the rest of the Middle East did not go untouched by new thinking. Having been an active participant in the ongoing Arab–Israeli conflict since 1955, the Kremlin in 1985 was, in the words of one observer, a superpower in eclipse.[3] The Soviet Union could not offer its services as broker for a peace settlement because it had severed diplomatic relations with Israel in the aftermath of the 1967 war. This void left the field open for, first Henry Kissinger, and then Zbigniew Brzezinski to negotiate disengagement agreements and the Camp David Accords respectively. Over the same period of time, Egypt abrogated its friendship and cooperation treaty with the USSR, leaving the latter with radical clients Syria and Libya.

Thus, within a few months of becoming the new Party Secretary, Gorbachev initiated contacts with Israel. In July 1985, then Soviet ambassador to France Iuli Vorontsov met with his Israeli counterpart at the home of pianist Daniel Barenboim. Reportedly, Vorontsov suggested that relations could be reestablished with Israel if Tel Aviv were to withdraw from part of the Golan Heights. Discussions also touched on the issue of Soviet Jewish emigration to Israel.[4] In July 1987 an official Soviet delegation arrived in Israel for a three-month stay ostensibly to inventory Russian church properties, and a year later an Israeli delegation was permitted to visit Moscow. These moves have been paralleled by the easing of emigration restrictions and the opening of a Jewish cultural center in Moscow. Finally in fall 1990 consular relations were formally reestablished.

On the Arab side of the ledger, Moscow's efforts have been directed toward modifying the policies of its radical clients and enhancing ties with moderate Arab states. When Syria's President Hafiz al-Assad traveled to the Soviet Union in April 1987, he was told by Gorbachev that the absence of relations between Tel Aviv and Moscow was not normal.[5] A year later, at a Kremlin reception, Gorbachev lectured visiting PLO Chief Arafat that Israel also was concerned about its security and borders.[6] Later that year, Moscow reportedly pressured the PLO to alter fundamentally its stand on the nonrecognition of Israel. Following the Palestine National Congress's historic meeting in Algiers in November 1988, Yasir Arafat announced that the PLO would accept United Nations resolutions 242 and 338 and that it was anxious to pursue negotiations with Israel.

Many of the changes in the PLO position and in the Soviet response thereto resulted from the *intifadah*, or Palestinian resistance to Israeli occupation, which has become a major fact of life in the Middle East. It riveted world attention on the Arab–Israeli conflict and laid the groundwork for the increase in the PLO's stature and declaration of Palestinian statehood. When the uprising began in December 1987 Moscow initially was restrained. Surprised by its outbreak, the USSR stressed both its indigenous origins and its peaceful nature. As it has continued, the Kremlin has emphasized its legitimacy and supported the declaration of Palestinian statehood.

In February 1989 the Soviet Union made clear its intention to restore its Middle East standing. In a high-profile trip to the Middle East, Soviet Foreign Minister Eduard Shevardnadze met with Arab leaders (Egyptian President Mubarak, Yasir Arafat, and Syrian President Hafiz al Assad) and Israeli leaders, with Iraqi President Saddam Hussein in Baghdad, and the Ayatollah Khomeini in Teheran. Shevardnadze worked to sustain the momentum in Soviet–Israeli affairs and to garner support for an international conference on the Middle East, as well as for a withdrawal of US and Soviet ships from the Gulf.

That Foreign Minister Eduard Shevardnadze's itinerary included Baghdad and Teheran indicated Moscow's ongoing concern over events in the Gulf. Although by then a cease-fire between Iran and Iraq had taken hold, the course of the war had forced the USSR to walk a tightrope between the combatants. Indeed, Soviet policy until almost the end of the conflict was directed toward avoiding a choice between Iraq and Iran. Following the Iraqi attack on Iran in September 1980, the Soviet Union officially declared neutrality; however, it held up military supplies to Iraq and permitted its allies, Syria and Libya, to transport Soviet equipment to Iran. Simultaneously, Moscow permitted several Warsaw Treaty nations to ship spare parts to Iraq. When the fortunes of war changed in 1982 as Iran repulsed Iraqi forces and crossed into Iraqi territory, the Soviet Union reopened Baghdad's arms pipeline and took up an increasingly anti-Teheran position. By 1983, the clerical regime in Iran had cracked down on the Tudeh (Communist) Party, making Iran's anti-Soviet leanings clearer.[7] While Moscow pursued a more overtly pro-Iraqi policy between 1983 and 1985, it also grew increasingly concerned over the shifting superpower balance in the region and the realignments in the Arab world – all caused by the war.

When Shevardnadze succeeded Andrei Gromyko as Foreign Minister, the USSR shifted to a more even-handed approach. The Kremlin criticized domestic trends in Iran plus Teheran's refusal to negotiate, but also exchanged several diplomatic and economic delegations with Iran. These contacts culminated in the trip of Soviet Deputy Foreign Minister Georgii Kornenko to Teheran in early 1986. According to Iranian dispatches, the discussions held with Ali Akbar Velayati and Hashemi Rafsanjani were "extensive," and Kornenko emphasized Soviet interest in expanding relations between Moscow and Teheran. Further discussions were then held on the resumption of Iranian natural gas exports to the USSR.[8] The late 1986 revelations that the United States had sold arms to Teheran provided Moscow with a tremendous propaganda opportunity. Underneath the bravado, however, lay a very real concern that Iran might reestablish diplomatic relations with the United States. Thus, throughout the first half of 1987, Moscow continued to pursue the compartmentalized policy of condemning Iranian intransigence about negotiations and seeking bilateral economic agreements and high-level political contacts.

By the spring of 1987, Soviet concerns centered on Kuwait's requests to both superpowers to protect its shipping from Iranian raids. As Kuwaiti ships increasingly came under Iranian attack and as Kuwait found itself a target for Shi'a terrorism at home, it sought international protection for its tankers. Moscow offered to lease three tankers, and Washington agreed to reflag eleven tankers and provide them with escort through the waters of the Gulf. The Kuwaiti appeal offered the USSR a formal invitation to the Gulf; yet, it also provided further legitimacy for American naval activity. The USSR, therefore, could not condemn the reflagging operation per se without calling into question its own assistance to the Kuwaitis.[9]

These complications of diplomacy led the USSR to join with other members of the United Nations Security Council to vote for a cease-fire resolution (UNSC 598). The Soviet Union undertook, almost simultaneously, independent mediation efforts: in mid-June 1987, Deputy Foreign Minister Iuli Vorontsov was sent to the region as Gorbachev's personal emissary. According to reports, Vorontsov proposed an end to the tanker war and the start of negotiations. Despite Teheran's objections to parts of the plan, Vorontsov was then sent on to Baghdad. Discussions continued in Moscow with officials of both countries.

Because talks with the Iranians yielded a new pipeline agreement and other economic benefits, Moscow assumed an increasingly pro-Iranian stance. The Kremlin refused to support sanctions against Teheran and shifted closer to the Iranian position on UNSC 598 by calling for the cease-fire to occur concurrently with the investigation into responsibility for the war. The pro-Iranian tilt led many in the Arab world to question Moscow's support for the Arab cause. At the Arab League's Amman summit meeting of November 1987, the Arab representatives focused on the Gulf War and, for the first time, not on the Arab–Israeli dispute. Even Syria acquiesced to a resolution that strongly condemned the Teheran regime for continuing the war and ignoring UNSC 598. Yet, if the USSR was losing points with the Arabs, Iran, too, seemed to blame Moscow for the fortunes of war. In the winter of 1988, when Iraqi-modified, Soviet-made missiles hit Teheran, Iran held the Soviet Union responsible. Thus, the winter and spring of 1988 appeared to be the low point of Moscow's fortunes in the region.

Battlefield operations ended within weeks of the US downing of an Iranian airbus over the Gulf in early July. Two weeks later, on 18 July 1988, Teheran announced its acceptance of UNSC 598. Simultaneously, Iuli Vorontsov traveled to the war zone, arriving in Baghdad on the 17th and spending the 20th to the 22nd in Teheran. According to several reports, Vorontsov offered the auspices of the USSR to mediate between the two combatants.[10] The end to the Iran–Iraq war, at least on the battlefield, lessened the pressure on the USSR to choose sides and reduced the likelihood that the Kremlin could be denounced for tilting openly toward Teheran. It also allowed Moscow greater flexibility in pursuit of the mutually beneficial economic relationship with Teheran.

This survey makes clear that Moscow is utilizing old and new techniques and approaches to attempt to influence the courses of Middle Eastern events, which will be analyzed in the next section.

Gorbachev's imprint

The bare outlines of Gorbachev's imprint on Soviet policy in the Middle East should now be visible. The main points include the desire to alter the international image and reputation of the USSR as well as the search for Middle Eastern (and Third World in general) trading partners whose expertise, manufactured goods, and even raw materials can benefit the

Soviet economy. To that end, Moscow has demonstrated a flexibility and moderation not seen previously in Soviet policy.

As noted above, the Soviet search for participation in the international economic system and for credits from and trade with the West necessitates a new, less threatening Soviet image. Personnel changes began the process. Shevardnadze replaced the dour Gromyko, and Gorbachev himself cuts a very different image from his predecessors. His trips abroad have been nothing but triumphant. Additionally, there has been a remarkable change in the diplomatic corps with old-time party hacks replaced by "new thinkers." Yet, it has been the significant policy alterations that will do the most to enhance Moscow's image.

In addition to pulling out of Afghanistan and initiating contacts with Israel, the Kremlin had pressured the radical Arabs to moderate their policies and sought a more centrist position in the Middle East. Even after Yasir Arafat's welcome public pronouncements about Israel, Moscow has continued to push for alterations in the policies of its radical clients, especially Syria. In late November 1989, Soviet ambassador to Damascus Aleksandr Zotov indicated that the Soviet Union no longer supported Syria's goal of strategic parity with Israel. In January 1990 several reports appeared in the Middle East press that the USSR resolved to cut its military presence in Syria. By one account, the Soviets were looking to reduce their presence by 50 percent and according to another, Moscow withdrew 500 troops in December 1989 and an additional 400 to 500 soldiers were to leave by the end of 1990.[11] The seriousness of the Soviet intent may be seen in the fact that Syrian media took pains to dispel rumors of a Soviet–Syrian rift.

The desire to play the centrist part or, at the least, to appear as the backer of the centrist Middle East forces is also manifest in Soviet–Egyptian relations and in Moscow's ties with the Gulf sheikhdoms. Egyptian President Sadat's signature on the Camp David Accords represented the end of an era. From the halcyon days of Soviet assistance to Egypt during the War of Attrition, Egypt by 1979 had moved fully into the US camp. Long isolated by its treaty with Israel, Cairo was reintegrated into the Arab world in November 1987 because of its solid support for Iraq in the Gulf War. Given Egypt's new acceptability, Moscow moved to restore the long-attenuated links: Egypt's debt has been rescheduled and, as noted above, Cairo was the first stop on Shevardnadze's tour in February of 1989. Finally, Gorbachev hosted Hosni Mubarak in the Kremlin in spring 1990. The two countries signed a joint statement of principles that included recognition of new political thinking, a call for an international conference on the Middle East, and criticism of continuing Israeli occupation of the West

Bank and Gaza and of the resettlement of Soviet Jews there. In the Arabian Peninsula Kuwait was Moscow's only link to the conservative Gulf sheikhdoms until 1985. Gorbachev's diplomatic offensive resulted in the establishment of relations with Oman, the United Arab Emirates, Qatar, and in the fall of 1990, with Bahrain and Saudi Arabia. Each for its own reasons decided that the time was propitious for links to the Soviet Union. The new embassies mean that Moscow in effect has broken into the region and created ties with the conservative Gulf Cooperation Council.

In addition, Moscow clearly hopes to enhance its new image by positioning itself to play the mediator's role, whether it be between Iraq and Iran or between Israel and the Arabs. As noted above, the USSR offered its auspices to Baghdad and Teheran at the same time as UNSC 598 was being discussed. At that time, it seemed that Moscow indeed might be the one country with reasonable links to both sides. This possibility may explain the move to improve ties to Teheran in the fall of 1987. In spring 1990, the Kremlin again offered to mediate the dispute. While both Iran and Iraq appeared more receptive to these 1990 Soviet initiatives, Moscow was careful to make clear that its intended role should complement UN efforts.

In terms of the Arab–Israeli dispute, once peace – not war or stalemate – determined the Middle East agenda, the Soviet Union had to prove its credentials as a moderate broker. This strong desire to remain an active player in the Middle East, to avoid being eclipsed again by the United States, underlies the renewal of contacts with Israel. It is as though the Kremlin realizes that its oft-repeated calls for an international conference on the Middle East were ignored as long as it was seen only as being a biased participant. To this end Moscow has pushed for direct talks between Israel and the PLO and continued to condemn the Israeli occupation of the West Bank and Gaza.

Political image making is just one side of the perestroika impulse; trade to benefit the ailing Soviet economy is the other. Examples abound. Although this chapter has not focused at all on the Maghreb, Soviet policy there illustrates the drive for trade. In October of 1987 Algeria's finance minister traveled to Moscow where he signed a new cooperation protocol. Then in February 1988 *Izvestiia* announced an accord whereby Algeria would export construction equipment to the USSR. The *Izvestiia* article stressed that the USSR needed this equipment and that it was part of a new Soviet policy toward the Third World that focused on manufactures, not only on raw material exports.[12] One of the manufactures to be imported by the Soviet Union are Algerian bathroom fixtures – items much needed in the USSR.

Trade, in addition to the political and diplomatic considerations previously noted, also may explain the renewal of contacts with Israel. Tel Aviv, with its international reputation for sophisticated technology and for such things as pharmaceuticals, seems an obvious target for Soviet cultivation. Indeed, within the last several months, the USSR and Israel have agreed to open a Soviet trade office in Israel. According to the *Jerusalem Post*, Soviet officials were interested in tourism, health care, and dairy technology. It was reported also that the USSR might be interested in buying Israeli produce.[13] It also should be noted in this context that Shimon Peres, the leader of the Labor Alliance, was scheduled to visit Moscow in December 1989. He had been invited by the Moscow Peace Committee and he supposedly was bringing with him proposals for joint ventures in pharmaceuticals.

During this same period, Soviet–Iranian trade has blossomed. There have been numerous exchanges of trade delegations resulting in new agreements about joint fishing ventures, railroads, shipping on the Caspian Sea, and Soviet aid to modernize the Isfahan steel mill. Most notably, the Iranian press announced a new natural gas agreement and the provision of Soviet credits to Iran totaling 1.2 billion rubles.[14] The USSR also has found new sources of capital in the Gulf. The Kuwaiti news agency announced a loan of $300 million to the Soviet Union.[15]

Overall, the volume of Soviet trade with Middle Eastern countries has increased. In particular, the statistics on Soviet trade with selected Middle Eastern countries indicates a significant increase in imports from these states to the Soviet Union. This increase reflects not only Moscow's need for certain items, but also an attempt to settle outstanding Third World debt.

Finally, the Soviet initiatives in the Middle East over the past five years show conclusively that Moscow intends to remain an influential player in the region. The Soviet Union has more than thirty years of diplomatic, military, and economic investment in the Middle East that it is unwilling to abandon. With the possible exception of Afghanistan, the USSR has not indicated that it is about to pack its bags and go home.

Even in Afghanistan, Moscow has shown a remarkable staying power. The Gorbachev regime has gone out of its way to try to stabilize the Afghan situation subsequent to the withdrawal. Contrary to expectations, the Najibullah government survived the exodus of the Soviet troops because of dissension among the mujahideen groups. Nonetheless, they remain a formidable threat to the regime and an obstacle to normalization. It is for these reasons that Iuli Vorontsov, the ambassador to Kabul and a deputy foreign minister, has been trying to negotiate both with and among the various rebel groups. In attempts at

Table 10.1 *Soviet trade with selected Middle East countries (in millions of rubles)*

Country	1987	1988
Algeria		
Exports	132.4	145.4
Imports	113.4	223.5
Egypt		
Exports	295.7	271.2
Imports	296.5	314.2
Iran		
Exports	110.4	119.2
Imports	49.5	77.0
Iraq		
Exports	324.3	309.1
Imports	788.3	961.4
Saudi Arabia		
Exports	12.4	12.8
Imports		12.6
Syria		
Exports	250.1	170.5
Imports	190.5	239.1

Source: Vneshnie ekonomicheskie sviazi SSSR v 1988 g. (Moscow: Finansy i statistiki, 1989)

establishing a coalition government, Vorontsov met with mujahideen in Saudi Arabia and in Iran and with former Afghan King Zahir Shah. Moscow's attitude toward these negotiations indicates that stabilization is the ultimate goal. It will not, however, stop supporting the regime until such time as there is a negotiated coalition government. Until then, the USSR continues its military support to Kabul, including the provision of Scud missiles, tanks, armored personnel carriers, and trucks.[16] Moscow has thus far withdrawn, but not disengaged from Afghanistan.

That the Soviet Union intends to remain involved in regional politics and that it fully intends to shore up its long-term alliances may be seen in Soviet–Syrian relations as well. It would seem, for example, that although Moscow wanted to push for Syrian moderation, those pressures were limited. Just prior to Assad's spring 1990 visit to Moscow, the Soviets seemed to backtrack. The Gulf press reported that not only were the Soviet Union and Syria negotiating a secret contract to refurbish Syrian air defense systems, but also that Moscow continued to supply SS-21s and Sukhoi-24s to Syria.[17] Apparently, Assad's trip to

Moscow was relatively successful for the Syrians. Despite differences regarding Lebanon and Jewish emigration, both sides reiterated the strength of the Soviet–Syrian relationship. Additionally, *Pravda* noted that they had discussed "Syrian military modernization."[18] This would seem to corroborate other reports from the Arab media.

Soviet support for Syria includes the search for creative ways to finance Damascus' debt to the USSR. According to A.S. Skripkin, a Soviet envoy in the Syrian capital, the USSR is looking to find investment opportunities for Syria in the southern parts of the USSR.[19] *Izvestiia* then reported that Syrian workers were on the job at USSR construction sites. Moreover, Syrian construction companies were to deliver equipment and finished materials, items in short supply in the Soviet Union.[20]

Finally, in what might be considered an example of old thinking, the USSR recognized that Iran is truly the strategic prize in the Gulf and, therefore, never abandoned its desire to take advantage of the Islamic revolution's anti-American nature. Following the Iran–Iraq cease-fire, the amelioration of Soviet–Iranian relations accelerated. In January 1989 the Ayatollah Javadi Amoli delivered a letter from Ayatollah Khomeini to Gorbachev. According to Teheran television, Khomeini praised Gorbachev's courage, boldness, and bravery. Ironically the letter also included the following: "It is clear to all that henceforth communism must be sought in the museums of world political history and that it is not possible for materialism to save humanity from the crisis of lack of spiritual conviction."[21] Thus, despite its anti-communism, the message held out the promise of better relations.

The flourish of diplomatic activity between Iran and the USSR included trade negotiations and a meeting between Velayati and Shevardnadze in Paris. The USSR welcomed not only the advance in Soviet–Iranian relations but also the improvement in Teheran's ties with the Western European countries. When Shevardnadze arrived in Teheran, he brought a letter from Gorbachev to the Iranian leadership. The Teheran press characterized the exchange of letters as a turning point in Soviet–Iranian relations.

Despite a slight disruption in the warming trend caused by the Salmon Rushdie affair, contacts were maintained throughout the spring. When the Ayatollah Khomeini died in early June, the Kremlin leadership sent condolences to the Iranian people, and a delegation of Soviet Muslims traveled to Iran during the official mourning period. The high point came in late June when Rafsanjani met with Gorbachev and other Soviet leaders in the Kremlin. The visit produced additional economic accords, reportedly an arms deal, and a declaration of principles governing relations between the two neighbors. The pronouncement of official friendship included pledges of mutual respect, economic cooperation, Soviet assistance in increasing Iran's defensive capabilities, promises of exchanges, support for the North–South dialogue, and support for the United Nations.[22]

It should be noted that the language of the declaration approximates that in earlier friendship and cooperation treaties, especially the phrase "strengthening Iran's defensive capabilities." The Soviet Union never publishes details of arms agreements, but the Iranian and Gulf presses did reveal some statistics. In early May 1989 the Iranian news agency quoted First Deputy Foreign Minister Ali Muhammad Besherati when he announced that Iran and the Soviet Union were on the verge of signing a series of arms agreements.[23] Even earlier, *Keyhan* reported Czech and Romanian deals that included weapons production facilities as well as 180 tanks.[24] Finally, the Kuwaiti and Abu Dhabi media indicated that the Soviet Union had promised to sell Teheran sophisticated weaponry and advanced radar in return for Iranian pledges of non-interference in Soviet Muslim areas.[25]

Gorbachev's imprint is thus a curious blend of the new, supporting moderation and flexibility, and the old, shoring up allies and remaining involved. Perhaps the best way to view the imprint is to say that the old and the new mix in a policy designed generally to find newer less confrontational and less costly ways of remaining an influential power in the Middle East. Nonetheless, there remain serious contradictions in the new Soviet Middle East policy which will be examined in the next section.

Contradictions, Gorbachev's imprint, and regional conflict

The very existence of contradictions in Soviet Middle East policy suggests that the transition to new thinking will be difficult. Some of the contradictions stem from glasnost: for the first time, foreign policy is subject to public scrutiny. Others are derived from the fact that old tools are used to achieve new objectives and from conflicts among the policies themselves.

Over the past five years, as the parameters of acceptable debate have widened because of glasnost, there is more in the press and in official statements about past policies. Soviet international relations specialists are free to analyze the USSR's policy in Afghanistan and Moscow's attitudes toward the Arab–Israeli dispute. As a result, solutions to the problems of these historical legacies – specifically Moscow's impulse to manage conflict while staying involved – are called into question.

For example, in the pre-glasnost era, casualty figures and the trauma of fighting in Afghanistan were hidden from the Soviet population. Since Gorbachev's accession to power, the horrors of Afghanistan have been exposed, casualty figures have been cited, and the decision-making process itself has been questioned. Eduard Shevardnadze in the fall of 1989 claimed that four people in the Politburo took the decision to intervene and that he and Gorbachev were not among them.[26] Glasnost also has meant that Moscow had to confront the internal origins of the Afghan conflict, and journalists have been forced to admit lying to the Soviet public.[27]

In other cases, articles have appeared since 1989 that question the extent of Soviet support for the Arab cause. A Moscow television report criticized the militarization of Soviet policy in Egypt (a reference to the War of Attrition) and drew the conclusion that this was but one example of the "habit of using force."[28] The press also contained allegations that the USSR was far too concerned about Egyptian domestic politics in the Sadat period and that Soviet meddling sped the rupture in relations.[29] The author of another article took a relatively even-handed approach to the Arab–Israeli conflict. He argued that Soviet policy initially was too pro-Israel and then became biased toward the Arab cause.[30] Soviet policy toward Iran, especially the handling of the Rushdie affair, also has elicited comment from the media. Moscow never overtly criticized the Iranian death threats against Salmon Rushdie; indeed, the theme of Soviet commentaries was generally that Muslim sensitivities should be understood. When Shevardnadze was in Teheran as part of his 1989 Middle East trip, he even offered to mediate between Iran and the West over Rushdie. The lack of Soviet censure led the outspoken Aleksandr Bovin to write the following commentary in *Moscow News*: "And one can only hail the decisive rebuff and the moral indignation which met [the death threats against Rushdie]. Sadly, this can't be said about our government. . . . Glasnost, I'm sorry to say, ended in this instance right where it should have begun."[31]

Specific policy options also may come under increasing scrutiny because of glasnost. We already have witnessed discussions in the new Supreme Soviet about foreign aid and about arms transfers. The latter is particularly relevant to the Middle East where the major recipients of Soviet arms are located. Although the subject is no longer shielded from public view, details are not printed in the Soviet press. In fact, articles that discuss arms trade frequently lament the absence of Soviet statistics. Nevertheless, over the past year or so several articles have appeared that criticize the international arms markets and implicitly what the USSR receives in return for its arms shipments.

Table 10.2 *Soviet military supplies to selected Middle East states, 1983–1987 (in millions of current dollars)*

Country	Amount	Country	Amount
Algeria	2,500	Jordan	825
Iran	100	Kuwait	240
Iraq	13,900	Syria	8,900

Source: World Military Expenditures and Arms Transfers, 1988, Arms Control and Disarmament Agency, publication 131, 1989

With or without the public criticisms of arms transfers, the subject of arms trade raises questions about the intentions of new thinking. For many years, the USSR earned hard currency, especially from its Arab clients, for arms exports. At the height of the oil boom, arms exports to the Middle East totaled some $19.1 billion.[32] Despite the decline in oil revenues, arms remains a hard currency earner. Thus the impulse for trade to earn convertible currency contradicts the creation of the new Soviet image. This fact has not escaped notice. In an article entitled "Merchants of death," a veteran Middle East correspondent stated that whether or not these sales generate hard currency, the problems incurred when these weapons are sold to unstable regions far outweigh any short-run financial gains.[33]

One can legitimately question just how serious the USSR is about solving regional conflicts when it continues to trade arms to Libya and Syria. Within the last year, the Soviet Union had sold Sukhois to Libya and, according to Middle East sources, continues to supply weapons to Syria. In the Iranian case, the Soviet Union seems to be trading "defensive" weapons for natural gas. When asked about the sale to Libya, one Soviet official charged with overseeing Soviet policy in the Middle East answered: hard currency.[34] And when the same question arose in discussions with Soviet international affairs experts, the response was that the money impulse could easily win out over new thinking.[35] In fact, current data indicate that Moscow continues to be a major arms supplier to the region.

A new realism seems to be taking hold in Soviet commentary and analyses about involvement in Third World conflicts. According to the old class-based thinking, regional conflicts resulted from imperialist meddling and "progressive forces" fighting reactionary regimes. By the late 1970s, when many Soviet-supported regimes found themselves fighting insurgencies, scholars added a category: radical regimes that defended themselves against anti-progressive insurgencies. By using these categories, the USSR could justify its internationalist duty to recipients of its aid. Disputes based on territory or religion did not fit this typology, nor did they fit neatly into the Soviet desire to be on the "just" side of the conflict. The removal of class struggle as an operative force in international politics means that local disputes may not have a "just" party and that they may be more intractable.

Soviet international affairs specialists now warn against oversimplifying events in the Third World. They argue that the chief reason for Third World conflicts lies in the states themselves, and in relations among them, and not in the rivalry between the East and the West. Prodding their colleagues to develop more sophisticated analyses, these observers urge, among other things, the abandonment of the zero-sum world view.[36] Moreover, given the indigenous causes for these numerous conflicts, Soviet observers increasingly have come to recognize that the patron frequently becomes the captive of the client, thereby complicating diplomacy.[37]

Soviet writers, keeping in mind the more sophisticated analysis of Third World politics that characterizes the glasnost era, suggest a three-stage process for the resolution of local conflicts. Efforts are to be made toward national reconciliation to be followed by a US–Soviet dialogue on the issues. Finally, in the last stage, the UN General Secretary is to engage in "peacemaking" activities.[38]

This formulation presupposes the possibility of national reconciliation, notwithstanding either US–Soviet agreement or the well-intentioned efforts of the United Nations. One need look only at Middle Eastern political dynamics to understand how Soviet policy objectives are, in many respects, hostage to local politics.

Despite the continuing contacts between Soviet and Israeli officials, many obstacles remain in the quest for diplomatic relations. Deep divisions in the Israeli polity prevent any agreement on negotiations with the PLO or acceptance of an international conference on the Middle East. What this means is that the often enunciated Soviet condition for the reestablishment of full diplomatic relations, the convening of an international conference on the Middle East, remains to be met. Even though the Soviet Union recently has softened its stand, saying that any negotiations would be acceptable,[39] the dialogue remains incomplete. An issue of even greater salience has been the question of where Soviet émigrés would be settled. When Prime Minister Itzhak Shamir stated that new arrivals from the Soviet Union would be settled on the West Bank, the Kremlin came under increasingly intense Arab pressure to stop emigration. Arab states always have objected to the flow of Soviet

Jews to Israel, but the fact that they would be settled on the occupied territories was intolerable.

Even the Soviet–Iranian relationship is not without its problems. Both are intensely interested in the flowering economic links – natural gas, shipping, refurbishing the Isfahan steel mill. By the same token, stubborn political issues dividing the two sides not only persist but can at any time disrupt the amelioration process. First, the Iranians continue to support the mujahideen and have tenaciously called for protection of Afghanistan's Islamic character in any future government. Second, Moscow, because of its interest in a cooling off in the central Arab–Israeli nexus, is irritated about Iran's continuing aid to the Hezbollah and other Shi'a groups in Lebanon.[40] Last, the 1990 clashes in Baku between local nationalities and Soviet troops elicited strong criticism from the Iranians. As champions of the international Islamic cause, Iranians condemned the use of force and urged respect for Islamic rights. The Soviets, for their part, urged caution on Teheran.

Finally, trade in the volatile Middle East may create policy conflicts for the Gorbachev regime. First, the desire for Israeli imports may run into Arab hostility. How far can the Kremlin go in its trade relations with Tel Aviv and still retain its standing in the Arab world? Second, an even more basic conflict may lie in the desire for US trade credits and Soviet ties with the Arabs. Can the USSR continue to allow emigration – especially if the Likud government entices the émigrés to settle on the West Bank – without damaging its ties to both moderate and radical Arabs? And, the same kinds of questions must be asked about enhanced economic ties with Iran. Is there a point at which the Soviet Union might be forced to choose between natural gas imports from Iran and its longstanding relations with the Arabs?

The Iraqi invasion of Kuwait

The Iraqi invasion and occupation of Kuwait altered once again the pattern of Middle East politics and consequently the role played by the Soviet Union. Baghdad's aggression forged new Arab alliances, seemed to end the stalemate between Iran and Iraq, facilitated a huge US presence in the Gulf, and allowed Moscow to cooperate with the Western powers in an unprecedented manner.

In the days following the attack, Moscow resolutely condemned Iraq and announced that it was severing the arms pipeline to Baghdad. The USSR also backed the UN Security Council resolutions calling for an international blockade of Iraq. Yet, the Soviets hesitated when it came to authorizing the use of force if Iraq did not withdraw from Kuwait. After two unsuccessful mediation efforts undertaken by Evgenii Primakov, Moscow somewhat reluctantly supported the UNSC resolution authorizing force against Iraq. However, behind the façade of agreement with the United States and the United Nations lay hesitations and even limits on Soviet policy, all of which illustrate the themes discussed above.

The choice to denounce the invasion was in reality relatively easy. Despite the Iraqi–Soviet arms connection and historical support for Baghdad, the Soviet Union could not maintain its new image and prestige if it did not condemn the attack. In fact, many Soviet commentators and spokesmen emphasized the significant shift in Moscow's policy. Several articles noted that in the pre-Gorbachev era, the Soviet Union would have declared its neutrality and probably criticized the US deployment in Saudi Arabia. Still others openly acknowledged that the USSR bore responsibility for helping to create the most aggressive force in the region.[41]

Through the condemnation Moscow expressed its resentment at Saddam's grab for Kuwait because it disrupted what the Soviets see as the emerging new world order. At the same time, Moscow's hesitation about a war stemmed from several sources. First, there was serious Soviet reluctance to becoming involved in yet another Third World conflict. Having learned in Afghanistan that such regional conflicts may be intractably long-term affairs, Moscow's policy makers were timid about overt military involvement in a war against Iraq. There were also pressures from deputies to the Supreme Soviet regarding Soviet deployments. In contrast to Shevardnadze's repeated statements that Soviet troops could be sent under the UN flag, the Soiuz group in the Supreme Soviet seemed inalterably opposed to any USSR involvement. What is clear is that any direct Soviet participation would have had to be authorized by the parliament.[42]

Second, old thinking had not disappeared entirely from the public and not-so-public debate. Both *Izvestiia* and *Krasnaia Zvezda* were critical of the size of the US deployments and the speed with which they confronted Iraq. Moreover, there were apparently forces within the decision-making establishment that were reluctant to see Moscow lose its standing in the Arab world. Evgenii Primakov, Gorbachev's foreign policy advisor and emissary to Baghdad, is an Arabist; he hoped that a solution could be found to the crisis that would not entail the USSR coming squarely behind the US-led coalition in the Gulf.

Finally, Soviet hesitation derived from the USSR's desire to remain a superpower. Superpower status accrues to active participation in

Security Council debates and to cooperation with the United States. The Soviet Union must retain some independence if it is to hold on to its already diminished superpower status. It is one thing to gain a position as a responsible power and player in the international community but quite another to appear to be dancing to your former rival's tune. In fact, Evgenii Primakov intimated as much in an interview with Moscow television. He argued that he was concerned about Moscow's superpower status and, therefore, it was appropriate for the USSR to pursue its own interests and perhaps own policy, including his mediation efforts.[43]

In this vein, Moscow also hoped that its earlier ties to Baghdad might enable it to mediate between Saddam Hussein and the US-led multinational coalition. In fact, when it became known that Moscow still had military personnel in Iraq, the Gorbachev regime took great pains not only to downplay the role of its advisors in Iraq, but also to avoid acting precipitously in withdrawing the personnel. Keeping the connection open would permit Moscow to play the broker, if Saddam were willing. Even after the opening of hostilities on 17 January, Gorbachev indicated that his government would continue to pursue a diplomatic solution.

Ultimately, regional politics will dictate what the Soviet Union can and cannot accomplish. Politics never cease, especially in Middle East conflicts. The Gulf cease-fire aided the increasing economic ties between Moscow and Teheran and the Palestinian *intifadah* refocused Soviet, and for that matter, Arab attention on the Arab–Israeli dispute. The Likud's refusal to negotiate with the PLO limits peace initiatives, while PLO moderation has been rewarded by the upgrading of its representation in Moscow to full ambassadorial status. Finally, Saddam Hussein's attack on Kuwait, the international crisis it created, and the war it unleashed disrupted the global push to end regional conflicts. As noted above, the Kuwaiti crisis created opportunities for the Soviet Union to enhance its image as a responsible power. In the end, the Soviet Union will remain involved in the Middle East because of its longstanding investment and because of the region's proximity to the USSR. Gorbachev's imprint, however, is to look for less confrontational and less costly ways of remaining a major player there.

Notes

1 Conversations with a Soviet official, Cambridge, September 1987.

2 In a February 1988 *Pravda* article, Gorbachev claimed that as early as April 1985, the Politburo began to reassess the situation in Afghanistan. *Pravda*, 19 February 1988.

3 Karen Dawisha, "The USSR in the Middle East: superpower in eclipse?" *Foreign Affairs*, vol. 61, no. 2 (1982–83).
4 Jerusalem Domestic Service, 19 July 1985, in *FBIS-SOV-85-139*, 19 July 1985, pp. H1–H2.
5 *Pravda*, 25 April 1987, p. 2.
6 *Pravda*, 10 April 1988, p. 1.
7 For the first three or so years after the Iranian revolution, Soviet observers bent over backwards to excuse the religious content of the upheaval in Iran. It was only as the Teheran regime resisted Soviet cultivation efforts and arrested the leadership of the Tudeh (communist party), that Moscow observers were forced to acknowledge publicly the Islamic fundamentalist ideology of the Iranian revolution.
8 It is entirely possible that this 1986 renewal of contacts was designed by Teheran. Although a new natural gas deal and further economic contacts would be mutually beneficial, Teheran may have hoped to convince Moscow of the importance of improved relations. Indeed, the promise of an ameliorated economic relationship may have been dangled in front of the Soviets in return for a limitation on the Soviet arms shipped directly to Iraq.
9 As Moscow Domestic Service claimed: "Incidentally, the actual intention of the United States to raise the U.S. flag, at Kuwait's own request, over its tankers is hardly objectionable." Moscow Domestic Service, 6 July 1987, *FBIS-07-129*, 7 July 1987, pp. 2–3.
10 Iran officials rejected the offer. In the words of Besherati: "In this way [the mediation offer] the Soviet Union wants to give the appearance that it is impartial in this war. The point is that not only are they not impartial in this war, but by the blatant and hidden support for the Baghdad regime, they have encouraged Saddam and therefore, the Russians are a partner to and share in Saddam's crimes." As quoted in Teheran Domestic Service, 27 July 1988, *FBIS-NES*, 28 July 1988, p. 36.
11 The first report is from Radio Free Lebanon, 16 January 1990, in *FBIS-NES-90-011*, 17 January 1990, p. 33 and the second is from *Al Ra'y al'Amm*, 15 January 1990, pp. 1, 23 in *FBIS-90-012*, 18 January 1990, p. 36.
12 *Izvestiia*, 2 February 1988, *FBIS-SOV*, 16 February 1988, p. 43. See also the report from the Algiers domestic service that indicates that the USSR was going to import bathroom fixtures from Algeria. Algiers Domestic Service, 12 February 1988, in *FBIS-SOV* 16 February 1988, p. 44.
13 *Jerusalem Post*, 31 January 1990, p. 1.
14 See details in *IRMA*, 15 May 1989, *FBIS-NES-89*, 15 May 1989, p. 50.
15 KUNA, 7 May 1990, *FBIS-NES-90-089*, 8 May 1990, p. 12.
16 Cited in W. Raymond Duncan and Carolyn McGiffert Ekedahl, *Moscow and the Third World under Gorbachev* (Boulder: Westview Press, 1990), p. 104.
17 *Al-Ra'y al'Amm*, 6 March 1990, p. 1, in *FBIS-SOV*, 8 March 1990, p. 37, and *Al-Ittihad*, 6 April 1990, p. 1 in *FBIS-NES*, 9 April 1990, p. 29.
18 *Pravda*, 29 April 1990, pp. 1, 4.
19 Interview with *Sovetskaia Rossiia*, 17 April 1990, p. 3.
20 *Izvestiia*, 1 May 1990, p. 3.
21 Teheran TV, 4 January 1989, *FBIS-NES*, 5 January 1989, p. 40.

22 See the text in *Pravda*, 24 June 1989, p. 1.
23 IRNA, 1 May 1989 *FBIS-NES*, 1 May 1989, pp. 46–47.
24 *Keyhan*, 30 March 1989, *FBIS-NES*, 4 May 1989, pp. 50–51.
25 *Al Qabas*, 26 June 1989, p. 22, in *FBIS-SOV*, 29 June 1989, p. 15, and *Al-Ittihad*, 25 June 1989, pp. 1, 21, in *FBIS-NES*, 30 June 1989, pp. 37–38.
26 Speech by Eduard Shevardnadze to Supreme Soviet, as reported in *Pravda*, 24 October 1989.
27 For example, in a remarkably candid piece, *Izvestiia* commentator Aleksandr Bovin admitted that his earlier analyses had been "fabricated." He added, "The deep roots, the sources of the anti-government actions were within the country. Help from abroad did not play an appreciable role, especially in the first stages of the civil war." *SShA*, no. 7, 1989, pp. 44–49, in *JPRS-USA*, 29 November 1989, p. 13.
28 Moscow TV report, 25 February 1990 in *FBIS-SOV*, 1 March 1990, pp. 32–33.
29 See interview with Georgii Mirskii, in *JPRS-USIA*, 25 July 1988, pp. 46–47.
30 Dmitrii Zgerskii, "Tolerance is needed on both sides," *New Times*, no. 15, 1990 (10–16 April), pp. 26–27.
31 Aleksandr Bovin, "In the world: politics and morals," *Moscow News*, no. 12, 1989, p. 3.
32 Calculated from US Arms Control and Disarmament Agency, *World Military Expenditures and Arms Transfers, 1971–1980*, ACDA Publication 115.
33 Peter Gladkov, "Merchants of death," *Moscow Times*, no. 17, 1990, p. 13. Gladkov then added, "Having received Scud missiles from Egypt, the People's Democratic Republic of Korea modified them . . . [and] they were then used by Iran in its war against Iraq . . . Iran then made its own modification . . . and used it against Iran, causing serious problems in Soviet–Iranian relations."
34 Discussions in Cambridge, MA, March 1990.
35 Discussions in Cambridge, MA, May 1990.
36 See for example, A. Kolosovskii, "Regional'nye konflikty i global'naia bezopasnost'," *Mirovaia ekonomika i mezhdunarodnye otnosheniia*, no. 6 (1988), especially p. 35.
37 See for example, Andrei Kozyrev and Andrei Shumikhin, "East and West in the Third World," *International Affairs* (March 1989).
38 V. Kremeniuk, "Sovetsko-amerikanskie otnosheniia i regional'nye konflikty," *Aziia i Afrika Seqodnia*, no. 3 (1989), p. 6.
39 See report in *FBIS-SOV-90-042*, 2 March 1990, p. 17. Radio Peace and Progress reported that Nikolai Ryzhkov stated that diplomatic relations with Israel could be resumed at the beginning of an Israeli–Palestinian dialogue.
40 For example, in a radio broadcast to Iran, the commentator claimed, "Iran can do a great deal to normalize the situation. We know that Teheran provides considerable financial and military assistance to the Hezbollah . . . to the tune of $100–150 million annually." 28 December 1989, *FBIS-SOV*, 2 January 1990, pp. 20–21.
41 See for example, *Komsomolskaia pravda*, 10 August 1990, p. 1 in *FBIS-SOV*, 10 August 1990, pp. 26–27.

42 Moscow World Service stated on 30 October 1990: "Not a single Soviet soldier will be found in the conflict zone without the approval of parliament." Cited in *FBIS-SOV*, 31 October 1990, p. 11.
43 31 October 1990, *FBIS-SOV*, 1 November 1990, pp. 8–9.

11 The implications of perestroika for the Third World, particularly Asia

Zafar Imam

Over the past six years the policies of perestroika and new thinking of Soviet General Secretary Mikhail Gorbachev have shaken the entire world, including the countries of the Third World. These countries, of course, are far from homogeneous, although they do share some common essential features, especially the wide spectrum of underdevelopment. Consequently, the implications of Soviet perestroika and new thinking for Third World countries are largely similar, although they do have marked variations. This impact is primarily centered on the external aspects of perestroika, what Gorbachev himself has categorized as new thinking.

The purpose of the present chapter is to specify the implications of perestroika for the countries of the Third World. The focus here is on identifying general patterns, as well as those patterns that are specific to Asia. The starting point of the analysis is an overview of the background of Soviet relations with the Third World. Perestroika in the USSR has developed in stages, as have external perceptions of the process. Hence, this chapter examines the perceptions of perestroika and new thinking held by Third World countries, especially those in Asia. The emphasis is first on understanding the nature of Gorbachev's Third World policy, then on its effects on the global role of developing countries themselves, and finally on the foreign policy postures of Asian states in particular. The domestic situation in various Third World countries is also given consideration. Lastly, the overall implications of perestroika for the Third World, especially in the context of Asia, are assessed.

The pre-Gorbachev background

Until recently the Soviet Union enjoyed a favorable reputation in Third World countries, with the exception of a few which were formally aligned with the West. The reasons for such a positive image are fairly well known.[1] First, the Soviet Union was considered to be free of a colonial past. The fact that, unlike the leading countries of Europe, the

Soviet Union never had a colonial empire in a classical sense of the term, was viewed favorably. Second, the strategy of rapid socio-economic development that took place in the Soviet Union was regarded as a model worth emulating – at least until the mid-1970s. Third, the Soviet Union had expanded its ties with the majority of Third World countries and had, thereby, emerged as an alternate source of economic aid, weapons, and political support on various global and regional issues vital to Third World countries. Hence, the Soviet Union was generally viewed as a countervailing influence to check the power of the Western countries, particularly the United States, and later to frustrate China's ambitions in Asia. Fourth, among the intelligentsia, communists, and other leftist groups in the Third World there existed the image of the Soviet Union as a revolutionary power standing against exploitation and the status quo and committed to change and development. This image was no doubt consistently built up by official Soviet propaganda, as well as by indigenous communist and other leftist groups.

Finally, the Western assessment of the USSR as a closed society controlled and run by a power-hungry and highly centralized communist party without the benefits of democracy, freedom, and human rights was hardly convincing to most of the national leaders of the Third World. From the days of Secretary of State John Foster Dulles' almost religious crusade to roll back communism until the time thirty years later of President Ronald Reagan's denunciation of the Soviet Union as an "evil empire," Third World leaders were not generally convinced of the threat to their security presented by the Soviet Union. Moreover, with the exception of a few leaders such as Jawaharlal Nehru, most Third World statesmen had little inclination to consider the niceties of democracy and freedom and to give serious attention to questions of ends and means. Indeed, many Third World leaders had no qualms about becoming mini-Stalins themselves.

Not one, but a mix of the above-enumerated factors, had built up a generally favorable image of the Soviet Union throughout the Third World. There was, of course, no uniform pattern, and the perception of the Soviet Union certainly varied as the Third World itself became more diversified and fragmented. For example, this image was clear in African countries, less clear in Asian countries and Latin America, and hazy throughout the Arab world. Besides, there also emerged Soviet-baiters such as Saudi Arabia, Iran, Mali, and Singapore. On the other hand, favorable images of the Soviet Union had little effect on the attitudes of national leaders toward their domestic communist movements.

Early reactions to perestroika and new thinking

It is against this backdrop that the implications of perestroika and new thinking for the Third World, particularly Asia, must be examined. The process of perestroika in the Soviet Union as it began to unfold, immediately drew attention throughout the developing world. In the past Soviet foreign policy had been the primary focus of the press throughout the developing countries. However, increasingly, the Soviet domestic debate on economic and political reform became a matter of major interest in countries throughout the Third World. Gorbachev's frank pronouncements about the nature and problems of Soviet society and the emergence of glasnost in the Soviet news media contributed to this expanded interest throughout much of the Third World. Curiosity grew concerning the ways in which the new Soviet leader would implement his ideas. As Gorbachev's perestroika was launched in earnest toward the beginning of 1986, the realization arose that he was not merely initiating a set of reforms comparable to those introduced by every new leader in the Soviet Union in the past, but rather a much more far-reaching restructuring of Soviet society. The complexity of the task that he had set for himself slowly dawned upon Third World observers. In mid-1988, for example, the secretary of the traditionally pro-Moscow Communist Party of India (CPI) recognized that the Soviet Union was moving toward a more democratic form of governance and concluded that "progressive circles in India are happy that democracy is being given so much importance in the building of socialism."[2]

The deliberations and decisions of the 27th CPSU Congress were considered crucial for the future of the Soviet Union. As a leading Arab daily, the *Kuwait News*, commented on the eve of the Congress: "How far Gorbachev's realism can go in salvaging and reviving the Soviet Union's moribund economy, restructuring Soviet society in the process, and thereby giving him power in dealing with the rest of the world is a question the Congress may go some way to answering."[3] A perceptive Indian observer of the Soviet scene and a former diplomat categorized the new program as a "remarkable example of both continuity and change, more continuity than change."[4] A leading Indian Marxist theoretician summarized the implications of the new party program of the CPSU as follows: "What is envisaged, therefore, is not merely a major upsurge of production but a qualitative revolutionary advance on all fronts. What is envisaged is an unprecedented accelerated and novel revolutionary transition from a developed or integral socialism to communism."[5]

Gorbachev's emphasis on entering into a dialogue with the United

States for the purpose of a phased scrapping of nuclear weapons was seen in the Third World as a courageous step toward the relaxation of tension in international politics. Hence, Gorbachev's summit diplomacy beginning in November 1985 was hailed by most of the Third World countries.[6] It is interesting to note that during the initial preparations for launching perestroika, Gorbachev assiduously avoided any impression that he was interested only in the West. While reporting to the Supreme Soviet in November 1985 on the Geneva Summit, the first of a series of meetings with President Reagan, he underlined the importance of Asia and the Pacific region: "The Soviet Union's longest borders are in Asia. We have there loyal friends and reliable allies, from neighboring Mongolia and Socialist Vietnam. It is extremely important to ensure that this region is not a source of tension and an area of armed confrontation."[7] Earlier, in July 1986, in his Vladivostok speech Gorbachev had launched his peace initiatives in Asia and targeted his attention toward *rapprochement* with China and toward a nuclear-free-zone in the vast Asian-Pacific region. Even during 1988, when he was engrossed in domestic problems and in dealings with the West, he worked to find a face-saving formula to end Soviet military intervention in Afghanistan. By February 1989 he had actually withdrawn Soviet troops from Afghanistan, thus ending a futile exercise in exporting revolution through direct military intervention. It was also during 1987–88 that Gorbachev unfolded his comprehensive plan for the Asian-Pacific region and paid an official visit to India. Gorbachev's proposal, however, proved to be a non-starter. The *Japan Times* correspondent in Jakarta rightly pointed out that "These proposals have not elicited much positive response either in Jakarta or in other parts of Asia."[8]

The reappraisal of Soviet Third World policy

All these initiatives in the foreign policy area occurred at a time of growing domestic crisis in the Soviet Union. Throughout 1988 it became obvious that perestroika had not brought about concrete results, particularly in salvaging the Soviet economy. The growing crises inside the Soviet Union encouraged Gorbachev to look more intently toward the West in the hope of preserving scarce resources through agreements on cuts in nuclear arms and the consequent reduction in defense expenditures. He was also hopeful that the West would provide the capital and technology that the Soviet Union so desperately required. By early 1989 it was evident that the Soviets had begun cutting down their global role in order to concentrate on relations with the United

States and Western Europe. As Soviet society itself, Soviet foreign policy was being Westernized.

In summer 1989 the process of change in Eastern Europe moved ahead at breakneck speed, largely with Gorbachev's approval. At the same time, efforts at internal economic reform in the USSR continued to fall behind. These developments further encouraged Gorbachev to look to the West for assistance and to view the Third World in a new way. Earlier, in February 1989, he had withdrawn the final Soviet troops from Afghanistan at a time when it was still devastated by the civil war. Leaving behind its traditional Third World policy, the Soviet Union began to advocate "mutual economic advantages" in its bilateral relationships with developing countries. Gorbachev's visit to China in May 1989 also signified the practical application of such a bilateral framework. A Moscow-based correspondent of the *Far Eastern Economic Review*, correctly summarized the situation in August 1988: "The message has gone out to third world allies that Soviet foreign relations are becoming multipolar, and that normal economic relations must replace grant aid."[9]

These trends coincided with the process of reappraisal of the entire spectrum of past theory and practice of Soviet Third World policy. This process was, indeed, signaled by Gorbachev himself from the very beginning. As early as May 1985, in a Kremlin banquet in honor of the visiting Indian Prime Minister, Gorbachev called for a "pooling of efforts by Asian states themselves for a common and comprehensive approach to the problem of security in Asia."[10] The speech was conciliatory in tone and pragmatic in content. With its stress on multilevel cooperation among Asian states, it was distinctive from statements during the Brezhnev years. A few months later, the draft of the new party program admitted that a number of Third World countries had in fact established capitalism, and not socialism. In his book *Perestroika*, Gorbachev also dealt at length with the basic problems facing the Third World: "the debt-trap, the growing impoverishment, unequal economic relations, regional conflicts and tensions."[11] It was as though he was hinting that, in spite of the best efforts of the Soviet Union involving a considerable self-sacrifice, the Third World countries were in fact no better positioned today than they had been four decades earlier. In other words, Gorbachev was tacitly recognizing the failure of earlier Soviet Third World policy. At the same time, he assured the West of its traditional relationship with the Third World:

> I have explained on many occasions that we do not pursue goals inimical to Western interests. We know how important the Middle East, Asia, Latin America, other Third World regions, and also Africa are for American and

West European economies, in particular as raw material sources. To cut these links is the last thing we want to do, and we have no desire to provoke ruptures in historically formed, mutual economic interests.[12]

It is clear, however, that it was the costly Soviet military intervention in Afghanistan that gradually made the traditional Soviet Third World policy untenable and even unpopular inside the country. Emboldened by glasnost, not only resentment of the Afghan crisis, but also criticism of the entire gambit of Third World policy was openly expressed. The question was raised whether that policy had brought advantages to the USSR, and the answer seemed to be negative, except in the case of relations with India. On the contrary, Soviet foreign policy toward the Third World had caused unnecessary friction and had aggravated relations with the West. It had sought to "provoke ruptures," as Gorbachev put it, "in historically formed mutual economic interests."[13]

Some basic theoretical issues in Soviet Third World policy now came up for critical scrutiny. These issues revolved around the non-capitalist path of development, the idea of socialist-oriented states, and above all, the very methodology of understanding the socio-economic development of the Third World. Early in 1988 Vadim Medvedev, a Politburo member and ideological chief, set the trend by asking in *Kommunist* for a thorough reexamination of the concept of socialist-oriented states.[14] During 1988 and 1989 a sort of debate raged among Soviet academics and intellectuals in the pages of a number of major journals that had wide circulation in Third World countries themselves – for example, *Socialism: Theory and Practice*, *New Times*, and *International Affairs*. The general consensus was that the theoretical foundations of Soviet policy in the Third World were unsubstantiated and faulty. For instance, commenting on the traditional Soviet approach of blaming imperialism, neo-colonialism, and the legacy of colonialism for the ills of the Third World, one discussant commented: "It obscures the fact that the crisis which has hit many third world countries in the 1980s is explained not so much by external causes as by mistakes in the economic policies of their regimes."[15] Furthermore, the theoretical category of socialist-oriented states in the Third World was now seen as an extension of the administrative command system that existed in the USSR.[16] Special criticism was directed against the economic assistance program of the USSR. In January 1990 it was disclosed for the first time in the Supreme Soviet that the USSR had provided through November 1989 approximately 78 billion rubles of assistance to the non-socialist Third World countries, and that this aid was now considered an unnecessary burden on the Soviet economy.[17]

In November 1988 the Soviet journal *International Affairs* published an important article by a foreign ministry official on Soviet policy in the Third World. Given the importance of the article in explaining the new thinking about developing countries, it is worth citing at some length. First, the author discusses the basic framework of Soviet–Third World relations:

> The myth that the class interests of socialist and developing countries coincide in resisting imperialism does not hold up to criticism at all. The majority of developing countries already adhere to or tend toward the Western model of development and they suffer not so much from capitalism as from a lack of it. They are interested not in struggling against former metropolises but in cooperating to defend their own and international stability.

On the issue of Soviet economic assistance the article notes:

> The unsolved nature of key national problems within the group of left-wing states stands out in particular contrast to the increasing tendency in Asia and Africa to seek ways toward accelerated economic development and involvement in the international division of labour. Unfortunately, there are no data about what it costs the Soviet Union to assist these countries. Estimates published in the West give rise to grave reflections about the returns from, and expediency, of this aid.

A third issue developed in the article concerns the ways in which these relations with developing countries had aggravated East–West tensions:

> Our direct and indirect involvement in regional conflicts leads to colossal losses by increasing general international tension, justifying the arms race and hindering the establishment of mutually advantageous ties with the West.

Finally, the author describes the type of policy that the Soviet Union should no longer follow in its relations with the developing world:

> Out interests in the developing countries must be defined above all by the real potential for setting up mutually advantageous economic and technological cooperation. From this point of view, it is not difficult to see that the West's interests of this kind are immeasurably deeper and broader. To attempt to balance this asymmetry by building up the potential of one's naval presence and strengthening one's strategic ties with individual states that might 'act in opposition to Western influence' would be to construct one's relations with the developing countries on a very shaky and short-term basis.[18]

Here we may note the changing perspectives of the Soviet Union on the non-aligned movement, of which almost all Third World countries are members. As the official report of the Soviet Foreign Ministry put it in 1989: "Within the framework of deideologising state-to-state relations . . . our country does not view the Nonaligned Movement from the standpoint of East–West differences . . . We recognise the Nonaligned

Movement as an independent factor in world politics and respect its principles and objectives."[19]

Although the issue is not yet finally settled, perestroika and new thinking have impelled the Soviet Union to play the new role in the Third World determined by the traditional pursuit of its national interests, free of ideology. The practice of fraternal help and support to national liberation movements and the special relationship with treaty partners, such as India, and allies, such as Vietnam, is over. This means the tapering off of economic aid, restricted sales of arms on less favorable terms, and non-involvement in regional disputes and conflicts. The main thrust of emerging Soviet policy appears to be toward bilateral trade and commercial ties. Such a general pattern is already noticeable in South Asia, the Middle East, and Africa. This policy has stemmed from the drastic overhauling of the very framework of Soviet foreign policy. As Gorbachev is fond of explaining, a balance (not a clash) of interests with the West and making the world safe from a nuclear holocaust (not international class struggle) are now the primary goals of Soviet foreign policy. These objectives need to be operationalized through compromise, negotiations, and accommodations. The new Soviet role in world affairs is no longer to play the antagonist to the United States and other Western capitalist powers, but to cooperate and to find accommodation with them.

The implications of new thinking for developing countries: common patterns

The implications of the new Soviet policy in the Third World are linked to the realities of the Third World itself. As is well known, the Third World state system as a whole is the weakest component of the international system. The situation in Africa is particularly precarious – with hunger, famine, and instability looming large. Latin American countries are reeling under the debt burden. Asian states, especially those in Southeast Asia, have done a somewhat better job than the others economically, but they are at the epicenter of regional conflicts and tensions. In addition, the non-aligned movement, which encompasses a large majority of the Third World states, is now groping for new directions and new causes to espouse, thus weakening even further the position of the Third World states. Now that bipolarity in the international system is nearly over, Third World states will likely become more open to economic pressure and political arm-twisting from the industrialized North, with the Soviet Union turning a blind eye.

Yet, more disturbing is the growing fear of a joint US–Soviet condominium overseeing the issues vital to them. A case in point has been the Soviet willingness to back US efforts to find a solution to the Afghan tangle, even at the cost of destabilizing the Najibullah government. Another example is the present precarious economic situation in Cuba. What indeed is surprising is Gorbachev's inclination to surrender his traditional advantages in the Third World so easily, almost without being asked. In the first formal summit with President George Bush in Washington in June 1990, he even agreed to include the issues of Kashmir and Indo-Pakistani relations, bypassing the vocal opposition to the move by the Soviet Union's traditional friend, India.[20]

It appears that most of the Third World countries, particularly those with a fairly long experience in dealing with the Soviet Union, may now have three different perceptions of Soviet Third World policy under perestroika and new thinking. The first perception assumes the shifts in Soviet policy are, in the main, generated by the domestic problems and crises arising out of perestroika and, thus, that the new foreign policy may be temporary in character. Hence, when the Soviet Union bounces back with renewed strength and vigor, the old policy in the Third World will be revived with more clarity and intensity. The second view maintains that, because perestroika has turned out to be a long-drawn-out process, essentially irreversible with or without Gorbachev, these changes in Soviet policy may be treated as a response to a difficult situation. Hence, necessary policy adjustments have to be made by developing countries. Bilateral relationships will be based on mutual advantages, and nothing more. Obviously, such a relationship is more easily operationalized in relations with the more developed countries of the Third World. Exceptions to this case may exist in the emergence of special ties between the USSR and countries that lie near the Soviet border (for example, Afghanistan, Iran). Logically, policies based on mutual advantage will be more relevant for Asian countries and less applicable to the countries of Africa and Latin America. The third perception of the new Soviet foreign policy is based on the assumption that the Soviet Union is fully preoccupied with domestic problems and with Europe and that it has neither the will nor the potential to maintain an all-embracing Third World policy as it did in the past. Hence, Soviet interests in the Third World are likely to be centered nearer its borderlands and on traditional friends. Most Third World countries in Asia, thus, may opt for regional cooperation efforts in ASEAN and SAARC. They may even be favorably disposed to strengthen relationships with Japan, United States, and Europe.[21]

As of early 1991 it is difficult to foresee which of the three perceptions and attendant options will become a prevalent general feature of the policies of the Third World countries toward the Soviet Union. However, the first interpretation and option – namely, that the present situation in the Soviet Union is temporary and transitory in nature – can safely be ruled out, for no Third World policy maker is willing to bet that the basic system in the Soviet Union will not eventually follow the example of the Eastern European countries. It is more likely that Third World countries, certainly in Asia, will pursue policies that are a mix of the second and third options – based on the view that perestroika and new thinking will continue and that developing countries will be required to adjust their policies toward long-term change in the overall Soviet orientation. As a result, most Third World countries are likely to move away from their past close ties with the Soviet Union. However, traditional friends such as India, long-term adversaries such as China, and other countries situated close to Soviet borders, such as Afghanistan and Iran, are likely to find a basis for maintaining and even expanding bilateral relationships with the USSR.

The economic impact of the dilution of the traditional Soviet role in the Third World is indeed of considerable significance. Until 1989 the Soviet Union had, as noted earlier, provided approximately 78 billion rubles in economic assistance to developing countries. The major recipients of that aid, in order, were Cuba, Mongolia, Vietnam, India, Iraq, and Afghanistan.[22] Although the amount of Soviet aid, when compared with that of the West, has not been great, it has represented a substantial amount for the Soviet economy. Based on comments in the Soviet media, it appears that a consensus is growing to write off past aid, which is increasingly considered unrecoverable, and to advance no additional aid in the future other than for normal commercial transactions.[23] As a matter of fact, the flow of Soviet economic aid now appears to have considerably slowed down. For instance, after Gorbachev's visit to India in 1986 no fresh aid commitments were made to India, while Soviet exports to India declined from 3.1 billion rubles in 1985 to 2.3 billion rubles in 1988.[24] This declining trend in Soviet exports is noticeable in its trade with all Asian countries. Likewise, there have been reports in the Western media that the Soviet Union has ceased supplying arms to the Middle East, Afghanistan, and Nicaragua, and that it has begun requesting cash payments and higher hard currency cash payments and higher prices from other countries, as perhaps in the case of India. All of this seems to fit into a policy of shifting to bilateral transactions based on mutual benefit, rather than Soviet credits.[25]

The diminution of the Soviet economic role in the Third World is likely to contribute to a growing sense of competition between the more developed Third World countries and the Soviet Union. The Western capitalist economy has now emerged as the only viable source of capital outflows and high technology, and both the Soviet Union and the more developed Third World countries may vie with each other in attempting to attract it. Here the economic impact on Africa of the system changes in Eastern Europe are relevant. In 1988 the countries of sub-Saharan Africa together received commitments of $850 million in economic aid from the United States, at a time when the US had already allocated $2 billion in aid to Eastern Europe. General Olusegun Obasanjo, former Nigerian head of state, lamented at an international seminar held in Paris in April 1990:

> Today, the question is no longer when and how European capital flows to Africa would be channeled and utilised, but whether the resources which hitherto had been coming to us in a trickle, will continue to come at all. Africa watches in awe as financial resources are being appropriated to selected Eastern European countries.[26]

Moreover, the pressure on the foreign aid and credit potentials of the United States and the international financial agencies, such as the World Bank and the IMF, is likely to increase. This mounting demand can hardly be met even partially in the case of most Third World countries. Moreover, the economic benefits of a united Germany and of a unified Europe may accrue only marginally in the Third World,[27] while Japan continues to focus most of its interest on the Chinese and Soviet markets. However, a possible economic rivalry among the United States, Japan, and a unified Europe may improve the overall bargaining position of Third World countries in the emerging new international system. This might lessen the strains of the competing economic interests of the Soviet Union and Eastern Europe, on the one hand, and the Third World countries, particularly the more developed ones, on the other. On balance, however, the economic situation in the Third World countries – with a few notable exceptions in places such as Singapore and South Korea – is bound to worsen, thus turning them into an inflammable material in world politics.

Yet another implication of perestroika and new thinking for the Third World is the end of the attraction of the Soviet Union as a socialist country. The growing domestic crisis in the USSR and Gorbachev's efforts to stem the disintegration of the Soviet state imply that it is only a matter of time before the CPSU loses its dominant position in the Soviet Union.[28] Thus, it is not suprising that most Russophiles and communists in the Third World, after their initial euphoria about perestroika, have begun to show reservations about it. For example, India's Communist Party (Marxist) has become vocal in criticizing the Soviet Union and in lamenting the demise of the socialist system throughout Eastern Europe.[29] In fact, a consensus is building among Third World communists that the demise of socialism in Eastern Europe and its deepening crisis in the Soviet Union has been generated in main by the characteristic experiences of these European countries and, hence, cannot be universalized. They themselves had erred earlier in considering these countries as a model without reservation.[30] The specific characteristics of the Third World countries, particularly those in Asian countries where democracy has taken root, are quite different from those of the USSR and Eastern Europe, where a command administrative mechanism prevailed over democracy. Thus, socialism remains relevant for the Third World, while Marxist ideas and movements likewise continue to have appeal. In other words, we find here an assertion of the legitimacy of non-European Marxist movements, with a mission to establish socialism of their own type.

In practical terms the end of the Soviet Union as a model revolutionary power implies an elimination of Soviet support and encouragement for national liberation movements. Conversely, it also implies that the Soviet Union will be viewed by Third World communist movements as a great power primarily interested, as other great powers, in the pursuit of its own national goals, and no more.

The end of the glory of the Soviet Union as a revolutionary power is momentous and has deep ramifications. After all, it is precisely in this respect that the Soviet Union has enjoyed unique advantages. Few in the Third World now look to the Soviet Union for hope and inspiration, and most have ceased to take it as a model worth emulating. For the communist movements in the Third World, and certainly in Asia, this unprecedented development may eventually turn out to be fruitful. To survive, these movements must change their habits of looking toward Moscow for guidance and sustenance, and they must become truly indigenous. This is a difficult process, akin to beginning all over again. Yet, this makes them more responsive to the specific requirements in the pursuit of their distinctive programs. As far as the Soviet Union is concerned, perestroika and new thinking deprived it of its traditional foreign policy advantages over other developed countries.

Implications of new thinking for developing countries: specific dimensions

Our discussion now brings us to some specific dimensions of the implications of perestroika for the Third World. As noted earlier, as a program of overhauling Soviet society Gorbachev's perestroika initially touched a harmonious cord almost everywhere in the Third World. Of particular interest was the introduction of democracy and the beginning of an assertive political culture, freedom of the press under glasnost, and the new trends toward a civil society in the USSR.[31] The very fast pace of these developments was, however, bewildering. Perestroika's swift transformation from a program of developing a humane socialism to a program of systemic changes in the USSR was all the more confusing. Gradually a romanticized view of perestroika became less prevalent and gave way to a realistic view of the problems and crises facing the Soviet leadership.[32] A consensus emerged that, notwithstanding its positive features, perestroika has engulfed the USSR in unprecedented crises and problems and, as such, the outcome is problematic. However, interest remained riveted to the question of how a crisis-ridden Soviet Union would play its role in world affairs, particularly in the Third World.

In fact, new thinking, the external dimension of perestroika, came to be regarded as a major weak point of perestroika. Gorbachev's vision of a world free of nuclear arms commanded attention. Likewise, his penchant for compromise in negotiations for the relaxation of tension in East–West relations evoked admiration. Most of the leaders and opinion makers were also impressed by the fact that the system changes in Eastern Europe were accomplished by and large peacefully by the masses themselves, with the Soviet leadership accepting the dramatic changes. However, as noted earlier, by the end of 1988 the dramatic shifts in Soviet foreign policy, the Soviets' growing reluctance to act globally, and their conservatism and concentration on relations with the United States and Western Europe had unnerved most leaders of the Third World. Meanwhile, the Soviet withdrawal of troops from Afghanistan in February 1989 left behind a raging civil war, although it removed an irritant in Soviet relations with most of the Afro-Asian countries. However, this action signaled the beginning of a new phase of low-key Soviet policy in the Third World. Apprehensions surfaced about how all these new trends in the international system would affect the Third World. As the present Indian ambassador to Washington put it: "When this new syndrome of love [between the United States and the USSR] is getting developed, we have to see what it is that is going to happen to the Third World. Will we be left out? . . . How do we really ensure that the new power combination which is going to take place will be meaningful?"[33]

We turn now to a brief assessment of the domestic situation in the countries of the Third World, especially Asia, and the relevance of Soviet new thinking and new behavior for these developments. It remains to be seen whether the shrinking of the role of the Soviet Union in the Third World will further aggravate the tensions and instability throughout it. Economic aid from the Soviet Union was never large in absolute terms. However, in qualitative terms, it was a much needed input into the industrialization and technological advancement of a substantial number of South Asian and Arab countries (for example, India, Algeria and Egypt). Substituting Soviet aid with equitable trade and commerce with the Soviet Union on the basis of comparable advantage will take time and cannot be a smooth process. Hence, immediate problems are likely to arise in most of these countries. Besides, the tapering off of the sale of arms from the Soviet Union may impel some developing countries to embark upon costly programs of developing their own high-tech armament industries. Some may even squander scarce resources on expensive arms deals with the West or on costly local adventures. All this would contribute to the aggravation of existing economic difficulties.

Throughout this chapter the implications of perestroika for legal communist movements in the Third World have been discussed. It is interesting that not only Third World communists are concerned about the withdrawal of the traditional role of the Soviet Union in the Third World. In addition, these concerns are also felt by most of the ruling classes and by affluent groups and elites throughout the Third World. In fact, ever since the mid-1950s the Soviet Union has supported and sustained them, in practice if not in theory. Whatever might have been the intention of Soviet assistance, as was belatedly recognized by the CPSU itself in the revised party program of 1986, in most cases ruling elites had profitably used Soviet economic aid and diplomatic support to strengthen their position against domestic adversaries, including communists and others. Besides, many of them had sought to maneuver and bargain to their advantage within the context of strained East–West relations. Now that this additional leverage of Soviet support and commitment is not likely to be at hand, these leaders are liable to feel more insecure and to show more intolerance toward local leftist political forces. Thus, domestic crisis situations may multiply, as for example terrorist and separatist tendencies which may expand in a number of countries.

A number of professed Marxist regimes in Africa have now officially dropped their adherence to what they termed Marxist ideology. They are poised for the introduction of some type of multiparty system. Likewise, in Latin America Nicaragua has succeeded in holding democratic elections and brought to an end a bloody civil war. Even Fidel Castro's Cuba is reported to have loosened its traditional mechanisms of internal control, although its future policy orientations depend in part upon US policy toward it.[34]

As far as Asia is concerned, few structural changes are yet noticeable. However, some countries such as Pakistan have restored their democratic framework through elections. During the early part of 1990 Nepal also witnessed an upsurge in democratic feeling. In general, there are trends developing in major Asian countries, such as India, to move away from heavy industrialization under a government-controlled state sector toward liberalization and decentralization in economic administration. The shift now being registered is toward rural-oriented growth and a free market mechanism. It is, of course, debatable whether these trends for change can be linked with Soviet perestroika or whether they are indigenous responses to distinctive national requirements. But one thing is obvious: the Soviet political system and its strategy of socio-economic development are no longer viewed favorably. On the contrary, the dismal record of the Soviet Union is now taken as a warning against following its path. The current tendency in the Soviet Union of debunking everything in its past has surely gone a long way in promoting this new attitude toward the Soviet model.

We must introduce a note of caution at this point. The implications of perestroika for domestic socio-political structures and societies of the Third World should not be overstated. These have to be seen primarily in the context of the perception of the Soviet Union as a socialist state system. Now that the end of the socialist system in the USSR is a distinct possibility, these implications may turn out to be of little relevance in the long run. But their short-term nature is nevertheless significant, particularly in its economic dimensions.

Toward an assessment

Of real significance are the implications of perestroika for the place and role of the Third World countries in the emerging international system of the 1990s and beyond. Keeping in mind the discussion in the preceding pages, it is no exaggeration to suggest that a new international system has begun to emerge at the beginning of the last decade of the twentieth century, wherein the Soviet Union is incapable of playing a role of parity with the United States. This new international system may well be dominated by the United States, although rival centers of power may also compete – such as a unified Germany, an all–European community, Japan, and even the Soviet Union. The bipolar world has now disappeared, and there seems to be a transition toward such a system.

In such a scenario the Third World countries as a whole are likely to be natural losers. Not only may it lead to their further impoverishment, but it may also revive their old fear of insecurity and domination by others including by their powerful neighbors. Yet they will have to face these realities of the emerging international system. Certainly there has been some evidence of a willingness to do so from the very beginning of Gorbachev's policy of perestroika and new thinking. A few significant examples may be fruitfully noted.

A common problem of Third World countries remains the clash of nationalisms, in which in the past outside powers had actively intervened directly or indirectly. Now that there is hardly any prospect of Soviet involvement, direct or indirect, in these clashes nations across the Third World may be more disposed to settle them through direct bilateral negotiations. Some recent examples may be quickly summarized: Vietnam's willingness to settle the future of Cambodia through negotiations; Afghan President Najibullah's initiatives for the peaceful settlement of the Afghan civil war through direct negotiations with the rebels; the relaxation of tensions between India and China; India's reiteration of its willingness to resolve the Kashmir dispute with Pakistan through direct bilateral talks; and, above all, the willingness of the Palestine Liberation Organization and a number of front-line Arab states to recognize Israel's right to exist. Similar trends have surfaced in the Horn of Africa and in Nicaragua. In general a relaxed international environment has contributed to a climate of opinion in the Third World favoring the resolution of contentious issues through negotiations and cooperation.

Another indication is the trend toward regional economic cooperation and collective self-reliance. Although these efforts have a long history, they have been accelerated by the emergence of an international environment characterized by the relaxation of tensions and by increased cooperative efforts. The emerging international system of the 1990s brought an urgency to translate words into actions. Third World countries have begun to realize that one of the effective ways for softening the shock of growing inequality is through regional cooperation and collective self-reliance. Such organizations as ASEAN, the South Asia Association for Regional Cooperation (SAARC) and various other collective forums across Asia may even get a new least on life, despite the diversities and clashes of interest of the nations involved.

Finally, there is the problem of dealing with the Soviet Union in the 1990s and beyond. Obviously this is a vital issue, especially for those Asian countries situated near the Soviet border. A bilateral relationship of mutual and comparative economic benefits is likely to be the main framework of these relations. Old and traditional commitments to friendly states (such as India, Afghanistan, Vietnam, North Korea, and Syria) through long-term bilateral treaties of friendship and cooperation may remain operative, although in a diluted form. Certainly the Soviet Union will not receive more from them than it gives to them. In essence a new type of relationship of equality and mutuality of interests is likely to evolve.

But there is also the danger of the development of adversarial relationships, if the Soviet Union opts for extending its cooperative bonds with the United States to the Third World. The specter of a joint US–Soviet hegemony has already come to haunt the Third World. The June 1990 US–Soviet Summit touched a sensitive cord because of its effort to reach agreement and to sign joint declarations concerning regional disputes and conflicts. In the May 1990 summit of Arab states King Hussein of Jordan voiced his apprehension when he noted that the Arabs could no longer take the support of either Washington or Moscow for granted as a result of the US–Soviet detente and the sweeping changes in Eastern Europe. He declared: "We are all facing a totally new situation which makes it imperative for us to stand together and rely on ourselves within the framework of a unified bloc in order to maintain our existence, ensure our future and preserve our vital role in the world."[35] In addition, the settlement of large numbers of emigrant Soviet Jews in areas annexed by Israel complicates Soviet relations with the Arab states, as did the Iraqi invasion of Kuwait and the ensuing crisis of war in the Gulf. Relations with the East European states are also undergoing change. At the May 1990 summit the Arab states agreed to review these traditional cordial relations following the decision by the new regimes in Eastern Europe to improve estranged relations with Israel. However, much depends on how the Soviet Union as a major continental power shorn of its past ideological focus, deals with the traditional susceptibilities and interests of the large majority of the Third World countries.

The implications of perestroika and new thinking for the Third World are complex. New thinking has led to more civilized relations among the great powers. Yet, the emerging international system does not promise to produce equivalent gains for the Third World. The developed North is once again poised to partake of a disproportionately large share of the benefits of the system. The self-inflicted process of downgrading the superpower status of the Soviet Union has not brought about tangible benefits to the Third World as a whole; yet it has put in sharp focus the imperative need for the Third World to move in the direction of self-reliance.

Notes

1 For details, see Zafar Imam, "The impact of the October Revolution on the Third World: an overview," in *The USSR: Sixty Years. Economic and Political Development*, ed. Zafar Imam (New Delhi, Tulsi Publishers, 1982), pp. 58–69.
2 M. Farooqi, "Socialism and democracy," in *The Second Revolution* (New Delhi: Patriot Publishers, 1989), pp. 12–13.
3 *Kuwait News*, 1 February 1986.
4 A.K. Damodaran, "The new Soviet party programme in historical perspective," in *Restructuring Soviet Society*, ed. Zafar Imam (New Delhi: Panchsheel Publishers, 1989), p. 8.
5 Mohit Sen, "The updated CPSU programme," in *Asian Dimension of Soviet Policy*, eds., D.D. Narula and R.R. Sharma (New Delhi: Patriot Publishers, 1986), p. 10.
6 See, for example, the speeches and comments of Indian Prime Minister Rajiv Gandhi during Gorbachev's first official visit to India, in *Indian Press*, 26–28 November 1986.
7 Cited in Zafar Imam, "Some added dimensional inputs in the framework of Soviet policy to the developing countries," in *Asian Dimension*, eds., Narula and Sharma, p. 31.
8 *The Japan Times*, 30 September 1988. For an analytical study of views of Indonesia and other Southeast Asian countries see "Gorbachev's Soviet Union and South-east Asia," *Indonesian Quarterly*, vol. 17, no. 2 (1989), pp. 113–83.
9 *Far Eastern Economic Review*, 4 August 1988, p. 24.
10 See the text of the speech in *The Times of India* and *Patriot*, 22–23 May 1985.
11 Relevant excerpts from the book dealing with the Third World can be found in V.D. Chopra, ed. *Mikhail Gorbachev's New Thinking: Asia Pacific* (New Delhi: Patriot Publishers, 1988), pp. 70–84.
12 *Ibid.*, p. 77.
13 These views were articulated after mid-1986 by what may be called the radical reformers in the Soviet Union who wrote for such publications as *Moscow News*, *Literary Gazette*, and *New Times*. These views were reiterated in discussions that the author had with radical reformers in the Institute of Orientology during the summer of 1987 in Moscow.
14 *Kommunist*, no. 2 (1988).
15 See, *New Times*, no. 44 (October 1988), p. 21.
16 *Ibid.*, no. 25 (June 1989), p. 30.
17 *Soviet Land*, Soviet Embassy, New Delhi, no. 4 (April 1990), p. 10.
18 "The USSR and the Third World," *International Affairs*, no. 12 (1988), pp. 133–36. See the discussion of this article in *International Herald Tribune*, 9 January 1989.
19 "Report of the Soviet Foreign Ministry," *International Affairs*, no. 1 (1990), p. 76.
20 See *The Times of India*, 31 May 1990.
21 These varying interpretations are based on personal interviews and discus-

sions of the author with Soviet academics of the Institute of World Economy and World Politics, USSR Academy of Sciences, during an extended stay in Moscow in December 1989. See, also, Zafar Imam, "New Soviet–Third World policy?" *Hindustan Times*, New Delhi, 31 March 1990.

22 *Soviet Land*, no. 4 (1990), p. 10.

23 See, for example, V. Skosyrev, "On Soviet–Indian relations," *Izvestiia*, 26 July 1990.

24 "Report of the Soviet Foreign Ministry," p. 100.

25 "Born of perestroika," *New Times*, no. 7 (1989), p. 26.

26 Report in *Times of India*, 23 May 1990.

27 Muchkund Dubey, "Europe 1991 and developing countries," *Mainstream*, New Delhi, 25 November 1989, pp. 15–17.

28 Sumanta Banerjee, "Curse of history," *Economic and Political Weekly*, Bombay, 15 October 1988.

29 See CPI(M) Central Committee statement on "Certain ideological questions pertaining to Comrade Gorbachev's Report on the 70th Anniversary of the October Revolution," adopted at the Central Committee meeting held from 3 to 6 May 1988, New Delhi, 1988.

30 See "CPI statements on East Europe," in *Indian Press*, March 1988; see, also, Achin Vanaik, "End of an era: turmoil in USSR and Eastern Europe," *Mainstream*, New Delhi, 10 February 1990.

31 Zafar Imam, "The politics of perestroika," *Mainstream*, 29 February 1987, pp. 7–8.

32 See the collections of articles in Imam, ed. *Restructuring Soviet Society*. See, also, Ajit Roy, "Perestroika and problems of socialist renewal: compulsions, constraints and contradictions," *Economic and Political Weekly*, 24–31 December 1988.

33 Abid Hussain, "Time for a new framework of policy," in *India's Foreign Policy in the 1990s*, ed. M. Rasgotra, *et al.* (New Delhi: Patriot Publishers, 1990), p. 23.

34 "Cuba admits the thin end of a capitalist wedge," in *Le Monde* (English Section), Paris, 8 February 1989.

35 Reported in *The Times of India*, 3 June 1990.

12 The Soviet Union and Indochina

Carlyle A. Thayer

Political relations between Vietnam and the Soviet Union date back to 30 June 1923, when Ho Chi Minh made the first journey by a Vietnamese revolutionary to Bolshevik Russia.[1] Shortly after his arrival, Ho joined the Communist International (Comintern) and actively worked to establish a firm institutional relationship between the Comintern and Vietnam. In February 1930, Ho, acting on behalf of the Comintern, presided over the founding of the Vietnam Communist Party (VCP). Party-to-party ties were formally established in October 1930 when the VCP, now renamed the Indochinese Communist Party, joined the Comintern.

The Soviet Union granted diplomatic recognition to Ho Chi Minh's fledgling Democratic Republic of Vietnam on 31 January 1950, nearly five years after it was founded. However, it was only after the end of the First Indochina War (1946–54) that formal state-to-state relations were established, when a Soviet embassy was opened in Hanoi. In July 1955 Ho Chi Minh paid his first visit to Moscow as president of the DRV. During the course of this visit, the Soviet Union announced its first grant of large-scale economic assistance. The Soviet Union also contributed heavily to Vietnam's first three-year plan (1958–60) and first five-year plan (1961–65).

On the political front Soviet-Vietnamese relations were not particularly close during the Khrushchev period.[2] This was reversed during the Brezhnev years, partly as a result of Moscow's military and economic aid to Vietnam during the Second Indochina War (1965–75). The basis for postwar relations was formalized in November 1978 with the signing of a comprehensive Treaty of Friendship and Cooperation between the USSR and Vietnam. The treaty served the security interests of both signatories as Moscow and Hanoi shared the common aim of containing China.

Since 1978 the Vietnamese have termed their "all-round relationship" with the Soviet Union as the "cornerstone" of their foreign policy. Some Vietnamese military leaders even went so far as to assert that Vietnam, as as outpost of socialism in Southeast Asia, was a part of the alliance network of the socialist states system.[3] In reality there was no one else to whom the Vietnamese could turn. Attempts to normalize relations with the United States foundered in 1978. After Vietnam's invasion of Cambodia, an international trade and aid embargo was imposed by the ASEAN states and their Western allies.

In the period since 1978 Vietnamese dependency on the USSR has grown in all fields. Vietnam's Cambodian venture would not have been possible without Soviet assistance and support. Vietnam relies overwhelmingly on the Soviet Union for weapons and military equipment. Dependency also prevails in the economic sphere. Nearly two-thirds of Vietnam's trade is conducted with the Soviet Union, and the Soviet Union is the source of virtually all Vietnamese development aid. Vietnam is also dependent on the Soviet Union for the supply of various strategic goods such as petroleum, oil, and lubricants. Recent estimates suggest that Soviet combined aid accounts for one-fourth of the Soviet Union's worldwide assistance program and that Vietnam ranks second only to Cuba as a recipient.[4]

Vietnamese dependency has entailed a price. Tens of thousands of Vietnamese "guest workers" have been sent to the Soviet Union to fill labor shortages. A portion of their wages is retained to pay off state debts.[5] Large amounts of Vietnamese raw materials and agricultural produce are shipped to the Soviet Far East as payment for Soviet imports. Vietnam is not free to sell these commodities on the world market for hard currency. More importantly, Vietnam has had to make political concessions. Under Soviet pressure it joined COMECON, and after 1978, acquiesced in hosting Soviet naval and air forces at Cam Ranh Bay.

Since 1978 Soviet–Vietnamese relations have developed both extensively and intensively. There has been frequent and regular contact and consultation at all levels by the party, state, and military bureaucracies and mass organizations of each country. On the political level, for example, there have been nine high-level summits held between the general secretary of the CPSU and the secretary general of the Vietnam Communist Party (VCP) in the period from March 1985 to November 1990. There are also frequent exchanges between delegations representing the various Central Committee departments. Field grade Vietnamese military leaders attend higher-level military academies in the Soviet Union, while the vast majority of Vietnam's science and technology elite has been either trained or educated at Soviet educational institutes.[6] The main symbol of cooperation in this sphere was the participation of a Vietnamese cosmonaut in the Soviet space program.

Despite whatever underlying tensions exist in the Soviet–Vietnamese relationship, involving as it did two starkly different cultural traditions, it would appear that adherence to Marxist–Leninist ideology created a genuine bond between the political elites of both countries. This was reinforced by the longstanding historical nature of the relationship as well as the weight of cross-cutting personal and institutional linkages.[7] In addition, both shared a strategic antipathy toward China.

Changes in these two areas – ideology and relations with China – have put severe strains on the Soviet–Vietnamese relationship. The Soviet Union's attempts to normalize relations with China, begun in the final years of the Brezhnev regime and intensified during the short-lived Andropov interregnum, were not well received by the Vietnamese leadership.[8] In their view, at that time China was "the direct and most dangerous enemy of the Vietnamese people."

Gorbachev's foreign policy initiatives in the area of arms control and regional security in the Asia–Pacific region were generally well received in Hanoi.[9] Vietnam also initially applauded Gorbachev's policies of glasnost and perestroika. Gorbachev's domestic policies were adopted by Vietnam's own reformers who succeeded in 1986 in having a Vietnamese variant – *dôi mói*, or renovation – adopted as party policy. However, as the events of 1989 unfolded, Vietnam's leaders stepped back aghast at developments unleashed by this process. They remained firm that the leading role of the VCP should not be challenged and that the tides of pluralism and multiparty democracy sweeping the socialist community should not crash upon Vietnam's shores. In public Vietnam's leaders blamed the machinations of "imperialism and international reactionaries" as well as the failure of fraternal parties to adhere to the tenets of genuine Marxism–Leninism for these developments. In private, Vietnam's leaders blame Mikhail Gorbachev himself for letting the reform process get out of hand. Quite clearly the bonds between the Soviet Union and Vietnam are being eroded by differences in how to interpret and apply what was once a shared ideology.

This chapter presents an overview of Soviet–Indochinese relations, with major emphasis on Soviet–Vietnamese relations, in the period since Mikhail Gorbachev became general secretary of the CPSU to the present. The main focus is on the impact of Soviet new political thinking in four areas of the relationship: economic, political, foreign policy, and military.

The economic relationship

In the late 1950s the Soviet Union became Vietnam's largest provider of economic aid and assistance, overtaking China. In 1973, with the signing of the Paris peace agreements, the USSR, along with other members of the socialist camp, canceled all of Vietnam's outstanding debts. After the unification of the country, the USSR substantially increased its funding of Vietnam's economic development program, doubling its financial contributions in each of the three five-year plans (FYP), as Table 12.1 indicates.

This funding has gone toward the construction of nearly 300 projects, including 100 major ones, in all areas of the Vietnamese economy.[10] An estimated 30 percent of this aid has been earmarked for industrial development. Soviet assistance in this area has been mainly in large showpiece projects in the energy sector, such as the Hoa Binh, Tri An, and Pha Lai electricity generating complexes, and Vietnam's oil and gas industry. Vietnam also has come under Soviet pressure to take part in the socialist international division of labor within the COMECON context.

At the same time the USSR has pressured the European members of COMECON to share the burden of "lifting up" Vietnam's economy (along with Cuba and Mongolia).[11] In October 1987, COMECON announced a special long-term program of multilateral assistance to Vietnam to cover the period 1991 to 2005. This program played down the importance of foreign aid and stressed instead a "more effective mechanism for managing [Vietnam's] foreign and economic relations and of a structural policy of a new type."[12]

Initially Soviet criticism of Vietnam's performance was muted and generally confined to private discussions. One of the first exceptions came in 1982 when Mikhail Gorbachev, then a relatively junior member of the CPSU Politburo, was dispatched to attend the 5th national congress of the VCP held in March 1982. At that time the Vietnamese were berated for their inefficiency and threatened with decreased Soviet

Table 12.1 *Soviet economic aid to Vietnam*

2nd FYP (1976–80)	US $1.45–3.5 billion
3rd FYP (1981–85)	US $6.5 billion
4th FYP (1986–90)	US $14.5–18.35 billion

FYP=five-year plan
Source: Far Eastern Economic Review, 5 July 1990, p. 44

support.[13] Indeed, the Soviet Union withheld long-term support for Vietnam's third five-year plan until it was well underway.

Since Gorbachev's rise to power the Vietnamese leadership has been put on notice that they must undertake strenuous efforts to improve the efficiency of Soviet aid. Soviet officials have become increasingly critical of Vietnamese ineptitude. Gorbachev's new economic specialists and advisers are wary of continuing to throw good money after bad.[14] They see their prime task as the successful restructuring of the Soviet economy, including its external economic relations. Toward this end they have endeavored to put their economic relationship with the Vietnamese on a more business-like footing. Additional Soviet concerns have focused on the problem of Vietnamese mismanagement, the appropriateness of Soviet aid projects, and the ability of the Vietnamese to absorb large-scale aid.

Vietnam also has experienced a similar attitude on the part of its allies in COMECON. In March 1990 COMECON decided to end multilateral cooperation and coordination of plans.[15] COMECON also initiated plans to abolish its present barter arrangements and shift to trade based on world prices using hard currency. In these changed circumstances, it is unlikely the 1987 multilateral aid program to Vietnam will be carried out.

Vietnam's leaders are aware of these changing attitudes and have responded with public admissions of their own faults. In July 1986 Truong Chinh, Vietnam's new party Secretary General, was reportedly berated by Gorbachev himself.[16] On his return to Hanoi, Truong Chinh stated publicly that Vietnam had squandered Soviet aid.[17] Both the Central Committee of the CPSU and the Politburo of the VCP held special meetings to consider what steps to take to rectify the situation.[18]

In May 1987, during the course of a visit to Moscow, Vietnam's present Secretary General, Nguyên Vân Linh, was pressed by his Soviet counterpart to accept Soviet "new forms of cooperation" such as joint enterprises and direct links between enterprises to ensure greater cost-accounting.[19]

Friction over Soviet aid surfaced in mid-1988 when the Tri An project shut down within days of opening because of a malfunction. Soviet commentary blamed the problem on hasty construction and lack of coordination among the Vietnamese ministries responsible.[20] The Vietnamese said it resulted from the flawed design drawn up by Soviet engineers. Complaints also have arisen over Soviet pricing policies. In 1988, for example, the Soviets reportedly doubled the price of goods delivered to Vietnam; goods which the USSR had purchased in third countries. The Vietnamese also grumble to visitors that they are frequently overcharged by the Soviets for outmoded technology, while receiving below-market prices for their exports of fruit and vegetables, seafood, and industrial crops. Soviet economic managers, who demand prompt fulfilment of commercial contracts by the Vietnamese, have begun writing penalty clauses into such contracts.

Soviet commentators have become openly critical of their aid program to Vietnam and have admitted their failings.[21] Such views surfaced on the tenth anniversary of the USSR–SRV Treaty of Friendship and Cooperation. One Soviet economist, after noting that several long-term construction projects were standing idle while others worked at half capacity, stated, "But instead (of advocating a Leninist NEP) we gave them chemical plants, large hydroelectric plants. They were attracted by the Chinese Great Leap Forward and had studied our Stalinist model of industrialization."[22] Vietnam's debts to the Soviet Union as of November 1989 totaled 9.13 billion rubles.[23] Vietnam is scheduled to start making repayments in 1991 over a five-year period. It is recognized that this probably will not be possible.[24] There is also a marked trade imbalance between Vietnam and the Soviet Union, with Vietnam importing far more than it can afford to pay via exports. This state of affairs has prompted a review, and in the next five-year planning cycle (1991–95) Vietnam will be expected to make payment in hard currency.

Changes in Soviet domestic and external economic policy have altered the nature of the Soviet–Vietnamese relationship. Hanoi can no longer count on the USSR – or its fraternal allies in Europe for that matter – for continued large amounts of economic largess. Recent reports suggest that the USSR is unable to meet its commitments to the final year of Vietnam's current FYP and that Soviet support for the 1991–95 FYP will decrease. Similar trends are evident in Moscow's relations with Vientiane and Phnom Penh.

Both Laos and Cambodia are indebted to the Soviet Union, with published figures setting their respective debts at 758.2 and 714.5 million rubles.[25] According to Soviet diplomatic sources, the USSR's assistance to Laos' current five-year plan (1986–90) totals $250 million. Laos also has a large trade deficit with the Soviet Union, with exports covering less than one-third of imports (estimated at $90.1 million).[26] This state of affairs has given rise to mutual recriminations. According to one review of the Lao–Soviet relationship:

> Strains focused on the question of Soviet aid to Laos have surfaced for the first time (in 1989). The Soviets hint that they expect more efficient use of their assistance, which they say makes up more than half of Laos' total foreign aid.
>
> The Lao, on the other hand, complain that they cannot afford Moscow's aid because the Soviet demand for Lao inputs of labour and local materials is too

expensive. Some Laos also complain that Laos loses money because too many of its products such as coffee, wood and tin ore, which could be exported for hard currency, are locked into long-term barter agreements with the Soviet Union.

But Soviet officials deny that this arrangement works to Laos' disadvantage. In exchange for sending its coffee and wood to the Soviet Union, Laos receives convertible currency goods such as oil, Soviet diplomats say.[27]

In 1989 Laos and the USSR reached agreement on Soviet support for Laos' next five-year plan for the period 1991–95. It is likely that the number of Soviet advisers will be reduced greatly and that future cooperation will take the form of Soviet–Lao joint ventures and direct contractual arrangements between Lao and Soviet enterprises. The amount of Soviet support for Laos was not indicated. One radio commentary declared:

In 1989, the concerned planning organizations of the Soviet Union and the LPDR (Lao People's Democratic Republic) have begun to consult with one another on determining a feasible number of cooperation projects which will be implemented during the period from 1991 to 1995. It is certain that the two sides will continue cooperation in building more roads and bridges and in implementing social welfare projects and a new project to lay an oil pipeline from Vinh (in Vietnam) to Vientiane which will eventually help facilitate oil supply and considerably reduce transport costs of oil products to Laos.[28]

Cambodia has attempted its own program of internal economic reform, and in 1989 foreign visitors to Phnom Penh reported a dramatic increase in economic activity. In August of that year a program of economic liberalization was announced by which Cambodian citizens were allowed to run private enterprises and undertake joint ventures with the state. Farmers were given long-term tenure of their lands and the right to pass it on to their children. Private property rights have been restored in urban areas.

Despite evident progress, a report commissioned by the European Community's NGO Forum on Cambodia revealed in May 1990:

The changes that have occurred in the countries of Central Europe and in the Soviet Union, countries which were until now partners of Cambodia within COMECON, have appalling consequences for Cambodia.

At present, these countries are giving priority to their own economic development. As applicants for IMF means, they are no longer allowed to provide aid to third parties.

From January 1991 on, the relations between these countries and Cambodia will consist of trade and no longer of technical assistance.

Up until now, all forms of aid combined coming from these countries constituted about 80 percent of the annual budget of Cambodia.[29]

In addition, Cambodia will be required to repay in hard currency an outstanding loan to the Soviet Union, estimated at 250 million rubles, when it falls due early in 1991. Also, as a consequence of this development, the Cambodian government has decided to retrench 56,000 employees and to sell off government-held gold reserves to meet pressing needs. For example, Cambodia must now pay on delivery for all imports of petroleum and oil supplies.[30]

A Soviet foreign ministry survey of relations with Vietnam, Laos and Cambodia, which it termed the "other socialist countries," stated:

> Cooperation in the economic sphere is of key importance at the current stage. Over the past few years the CPSU Central Committee and the USSR Council of Ministers have adopted a number of decisions to overhaul economic ties with Vietnam, Laos and Cambodia and ensure the effectiveness of bilateral cooperation.
>
> The efforts taken by both sides to improve economic ties have yielded certain results. Soviet credits were reorientated in part to cooperation in implementing the priority economic programmes of Vietnam, Laos and Cambodia. Utilization of the production potential created with Soviet assistance improved somewhat. Exports from the Indochinese countries to the USSR, including foods and some industrial consumer goods, began to increase . . .
>
> However, we have failed thus far to attain the main goal, that of creating a thrift model of economic cooperation. The present practice of financing cooperation from the state budget prevents input-maximizing methods of interconnections from being broken down, allows crediting of excessively protracted construction projects, hampers reductions in the size of Soviet personnel at sites, etc. Both sides are focusing on efforts to resolve these problems without delay.[31]

The political relationship

As mentioned previously, Vietnam initially welcomed the process of glasnost and perestroika in the Soviet Union and endorsed the domestic economic reform program of the CPSU's 27th Congress (February 1986). In December 1986 the 6th Congress of the Vietnam Communist Party formally adopted *dôi mói*, or renovation. In the political sphere this meant a gradual process of political change in three main areas: more "openness" and honesty in press reporting, separation of party–state relations to end party interference in day-to-day governmental affairs, and enhancement of the role of law through reform of the National Assembly, its electoral procedures and committee structures.

Political reform in Vietnam has not embraced political pluralism or multiparty democracy. The leading role of the VCP, as enshrined in the state constitution, is sacrosanct. Quite simply, political renovation was not intended to alter radically the structure, functions, or policies of the Vietnam Communist Party. In the era of *dôi mói* the public was asked to assist the party in combating corruption, bureaucratism, and other so-called negative phenomena. But the party itself would take charge of its own reform.

The VCP reacted negatively to the pro-democracy and anti-socialist movements in Poland and Hungary. Developments in Poland were termed a "counter-revolutionary *coup d'état*."[32] Demonstrations protesting these developments were organized in Hanoi and petitions delivered to the Polish Embassy. When the Polish government reacted sharply to what it considered interference in its internal affairs, Vietnamese authorities retreated quickly.[33]

The events in Hungary and Poland, as well as the emergence of pluralist tendencies in the Soviet Union, eventually attracted attention and some support within the VCP. Soon there were calls for a modification of the state constitution's clause on the leading role of the party and the direct election of the chairman of the National Assembly (in effect Vietnam's president). At the same time as the VCP's leadership resisted these demands, Gorbachev led the Soviet Union down the path of political reform, and the other fraternal states (Czechoslovakia, the GDR, Romania, and Bulgaria) embraced multiparty democracy, political pluralism, and free elections. The emergence of a pro-democracy movement in China and the swift collapse of the Ceauşescu government in Romania startled the VCP. It now faced growing pressures to speed up the process of political reform in Vietnam.

It was in these circumstances that the VCP convened the 8th plenary session (6th congress) of the Central Committee. In an unprecedented move, a draft program was circulated in public in an effort to solicit comment from the population at large.[34] The Central Committee then met in secret for several weeks. At the end of these deliberations economic renovation was reendorsed but not political reform.[35] Trân Xuân Bách, a member of the Politburo, secretary of the Central Committee, and a leading advocate of political reform, was dismissed from all his posts in a clear negative signal to advocates of change.

In brief, the VCP has fallen back on orthodox ideological tenets to argue it is the upholder of "true socialism" as opposed to "deformed socialism" elsewhere.[36] The party-controlled media repeatedly have stressed the primacy of the party and the objective of building socialism in Vietnam.

Changes in Central and Eastern Europe and the USSR – the end of the cold war, the disintegration of the Warsaw Pact, the overthrow of communist regimes by more or less peaceful means, and the threat of secession in the Soviet Union – have posed severe ideological challenges to the Vietnamese leadership. Past declarations that they are part of the "socialist community headed by the Soviet Union" ring hollow in the face of the momentous changes now unfolding. The ideological glue which has bound the Vietnamese to the Soviet Union has dried up and no longer appears to be serving its purpose.

Strains in Soviet–Vietnamese relations are now appearing on the political plane, especially in the area of socialist ideology. Vietnam endorses economic renovation at home, but adamantly eschews political reform of the type which is unfolding in the USSR and elsewhere in the socialist community. Adherence to outmoded ideological conceptions leaves open the possibility that Vietnam may be left politically isolated from its current economic benefactors.

Laos initiated its program of economic reform in 1986 at the fourth congress of the Lao People's Revolutionary Party. These reforms have included economic liberalization (utilizing market forces) and limited political reform. Collectively they are referred to as *chin tanakan may*, or new thinking. A major watershed was reached at the February 1988 plenary session of the Supreme People's Assembly. At this time, midway through the second five-year plan (1985–90), Laos decided to scrap its system of central planning, state subsidies, and agricultural collectivization. Laos has since adopted a new economic management system and policies which give play to market incentives and autonomy for state enterprises.

In the political sphere, Laos held its first elections in 1988 starting at the district level in June and province level in October. These were followed by national level elections for the Supreme People's Assembly in March 1990. In June of the same year, Laos made public the draft text of its first written constitution.[37]

Soviet–Lao relations in the political sphere appear to be developing without the strains evident in Soviet–Vietnamese relations. The events in Eastern Europe and the Soviet Union in 1989–90 do not appear to have affected Lao society with the same force as they did in Vietnam. Some concern, however, has been expressed that domestic reform and Laos' opening to the outside world "may create phenomena which run counter to our fine culture and customs."[38]

In 1989 Cambodia embarked on a program of limited political reform and appeared to be shedding the trappings of orthodox communism. In addition to the economic reforms mentioned which created a free-market economy, Cambodia moved to allow greater political diversity. The National Assembly amended the state constitution and restored Buddhism as the official religion. The country was renamed the State of Cambodia (previously it was known as the People's Republic of Kampuchea). The death penalty has been abolished, and freedom of press, freedom of political association, and freedom of movement were all guaranteed. Nevertheless, Cambodia remains a one-party state. The last national elections were held in 1981, and although new elections have been mooted, they have become a hostage to the protracted peace process.

Generally the reform efforts in Indochina have received praise from the Soviet Union. Eduard Shevardnadze, for example, in his 1989 survey of Soviet foreign relations, stated in this regard: "The leadership of Vietnam, Laos and Cambodia embarked upon the path of sweeping economic and political reforms. The Indochinese countries as a whole assessed positively the concept of new political thinking."[39]

Prospects for continued reform in Cambodia took a downturn in mid-year when the government announced it had uncovered a plot to stage a *coup d'état* by persons seeking to overthrow one-party rule. According to the official communiqué:

> The enemies – including foreign espionage circles – took advantage of the political and economic liberalization policy of our party and state to set up a treacherous force within our inner ranks with the intention of overthrowing the State of Cambodia through attacks from the rear in addition to military attacks from the front.[40]

This announcement followed the reported arrest earlier of the Minister for Communications, Transport and Posts Ung Phan, two colonels, and three civil servants. According to an official source, these individuals were charged with trying to form a liberal social democratic party. At the same time, Khieu Khanarith, an outspoken journalist, was removed from his post as editor-in-chief of *Kampuchea*, and Men Sam An was dropped from her position as head of the party's Organization Commission.[41]

These developments came at a time when the Phnom Penh regime was under increased pressure from the Soviet Union to achieve a negotiated peace settlement and increased pressure from the Khmer Rouge, and other resistance forces, who were stepping up attacks on the battlefield. Outside observers concluded that regime hard-liners were attempting to consolidate their positions in the face of these challenges. Continued Soviet pressures on the Cambodian government, coupled with a decline in economic assistance, will place severe strains on the political relationship between Moscow and Phnom Penh. In March 1990, at a meeting of the UN Security Council Permanent Five held in Paris, for example, the USSR agreed to drop references to "genocide" in a concession to China. Hun Sen, Cambodia's premier, said in a later interview that this "was not in any way to our satisfaction."[42]

The foreign policy relationship

New political thinking in the USSR has brought about dramatic shifts in the Soviet Union's foreign policy. The Vietnamese have easily adjusted to Soviet arms control initiatives and to the improvement in Soviet–American relations. However, Soviet efforts to normalize relations with China have posed particular problems for the Vietnamese. Vietnam is a regional power with regional interests. The Soviet Union is a global power with global interests. Put simply, the utility to Moscow of Vietnam as an ally has faded in the face of Sino-Soviet normalization.

Soviet efforts to improve relations with the People's Republic of China may be traced back to the last years of the Brezhnev government. They were intensified under Andropov, much to the discomfort of Hanoi. A swing back during the Chernenko period gave Vietnam momentary respite. Efforts to normalize Sino-Soviet relations were intensified by Gorbachev and were highlighted in his landmark speech at Vladivostok in July 1986.

China had long identified three obstacles which it stated had to be overcome if relations were to improve. Among them was ending Vietnam's occupation of Cambodia. Initially the Soviet Union was unwilling to become involved in pressuring the Vietnamese on this issue. It told Beijing it would not discuss third-party issues. Moscow called for bilateral Sino-Vietnamese discussions. However, as the normalization process developed, Moscow changed tack and permitted China to place Cambodia on the agenda of their bilateral discussions.

Vietnam then came under sustained pressure from the USSR to withdraw its forces.[43] The Soviet Union argued that Vietnam should follow its model in Afghanistan. Vietnam resisted, arguing that the two situations were fundamentally different. The Soviets also pressed the Vietnamese to pursue a policy of "national reconciliation of all the Cambodian nationalist forces," a coded expression for the inclusion of elements of the Khmer Rouge in a political settlement.

In April 1989, on the eve of the long-awaited Sino-Soviet summit, Vietnam made the expected concession and announced that it would withdraw all its military forces by September without precondition. At this point the tragic events of Tiananmen intervened to freeze Chinese policy on Cambodia and to take the gloss off Sino-Soviet normalization. Although the Soviet Union is no longer playing the activist role which it pursued in 1987–88, the Cambodian question is no longer an obstacle to Sino-Soviet relations.

Soviet new political thinking in foreign relations has had a major impact on Laos' foreign relations. Laotian leaders quickly adopted the central tenets of Soviet new political thinking. They redefined the meaning of national security to incorporate economic growth as a central element and took steps to move Laos from a "natural" or subsistence economy to a goods economy. Laos thus stressed the importance of private foreign investment, international trade, and technological cooperation with a diversity of foreign countries including capitalist states. A foreign investment code was adopted in April 1988. Relations with Thailand improved dramatically, and relations with China have shifted from hostility to normalization. Laos, of course, benefits from the fact that since the formation of the LPDR in December 1975, it has maintained relations with and has received aid from a wide variety of foreign countries, including the United States. Laos was not subject to the trade and aid embargo clamped on Vietnam.

With respect to Cambodia, Soviet new political thinking in foreign relations has been mainly focused on obtaining a negotiated resolution to the armed conflict. Soviet policy under Gorbachev has passed through several phases from passive involvement to an activist stance in support of a settlement based on coordination of diplomatic efforts by the Permanent Five Members of the UN Security Council. Until such a settlement is reached, Cambodia will remain isolated in its foreign relations to members of the former "socialist community" and India.

The military relationship

During the pre-Gorbachev era it was common among Western analysts of Soviet behavior in the Third World to highlight the saliency of military aid as an instrument of Soviet influence.[44] Quite clearly the military dimension of the Soviet–Vietnamese relationship was of great importance. Vietnam served the USSR's strategy to contain China, and it offered a base from which Soviet power could be projected into the South and Southeast Asian regions. To the Vietnamese, Soviet military assistance was vital, since Vietnam possesses no modern armaments industry. All major items of military equipment from jet aircraft and air defense missiles to field guns and tanks must be imported from abroad. Table 12.2 sets out the value of Soviet arms shipments to Vietnam in recent years.

The Brezhnev years were a period of military overextension. For example, Vietnam could not have invaded and occupied Cambodia without prior Soviet approval and support. The Soviet invasion of Afghanistan followed a year later. During this period Soviet Defense Minister Ustinov was quoted as calling for the integration of Vietnam's military into the armed forces of the socialist community.[45] Vietnamese

Table 12.2 *Soviet military aid to Vietnam (in billions of $US)*

Year	1974	1975	1976	1977	1978	1979	1980	1981
Amount	negl.	$0.25	$0.30	$0.10	$0.19	$1.5	$0.24	$0.45
Year	1982	1983	1984	1985	1986	1987	1989	1989
Amount	$0.90	$1.2	$1.3	$1.7	$1.5	$1.5	$1.3	n.a.

Sources: NATO, *Soviet Economic Relations with Selected Client States in the Developing World*, 14 October 1982 (1974–80); Douglas Pike, *Vietnam and the Soviet Union: Anatomy of an Alliance* (Boulder: Westview Press, 1987), p. 196 (1981–86); Thailand, National Security Council sources cited in *The Nation* (Bangkok), 10 May 1987, p. 1 (1982–86). Figures for 1987–88 were provided to the author by knowledgeable sources. There are discrepancies among the various sources cited.

officials made similar statements. Some analysts even speculated that Hanoi had accepted integrated war planning and that the Vietnam People's Army would open a second front against China in the event of a Sino-Soviet war.[46]

The Gorbachev period has brought about a marked alteration in the relationship with Vietnam in the military sphere. The Soviet Union has adopted a doctrine of "defense self-sufficiency" and has extricated itself from Afghanistan. The Soviet Union has moved also to assist in resolving regional conflicts, such as Cambodia. It has begun also to scale down its naval presence in the Indian Ocean. In January 1990, Foreign Minister Shevardnadze told visiting US senators that the USSR would withdraw all its military forces in Asia behind Soviet borders.[47]

In 1979 when the Sino-Vietnamese border war broke out, the Soviet Union signaled its support for Vietnam by dispatching a naval flotilla to the South China Sea. It later called in at Cam Ranh Bay. Cam Ranh then became an important Soviet staging point for operations in the region (and an important bargaining chip for the Vietnamese). Nine years later (March 1988), when Chinese and Vietnamese naval forces fought an engagement in the Spratly Island area, the Soviet response was quite different. In a clear signal of the changing relationship, the USSR adopted a more or less even-handed approach calling on both parties to refrain from the use of force. This was quite remarkable given that the naval clash appeared to have been provoked by China. Vietnam's leaders were reported as being shocked at the Soviet attitude.[48]

The Soviet Union's military presence in Vietnam also has decreased. In his speech at Vladivostok in 1986, Secretary General Gorbachev stated that a US withdrawal from its military bases in the Philippines would not go unanswered.[49] Later, in a speech given in Krasnoyarsk in September 1988, Gorbachev offered an explicit trade.[50] This statement clearly angered the Vietnamese[51] and later the next year they staged several anti-Soviet incidents at Cam Ranh in a symbolic assertion of their sovereignty.[52] As a result of changes in Soviet strategic doctrine, the utility of a base at Cam Ranh has diminished. In late 1989 the Soviets unilaterally withdrew most of their planes and warships from the base. In April 1990 the Soviets stated they would withdraw all their military forces by 1992[53] and by year's end this process apparently had begun.[54] Thus the Vietnamese have lost an important lever in their relationship with Moscow.

In the aftermath of its military withdrawal from Cambodia, Vietnam announced long-term plans to demobilize the Vietnam People's Army. In late 1990 it was reported that Vietnamese troop strength had been reduced by half.[55] At the same time, the Soviet Union has indicated that its military assistance will decline by one-third starting in 1991[56] and that Vietnam will be expected to pay for military equipment.[57] Given the parlous state of the Vietnamese economy, Vietnam will be hard pressed to pay for major equipment purchases, and to modernize its armed forces to keep up with regional developments. Vietnam thus faces a future of declining military influence in the region which will make it more vulnerable to Chinese pressures.

The Soviet Union and Vietnam are the main providers of military assistance to Laos. Few details are available but the amounts would appear to be modest. Laos' foreign military assistance in 1983 was estimated at $125 million and has probably decreased since.[58] In 1988–89 Vietnam began a run down of its military forces stationed in Laos. At their peak, Vietnamese forces were estimated at being in the 40,000 to 50,000 range and current estimates place their size at between 4,000 to 10,000.

There are no accurate public figures for the amount of Soviet military aid to Cambodia. The Soviet Union declared in 1990 that it had unilaterally ended all military assistance to Cambodia. Presumably this refers to free military aid channeled directly to the government in Phnom Penh. In contrast, the Khmer Rouge radio station regularly broadcasts reports on the arrival by sea of Soviet military equipment and supplies at the port of Kampong Som.

Conclusion

The nature of Soviet–Indochinese relations is undergoing a fundamental transformation as a result of marked changes in Soviet domestic and foreign policy priorities. The salience of ideology as a factor uniting these dissimilar states is fast eroding. As a global power, the Soviet

Union has a greater stake in improving its relations with Washington and Beijing than in maintaining the historically close and costly relations with the three states of Indochina. Quite plainly the Soviet Union can no longer afford to dish out lavish amounts of economic and military credits to Vietnam, Laos, or Cambodia.[59] Soviet economic relations with the three Indochinese states can be expected to continue, but on a more pragmatic and less ideological basis.

Soviet–Indochinese economic, political, and military ties also can be expected to lessen, but not diminish entirely, as the Soviet Union turns inward to solve its mounting domestic problems. Vietnam, Cambodia, and Laos[60] have reacted to the changing nature of their relations with Moscow by trying to hold firm on the domestic front in order to ensure political stability and to forestall internal challenges to the legitimacy of one-party rule. In all three states the ruling communist party has made clear its intention to insulate domestic society from the political changes sweeping the Soviet Union and Eastern Europe.

The Vietnam Communist Party, which has always seen itself as a member of the socialist community headed by the Soviet Union, now appears to be isolated and to have more in common in ideological terms with neighboring China,[61] Laos, Cambodia, and hard-line socialist states such as North Korea and Cuba than with its Soviet and European allies. An *Izvestiia* interview by Secretary General Nguyên Vân Linh highlighted this point.[62] Linh once again stressed the "three no's" – no pluralism, no multiparty system, and no opposition party. In discussing relations with the USSR, Linh could only stress Vietnamese gratitude for Soviet aid.

All the states of Indochina have embarked on programs of economic reform. One aspect of this process involves restructuring their present relations with the USSR (and other Eastern European states) in a manner acceptable to both. Another aspect involves opening up Indochina to the free-market economies of Asia and the Pacific (the ASEAN states, Taiwan, and South Korea), as well as the European Community and Australia. This process involves a concerted attempt by Laos, Vietnam and, to a lesser extent, Cambodia, to normalize relations with China[63] and the United States.[64] Economic imperatives will likely mitigate against the formation of a "red brotherhood" of conservative Asian states.

Notes

1 Evgenii Kobelev, *Ho Chi Minh* (Moscow: Progress Publishers, 1989), p. 59.

2 For background, see Carlyle A. Thayer, "Vietnam and the Soviet Union: perceptions and policies," in *The Soviet Union and the Asia-Pacific Region:*

Views from the Region, ed. Pushpa Thambipillai and Daniel C. Matuszewski (New York: Praeger Publishers, 1989), pp. 134–53.

3 General Hoang Van Thai, "Ve Quan He Hop Tac Dac Biet Giua Ba Dan Toc Dong Duong" [On the Special Relations of Cooperation Among the Three Nations of Indochina], *Tap Chi Cong San*, vol. 1 (January 1982), pp. 11–17.

4 Thai Quang Trung, "When the cornerstone is crumbling: Soviet–Vietnamese military cooperation reassessed," *Vietnam Commentary*, no. 13 (January–February 1990), p. 2.

5 Bruno Franceshi, "Eye on Indochina," *Business Times* (Kuala Lumpur), 11 February 1984, p. 4; Ly-Binh Berges dispatch from Prague, *The Australian*, 13 October 1986; and Giles Campion dispatch from Hanoi, *The Bangkok Post*, 7 April 1987.

6 Carlyle A. Thayer, "Soviet studies in Vietnam," in *Soviet Studies in the Asia-Pacific Region*, ed. Charles E. Morrison and Pushpa Thambipillai (Honolulu: Resource Systems Institute, East–West Center, 1986), pp. 101–22.

7 Thayer, "Vietnam and the Soviet Union," pp. 134–53.

8 Robert C. Horn, *Alliance Politics Between Comrades: The Dynamics of Soviet–Vietnamese Relations* (Los Angeles: RAND/UCLA Center for the Study of Soviet International Behavior, August 1987), pp. 12–27.

9 Carlyle A. Thayer, "Kampuchea: Soviet initiatives and regional responses," in *The Soviet Union as an Asian Pacific Power: Implications of Gorbachev's 1986 Vladivostok Initiative*, ed. Ramesh Thakur and Carlyle A. Thayer (Boulder, CO: Westview Press, 1987), pp. 171–200; and interviews conducted in Hanoi with Vietnamese Soviet specialists in October 1987.

10 Hanoi Radio international service, 21 September 1989.

11 Communiqué of the VCP Politburo, Hanoi Radio home service, 13 November 1986.

12 M. Trigubenko, "Co-operation between CMEA and Vietnam: checking the slowdown," *Far Eastern Affairs* (Moscow), no. 4 (1988), p. 24; see also Vietnam News Agency, 15 October 1987 and address by Vo Van Kiet to the 43rd special CMEA session held in Hanoi; Hanoi Radio domestic service, 15 October 1987.

13 Hoang Huu Quynh, "Gorbachev and the Vietnamese stake: deflating an inflated value," *Vietnam Commentary*, no. 13 (January–February 1990), p. 10; and Nayan Chanda, "As Moscow's ardour cools, Hanoi looks elsewhere," *Far Eastern Economic Review*, 16 April 1982, p. 18.

14 This is based in part on discussions with Soviet specialists in May 1988 and January 1989.

15 Dispatch from Prague in *The Sydney Morning Herald*, 29 March 1990.

16 Hoang Huu Quynh, "Gorbachev and the Vietnamese stake," p. 9.

17 AP dispatch from Moscow, citing TASS, *The Bangkok Post*, 28 July 1987, p. 10; UPI dispatch from Bangkok, *The Straits Times*, 23 October 1986.

18 Moscow Radio home service, 5 January 1987; and communiqué of the VCP Central Committee Politburo meeting, 7 May 1987, broadcast by Hanoi Radio home service, 7 May 1987.

19 Full text of Soviet–Vietnamese joint communiqué carried by TASS, 21 May 1987.
20 Blagov, V. Burbulis, and M. Kalmykov, "Taking account of mistakes for the future," *Sotsialisticheskaia Industriia*, 23 March 1988 translated in BBC, Summary of World Broadcasts, FE/0110 A2/1, 26 March 1988.
21 Soviet Television, 7 January 1988, in BBC, Summary of World Broadcasts, FE/W0009 A/14, 20 January 1988.
22 Sophie Quinn Judge and Murray Hiebert, "Ten year itch," *Far Eastern Economic Review*, 10 November 1988, p. 23.
23 *Chas Pik* [Rush Hour], newspaper of the Leningrad Division of the USSR Journalists' Union, 26 February 1990, no. 1, reprinted in "To whom we have 'loaned' 85.8 billion rubles," *Izvestiia*, 1 March 1990, p. 3, and translated in *The Current Digest of the Soviet Press*, vol. 42, no. 9 (1990), p. 9.
24 Vinogradov, "Toward a restructuring of Soviet–Vietnamese economic ties," *Izvestiia*, 4 February 1990, translated in the current *Digest of the Soviet Press*, vol. 42, no. 5 (1990), pp. 20–21.
25 *Chas Pik*, 26 February 1990.
26 Murray Hiebert, "Hammer blow for Hanoi," *Far Eastern Economic Review*, 5 July 1990, p. 45.
27 "Laos," *Asia Yearbook 1990*, p. 164.
28 Vientiane Radio domestic service, 12 May 1989.
29 Raoul M. Jennar, *Cambodia Mission Report 19th April–10th May 1990*, p. 3.
30 Elizabeth Becker dispatch from Paris, *The Washington Post*, 7 June 1990.
31 "The foreign policy and diplomatic activity of the USSR (April 1985–October 1989) a survey prepared by the USSR Ministry of Foreign Affairs," *International Affairs* (Moscow), January 1990, p. 74.
32 Commentary, "Political crisis in Poland," *Nhân Dân*, 25 August 1989; Hanoi Radio home service, 25 August 1989; and Vietnam News Agency, 26 August 1989. Solidarity was termed a "reactionary organization."
33 Based on conversations in Hanoi with Western diplomats during the course of a visit in October 1989.
34 Broadcast by Hanoi Radio domestic service, 5 February 1990.
35 See text of the communiqué of the 80 plenum of the 6th Communist Party of Vietnam Central Committee, Hanoi Radio domestic service, 28 March 1990.
36 See the perceptive analysis by Tony Hill, based on interviews with Vietnamese officials; ABC Radio, "Correspondent's report," 21 January 1990.
37 "Draft Constitution of the Lao People's Democratic Republic," *Pasason*, 4 June 1990.
38 Vientiane Radio commentary cited in *Asia Yearbook 1990*, p. 161.
39 "The foreign policy and diplomatic activity of the USSR," p. 73.
40 Voice of the People of Cambodia, Phnom Penh Radio home service, 20 June 1990.
41 AFP dispatch from Bangkok, *The Australian*, 22 June 1990.
42 See "On the offensive" (Nayan Chanda's interview with Hun Sen) *Far Eastern Economic Review*, 7 June 1990, p. 30.
43 See Carlyle A. Thayer, "Prospects for peace in Kampuchea: Soviet

initiatives and Indochinese responses," *The Indonesian Quarterly* (Second Quarter 1989), vol. 17, no. 2, pp. 157–72.

44 Daniel S. Papp, *Soviet Policies Toward the Developing World During the 1980s: The Dilemmas of Power and Presence* (Maxwell Air Force Base, Alabama: Air University Press, 1986), pp. 119–52.

45 Thai Quang Trung, "When the cornerstone is crumbling," p. 2.

46 Douglas Pike, "Vietnam, a modern Sparta," *Pacific Defence Reporter* (April 1983), p. 38.

47 UPI dispatch from Moscow, *The Australian*, 19 January 1990.

48 Nayan Chanda, "A troubled friendship," *Far Eastern Economic Review*, 9 June 1988, p. 17.

49 Text of speech by Mikhail Gorbachev in Vladivostok, 28 July 1986 in *The Soviet Union as an Asian Pacific Power*, p. 224.

50 Text of broadcast of Gorbachev's speech at a meeting with people from Krasnoyarsk Krai, Moscow Radio home service, and Soviet Television, 16 September 1988.

51 See Kyodo dispatch from Ho Chi Minh City, 17 September 1988, citing the reactions of Vietnam's Foreign Minister Nguyen Co Thach; and Murray Hiebert, "Carping about Cam Ranh," *Far Eastern Economic Review*, 27 October 1988, p. 27.

52 Based on information provided by Western intelligence analysts, 3 August and 5 and 18 December 1989.

53 AP dispatch from Washington, citing a senior member of the House Armed Services Committee, *The Australian*, 23 April 1990.

54 See Kyodo News Agency dispatch from Hanoi quoting the Soviet Ambassador to Vietnam, 31 October 1990.

55 Kyodo News Agency, 1 November 1990, citing Vietnamese military sources.

56 Louise Williams dispatch from Bangkok, *The Sydney Morning Herald*, 31 January 1990, citing Western diplomatic sources. The decision was conveyed to the Vietnamese government late in 1989.

57 "Soviet sales of military equipment to Vietnam are likewise being converted to a market cash-based system for implementation next year," see Michael Byrnes, *The Australian Financial Review*, 12 April 1990.

58 *Pacific Defence Reporter 1987 Annual Reference Edition* (December 1986/January 1987), p. 152; subsequent issues provide no estimates for the Lao defense budget or foreign military assistance.

59 Murray Hiebert, "Straitened superpowers," *Far Eastern Economic Review*, 4 January 1990, pp. 6–7.

60 In October 1990 it was reported that Lao authorities had arrested about six persons who had been agitating for a multiparty democracy; AFP dispatch, *The Age*, 24 October 1990, and *Pasason* quoted by KPL News Agency, 3 November 1990.

61 See the suggestion that China and Vietnam might agree to a "red solution" to the Cambodian conflict, James Pringle dispatch from Phnom Penh, *The Weekend Australian*, 3–4 November 1990.

62 Excerpts of which were broadcast by Voice of Vietnam, 9 May 1990.

63 There have been reports of contacts between Chinese diplomats and officials of the Phnom Penh regime.

64 Vietnam has even suggested that the United States could avail itself of the facilities of its former base in Cam Ranh Bay; AP-Dow Jones, "Vietnam woos US with base," *The Australian Financial Review*, 13 November 1990.

13 Gorbachev's Southeast Asia policy: new thinking for a new era?

Bilveer Singh

The Soviet Union's role in Southeast Asia has gone through a metamorphosis. For most of the postwar period, it had only peripheral interests in the region. Indeed, the Southeast Asian countries viewed the Soviet Union largely as an outsider, a "white power" with no concerns or legitimate interests in Southeast Asia. But by the 1980s, after a shift in its policies, the Soviet Union had emerged as an important actor in Southeast Asia. This chapter traces the growth of the Soviet Union as a Southeast Asian power and compares Moscow's old and new thinking toward the region. The object is to show how the Soviet Union has become a major power in the region and to delineate the changing focus and policies of the Soviet Union, especially under Mikhail Gorbachev, toward Southeast Asia.

Soviet postwar policy toward Southeast Asia

For years the Soviet Union had no direct interests in Southeast Asia. Even after World War II, when tremendous political and social changes were taking place in Southeast Asia, Stalin continued to neglect the region. Moscow exhibited this neglectful, even hostile, posture toward the Southeast Asian countries in many ways: by its refusal to recognize states like Burma, Thailand, and Indonesia; by its failure to recognize the government of Ho Chi Minh until 1950; and by its continued call for revolutionary struggle in Southeast Asia, such as the endorsement of the communist uprisings in the region that broke out in 1948 in Malaya, Indonesia, Burma, the Philippines, and Thailand.

By the early 1950s, and especially after 1953, the Soviet position had changed. The change was inaugurated by Josef Stalin at the 19th Congress of the Communist Party of the Soviet Union (CPSU) in October 1952, but it was left to Nikita Khrushchev to implement the new policy. Stalin changed his position for two reasons: the failure of his earlier policies in the region, and the realization of the faulty nature of the "two camps" theory. Moscow discovered that the actual situation in the

Third World was far more complex than previously thought, especially as a result of actions by countries such as India, Burma, and Indonesia. These states showed that they were not "neo-colonies" and could, indeed, act against their former colonial masters. For example, they played a role in the resolution of the Korean War, criticized the San Francisco Peace Treaty, and refused to condemn China as an aggressor in the Korean War.

The real change in Soviet posture toward Southeast Asia, however, occurred during Khrushchev's leadership, the high-water mark being the official visits by Khrushchev, Voroshilov, and Bulganin to Burma and Indonesia. Changes in policy were enunciated clearly at the 20th Party Congress in February 1956, where the Third World was viewed as a "zone of peace" which could be an ally of the socialist bloc in countering the expansionism of the "imperialist bloc." The Soviet Union, however, did not view all countries in the region as equally important. Rather, Moscow focused on Vietnam, Burma, and Indonesia. Vietnam was, however, under strong Chinese influence, and Burma was moving toward self-imposed isolation. Therefore, only Indonesia was left open to Soviet approaches.

Moscow targeted Jakarta for several reasons. First, President Sukarno was a charismatic leader who opposed the old established forces and pursued a foreign policy of "positive neutralism." Second, after the Bandung Conference, Sukarno and Indonesia were emerging as leaders of the Afro-Asian movement, the forerunner of the non-aligned movement. Third, the revamped Communist Party of Indonesia under the leadership of D.N. Aidit – and Sukarno's willingness to cooperate with it in line with the Soviet concept of "national democracy" – provided a semblance of ideological legitimacy to Indonesia and for Soviet involvement in Indonesia. Fourth, the United States' refusal to provide military and economic aid to Indonesia and the implication for the separatist movement in Sumatra and Sulawesi led to a deterioration of American–Indonesian relations and provided Moscow with an opportunity to increase its influence in the archipelago. Similarly, the deterioration of Sino-Indonesian relations caused by the overseas Chinese issue between 1959 and 1961 provided the Soviet Union with a clear opportunity to improve its image at the expense of its adversary. In addition, the size of Indonesian territory, population, and resources made Indonesia a natural leader of the region – an important consideration for the Soviet Union, which targeted Egypt in the Middle East and India in South Asia for similar reasons. The issue of West Irian, where the Western powers were seen to be backing the Dutch, provided Moscow with an opportunity to back Sukarno's "just war" and hence win Indonesia's favor as well as improve its status as a supporter of national liberation movements in the Third World.

Following the resolution of the West Irian issue, Soviet–Indonesian relations deteriorated, partly because Moscow played no direct role, compared with the United States, in ending the conflict. Moreover, after the Cuban Missile Crisis in October 1962, the Soviet Union began to oppose Indonesia's policy of brinkmanship, fearing that it could become involved in a war with the United States. In this regard, Indonesia's *konfrontatsiia*, or confrontation, against Malaysia in 1963 embarrassed the Soviet Union whch had to bail Jakarta out diplomatically in the United Nations. Jakarta's decision to leave the United Nations was equally unexpected and embarrassing. In fact, a direct result of the increasingly strained Soviet–Indonesian relations was the warming of Sino-Indonesian relations; Sukarno and the PKI became pro-PRC in the Sino-Soviet conflict. In this context, Indonesia's estrangement from the Soviet Union represented a major political and diplomatic defeat for the Soviet Union in Southeast Asia, especially in view of the fact that between 1958 and 1962, Indonesia was the largest recipient of Soviet military and economic aid in the Third World, except for Egypt. That Soviet investments in Indonesia did not pay dividends also represented one of Moscow's initial failures in the Third World.

In many ways, 1965 marked a major turning point for Soviet policies and posture in Southeast Asia. Within the Soviet Union itself, following the ouster of Khrushchev in October 1964, a new leadership came to power under Leonid Brezhnev and implemented new policies toward the Third World. More significant were the developments in the region itself. In Indonesia, following the GESTAPU "coup" in September 1965, the PKI was obliterated and Sukarno deposed. A new leadership under General Suharto led to a reorientation of the country's domestic and foreign policies toward the capitalist West. The United States also escalated its war in Indochina and began bombing North Vietnam following the Gulf of Tonkin incident. Finally, the Cultural Revolution in China, which inaugurated militant domestic and foreign policies, provided the new Soviet leadership with an opportunity to discredit Beijing as well as make inroads into the region. At the same time, Moscow's policies shifted from Jakarta to Hanoi. The Kremlin realized that Hanoi needed support, especially in the area of modern weaponry. And since the PRC was in domestic turmoil and in no position to provide sophisticated conventional weapons, the Soviet Union moved in to exploit Vietnamese helplessness in the war in Indochina. A major Soviet consideration in investing in Vietnam was the growing Sino-Soviet rift, and the object was to gradually edge the Chinese out of their traditionally dominant influence in Indochina.

An additional impetus for change in policy toward the region was provided by international developments in 1969. First, Sino-Soviet rivalry intensified, as manifested by the violent border clashes between the two countries in March and November 1969. Second, in April, the PRC held its 9th Congress of the Chinese Communist Party (CCP) leading officially to the end of the Chinese Cultural Revolution and the inauguration of a more pragmatic foreign policy. One result of this pragmatism was the growing warmth in relations between the PRC and the United States. Third, in 1969, President Nixon announced the Guam Doctrine, inaugurating a decreased American military presence in Southeast Asia. Finally, the British effected their policy of withdrawing militarily from the "East of Suez," opening the race for naval domination of the Indian Ocean. In direct response to these developments, the Soviet leadership floated the idea of an Asian Collective Security System and dispatched a naval squadron to the Indian Ocean.

These developments also led to a reevaluation of Chinese policies toward Southeast Asia, especially with regard to the war in Indochina. A growing convergence of perceptions with the United States resulted in the belief that the country which posed the greatest danger to American security and interests in Indochina was the USSR. This also marked the beginning of the Chinese problem with the Vietnamese. Following the military withdrawal of the United States from mainland Southeast Asia, amid the soul-searching that accompanied its defeat there, Beijing feared that the Soviets would dominate Southeast Asia. That led to the Chinese policy of supporting a residual US military presence in the region, especially in the Philippines.

The fall of the non-communist regimes in South Vietnam and Laos led to the birth of a new ideologically polarized Southeast Asia. To be sure, the communist regimes in Indochina were not united. With the disappearance of anti-imperialism and anti-colonialism as national issues, traditional problems and rivalries reemerged in Indochina between Vietnam and Cambodia, Thailand and Cambodia, China and Vietnam, Vietnam and Thailand, and China and Laos. It was in these circumstances that the Soviet Union sought to maximize its influence in the region. At the same time, in the context of the growing Sino-American *rapprochement*, there was a concomitant warming between China and members of the Association of Southeast Asian Nations (ASEAN), which the Soviet Union watched anxiously. In this context, Moscow decided to cash in on Indochina, especially Vietnam, which led to great success for its policies. This was, however, due more to circumstances than to design.

Soviet–Southeast Asian relations: April 1975 to March 1985

Indochina, especially Vietnam, became the principal focus of Soviet policy in Southeast Asia after 1975. Soviet interests in Vietnam were three-fold. First, the Soviet Union wanted to encourage Sino-Vietnamese hostilities, to tie down Chinese forces and resources in the south so as to deal with the Vietnamese menace, as well as to increase Hanoi's dependence on Moscow. Second, especially in relation to the rapid expansion of the Soviet Pacific Fleet, the Soviet Union wanted to gain access to warm-water ports in the region. This goal was all the more pressing in view of the American presence in the region and its access to basing rights in the Philippines, Japan, and South Korea. Finally, Vietnam was viewed as an important Soviet beachhead in the region to gain acceptance of Soviet influence in Southeast Asia, to contain the growing Sino-American presence, and to check the growing influence of ASEAN as well as the association's relations with the West and China.

Compared with its past position in relation to the other major powers, the USSR achieved great success in Indochina. This fact was evident in Vietnam's near total dependence on the Soviet Union for economic, political, military, and diplomatic support. Soviet gains in Vietnam were clearly evident also in its acquisition of military facilities at Cam Ranh Bay and Da Nang. The final evidence of Soviet success could be seen in the fact that Moscow had gained an ally which was militarily the most powerful country in Southeast Asia. The Soviet–Vietnamese alliance was finalized in the Treaty of Friendship and Cooperation signed between the two countries in November 1978.

While it was clear that Moscow had made gains in Indochina, they proved not to be cost-free. By establishing an alliance with Vietnam, during the Brezhnev period, Moscow came to be identified largely as a pariah state in the international system. For a superpower concerned with its image, the Soviet Union found that Vietnam was certainly more of a liability than an asset in this respect. Second, while Moscow made gains in Indochina, they were made at the expense of the ASEAN states. The non-communist states, with dynamic economies, high growth rates, abundant resources, and control of the strategic waterways, were alienated by Moscow's open support for Vietnam's aggression in the region. Not only did Moscow lose goodwill in the region but it also wasted its years of investment and efforts aimed at cultivating relations with the ASEAN states. In global terms, the Soviet Union became linked with aggression and was regarded as an indirect aggressor in Cambodia. In this context, the Soviet Union's regional policy with regard to Vietnam did not benefit its global aims *vis-à-vis* China and the United States. Instead of containing the growing influence of these powers in the region, the reverse took place. Notwithstanding its clear gains in Indochina, the Soviet Union very definitely lost prestige and influence in the non-Communist region of Southeast Asia.

As in Indochina, Soviet relations with ASEAN were largely a function of its foreign policy toward Southeast Asia. The rise of the Brezhnev regime in 1964 in many ways marked a watershed in Soviet–Southeast Asian relations. The Soviet leadership shifted its attention away from insular Southeast Asia toward Indochina largely because of the American escalation of the war there and the intensification of Sino-Soviet rivalry. In this context the formation of ASEAN was condemned by the Soviet Union, which viewed it in cold war terms as an American tool similar to SEATO.[1] The Soviets believed ASEAN was set up to prop up the ineffectual SEATO, to stop the march of socialism, and to strengthen the members' relations with the Western capitalist states, especially the United States.

In broad terms this hostility toward ASEAN continued with only a slight change in emphasis in 1971. The slight modification resulted from changes in great power alignments involving the United States, China, and Great Britain, as well as from ASEAN's Zone of Peace, Freedom, and Neutrality (ZOPFAN) proposal, which the Soviet Union saw as being compatible with the Asian Collective Security System first propounded by Brezhnev in June 1969. Following this, the Soviets praised ZOPFAN but not ASEAN as an organization. This position continued right up to June 1978. In mid-1978, for the first time, the Soviet Union noted that ASEAN was a regional organization set up in its own right and for the purposes stated, namely, to cooperate in improving economic and social conditions.

A number of factors explained the change in Soviet attitude. First, Moscow hoped to gain influence in the region and be a dialogue partner similar to the United States, EEC, Canada, Australia, New Zealand, and Japan. Second, the Soviets must have realized that ASEAN, which was strong and successful, could not be wished away like SEATO and ASPAC. Third, it realized that ASEAN was not an "American running dog" as it had been portrayed by Soviet propaganda. Fourth, Moscow hoped to retard the growing Chinese influence in the region. Unlike the Soviet Union, China recognized ASEAN, supported the organization's initiatives, and increased contacts with ASEAN nations. Finally, the change in Soviet posture toward ASEAN can be explained by the developments in Indochina. As a result of the growing conflicts between Cambodia, Vietnam, and China, both Moscow and Hanoi began to court ASEAN in hopes of winning the association's support as well as expecting mellowed ASEAN reaction to Vietnam's membership of the COMECOM, its Treaty of Friendship and Cooperation, its refugee policy and, finally, its invasion of Cambodia.

The Soviet efforts to woo ASEAN did not pay off. Following the Soviet-supported Vietnamese invasion of Cambodia, ASEAN condemned the invasion and blamed the Soviet Union as a bankroller of Vietnamese aggression, a political opportunist and exploiter. ASEAN also condemned both Vietnam and the Soviet Union with regard to the "boat people" issue. Finally, ASEAN mobilized international efforts against Soviet–Vietnamese policies on Cambodia. In general, under Brezhnev, Soviet–ASEAN relations completed a full circle, starting off coolly, then improving and becoming cool again in the late 1970s and early 1980s. Basically, two sets of factors explain the general lack of Soviet success in the ASEAN region. The first set relates to the nature of ASEAN. Soviet penetration into the region was impeded by ASEAN's anti-communist, pro-West, capitalist political and economic orientation, its endorsement of a massive American, West European and Japanese presence, and its acceptance of growing state-to-state relations with China and hence a Chinese role in the region. The second factor related to the general failure of Soviet objectives in the region, in particular, the rejection of the Asian Collective Security System, opposition to the USSR's Cambodian policies, objections to the Soviet military presence in Vietnam, lack of acceptance of Soviet economic initiatives in the region and, finally, opposition to many of the Soviet Union's policies in the United Nations.

Soviet–Southeast Asian relations under Gorbachev

Gorbachev's foreign policy toward Southeast Asia is mainly a function of his policies toward the Asia-Pacific. On assuming leadership in March 1985, Gorbachev, together with new Foreign Minister Eduard Shevardnadze, reoriented his country's foreign policy from a primarily Gromykian Soviet–American focus to a more multipolar and global one. One of the most important innovations was the focus, for the first time since Lenin, on the Asia-Pacific. This could be seen in a series of speeches made by the new leader: his banquet speech in honor of Rajiv Gandhi's visit to Moscow on 21 May 1985; his Political Report to the 27th CPSU Congress in February 1986; the Soviet government statement on the Asia-Pacific in April 1986; his speech at Vladivostok in July

1986; his interview with B.M. Diah, the editor-in-chief of the Indonesian newspaper *Merdeka* in July 1987; his Krasnoyarsk speech on 17 September 1988; and, finally, his address at the United Nations on 7 December 1988. In all these addresses, Gorbachev stressed the Asia-Pacific credentials of the Soviet Union, called for peaceful coexistence in the region, initiated policies to reduce military conflicts, called for arms control and disarmament measures, and called for political dialogue with all countries in the region irrespective of their political, economic, and social systems. This aided the Sino-Soviet normalization, the Soviet–Japanese dialogue, the troop reductions along the Sino-Soviet border and in Mongolia as well as the all-around improvement in relations with all countries in the region.

Gorbachev's "peace offensive" in the region must be understood in the wider context of the problems the country was facing from within and without. The new leadership concluded that Brezhnev's foreign-policy legacy was a negative one and that Brezhnev had also failed to resolve domestic problems. By the time Mikhail Gorbachev emerged dominant in the Kremlin, the strategic situation in the Asia-Pacific region had undergone drastic change. Not only had the Soviet Union broken the American nuclear supremacy of the 1960s, but it was also in the lead in some areas of conventional forces. At the same time, the Soviet Navy had become a modernized, ocean-going offensive force. While the Americans suffered a serious débâcle in the mid-1970s in Indochina, forcing them into a strategic retreat, the Soviets, under Brezhnev's leadership, launched their "geographical momentum" into the Third World. This policy, however, had many costs and liabilities, which Gorbachev hoped to neutralize and reverse.

First, the gradual rise of anti-Sovietism almost amounted to an anti-Soviet bloc in the Asia-Pacific region. Several factors made it imperative for the Soviet leadership to halt the emergence of an "eastern front" against the Soviet Union: the growth of Sino-American relations and of America's military relations with Japan, South Korea, Taiwan, and the ASEAN states; the development of Japanese military capabilities; and the general political, economic, and diplomatic cooperation between the West and non-communist Asia-Pacific countries.

Second, the Asia-Pacific region had become increasingly important in Soviet strategic thinking due to the Reagan Administration's attention to the region, partly due to the volume of American trade with the region and the rate of increase in American investments there, which far exceeded those of Europe. The promotion of economic ties, especially with countries in the Asia-Pacific region also became increasingly an important goal of Gorbachev's Soviet Union. The Kremlin hoped to inject capital and technology from the developed industrial states in the Pacific Basin into Siberia and the Soviet Far East. Transfer of technology would prove indispensable for the Soviet economy, the reform of which would play a critical role in keeping the "balance of forces" in the Pacific against the United States. Realizing that the Asia-Pacific region was becoming the hub of economic and technological development, the Soviet Union found that it would like not only to participate in the region but also to keep abreast of technological developments so as to survive in the new economics-first era.

Third, the Reagan Administration's greater military focus in the region was also an important cause for Soviet concern. The United States expanded its military and especially its naval deployments in the region, and simultaneously persuaded its allies to play a larger military role in the region. Fourth, while the Soviet Union was a military giant in the Asia-Pacific region, it was an economic pygmy. This unidimensional assertion of power in the Asia-Pacific region was made more jarring by the fact that Soviet military-oriented developments in the later Brezhnev years had frightened the Chinese, Japanese, and ASEAN states into closer cooperation with the United States. By expanding militarily, the Soviet Union only succeeded in encircling itself and providing the United States with a strategic advantage in the region.

Finally, in order to implement his domestic agenda of political and economic perestroika, or reconstruction, Gorbachev had to stress the non-military instruments of Soviet policy and make the linkage between foreign and domestic policies manifest. In many ways, it can be argued that Gorbachev's attempts to tackle the Soviet Union's domestic problems – stunted economic growth, technological backwardness, negative productivity, ultra-centralization, stagnant industrial infrastructure, and various social problems – are reflected in his new thinking on foreign policy. Gorbachev stressed repeatedly that without domestic reforms, the Soviet Union would lose its superpower preeminence. The USSR needed a respite from international competition and commitments to create an international environment more conducive to domestic growth. The fact also shows that, while noted as a European power, the Soviet Union is an Asia-Pacific power as well. It is the largest Asian state and has the longest Pacific coastline. Gorbachev's concerns in the Asia-Pacific region are, therefore, quite natural.

While Gorbachev adopted a broad-based peace offensive toward the Asia-Pacific region as a whole, he also made direct approaches to individual countries in Southeast Asia. It is in this context that Soviet new thinking toward the region can be discerned. A constant theme in Gorbachev's Southeast Asian policy was his willingness to work with

ASEAN, which he viewed as a positive force for peace in the region. In his Vladivostok address, Gorbachev argued: "Our views about security in the Asian-Pacific region did not come out of thin air. They take into account the experience of the past and of today." In this context, ASEAN was singled out for special praise: "Nowadays, too, we have witnessed the efforts of a number of states to solve in practice common problems and the attempts somehow to regulate conflicts. In the activities of the ASEAN and in bilateral ties, many positive steps have been taken."[2]

During the visit of Malaysian Prime Minister Mahathir Mohamad to the Soviet Union, Vsevolod Murakhovskii, the first vice-chairman of the USSR Council of Ministers, said on 30 July 1987 that: "The Association of Southeast Asian Nations, which is playing an ever growing role in regional and pan-Asian affairs, will soon be marking its 20th anniversary. In this connection, I would like to re-emphasize the Soviet Union's desire to continue working for mutually beneficial contacts with the ASEAN."[3]

In addition to the positive evaluation of ASEAN by the new leadership, the Soviet spokesmen also indicated Moscow's interest in joining the United States, Japan, the EEC, Australia, New Zealand, Canada, and South Korea in yearly high-level meetings with ASEAN. In other words, the Soviet Union showed its willingness to become ASEAN's dialogue partner. A good indication of the high regard the Soviet Union now has for ASEAN is the publication in May 1988 of the *USSR–ASEAN Relations Directory* by Novosti Press Agency. The first edition of the directory detailed Soviet relations with each of the ASEAN member states and presented official agreements between Moscow and countries of the association. The directory concluded on an optimistic note that relations between ASEAN and the Soviet Union should improve with ASEAN–COMECON cooperation. The positive evaluation was based on four factors: the steady growth of the economic potential of both the Soviet Union and ASEAN; non-competition between the USSR and ASEAN countries, either in regional or international markets, for their products; the development of long-term trade with the USSR as the planned nature of its economy proves more beneficial for the ASEAN countries' economies than that of the capitalist markets; and the accelerated economic development of Siberia and the Soviet Far East, which will create more opportunities for deepening Soviet trade and economic relations with Asia-Pacific countries.[4]

While the Soviet Union's evaluation of ASEAN as an organization improved markedly, the improvement in bilateral relations between the Soviet Union and member states of ASEAN proved even more dramatic. The only country in ASEAN with which the Soviet Union does not have diplomatic relations is Brunei. President Suharto of Indonesia, Prime Minister Mahathir of Malaysia, and Prime Minister Lee Kuan Yew of Singapore have all visited Moscow. Soviet Foreign Minister Shevardnadze has visited Thailand, Indonesia, and the Philippines, while Soviet Prime Minister Nikolai Ryzhkov has visited Thailand and Singapore. The visits were important signals of the new era of Soviet–ASEAN relations.

On the whole, the Soviet Union's aim in the ASEAN region is to improve its ties with the organization as well as its individual member states. In this endeavor, it would serve Moscow's interest if the association continued to disagree as to which external power is its main adversary; if it can be distanced from its pro-Western posture; if distrust and suspicions of China and the ethnic Chinese in the region can be imbibed; if it can be persuaded to accept the Kampuchean situation with only secondary changes; if ASEAN can be persuaded to establish a working relationship with Vietnam; and, finally, if the association can be made to accept the Soviet presence – political, economic, and military – in the region as a normal and natural one emanating from a superpower with intrinsic interests in the Asia-Pacific region. In other words, if the regional states can be made to accept the fact that the Soviet Union has come of age in the region and can be accepted as part of the regional balance of power, then Soviet foreign policy in the region will have succeeded.

An important barometer of the new relationship between the Soviet Union and ASEAN is the role of the Soviet Union with regard to the Kampuchean problem. The Soviets realized that as long as they continued to back Vietnam's aggression against the Khmer people, they would not be able to make any headway in their relations with the ASEAN states that had staked their prestige on a policy aimed at forcing the Vietnamese to withdraw from Cambodia. Moscow's Cambodian policy also would determine Soviet relations with China, Japan, and the United States. It was in this regard that Gorbachev took a major step in distancing himself from Brezhnev's Kampuchea policy, which was based on the premise that no "Kampuchea problem" existed and that the situation was "irreversible."[5] Brezhnev's policy required all countries opposed to the "democratic change" in Kampuchea – that is, the invasion and occupation of Kampuchea – to come to terms with Vietnamese military might and to accept the fact that the Heng Samrin regime was legitimate. The Soviet Union adopted this posture despite the fact that the United Nations General Assembly repeatedly voted for ASEAN's resolution on Kampuchea which rejected the Vietnamese-installed regime in favor of the Democratic Kampuchea, now represented by the Coalition Government of Democratic Kampuchea, a united front organization consisting of Prince Sihanouk, Son Sann, and the Khieu Samphan forces.

In an attempt to demonstrate a break from the Stalinist past, Gorbachev announced a series of foreign-policy measures aimed at playing a major role in the Asia-Pacific region. However, in his first year of office, no major initiatives emerged from the Kremlin, which adopted basically the Brezhnevite approach to regional problems. The first major indication of a possible willingness to discuss the "irreversible Kampuchean problem" was manifested in a Soviet government statement of 23 April 1986 in which it was suggested that an All Asian Forum would be held to search for "constructive solutions for regional problems."[6] This announcement was followed quickly with Gorbachev's Vladivostok address on 28 July 1986, in which he admitted that the Kampuchean problem needed resolution. However, Gorbachev tried to deflect Soviet responsibility in the issue by calling it a bilateral Sino-Vietnamese problem. According to him:

> As with other problems of Southeast Asia, much depends on the normalization of Sino-Vietnamese relations. It is a sovereign matter of the governments and the leadership of both countries. We can only express our interest in seeing the border between these socialist countries become again a border of peace and good-neighborly relations, in seeing friendly dialogue resumed and the unnecessary suspicion and mistrust removed.[7]

This statement, however, did not go over well with the ASEAN states, especially since no pressure of any sort was implied from the speech on Vietnam. If anything, it could be interpreted as a signal to Hanoi that there was no Soviet–Vietnamese problem and a business-as-usual climate could be expected.

The next major development to have emanated from the Kremlin with regard to the problem was the first ever visit in 1987 of its Foreign Minister, Eduard Shevardnadze, to the five countries in Southeast Asia. Expectations were high prior to the visit, but the Soviet Foreign Minister brought no fresh initiatives on Kampuchea. If anything, he reiterated his country's support for Vietnam and the Indochinese countries and echoed Gorbachev's Vladivostok line that both Vietnam and China should negotiate a resolution to the Kampuchean problem. The disappointment arising from the failure of Shevardnadze to bring forth new initiatives or pressure on Vietnam to resolve the issue, especially to withdraw its forces from Kampuchea, was best reflected in Singapore's Foreign Minister's report to parliament which dismissed the Soviet Foreign Minister's visit as nothing more than a ploy by Vietnam to give the impression that efforts were underway to solve the Kampuchea problem. In reality, however, "it was very difficult to find any positive steps," and Singapore officials concluded that "the flurry of activity is just part of a very subtle public relations exercise." According to Dhanabalan: "Expectations had been high that these visits, coupled with continuing leadership changes within Vietnam, would produce some new initiative to break the eight-year deadlock over Kampuchea's future. A variety of formulae had been put forward over the years but none have succeeded."[8]

The negative reactions, almost amounting to ill will toward the Soviet Union, must have come as a shock to the Soviet leadership. The Soviets expected that their Foreign Minister would be welcomed with open arms and his historic visit viewed positively as a Soviet commitment to pursue peace in the region. But the net result was almost exactly the opposite. The Soviet Union was accused of playing a negative role in the region by bankrolling Vietnamese aggression. Even the more friendly Indonesians were disappointed with the outcome of Shevardnadze's visit, as they had nothing to show by way of concrete results that the Soviet Union was a useful power to have as an ally. As Radio Republic Indonesia stated on 17 March 1987, "The Shevardnadze visit highlighted the limited leverage that Moscow can apply on Hanoi, given the relative strength the latter has achieved by establishing its presence in mainland Southeast Asia and its offshore."[9]

It was in these circumstances that, after Shevardnadze's visit, a gradual but subtle change took place in the Soviet line on the Kampuchean problem. With Gorbachev beginning his term as CPSU General Secretary with the policy that the Kampuchea problem was "irreversible," by the time of his Vladivostok initiative, he not only admitted that a Kampuchean problem existed, he also called for a negotiated settlement of the "bilateral problem" between China and Vietnam. This line was later replaced by a more general one arguing that the problem must be resolved politically, especially in line with the program of "national reconciliation," a program which the Soviet Union was implementing in Afghanistan. This policy was made explicit in Gorbachev's interview with B.M. Diah, the editor-in-chief of *Merdeka*, on 21 July 1987, when he argued that:

> There seem to be some promising indications of a possible settlement. It is now understood that this problem can be solved only by political means. A specific date for the withdrawal of Vietnamese troops has been announced and we are confident it will be respected. And, in our opinion, the most important thing is that the idea of national reconciliation slowly but surely is making headway. Here as well, dialogue must prevail over confrontation, and here too, a coalition of national forces is possible.[10]

Since then, the Soviet Union has not only supported peace moves to settle the dispute, but has for the first time announced that it will play an active role in the resolution of the dispute. In this spirit, the Soviet Union supported the "cocktail party" proposal as was initially agreed upon between Indonesia and Vietnam on 29 July 1987. Following its failure, the Soviet Foreign Ministry for the first time openly announced on 1 September 1987 that it was prepared to facilitate a political settlement of the problem in the interests of the Khmer people and to strengthen peace and international security.[11]

In many ways, the statement was a sharp departure from earlier expressions of support for endeavors by various countries to find a solution to the problem and indicated that Moscow would be willing to play an active role in the resolution of the problem as had been demanded by the ASEAN states. In this regard, when the Heng Samrin regime announced its policy of "national reconciliation," namely, to negotiate with the other Khmer resistance groups, Moscow immediately supported the move. The Heng Samrin government also called for the convocation of an international conference to work out guarantees to implement the agreement and ensure Kampuchea's independence. The Soviet Union not only supported the call, but also announced its readiness to participate in such a conference. When Hun Sen, chairman of the Council of Ministers of the People's Republic of Kampuchea, agreed to meet Prince Sihanouk in Paris to discuss the future of Kampuchea, Moscow immediately supported the move. Observers have argued that it was the Soviet Union which was principally responsible for persuading Vietnam and the PRK to accept Prince Sihanouk's terms for a meeting in Paris. The four-point accord reached between Hun Sen and Sihanouk was welcomed by the Soviet Union in the most glowing terms. According to Novosti Press commentator O. Antipovskii, "Light is now visible in the Kampuchean problem which until recently was believed by many to be in a hopeless deadlock." According to Antipovskii, three factors led to the understanding at Paris to break the deadlock. First, it was the result of developments in other volatile areas such as Nicaragua and Afghanistan, where a process of national reconciliation was taking place. Second, it was due to the specific steps Vietnam had taken, especially its partial withdrawal of two divisions of troops from Kampuchea. Third, it was due to the growing consensus in Southeast Asia as a whole that the national reconciliation process should be encouraged in Kampuchea in order to bring peace to the region.[12]

The Soviets similarly welcomed the second round of talks between Sihanouk and Hun Sen in Paris, even though the prince's outburst that both Moscow and Hanoi were scheming to "trap" him politically proved an embarrassment for the Soviet Union. In a statement issued in Paris on 12 January 1988, Sihanouk reiterated that he would never accept a settlement which did not include a total withdrawal of Vietnam's 140,000 troops from Kampuchea. Sihanouk also accused Moscow of pretending to be in favor of the negotiations even though its real intentions were to push him to integrate himself into the Phnom Penh government which Hanoi installed forcibly in January 1979.

In spite of this change, Soviet Deputy Foreign Minister Igor Rogachev, speaking at a news conference in Moscow, underscored the importance of promoting dialogue among the various Kampuchean factions and emphasized that the Kampuchean people themselves must solve Kampuchean problems.[13] Soviet Foreign Minister Shevardnadze reiterated this principle later that month by emphasizing that the Soviet Union not only welcomed the Sihanouk–Hun Sen dialogue but was prepared to participate in an international conference on Kampuchea to reach a fair and reasonable solution to the problem.[14] If anything, Shevardnadze's emphasis on a fair settlement indicates that the Soviet Union was willing to reach a certain compromise to settle the dispute.

Since 1988, the Soviet Union has called for the solution of the Kampuchean problem on the basis of a "balance of interests" of all parties concerned, indirectly calling on Vietnam and the Heng Samrin government to take into account the interests of the Khmer Rouge. That Kampuchea was a centerpiece for Soviet foreign policy in the region can be seen in the first Sino-Soviet meeting on Kampuchea in late 1988. From this time, the Soviet Union has played an active role in supporting the resolution of the problem and has backed all initiatives on the problem. It supported the Jakarta informal meetings and was involved actively in the International Conference on Cambodia in Paris. Moscow welcomed the Vietnamese announcement that all its troops had withdrawn from Cambodia by September 1989.

The Soviet Union also actively backed the Australian plan to involve the United Nations in finding a solution to the Kampuchean problem, similar to the one employed to resolve the Namibian question. It has participated so far in all of the "Big Five" meetings of the permanent members of United Nations Security Council and played an important role in helping the "Perm Five" to reach agreement on 28 August 1990 on the principles for a settlement of the Cambodian problem. Since then, Moscow has supported the 10 September 1990 agreement among the K-4 (the four Khmer factions) in Jakarta to establish a Supreme National Council to replace the coalition government of Democratic Kampuchea as the Cambodian representative in the United Nations and to provide a power-sharing mechanism acceptable to all the warring factions without requiring any of them to accept total defeat. This would mean that the Soviet Union has played an important role in the peace-making process of Cambodia, a move bound to win the Soviet Union much goodwill with ASEAN members, in spite of Vietnam's displeasure over a Soviet alliance with the permanent members of the Security Council, including China, to solve the problem.

Soviet military policy in Southeast Asia

As of February 1979, an important factor for the relatively cold Soviet–ASEAN relations was the fear caused by Moscow's military presence at Cam Ranh Bay and Da Nang. The Soviets always have maintained that they had no bases in Vietnam and that their military wherewithal was consistent with the relations between two countries and not directed at any country in the region. Strategically, however, Soviet military strength had an important psychological impact in the region, as it was the first time that Soviet military power had been deployed in Southeast Asia. That this deployment took place amid the backdrop of a steady American military disengagement made the Soviet military forward movement into Southeast Asia all the more formidable.

Since Gorbachev's rise to power, he has tried to address the "Soviet military presence in Southeast Asia enigma" on a number of occasions. In his Vladivostok and Krasnoyarsk addresses he called on the United States to start a military pullout from the region, a move rejected by the Americans as an unequal exchange. Since then, the Soviets have indicated that they may undertake a unilateral military withdrawal from Southeast Asia. For instance, Shevardnadze, during his visit to Manila in December 1988, announced that the Soviet Union would dismantle its military facilities in Vietnam without demanding a parallel American withdrawal from its facilities in the Philippines. On 22 January 1990, Shevardnadze announced, "The day is near when there will be no Soviet military presence in Asia beyond its borders."[15] At about the same time, the Soviet Foreign Ministry announced that the Soviet Union had decreased its military presence in Vietnam. It was reported that Soviet offensive capability, including the Mig-23 Squadron, TU-16 bombers and submarines, had been withdrawn as part of the Soviet Union's defense cuts in the Asia-Pacific region.

This development and the announcement that the Soviet Union eventually would withdraw completely from Vietnam could improve Soviet–ASEAN relations. It also could give greater credibility to utterances about peace and stability in the region and could make the Soviet Union more welcome in Southeast Asia, especially in the

ASEAN region. The withdrawal was timed to influence the debate about the future of American bases in the Philippines and to weaken any potential Soviet threat in Southeast Asia and to win friends in the Philippines, ASEAN as a whole, Japan, China, and even the United States. One direct impact of this decision was the American decision to close down four military bases in Asia, three in South Korea, and one in the Philippines. In many ways, the Soviet decision to scale down its military presence in Vietnam and the general scaling down of troops along the Sino-Soviet border can be regarded as the most important element in the operationalization of Gorbachev's new thinking in Southeast Asia and the advancement of Soviet–ASEAN relations. The affect on Soviet–Vietnamese relations remains to be seen, especially since Moscow's improving relations with China and ASEAN can be regarded as a good measure of its downgrading of its ties with Hanoi. Nevertheless, if the reordering of relations is well managed, it could lead to improved relations between the Soviet Union and Southeast Asia.

Conclusion

It is obvious that Gorbachev has initiated a new Southeast Asian policy and has reversed, albeit slowly, Brezhnev's approach to the region. This new policy is evident mainly from his policy of improving ties with the ASEAN states while downgrading to some extent his commitments to the Indochinese region. While these changes have much to do with the new foreign policy oriented to economic concerns, they have been caused by the superpowers' cooperative efforts aimed at resolving regional conflicts worldwide. As the Kampuchean problem has been a major obstacle to the improvement of Soviet relations with the non-communist countries of the world, it was, therefore, natural to expect Gorbachev to attempt to demonstrate that he was concerned with the resolution of the issue. Such a move would silence his critics in the region and would show the value of Soviet friendship. At the same time, a concerted attempt has arisen to discredit the notion of the Soviet Union as a threat to the region. This action has been achieved through three policies: by attempting to resolve the Kampuchean problem; by pushing arms control and disarmament initiatives, including supporting the proposal to turn Southeast Asia into a nuclear-free zone; and by reducing its military presence in Vietnam. There always has been a concerted attempt to improve the content of Soviet relations with Southeast Asian countries, especially the ASEAN states, all of which is clearly visible in the growing political, diplomatic, economic, and cultural ties between ASEAN and the Soviet Union.

Despite these positive developments, the Soviet Union continues to suffer from many handicaps in the region. Its historical record in the region has been a poor one. It will take a much longer time frame and change in attitude for the Southeast Asian nations to accept the Soviet Union as an integral actor in the region. The Soviet Union's economic weaknesses, as compared to the United States, Western Europe, Japan, and the Asian newly industrializing countries also have provided a major handicap to the improvement of Soviet relations with countries in the region. While Moscow has been able to make economic inroads into Indochina, it has had great difficulties in presenting itself as an attractive partner to the ASEAN countries, which have integrated very effectively into the Western capitalist system. The continued uncertainty about Gorbachev's future and the growing instability in the Soviet Union also have militated against a real improvement of Southeast Asian ties with the Soviet Union. While ASEAN is uncertain about the future of Gorbachev and the Soviet Union, the Indochinese are disturbed by the rapid pace of domestic reforms and democratization of the Soviet system which they fear may threaten their regime stability. While a notion exists that the Soviet danger has lessened, the fear remains that any backlash against Gorbachev could lead to the rise of conservative or extremist elements in the Soviet Union and thereby reverse Gorbachev's policies of accommodation with the region. Finally, many in the region believe that in light of growing American economic and political weaknesses, improved relations with the Soviet Union must not be undertaken at the expense of the United States, as the latter's presence is valuable for the security and stability of the region.

While the countries in the region welcome improved Soviet–American relations, and Soviet peaceful policies toward the region, they still would prefer to see a continued American presence in the region. In view of these circumstances, no matter how attractive Gorbachev may present the Soviet Union to be, it faces many inherent disadvantages in the Southeast Asian region. While the Soviet Union has difficulties in penetrating the developed region of ASEAN, at the same time, by directly and indirectly pressuring Vietnam to be more accommodating, it also is losing the confidence of the Vietnamese leadership and may end up with limited influence in the region as a whole. Gorbachev may have succeeded in reducing the fear of the "Russian Bear" in the region, but due to internal problems and a decreased tendency to be too active abroad, he may not have ensured that Soviet power and influence will increase in the region. Indeed, the Soviet Union may become merely a marginal power in the area with Southeast Asian countries looking more and more toward Japan, the United States, and Western Europe for development and even security. What Gorbachev's

Southeast Asian policy has meant is that the "big stick" slowly has been removed but it will have difficulty in "speaking softly" as it has little of substance to offer the region.

Notes

1 *Pravda*, 1 September 1967.
2 *Speech by Mikhail Gorbachev in Vladivostok, July 29, 1986* (Singapore: USSR Embassy, 1986), p. 34.
3 Cited in *Security in the Asia-Pacific Region, the Soviet Approach: Documents and Materials*, 1988, p. 165.
4 *USSR–ASEAN Relations Directory* (Moscow: Novosti Press Agency, 1988), p. 51.
5 See *Kampuchea: From Tragedy to Rebirth* (Moscow: Progress Publishers, 1979).
6 *Izvestiia*, 24 April 1986.
7 *Speech by Mikhail Gorbachev in Vladivostok*, p. 35.
8 Cited in *Foreign Broadcast Monitor*, no. 201/87, 2 September 1987, p. 7.
9 *Ibid.*, no. 63/87, 18 March 1987, p. 9.
10 See "Answers by M.S. Gorbachev to the questions of the Indonesian newspaper *Merdeka*," in *Press Release* (Singapore: USSR Embassy), no. 37/87, p. 3.
11 Cited in *Foreign Broadcast Monitor*, 201/87, 2 September 1987, p. 7.
12 *Soviet News* (Singapore), 5 December 1987, p. 8.
13 Cited in *Foreign Broadcast Monitor*, no. 10/88, 13 January 1988, p. 6.
14 *Ibid.*, no. 23/88, 28 January 1988, p. 11.
15 *The Straits Times*, 23 January 1990.

14 The impact of Gorbachev's new thinking on Soviet policy toward South Korea

Ho-Won Jeong

Along with the efforts to develop new ties with non-socialist developing countries in Asia, the Soviets have improved relations with South Korea during 1989–90. After the absence of any significant contacts for the last several decades,[1] the Soviets have actively sought a close relationship with Seoul at various levels since the 1988 Seoul Olympic Games. The Olympic Games provided a natural opportunity for the Soviets to recognize the economic development of South Korea and to establish contacts. In 1989, more than 2,000 Soviets, including politicians, government officials, journalists, scholars, and members of business associations, visited Seoul to promote cooperation in various fields. Major South Korean business corporations also opened liaison offices in Moscow in 1989, and they have negotiated economic deals. The ruling parties of the two countries also made political contacts in March 1990, and this led to a meeting between the presidents of the two countries two months later. Most significantly, several contacts between the officials of the two countries finally resulted in the establishment of full diplomatic relations between Moscow and Seoul in September 1990. As most Korean specialists in the Soviet Union agree, the two countries are expected to develop serious business relations beyond mutual understanding and curiosity. Many Soviets view the development of relations between South Korea and the Soviet Union as an inevitable historical process due to new thinking in Soviet foreign policy.[2]

Recent Soviet policy toward the Korean peninsula requires particular attention, not only because the Soviets began to downplay their military interests in the region in order to promote economic cooperation with the adversary of their traditional ally North Korea, but also because it represents changes in Soviet attitudes toward the newly industrialized countries (NICs) in Asia, which used to be viewed as antagonistic toward socialism.[3] Previously, military and strategic considerations in the Far East, ideological differences, and the existence of antagonistic alliance systems on the Korean peninsula were the major obstacles to the improvement in Soviet relations with the Republic of Korea (ROK).

The significance of North Korea in the Sino-Soviet rivalry and military competition with the United States in East Asia led Moscow to maintain close relations with North Korea and to ignore South Korea. In the past, despite fluctuations in the relationship between Moscow and Pyongyang, the Soviets remained a key ally to Pyongyang by maintaining a friendship treaty and supplying armaments to the North Koreans.

The new Soviet approach to South Korea is related to the emergence of new political thinking and the influence of its proponents in foreign policy making. The need for economic cooperation with economically growing East Asian countries and the decrease in the significance of military relations with the Democratic People's Republic of Korea (DPRK) led to Soviet efforts to develop better relations with South Korea. Most Soviet policy makers and specialists argue for the benefits of economic cooperation with Seoul and emphasize the expansion of contacts in scientific and cultural areas. On the other hand, Moscow's increasing contacts with Seoul and the establishment of a diplomatic relationship between South Korea and the Soviet Union produced tensions in Soviet relations with North Korea, which shares military and strategic interests in Far East Asia.[4] Now the Soviets are concerned about the way to develop a close relationship with the ROK while not antagonizing North Korea.

After examining the changes in Soviet policy toward the Korean peninsula under Gorbachev's new Asian policy framework, this chapter will analyze Soviet motivations and policy goals. It will look further at how the new perceptions of South Korea have emerged in Soviet policy-making circles and have helped the formulation of new policy perspectives. Soviet efforts to develop economic ties with South Korea will be explained in the context of new Soviet theories on the role of the NICs in the international economy. In addition, major policy issues and debates concerning Soviet policy toward the Korean peninsula among the policy makers and specialists will be examined. In conclusion, it will deal with the implications of improved Soviet–South Korean relations for changes in the existing international order surrounding the Korean peninsula.

A new Soviet approach to South Korea by the Gorbachev regime

Soviet reconciliation with Seoul has accompanied a new focus on Asia by the Gorbachev regime.[5] In particular, the various elements of the new thinking applied to Asia brought about improved Soviet relations with South Korea and several non-socialist Southeast Asian nations.[6]

Recent Soviet policy toward South Korea was affected by the Soviet program for promoting peace and security in Asia, set out in detail by Gorbachev during his speeches in Vladivostok (July 1986) and Krasnoyarsk (September 1988).[7] Compared with the policies of his predecessors, whose emphasis was on the military balance in the Far East,[8] Gorbachev's policy began to stress economic cooperation with neighboring countries, mutual security, and reduction in armed forces.[9] More specifically, new Soviet programs include participation in the international division of labor for the development of Siberia, the creation of a new, comprehensive security regime similar to security arrangements in Europe, the building of confidence measures for avoiding accidental wars, and the establishment of multilateral ccoperation for solving regional conflicts.[10] The new policy is a repudiation of the Brezhnev era's misplaced emphasis on military power as a means to bolster Soviet security. Gorbachev and his advisers recognize that, because the stability offered by competing alliances is precarious and costly, the Soviets should pursue security through political and economic means.[11] The new Soviet policy goal in East Asia is to establish a peaceful international political environment and reduce tensions for the development of the Soviet Far East.

With respect to Soviet policy toward the Korean peninsula, Gorbachev initially pursued his predecessors' policy aimed at improving relations with North Korea without any major changes in his policy toward South Korea.[12] The Soviets downplayed contacts with South Korea due to their concerns over relations with North Korea, and Moscow often supported North Korea's position in the struggle against imperialism.[13] The transition in the Soviet attitude came along with Gorbachev's cautious prediction that "there may emerge possibilities for establishing economic ties with South Korea within the context of the overall improvement of the situation on the Korean peninsula."[14] Especially as the Soviet domestic economy declined, Moscow needed economic cooperation with South Korea to boost the development of Siberia. In one Soviet commentator's view, "the establishment of enterprises in various parts of the Soviet Union, including the Soviet Far East and Siberia, and a plan to expand ties with all countries in Asia and the Pacific require that the Soviet Union improve its relations with the ROK."[15] Relations with North Korea considered in the context of competition with China for influence in Pyongyang became less important after Moscow became reconciled with China and looked for easing tensions in the region.

Whereas the primary Soviet motivation in its approach to South Korea is economic cooperation, there is an intimate relationship between economic ties and a new Soviet foreign policy role on the Korean peninsula. In the view of Institute of the Far East Director Mikhail Titarenko:

> South Korean trade and industrial corporations, with their own experience in overseas economic cooperation and financial potential, could beneficially participate in our grand-scaled plans for Siberian Far Eastern development. Apart from the economic interest, we see our possible economic contacts with South Korea as conducive to reduction of tensions on the Korean peninsula and to better relations between the North and South.[16]

The normalization of political and diplomatic relations with Seoul followed the expansion of trade and joint investment efforts and the expectation of further economic cooperation. The efforts to promote trade and economic relations with the ROK require various political arrangements between the two governments such as the treaties on the prevention of double taxation and investment guarantees.

The existing political and military relationships in the Far East have not been favorable to the implementation of the new Soviet foreign policy program. The Soviets need stability in the region and urge a dialogue between South and North Korea. In attempting to solve the Korean problems, Soviet policy makers proposed the end of military confrontation on the peninsula, the phased reduction of the North and South armed forces, the withdrawal of US troops and nuclear weapons, the transformation of the Korean peninsula into a nuclear-free zone, the conclusion of a non-aggression treaty between Pyongyang and Seoul, and the development of an inter-Korean peace dialogue.[17] The Soviets see opportunities for their proposed policy changes in the Korean peninsula with "the improvement in the overall world situation as a result of such events as the improvement of relations between the USSR and the United States, the USSR and Japan, and the progress in arms reduction in Europe."[18] The easing of tensions and the change in the status quo based on the military balance in the Far East will help the Soviets reduce their military budget and secure investment needed for domestic economic development.

By establishing diplomatic relations with the Republic of Korea without any reciprocal actions toward North Korea from the United States and Japan, Moscow is attempting to change, to an important degree, the political environment based on the antagonistic alliance system surrounding the Korean peninsula. Asian specialists at the Institute of USA and Canada contend that "it is important to note that the Soviet Union and the United States are coming to realize that neither the South nor the North are unanimous in their approach to a settlement. . . . Soviet–South Korean contact is as important as promoting dialogue between the DPRK and the United States as well as other industrialized countries."[19] It also is noted that "the development of relations between the USSR and South Korea will not only benefit the two countries economically, but might also help transform the security system in the Asian-Pacific region that still retains elements of the Cold War."[20] On the other hand, Moscow does not forget to stress that "the Soviet Union will not disrupt the Asia-Pacific countries' relations with the United States and Japan."[21]

While officially supporting North Korea's positions on various political issues, Moscow has begun to follow its own independent policy regarding its relations with South Korea. In support of North Korea, Moscow cautiously points out the necessity of a withdrawal of US forces and disarmament in the Korean peninsula. The Soviets also frequently emphasize that "the Soviet Union will not do any damage to its cooperation with the DPRK in developing its ties with South Korea. Solid, friendly relations have been established and diverse ties maintained with People's Korea."[22] On the other hand, the contacts with South Korea are inevitable given the fact that a two-state solution to the Korean problems is in the interests of the Soviets. The Soviets assert that gradual progress in Soviet relations with the ROK will contribute to stability on the Korean peninsula.[23] In the Soviet expectation, "the dynamics of our relations allow us to suppose that in a few years the Soviet Union will have equally intensive contacts with both North and South Korea."[24] The creation of stability and security on the Korean peninsula is seen as the top priority in resolving the Korean problems. Gorbachev wants to mediate North and South Korean relations and to promote the easing of tensions on the peninsula.

The emergence of new perceptions of South Korea

The new conceptualization of Soviet policy toward South Korea has developed as part of the new thinking in Soviet foreign policy, which reflects the necessity of different approaches to old and current problems, the redefinition of problems, and the creation of a new vision of the world. It generally is recognized that "this epoch is associated with politics, specifically with new political thinking which demands from us, apart from everything else, a calm recognition of objective realities, and with internal democratization which helps us to get rid of likemindedness inculcated in us for years." In this sense "the discovery of South Korea is not exception from the general rule but, on the contrary, one of its most vivid manifestations."[25] One Soviet Korean affairs specialist adds that "from the standpoint of new political thinking . . . modern

South Korea is now far from what it once was. And we are not talking just about the powerful economic leap forward that has occurred. The political sphere and the correlation of internal and external factors and the objective and subjective conditions of its development have undergone changes."[26]

A series of visits by Soviet journalists, scholars, and policy advisers to Seoul since the 1988 Olympic Games has created the new perception. Through their contacts with ordinary people, politicians, and businessmen in the South, the Soviets realized that another social system exists on the Korean peninsula. To most Soviets it was a big surprise that South Korea is now one of the most rapidly developing countries. Some Soviet journalists say that the "discovery" of South Korea was shocking and acknowledge that they had ignored the reality of the Korean peninsula because of their old ideological interpretation.[27] In one Soviet analyst's comment, "the ROK is now the world's tenth largest industrial state. In the meantime, the DPRK regards the ROK as completely subjugated to the United States and does not acknowledge this fact. I do not agree with this as I am a historian who views things from a realistic point of view."[28] Under new thinking the achievements of South Korea are an objective fact. This is quite a different description of South Korea, which previously was viewed as a fascist state full of crises generated by student demonstrations and working-class strikes.

The remarkable changes in Soviet thinking about relations between states helped the Soviets see the political situation on the Korean peninsula from a more realistic perspective. The political system of South Korea is a legal entity rather than only an opposing regime to the legitimate socialist North Korea. In the new Soviet view "from the standpoint of international law, South Korea is a sovereign state because it possesses all the indisputable attributes–territory, an integral economic system, legislative and executive bodies. Whether one likes or dislikes its policy and ideology, they are an objective reality independent of our wishes."[29] The current Soviet view is also well represented by an *Izvestiia* article which admits that "the most important thing is that the South Korean state existed for more than 40 years."[30] Along with a new understanding of the "reality," there are growing efforts to reinterpret Korean history and politics based on "objective" facts. There has emerged even a new interpretation of the origins of the Korean War. In one article, a Soviet historian provides a more candid view of the origins of the Korean War in which North Korea initially began the war; the official Soviet position had asserted that South Korea invaded the North. In contrast with an old description of South Korean society as dominated by conservative political forces and the state's coercive power, Soviet specialists now recognize diverse interests in society. Previously, capitalism in South Korea was characterized as imposed on an unwilling society, with the state as the major force behind the private sector. South Korea also was perceived as a pro-imperialist, dictatorial state subjugated to US military and economic interests. But a new Soviet observation records young South Koreans' anti-American sentiment and disinterest in Washington's strategic plans in addition to the desire of middle-aged and old people to keep American troops on the peninsula.[31]

The new, positive image of South Korea has generated support for more cooperation with Seoul. Soviet Asian specialist Titarenko stresses that South Korea is "one of the advanced countries of the world . . . I think we have something to learn from their business. Natural understanding is the key to peace and friendly relations. More contacts are needed."[32] One specialist even says, "We need allies and partners for joint economic development and the tackling of global problems. In this sense the Republic of Korea, a dynamically growing state, advancing from the authoritarian to democracy [*sic*] can become such an ally and partner."[33] Another specialist argues that "when the problem of mankind's survival confronts us, the main task of socialism is to struggle to avert nuclear catastrophe, secure peace, and eliminate trouble spots (and that includes the Korean peninsula)," and cooperation with South Korea is essential for this task.[34] The favorable image of South Korea and the expectation of promoting common interests also have been developed among the public, especially in the Soviet Far East. In June 1990, local politicians and businessmen in Sakhalinsk Oblast, including representatives of industrial and transportation enterprises and cooperatives, deputies of local Soviets, and people's deputies of the USSR and RSFSR, formed an association which promotes the prospects of a restoration of diplomatic, economic, cultural, and social ties with South Korea.[35]

Economic cooperation with South Korea

Economic cooperation with South Korea has become a dominant concern for most Soviet policy makers. It reflects a revolutionary change in the Soviet theory of global economic interdependence. In his interview for a Korean newspaper, Tiknomirov, a professor at the USSR Academy of Sciences, asserts that capitalist institutions are strong and that interdependence in a capitalist system is inevitable.[36] In the Soviets' new thinking, the interdependence of the global economy leads to cooperation with various types of non-socialist regimes. Moscow accepts the fact of worldwide economic interdependence and ecourages greater East–West–South cooperation. Thus, "instead of hoping to dominate the world market, the Soviets now show more tolerance for the economic map as it is drawn and a sober respect for the power of the advanced capitalist states – not just the United States but Japan and South Korea as well."[37]

Many Soviet policy makers are eager to involve South Korean firms in economic projects. Gorbachev and Aleksandr Iakovlev urged South Korean businessmen to invest more aggressively and complained about the slow progress in economic cooperation even despite the fact that the amount of trade between the two countries increased from $290 million in 1988 to $600 million in 1989. On his visit to Seoul in 1989, Director of the Institute of USA and Canada Georgii Arbatov admitted that there are some legal and bureaucratic obstacles to Korean investment and promised that he would advise a policy on foreign investment laws guaranteeing the protection of investment. To promote trade the Soviets agreed to grant South Korea most-favored-nation status when they established diplomatic relations.

Efforts to expand economic cooperation with South Korea are best understood in the context of a new Soviet perception of the NICs in Asia. Previously the NICs were viewed as surviving as capitalist-path states due to investment from multinational corporations. Now a new emphasis is given to domestic factors such as government economic policies in understanding the economic growth of South Korea, Taiwan, Hong Kong, and Singapore. The economic structure of these countries is viewed as compatible with the Soviet economy. Light industrial products from the neighboring countries can improve vastly the quality of life in the Soviet Far East, and these countries can buy Soviet commodities and invest in new Soviet projects. More importantly, rich Soviet natural and energy resources in the Far East can be combined with highly developed human resources and technologies of East Asian NICs. Compared with Japan and the West, the NICs are attractive partners given the competitiveness of the prices and quality of their products.[38]

In particular, the Soviets' focus on economic relations with South Korea stems from its proximity to the Soviet Far East and its "fortunate" combination of state control and planning with the market mechanism. The Soviets praise South Korea as having "a post-industrial type of development of productive forces even in the odd combination of manual labor and electronic control of the production process itself."[39] In the view of IMEMO Director Martinov, "large-scale long-term trade and economic cooperation holds great promise . . . Neither South Koreans nor ourselves are as yet aware of the magnitude of this promise."[40] To the Soviets South Korea, unlike Japan, is viewed as willing to invest in Siberia. Soviet officials show a keener interest in the possibilities for Soviet–South Korean trade than they did for Soviet–Japanese trade. Compared with other NICs, it has more experience in and industrial capacity for building plants and other production facilities. The Soviets especially expect help in building an economic infrastructure and supplying consumer goods in Siberia. The Soviets believe that Soviet technology in the military sector could be combined with the South Korean ability to develop commercial goods, and talks on cooperation between the two governments already have taken place in the computer industry and other complex technology areas, such as satellite communications and the production of high-resolution TV sets. The list of areas for cooperation recently suggested by the Soviet government also includes the development of chemistry and metallurgy, extraction of minerals, natural gas and oil, and implementation of technical aid in the engineering industry as well as the production of consumer goods and medical equipment.[41]

The Soviets and South Koreans have made some progress in establishing joint ventures in ship-building, mining, and forest industries. Soviet enterprises were encouraged to develop contacts with Korean business firms and help them form joint ventures. For the joint ventures South Korean business groups offer technology and investment, while the Soviets provide raw materials. The products are planned to be consumed in the Soviet Union and to be exported to their countries. Hyundai, the giant South Korean trade and industrial group, agreed to invest in a twenty-year, $54 million project with the Soviet Primorsklesprom (Maritime Regional Forest Industry Administration) industrial amalgamation to develop a large timber-processing complex near the city of Svetlaia on the coast of the Sea of Japan. South Korean firms also are expected to build a ship repair plant and furniture factories in the Soviet Far Eastern city of Nakhodka. Another joint venture, in which various types of foodstuffs with fish will be produced, can help the Soviets earn hard currency through the export of its products. One of the most ambitious projects includes the production of the next generation of videotape recorders in Voronezh in cooperation with the South Korean company Samsung; Soviet officials regard this as a program for the "Russian version" of the Korean model. In addition, Soviet and South Korean enterprises are considering forming joint ventures to process farm products in Uzbekistan and Kazakhstan – vast areas inhabited by Soviet Koreans.[42]

Soviet business groups expect many benefits from these joint ventures. A member of the Soviet national fisheries industry association, one of the first enterprises which forged direct connections with South Korean business counterparts, points to "the industrial potential of Korea" and asserts "its advanced know-how will be conducive to solving our pending problems in the future."[43] The Soviets note that cooperation will benefit both sides; the Soviet Far East with its abundant natural resources and "South Korea which has modern technology can be said to have a historical destiny of cooperation."[44] Viktor Benezhkov, mayor of Nakhodka, hopes his city's development will be spurred by cooperation with its sister city, the South Korean port city of Pusan, and further expects South Korean participation in the development of a free economic system. "We think it would be unreasonable if such companies as the Hyundai and Daewoo groups could not assist by using modern technology."[45]

Economic relations have been developed mainly through the Soviet Chamber of Commerce and Industry and the Korean Trade Promotion Corporation (KOTRA). The two organizations, which opened offices in each other's capitals in 1989, later performed consular functions before the two countries established diplomatic relations. Vladimir Golanov, deputy chairman of the Chamber of Commerce and Industry, signed an agreement with South Korea's Foreign Trade Associations on the exchange of information and delegations, the holding of seminars, and training of Soviet specialists in South Korea. Stepan Sitarian, chairman of the State Foreign Economic Commission, exchanged views with visiting South Korean politicians on prospects for developing commercial and economic ties between Soviet enterprises and organizations and South Korean companies. The elevation of the two countries' trade and economic relations to the state level has been discussed at meetings between South Korean economic officials and Soviet officials in the State Planning Committee, the Ministry for Foreign Economic Relations, and the Ministry of Finance.[46] The visits to Seoul by Gorbachev's top economic advisers, including Economics Department of USSR Academy of Sciences Secretary Abel Aganbegyan, Economics Institute Director Leonid Abalkin, and Chairman of the International Bank for Economic Cooperation Vitalii Khokhlov, also have promoted cooperation in financial and trade spheres.

Soviet policy making toward South Korea

Despite a strong consensus on the expansion of cultural and economic relations, there have been some disagreements within policy-making circles regarding how rapidly and under what conditions Moscow should develop political relations with South Korea. Because the establishment of diplomatic relations with the ROK would influence the military alliance system with North Korea, different foreign policy interests have been involved in the policy making.

Because the Soviet Foreign Ministry has been interested in maintaining normal relations with the DPRK ministry officials, they were not very active in developing immediate diplomatic relations with South Korea. In Soviet Deputy Foreign Minister Rogachev's view, "It is not right to ignore South Korea. Instead, the Soviet Union should develop economic ties with it." Until recently, Soviet Foreign Ministry officials maintained the position that "while maintaining relations with South Korea on a non-governmental level, mainly in the trade and economic field [the Soviet government] has no intention to grant that country diplomatic recognition."[47] They insisted that "establishing diplomatic relations could be only considered in the context of the general development of the situation in the Korean peninsula."[48] In addition, Shevardnadze often expressed solidarity with North Korea in solving the Korean problems.[49] Given bureaucratic contacts, the Defense Ministry also showed sympathetic views toward Pyongyang. In his messages to the North Korean government Defense Minister Dmitrii Iazov stressed the traditional relations of friendship and cooperation between North Korea and the Soviet Union, expressed his view that those relations would serve the interests of Soviet and Korean people and of peace, and wished the DPRK "a new success in its work to strengthen national defense for the fatherland."[50]

The military buildup of Seoul was criticized by Soviet commentators who asserted that South Korea's military budget increase and the purchase of modern US fighter aircraft are opposed to Gorbachev's peace initiatives and are harmful to the improvement in relations with socialist countries.[51] Some foreign policy specialists do not see any urgent change in Soviet policy toward the Korean peninsula as desirable, and contend that contacts at a non-governmental level best serve Soviet interests. They are not sure of the kind of relations that will develop after the establishment of diplomatic ties between Seoul and Moscow and are worried about the uncertainty following Soviet recognition of South Korea.[52] Some still argue that Soviet policy toward the Korean peninsula should be determined by "an essentially new type of international relations based on the principles of Marxism–Leninism and socialist internationalism."[53]

The major criticism of these positions comes from those who support new diplomatic ties with South Korea. They question "the theory of so-called strategic cooperation with the DPRK," and call for the reconsideration of the Soviet Union's continued supply of new weapons to

North Korea.[54] Some demand the reexamination of political relations with the DPRK and argue that the establishment of diplomatic relations with South Korea will help demolish the cold war structure in the Far East. In their view, "by maintaining close political and economic relations with the DPRK, the Soviet Union artificially restricted its ability to play a more active role in reducing tensions in [the] Korean peninsula."[55] They emphasize that "ideological fetters should be removed from foreign policy" and that "the thesis that socialist states' recognition of South Korea represents a violation of socialist duty and the principles of socialist internationalism by them" should be refuted.[56] The establishment of diplomatic relations between the Soviet Union and other socialist countries and South Korea is seen as helpful to the reunification of the Korean peninsula and the consolidation of durable peace on the Korean peninsula.[57] In addition, it "could . . . objectively promote the progressive processing taking place in South Korean society." Recognition of the South also would enhance Soviet prestige "because it is consonant with the new political thinking. . . . The times dictate the need for different measures and approaches to the Korean problem."[58] These analysts prefer the change in the status quo and want to put more pressure on Pyongyang to accept the mutual recognition of two separate Korean states by the major powers and their admission to the United Nations.

The establishment of diplomatic ties with Seoul was supported by the International Department of the CPSU Central Committee and Gorbachev's foreign policy advisers, officials in economic ministries, and specialists at various research institutes. When a group of South Korean ruling party members visited Moscow in March 1990, Karen Brutents, first deputy head of the International Department in charge of relations with developing countries, discussed with them how to improve political and economic ties between the ROK and the USSR and hosted a dinner on behalf of the International Department. The proposal to upgrade the consular department to consulate general, as a prelude to opening full diplomatic ties, was made during talks between Brutents and South Korean officials.[59] The involvement of the CPSU International Department is explained, to a great degree, by the interest of Iakovlev and Brutents in the newly industrialized states of the Third World.[60] Iakovlev, the head of the CPSU International Affairs Commission, is believed to have pressed the International Department to show increased concern with the newly industrialized countries of the Third World.[61] Primakov, a candidate Politburo member and former IMEMO director, developed contacts with South Korean politicians and advised Gorbachev on close ties with South Korea. Since he visited Seoul in

1988 he has viewed South Korea as having achieved significant progress despite its capitalist institutions and imperialist connections. Gorbachev's other top foreign policy adviser Anatolii Dobrynin personally visited Seoul in May 1990 and engaged in preparing for the summit meeting between the presidents of the two countries. The Supreme Soviet also was involved in establishing political contacts with South Korea by agreeing to inaugurate a friendship association between the parliaments of the two countries in March 1990. In September 1990, Gennadii Ianaev, member of the Supreme Soviet International Affairs Committee and CPSU Central Committee Secretary, exchanged opinions on the situation in Southeast Asia and the possibilities for further developing inter-Korean dialogue with South Korean congressmen and businessmen, and briefed them on the current problems of perestroika in the Soviet Union.[62]

In addition, various research institutes played a very important role in initiating contacts with South Korea. Several meetings between IMEMO and the ruling party of South Korea provided informal channels for discussing policy issues. The two sides agreed on the necessity of normalization of relations between Moscow and Seoul and called for regular talks between the two governments. In a joint statement signed in March 1990 by Kim Yong-Sam, a co-leader of South Korea's ruling Democratic Liberal Party and Vladen Martinov, director of IMEMO, the two sides emphasized that official relations are desirable along with cooperation in political, economic, and scientific fields, and that the relations between the two countries should be mutually beneficial and non-interventionist. They agreed that improved relations between South Korea and the Soviet Union will be conducive to the promotion of South–North dialogue on the Korean peninsula. Other research institutes, including the Institute of the USA and Canada, the Institute of Oriental Studies, the Institute of the Far East, and the Institute of Economics of the World Socialist System, also were engaged in discussions on various policy issues and staged symposiums. In February 1990, the Institute of the World Socialist System sponsored a conference in Moscow with the South Korean Institute of Parliamentary and Political Relations to discuss problems and prospects for Soviet–Korean relations. At an international meeting organized by the South Korean Institute of International Affairs in September 1990, the scholars from IMEMO, the Far East Institute, and the Oriental Studies Institute, headed by Oriental Studies Institute Director Mikhail Kapitsa, exchanged views about the situation on the Korean peninsula and the prospects for cooperation between the Soviet Union and the ROK with South Korean government officials and leading businessmen. These research institutes inform the leadership of policy options and are believed to have advised the normalization of relations between Moscow and Seoul. In particular, IMEMO, which maintains close ties with the CPSU's foreign policy-making apparatus, was reported to have finished preparatory work for the establishment of diplomatic relations with the officials of South Korea's ruling party in March 1990. The Institute of the USA and Canada, whose Asian specialists often are tapped by the party and government alike for their expertise, has been one of the main proponents of strong trade ties between the Soviet Union and South Korea.[63]

Those in support of the political recognition of South Korea have had more influence on policy making as economic cooperation and cultural contacts developed further between the Soviet Union and the ROK. The top Soviet leadership supported close ties with South Korea. Gorbachev and Iakovlev were reported to say that there were no insurmountable obstacles to establishing diplomatic relations with South Korea.[64] Developing political contacts with Seoul is compatible with Gorbachev's emphasis on the removal of tensions on the Korean peninsula and the beginning of solving national problems.

Conclusion

The Soviets have been concerned with the strategy for the development of the Soviet Far East, and economic cooperation with neighboring countries will continue to have a priority in Soviet East Asian policy in the 1990s. The development of economic resources in Siberia is related closely to foreign policy actions both because it needs a basis for expanded foreign trade with neighboring countries and because overcoming developmental problems requires economic help and cooperation.[65] While downplaying the military factor, the Soviet leadership pursues broader ties with countries in East Asia. South Korea's rise as a center of economic power prompted a new Soviet approach to Seoul, and it "would seem that South Korea is increasingly central to development plans in the Soviet Far East." The Soviet turn toward the Republic of Korea is considered "perhaps the most striking evidence of the East Asian 'new thinking' tactics in action."[66]

The new ties between the Soviet Union and South Korea may bring about some changes in the international political environment of East Asia. First of all, the improved relations with South Korea will help the Soviets participate in building a more stable international order in the Far East. By downgrading military and strategic relations with North Korea, the Soviets appear to want to reduce tensions on the Korean peninsula which can hamper Soviet efforts to promote economic cooperation in the region. Some Soviets even assert that "the close economic relations between the Soviet Union and the ROK have the mission of making an important contribution to the strengthening of peace and security in the Far East and East Asia."[67] To improve political and economic relations throughout the region, Gorbachev already has proposed the convening of a multilateral conference and is looking for fundamentally new constructive, and sustainable relations with leading Asian countries rather than pursuing military balance in the region. This new policy is compatible with the Soviet attempt to reconcile with China, improve relations with Japan, and reduce military competition with the United States.

Second, the Korean peninsula would appear to have a new priority in Soviet East Asian policy. Previously, the Korean peninsula was considered important only strategically given its geographic proximity to the Soviet Union. Given the expectation of economic cooperation with South Korea and the North–South talks about the reunification of the two Koreas, Soviet policy toward the Korean peninsula will have its own significance regardless of Soviet relations with China and Japan. In developing the Far East, Moscow probably sees South Korea as a counterweight to, or a substitute for, Japan because of the controversy over the Northern Territories and historical animosity between Russia and Japan.[68] Equally importantly, the Soviets now think "that without South Korea, without taking the South Korean factor into account, it is difficult to talk about those problems of security and stability in the Asian–Pacific region."[69]

Third, to pursue better relations with South Korea, Moscow seems to put less stress on its relations with North Korea. The old ideological dogma and concerns with strategic interests were replaced by the pursuit of economic cooperation and the emphasis on peaceful solutions to regional problems. Recent Soviet policy change is reflected in Shevardnadze's statement that the Soviets will "develop relations with South Korea, acting primarily on the basis of Soviet interests."[70] Perhaps, "Moscow's ravenous appetite for foreign capital and advanced Western technology, both of which Seoul possesses in abundance, could prove an irresistible lure to Soviet leaders."[71] In Soviet East Asian policy, North Korea has become less significant, and, consequently, the DPRK is the only country with which political relations have not improved for the last several years. Soviet newspapers recently have criticized the "cult of personality" of Kim Il-Sung and questioned the ally relationship between Pyongyang and Moscow. The establishment of diplomatic relations between Moscow and Seoul increased tensions in Soviet–North

Korean relations. The new ties between the Soviet Union and the ROK may lead to the weakening of the Soviet–North Korean military alliance system and may generate disagreements on various political issues, including reunification of the two Koreas and their membership in the United Nations.

Notes

1 Until recently the contacts between South Korea and the Soviet Union were minimal. In the 1970s, the Soviets even refused to participate in any athletic competition held in South Korea. Only very few scholars and government officials of South Korea were allowed to visit the USSR to attend international meetings in the early 1980s. During this period, Moscow recognized "only one Korea [North Korea] which symbolizes the bright future of the entire Korean people," *Pravda*, 12 October 1978. For Soviet policy toward the Korean peninsula before the Gorbachev regime, see Ralph N. Clough, "The Soviet Union and the two Koreas," in *Soviet Policy in East Asia*, ed. Donald S. Zagoria (New Haven: Yale University Press, 1982), pp. 175–200.

2 For example, see F. Shabshina, "Mozhno li rasputat' 'Koreiskii Uzel,'" *Izvestiia*, 1 September 1990.

3 Indeed, Gorbachev improved relations with Singapore, Hong Kong, and Taiwan, as well as South Korea.

4 This relationship has been reflected most vividly in the media of the two countries. The Soviets responded to North Korea's criticism of the recent establishment of Soviet–South Korean diplomatic relations by arguing that the establishment of diplomatic relations with South Korea is being done in the Soviet Union's interests and is a question which "must be decided by the USSR itself – a sovereign state – without anyone's permission," *Izvestiia*, 19 September 1990. For similar views, see also *Komsomolskaia pravda*, 22 September 1990. For North Korean views of Soviet policy, see *Minju Choson*, a daily North Korean Communist Party newspaper, 19 September 1990.

5 In his 1986 Vladivostok speech which outlined a new Soviet Asian policy framework, Gorbachev stressed that the USSR is an Asian power and that it wants to develop stable relations with other Asian countries by expanding ties with its friends and repairing relations with its foes. Until recently, the Soviet Union was restrained in East Asia because of its sparse population, an inhospitable agricultural environment, and the lack of a self-sufficient industrial base. For the text of Gorbachev's speech in Vladivostok see *Pravda*, 29 July 1986.

6 Carolyn McGiffert Ekedahl and Melvin A. Goodman, "Gorbachev's new directions in Asia," *Journal of Northeast Asian Studies*, vol. 8, no. 3 (1989), pp. 3–24.

7 Several Soviet commentators placed great emphasis on the significance of those speeches in the formulation of the new Soviet policy toward the Korean peninsula. For example, Iuri Kornilov, TASS in English, 5 June 1990, in *Foreign Broadcast Information Service, Daily Report: Soviet Union*

(Washington, D.C.) (hereafter, *FBIS-SOV*), 6 June 1990, p. 40. For the text of Gorbachev's speech in Krasnoyarsk, see *Pravda*, 18 September 1988.

8 Previous Soviet policies are characterized as a defense of the Soviet homeland, protection of Marxist–Leninist regimes, economic development of Siberia, expansion of Soviet influence, and import of technology through trade. Refer to Thomas W. Robinson, "The Soviet Union and East Asia," in Edward A. Kolodziej and Roger E. Kanet, eds., *The Limits of Soviet Power in the Developing World* (Baltimore: The Johns Hopkins University Press, 1989), pp. 170–200; Ray S. Cline, James A. Miller, and Roger E. Kanet, eds., *Asia in Soviet Global Strategy* (Boulder, CO: Westview Press, 1987); Harry G. Gelman, "Continuity versus change in Soviet policy in Asia," *Journal of Northeast Asian Studies*, vol. 4, no. 2 (1985).

9 For Gorbachev's policy toward Asia, see Scott Atkinson, "The USSR and the Pacific century," *Asian Survey*, vol. 3, no. 7 (1990), pp. 629–45; Coit D. Blacker, "The USSR and Asia in 1989: recasting relationships," *Asian Survey*, vol. 3, no. 1 (1990); Stephen M. Young, "Gorbachev's Asian policy: balancing the new and the old," *Asian Survey*, vol. 28, no. 3, March 1988, pp. 317–39; Herbert J. Ellison, *The Soviet Union and North East Asia* (Lanham: University Press of America, 1989); Rajon Menon, "New thinking and Northeast Asian security," *Problems of Communism*, vol. 38, no. 2 (1989), pp. 1–29; Gerald Segal, "The USSR and Asia in 1987: signs of a major effort," *Asian Survey*, vol. 28, no. 1 (1988), pp. 1–9; Ramesh Thakur and Carlyle A. Thayer, eds., *The Soviet Union as an Asian Pacific Power: Implications of Gorbachev's 1986 Vladivostok Initiatives* (Boulder, CO: Westview Press, 1987).

10 See Anatolii Dobrynin, "The Vladivostok Programme: progress and prospects," *World Marxist Review*, vol. 30, no. 9 (1987), pp. 5–15.

11 Menon, "New thinking and Northeast Asian security," p. 29. Indeed, Gorbachev pulled out the Soviet armies from Afghanistan, reduced armed forces on the Chinese borders, and showed a willingness to eliminate SS-20 missiles in Asia. He normalized relations with China and tried to improve relations with Japan. Moscow also showed an interest in developing relations with Southeast Asian nations.

12 For the first three years of his rule, Gorbachev eagerly pursued his predecessors' policy of providing long-sustained ties to North Korea. The Soviet Politburo member Aliev visited Pyongyang in August 1985 and Shevardnadze was there several times to show support for the North Korean proposals for Korean reunification and arms reduction. Chebrikov, the head of the KGB and a Politburo member, headed the Soviet delegation in September 1988 to attend a celebration of the 40th anniversary of the formation of the DPRK. In December 1988, Shevardnadze endorsed the North Korean proposal for the creation of a Democratic Confederated Republic of Koryo, rejected South Korean calls for the cross recognition of the two Koreas, and denounced the US military presence in the Pacific Asian region. *Pravda*, 25 December 1988.

13 For example, in his speech on the visit of North Korean leader Kim Il-Sung to Moscow, Gorbachev stressed the common struggle against imperialism: "For durable peace and international cooperation, two countries fight

against the threat of war and imperialism." He promised to work together to promote cooperation, exchange experience, and prevent nuclear catastrophe "into which the aggressive and dangerous policy of imperialism is pushing humanity," *Pravda*, 25 October 1986.

14 Gorbachev's speech in Krasnoyarsk, *Pravda*, 18 September 1988.

15 Moscow International Service in Korean, 6 January 1990, in *FBIS-SOV*, 17 January 1990, p. 25.

16 Mikhail L. Titarenko, "Asian and Korean security and stability: a Soviet perspective," *Korea and World Affairs*, vol. 15 (1989), pp. 278–96.

17 *Krasnaia zvezda*, 15 August 1990.

18 Mikhail Titarenko, interview, Moscow International Service in Korean, 16 January 1990, in *FBIS-SOV*, 2 January 1990, p. 13.

19 Alexei Bogaturov and Mikhail Nosov, "The Asia-Pacific region and Soviet-American relations," *International Affairs*, no. 2 (1990), pp. 109–17.

20 TASS in English, 5 June 1990, in *FBIS-SOV*, 6 June 1990, p. 41.

21 Igor Rogachev, Deputy Foreign Minister over the Asian and Pacific region, interview, Moscow International Service in Mandarin, in *FBIS-SOV*, 20 April 1990, p. 15.

22 Moscow International Service in Korean, 20 May 1990, in *FBIS-SOV*, 22 May 1990, p. 15.

23 Rogachev, interview, in *FBIS-SOV*, 20 April 1990.

24 G.V. Kireev, chief of the USSR Foreign Ministry Asian Socialist Countries Administration, interview, *Sovetskaia Rossiia*, 19 April 1990.

25 Vladen Martinov, director of IMEMO (Institute of World Economics and International Relations), interview, *New Times*, no. 47 (1989), p. 12.

26 Shabshina, "Mozhno li rasputat' 'Koreiskii Uzel'."

27 In one Soviet journalist's confession, "one gets the impression that a new land has been discovered. True, I've taken a mental note of the fact that my colleagues have difficulties in uttering the word 'country,' 'capital' and other such terms normally applying to a sovereign state . . . In my first reports from Seoul last year, the world 'capital' does occur, but only in the phrase 'the capital of the Olympics' . . . After Mikhail Gorbachev's Krasnoyarsk speech, South Korea suddenly appeared in our field of vision." See Vitalii Ignatenko, interview, *New Times*, no. 47 (1989), p. 15.

28 Vladimir Vorontsov, chief editor of *Far Eastern Affairs*, interview, Moscow International Service in Korean, 8 December 1989, in *FBIS-SOV*, 12 December 1989, p. 19.

29 Martinov, interview, *New Times*, no. 47 (1989), p. 15.

30 Shabshina, "Mozhno li rasputat' 'Koreiskii Uzel.' "

31 Leonid Mlechin, "Sitting on the fence," *New Times*, no. 10 (1990), p. 20; G. Kim, "The national liberation movement today," *International Affairs*, no. 4 (1981), pp. 27–37; I. Zorina, "Razvivaiushiesia strany v politicheskoi strukture sovremennego mira," *Mirovaia ekonomika i mezhdunarodnye otnosheniia*, no. 8 (1982), pp. 15–24; and Martinov, interview, *New Times*, no. 47 (1989), pp. 19–21.

32 Titarenko, interview, *FBIS-SOV*, 2 February 1990, p. 13.

33 Mlechin, "Sitting on the fence," p. 21.

34 Shabshina, "Mozhno li rasputat' 'Koreiskii Uzel.' "

35 *Rabochaia tribuna*, 12 June 1990, in *FBIS-SOV*, 15 June 1990, p. 20.
36 *Hankuk Iibo*, 11 February 1989, in *FBIS-SOV*, 14 February 1989, pp. 17–18.
37 Elizabeth K. Valkenier, "New Soviet thinking about the Third World," *World Policy Journal*, vol. 20 (1987), p. 655.
38 Kim, "The national liberation movement today." For the Soviet reassessment of the NICs, see Aleksandr Bogomolov, "Problems of cooperation in the Pacific region," *International Affairs*, no. 1 (1987), pp. 38–44.
39 I. Andreev, "Chto vpered? Razvivaiushchiesia strany na poroge novogo tysiacheletiia," *Pravda*, 7 June 1990.
40 Martinov, interview, *New Times*, no. 47 (1989), p. 15.
41 Segal, "The USSR and Asia in 1987," p. 104; Titarenko, interview, in *Choson Iibo* (in Korean), 29 July 1990, in *FBIS-SOV*, 3 August 1990, p. 21; Moscow TASS in English, 27 August 1990, in *FBIS-SOV*, 28 August 1990, p. 5; and Iurii Masliukov, chairman of the USSR State Planning Committee, interview, *New Times*, no. 33 (1990), p. 12.
42 Moscow International Service in Korean, 14 February 1990, in *FBIS-SOV*, 26 February 1990, p. 21; Moscow International Service in English to Great Britain and Ireland, 16 September 1990, in *FBIS-SOV*, 20 September 1990, p. 8; Moscow International Service in Korean, 24 February 1990, in *FBIS-SOV*, 9 March 1990, p. 4; Moscow International Service in Korean, 26 April 1990, in *FBIS-SOV*, 4 May 1990, p. 15; Iurii Masliukov, interview, *New Times*, no. 33 (1990), p. 13; and Moscow TASS in English, 27 August 1990, in *FBIS-SOV*, 28 August 1990, p. 5.
43 See Moscow International Service in Korean, 14 February 1990, in *FBIS-SOV*, 26 February 1990, p. 21.
44 See Moscow International Service in Korean, 3 May 1990, in *FBIS-SOV*, 9 May 1990, p. 23.
45 Moscow International Service in Korean, 13 September 1990, in *FBIS-SOV*, 17 September 1990, p. 16.
46 Moscow TASS in English, 12 June 1990, in *FBIS-SOV*, 13 June 1990, p. 16; Yonhap in English, 23 March 1990, in *FBIS-SOV*, 23 March 1990, p. 10; and Moscow TASS in English, 7 August 1990, in *FBIS-SOV*, 8 August 1990, p. 21.
47 Rogachev, interviews, Moscow International Service in Mandarin, in *FBIS-SOV*, 25 April 1990, p. 15; and TASS in English, 4 September 1989, in *FBIS-SOV*, 5 September 1989, p. 6.
48 Gremitshikh, first deputy of Soviet Foreign Ministry Information Administration, interview, *Izvestiia*, 13 April 1990.
49 Moscow International Service in Korean, 28 May 1990, in *FBIS-SOV*, 1 June 1990, p. 16; *Pravda*, 31 January 1990.
50 *Krasnaia zvezda*, 9 September 1990.
51 Moscow International Service in Korean, 17 August 1990, in *FBIS-SOV*, 20 August 1990, p. 11; M. Morozov, "Mir i 'Mig,' " *Komsomolskaia pravda*, 21 August 1990.
52 For instance, see S. Agafonov, "Inertsiia entuziazma, ili pessimistichnye mysli po povodu optimistichnykh faktov," *Izvestiia*, 9 June 1990, p. 7. He questions the urgency of such relations for the Soviets and warns that the Soviets will lose control of the situation completely if they send an

ambassador to Seoul before the end of the year. "If that happens, the Koreans will fulfil their 'maximum program' with respect to the Soviet Union. We, by contrast, having played our last trump card . . . will be left with an ambassador and looking like fools, since nothing solid and mutually binding can be put together in just two years' time."

53 V. Vanin, *SSSR i Koreia* (Moscow: Glavnaia Redaktsia Vostochnoi Literatury, 1988), p. 410.

54 Moscow International Service in Korean, 13 September 1990, in *FBIS-SOV*, 14 September 1990, pp. 10–11.

55 S. Maksimov, "Probil chas diplomatov?" *Komsomolskaia pravda*, 2 June 1990.

56 See Shabshina, "Mozhno li rasputat' 'Koreiskii Uzel.' "

57 Vorontsov, interview, in *FBIS-SOV*, 12 December 1989, p. 19.

58 See Shabshina, "Mozhno li rasputat' 'Koreiskii Uzel.' " Similar views are found in S. Maksimov, "Probil chas diplomatov?" "At present in South Korea there is a great interest in the USSR. The interest is evident in various spheres and among various sections of population . . . In considering by means of diplomatic measures what has been achieved in our relations, the Soviet Union can only enhance its prestige in South Korea and the Pacific region."

59 Yonhap in English, 21 March 1990, in *FBIS-SOV*, 21 March 1990, p. 11; and 23 March 1990 in *FBIS-SOV*, 23 March 1990, pp. 10–11.

60 Iakovlev often states that Soviet foreign policy should focus not only on the United States, Western Europe, and Japan, but also on the newly industrialized countries. See his book, *Ot Trumena do Reigana* (Moscow: Molodaia Gvardiia, 1984). Karen Brutents shares similar views with Iakovlev. He recognizes the limits of the Soviet role in the international arena and supports a shift away from the Marxist–Leninist states. Scott A. Bruckner, "From the ID to the International Affairs Commission: Karen Brutent's role in the USSR's programmatic approach to the Third World," in Center for the Study of Foreign Affairs, *The International Department of the CC CPSU under Dobrynin: Proceedings of a Conference on October 18–19, 1988 at the Department of State* (Washington, D.C.: Foreign Service Institute, US Department of State, 1989), p. 75.

61 See David Albright, "The CPSU International Department and the Third World in the Gorbachev era," in Center for the Study of Foreign Affairs, *The International Department of the CC CPSU under Dobrynin*, p. 150. The most recent restructuring of the Soviet foreign policy bureaucracy was made in 1988 with the creation of the International Policy Commission within the CPSU. Its role is to prepare policy options for the top leadership and supervise the work of the International Department. The current members include high-ranking Soviet officials and senior policy analysts, including a deputy prime minister, the KGB chief, two deputy foreign ministers, the chief of the Armed Forces General Staff, Gorbachev's aides, senior academics, and an *Izvestiia* editor. See Central Intelligence Agency, *Directory of Soviet Officials: National Organizations* (Washington, D.C.: Office of Directorate, 1989), p. 5. In addition, there were some personnel changes in the International Department in charge of matters involving non-ruling com-

munist parties. Dobrynin moved from chief of the International Department to Gorbachev's foreign policy adviser team, and Valentin Falin was newly appointed as head of the Department.

62 *Pravda*, 12 October 1988; Yonhap, 26 March 1990, in *FBIS-SOV*, 26 March 1990, p. 21; and Moscow TASS International Service in Russian, 7 September 1990, in *FBIS-SOV*, 11 September 1990, p. 20.

63 Yonhap, 26 March 1990, in *FBIS-SOV*, 26 March 1990, p. 21; *Izvestiia*, 14 February 1990, in *FBIS-SOV*, 16 February 1990, p. 14; Moscow International Service in Korean, 22 September 1990, in *FBIS-SOV*, 2 October 1990, pp. 17–18; and Yonhap, 26 March 1990, in *FBIS-SOV*, 26 March 1990, p. 21. For the role of Soviet research institutes in policy making, see Eberhard Schneider, "Soviet foreign policy think tanks," *The Washington Quarterly*, vol. 11, no. 2 (1988), pp. 145–56.

64 Yonhap in English, 22 March 1990, in *FBIS-SOV*, 22 March 1990; Seoul Domestic Service in Korean, 11 April 1990, in *FBIS-SOV*, 12 April 1990, p. 15.

65 Robert W. Campbell, "Prospects for Siberian economic development," in Zagoria, ed., *Soviet Policy in East Asia*, pp. 229–54.

66 Atkinson, "The Soviet Union and the Pacific century," pp. 643, 639.

67 Moscow International Service in Korean, 6 January 1990 in *FBIS-SOV*, 17 January 1990, p. 25.

68 Atkinson, "The Soviet Union and the Pacific century," p. 644.

69 Shevardnadze, interview, TASS International Service in Russian, 30 September 1990, in *FBIS-SOV*, 1 October 1990, p. 17.

70 Shevardnadze, interview, *Izvestiia*, 12 September 1990.

71 Blacker. "The USSR and Asia in 1989," p. 11.

Part V

Conclusion

15 The paradox in new political thinking in Soviet foreign policy

Tamara J. Resler

The rise of new political thinking in Soviet foreign policy has been both a blessing and a curse. While it has created warmer relations with many countries and has enhanced global security, the radical change in policy also has alienated some traditional Soviet allies and even has exacerbated domestic unrest in the Soviet Union. Not every region of the world has welcomed the changes in Soviet foreign policy during the first five years of Gorbachev's tenure. Many countries have benefited from the new, deideologized interstate relations based on mutual benefit, but others find those changes threatening. The revolutionary transformation in the East European countries reflects the most profound shifts in Soviet foreign policy. And the West European countries, and especially the Nordic states, have profited from the Soviet Union's desire to be an architect of the common European home. But for several traditional Soviet allies in the Third World, such as the Indochinese countries, new political thinking means a loss of financial and military support from the Soviet Union and a threat to their hard-line regimes.

The consequences of the changes in Soviet foreign policy, however, have not been limited to foreign relations. New political thinking has unleashed some forces, primarily in Eastern Europe, that have served as a catalyst to domestic discontent in the Soviet Union. The freedom given to the East European countries in particular has fueled the desire for independence in some of the Soviet republics, especially in the Baltic. This is not simply a domestic concern for the Kremlin, as "the Baltic question" has become a factor affecting Soviet relations with the West, especially with the Nordic states. In addition, the emergence of some of the republics as independent political actors in the international arena has complicated Soviet relations with foreign states and exacerbated domestic criticism of the changes in Soviet policy. Finally, the loss of the Soviet external empire, the abandonment of some traditional allies, and the national unrest fueled partially by new political thinking have created a reactionary conservatism that threatens the very core of perestroika and new political thinking.

At the heart of new political thinking is the emphasis on pragmatism rather than ideology as the basis for the Soviet Union's foreign relations. This shift stemmed from the realization that the Soviets' efforts to create world communism were in vain. As several contributors to this volume have noted, the economic crisis in the USSR also has threatened its position as a global superpower as well as the success of its reforms. Therefore, the Soviets began to focus on mutually beneficial economic relations with other states. Gorbachev stressed economic cooperation and global economic interdependence, ideological shifts that paved the way for expanded Soviet relations with capitalist countries, as Jeong observed. Along with the realization that developed capitalist countries were stable and thriving, the Soviets admitted that the socialist bloc was in crisis. As Chenoy and Botha have argued, this prompted the Soviets to question several key doctrinal concepts based on Marxism–Leninism, such as "national liberation movements" and "non-capitalist development" or "socialist orientation" as a model for Third World countries.

The emphasis on economic relations does not mean that the Soviets have abandoned political and diplomatic considerations. Indeed, as Saivetz noted, many of the Soviet Union's actions have been geared toward enhancing its position in the international community. As evidenced in its actions in the Middle East, especially during the recent Gulf crisis, the Soviet Union has tried to carve out a niche for itself as a mediator of regional conflicts. Adams delineated three broad prescriptions that new political thinking carried for superpower behavior in regional conflicts. In addition to seeking political rather than military solutions and secularizing interstate relations, the Soviets were to refrain from violating the sovereignty of another nation; that meant, for example, they could not export revolution.

These shifts in Soviet foreign policy carried profoundly different ramifications for various regions and countries. The Soviets began to focus on their integration into Europe and on cooperative relations with more developed countries that could benefit them. As a result, socialist-oriented regimes dropped on the list of Soviet priorities. No longer did Third World countries occupy the central position in Soviet foreign policy as they did under Brezhnev. As Kanet and Katner noted, the Soviet Union reassessed the place of those countries in international politics as well as the costs of pursuing Soviet objectives in those states. Moscow largely has abandoned its role of providing financial – and military – support for developing countries and leftist movements.

But these shifts, along with the abandonment of Marxist–Leninist ideology, have worried some Third World leaders, especially in Vietnam and Cuba. They believed that the Soviet leaders were compromising on issues vital to the future of Third World states in an effort to achieve peace and a deescalation of tensions, as Chenoy observed. Even the emphasis on a "common European home" seemed to indicate to them that Soviet new thinking was too Eurocentric and that security and economic interests in Europe have overridden the earlier commitment to the national liberation movements in the East. Thayer argued that Marxism–Leninism – in addition to a shared strategic antipathy toward China – was the glue holding the Soviet–Vietnamese relationship together, despite the stark contrasts in their cultural traditions. But because of new political thinking and the Soviets' "encouragement" of reform in the East European countries, the Vietnamese Communist Party has resorted to orthodox ideological tenets to argue that it is upholding "true socialism" as opposed to "deformed socialism" elsewhere. Indochina, however, has become less important to Moscow as it has normalized relations with Washington and Beijing. This change was evident in a change of attitude regarding aid to those countries. The Soviets wanted to ensure that whatever aid they gave to Vietnam, Cambodia, and Laos was used effectively. Indeed, Soviet leaders publicly berated Vietnamese ineptitude in the mismanagement of financial aid.

A similar pattern has occurred on the Korean peninsula, where the Soviet Union is turning away from its traditional ally in the north to form more profitable relations with other states. As Jeong observed, the Soviet Union has downplayed its military interests with North Korea in order to promote economic relations with South Korea and several other non-socialist, newly industrializing countries. The emphasis on trade and economic relations in turn required a certain level of political relations.

Despite the views of some Third World socialist leaders, the improved relations with non-socialist states, ASEAN, and the West, however, have not been to the detriment of the Soviet Union's traditional partners. As Chenoy and Singh pointed out, several longstanding conflicts have been settled in the Third World, largely because of the Soviets' economic-oriented foreign policy and partly because of the superpowers' cooperative relations aimed at resolving regional conflicts worldwide. In addition to helping to resolve conflicts in Afghanistan, Angola, and Namibia, Gorbachev has shown that he wants to resolve the Cambodian problem. The Soviet Union also has followed two other policies in an attempt to undermine the notion that it is a threat to the states in the region. It has supported arms control and disarmament initiatives, which include declaring Southeast Asia a nuclear-weapons-free zone, and has reduced its military presence in Vietnam. In addition, because of the warmer US–Soviet relations and the relaxed international environment largely resulting from perestroika, Third World countries are less likely to count on the backing of Washington or Moscow in conflicts. So, they have had to turn to the negotiating table for solutions, as Imam has noted.

The negotiating table is a key part of Soviet policy in the Middle East, as Saivetz has argued. In addition to trying to find reliable trading partners, the Soviets are trying to bolster their international image by playing the role of mediator in disputes – whether between Iraq and Iran or between the Arabs and the Israelis – in the Middle East. To counteract fears of bias in such roles, the Soviets have increased contacts even with Israel. Mediation is a way to keep involved in the region and thereby to remain a superpower – as evidenced by Moscow's attempts to find a solution after Iraq's invasion of Kuwait. Gorbachev's imprint on foreign policy, Saivetz argued, is a blend of an old desire to be involved and support allies along with a new emphasis on moderation and flexibility.

With states west of its borders the Soviet Union has been focusing on establishing mutually beneficial interstate relations and on integrating into the common European home. The Soviet Union's new relations with its East European neighbors reflect the most profound change in its foreign policy. Here, again, is a paradox. Not only did Moscow release its tight grip on those countries, it also on several occasions promoted the revolutionary changes that toppled the authoritarian communist leaders, Skak has argued. In East-Central Europe, normal interstate relations are replacing Soviet hegemony. Indeed, it is unlikely that the Soviet Union will be able to maintain even a role of primacy in the region, especially with the demise of the Warsaw Pact and the CMEA. The primary motivation guiding the Soviet Union in its relations with both the East European and West European, especially Nordic, states is Soviet national interest, defined in an economic sense free of ideology.

The importance of becoming a foundation for the common European home helped moderate Soviet behavior toward the Nordic countries. Granted, Soviet relations with the West had improved as the Soviets abandoned their ideologically based foreign policy. But the Soviets' desire to become part of the new European order has restrained Soviet criticism of those countries that run counter to Moscow's wishes by supporting independence-minded movements, in the Baltic republics especially. Jonson and Nørgaard emphasized the importance of the republics for Soviet–Nordic relations. Indeed, the emergence of the Baltic republics as political actors became an important factor – along with the changes in the international arena and new political thinking –

in shaping the new pattern of Soviet–Nordic relations, Nørgaard argued. That relationship no longer is characterized by an asymmetry in which the Soviet Union is dominant but by an asymmetry in which the Nordic countries have been able to draw upon their strengths and support the Baltic republics without jeopardizing relations with Moscow. This is partially because the Soviet Union is in no position to risk undermining its goal by enraging its neighbors to the northwest; its flexibility in policy is constrained by its goals.

New political thinking's emphasis on deideologized, mutually beneficial relations not surprisingly has led to an increased Soviet interest in neutrality as a possible model for relations in the common European home, as Kux has noted. Gorbachev believes that a highly integrated, regulated Europe would leave little room for non-participation and neutrality, especially given the dissolution of the traditional security blocs. Kux delineated three possible types of neutrality: a "Finnish solution" of non-alliance but good-neighborly relations and specific security guarantees toward the USSR in the form of bilateral treaties (neutrality plus); an "Austrian or Swiss solution," with an unconditional neutrality based on a unilateral declaration or a multilateral agreement; and a "Greek solution," the continued but loose membership in the Warsaw Pact combined with active efforts to weaken the Pact's military and political integration (internal neutralization).

The ramifications of new political thinking have gone beyond the Soviet Union's foreign relations with other states. The forces unleashed primarily in Eastern Europe also have created a ripple effect at home in the Soviet Union. The freedom given to the East European countries in particular has fueled some republics' desire for independence. Those republics, primarily the Baltic republics, have turned to the West and especially the Nordic countries for support in their bids for independence. In addition to achieving some success in internationalizing their plight, the republics also have presented another challenge to Moscow. They are developing their own foreign policies and are emerging as independent political actors in the international arena. These new developments have complicated Soviet relations with foreign states for several reasons. First, the support of some foreign states for the independence movements in the republics has piqued the Soviets. Second, the instability of the Soviet system, fueled by national assertiveness and ethnic strife, has prompted many countries to assume a "wait-and-see" attitude in terms of relations with the Soviet Union. Third, some political leaders also have begun at least to consider direct relations with the republics' governments, especially when confronted with the frustrating prospect of Western economic aid going to waste because of the inability of the central Soviet government to get it to where it is needed.

These new developments – as well as the "loss" of the Soviet external empire and the "abandonment" of some traditional allies – also have exacerbated domestic criticism of the changes in Soviet policy. These developments have provided ammunition to the reactionary conservatives who are seeking to undermine the very core of perestroika and new political thinking. As Miner has noted, the linkage of the nationality problem and the breakup of the union with political liberalization particularly has endangered the Soviet reforms, as the military high command, KGB, party loyalists, and government bureaucrats have united in a conservative coalition opposing such sweeping changes. So, paradoxically, the same policy changes that gave freedom to Eastern Europe and promoted warmer relations with many states throughout the world also may threaten the very essence of reform; the changes have snowballed beyond the limits of toleration of many Soviet leaders.

The reemergence of extremely conservative voices along with a collapse in the internal consensus on foreign policy, as Kanet and Katner noted, affect the prospects for reform in the Soviet Union and in its foreign relations. Indeed, the period since 1990 has been characterized by a fragmentation in Soviet foreign policy, as the Soviet leadership increasingly has been forced to devote its attention to domestic concerns, including the separatist forces and ethnic strife in the republics. In addition to the internal conflict in the Soviet Union, another factor affecting the fragmentation in foreign policy has been the gradual weakening of the position of reformers, most dramatically represented by Eduard Shevardnadze's resignation as Foreign Minister at the end of December 1990. This period followed two earlier stages in Soviet foreign policy, in Kanet and Katner's characterization: a "period of great expectations," from 1985 to 1988, when new political thinking was promoted but not put into practice; and a flurry in new foreign policy initiatives, from 1988 to mid-1990.

The economic crisis in the Soviet Union has created another paradox in terms of its foreign policy prospects. The Soviets realize, as Adams noted, that their economy cannot afford a return to the type of military expansionism which prevented the country from becoming a superpower in the economic, technological, and social spheres. Therefore, a key goal of new thinking is to bolster the Soviet economy through improved trade relations and more amicable political relations. But the means for achieving this goal are compromised both by the Soviet Union's historical record and by its current efforts. As Singh noted, the Soviet Union is not as attractive a partner as the United States in the view of the NICs and other non-socialist states. The Soviet Union's former antagonism toward many of these states, the sorry state of its economy, and the domestic instability offer little incentive for those countries to form relations with the Soviet Union, especially if they are at the expense of relations with more developed countries. In addition, the Soviet Union's efforts to earn hard currency paradoxically have undermined its attempt to bolster its international image, Saivetz argued. The Soviets sell armaments for hard currency, an action that contradicts the new image they are trying to achieve. Nonetheless, Skak noted that the Soviet Union will remain an important economic partner for Eastern Europe and that the new Soviet–German economic axis will provide it with some degree of influence in East–Central Europe.

It is less certain what kind of policy the Soviet Union will pursue in other regions, especially *vis-à-vis* the United States. By opting to take steps to hold the union together, the Soviet leadership at least temporarily has moved along an anti-reform path, Miner has argued. If the conservative coalition were able to dictate foreign policy, the Soviet Union might adopt a much less cooperative attitude, especially toward the United States. While it is incapable of playing a major global role, the Soviet Union could pursue a more region-oriented policy based on protecting its borders and securing aid from countries other than the United States. Given the conservatives' wariness of the United States, the Soviet Union also could work against US interests in various regions, for example, by not supporting the United States in the Third World. But ultimately, Miner argued, the Soviet Union will have to pursue a foreign policy that will allow it to reform. Without dramatic economic and political reform, the Soviet Union will not be able to function as a world power. And the desire to be a world power – along with the necessity of rising to the economic and technological demands of the international environment – is the goal largely dictating Soviet behavior in the international arena.

Index

SELECTED PAPERS FROM THE FOURTH WORLD CONGRESS FOR SOVIET AND EAST EUROPEAN STUDIES, HARROGATE, JULY 1990

Edited for the International Committee for Soviet and East European Studies by Stephen White, University of Glasgow

Titles published by Cambridge

Market socialism or the restoration of capitalism?
edited by ANDERS ÅSLUND

Women and society in Russia and the Soviet Union
edited by LINDA EDMONDSON

Soviet foreign policy in transition
edited by ROGER E. KANET, DEBORAH NUTTER MINER and TAMARA J. RESLER

The Soviet Union and Eastern Europe in the global economy
edited by MARIE LAVIGNE

The Soviet environment: problems, policies and politics
edited by JOHN MASSEY STEWART

New directions in Soviet history
edited by STEPHEN WHITE

For EU product safety concerns, contact us at Calle de José Abascal, 56–1°, 28003 Madrid, Spain or eugpsr@cambridge.org.

www.ingramcontent.com/pod-product-compliance
Ingram Content Group UK Ltd.
Pitfield, Milton Keynes, MK11 3LW, UK
UKHW042150130625
459647UK00011B/1266

* 9 7 8 0 5 2 1 0 6 3 4 1 8 *